Modern Language Association of America

Research and Scholarship in Composition

Lil Brannon, Anne Ruggles Gere, Dixie Goswami, Susan Hilligoss,
C. H. Knoblauch, Geneva Smitherman-Donaldson, and Art Young,
Series Editors

1. Anne Herrington and Charles Moran, eds. *Writing, Teaching, and Learning in the Disciplines.* 1992.
2. Cynthia L. Selfe and Susan Hilligoss, eds. *Literacy and Computers: The Complications of Teaching and Learning with Technology.* 1994.

Literacy and Computers

The Complications of Teaching and Learning with Technology

Edited by
Cynthia L. Selfe and Susan Hilligoss

The Modern Language Association of America
New York   1994

Library of Congress Cataloging-in-Publication Data

Literacy and computers : the complications of teaching and learning
   with technology / edited by Cynthia L. Selfe and Susan Hilligoss.
        p.   cm. — (Research and scholarship in composition)
     Includes bibliographical references and index.
     ISBN 0-87352-579-5 (cloth) — ISBN 0-87352-580-9 (pbk.)
     1. Computers and literacy—United States.   2. Language arts—
   United States—Computer-assisted instruction.   3. Reading—United
   States—Computer-assisted instruction.   4. English language—
   Composition and exercises—Study and teaching—United States—
   Computer-assisted instruction.   I. Selfe, Cynthia L., 1951–
   II. Hilligoss, Susan, 1948–   .   III. Series.
   LC149.5.L575   1993
   371.3'34—dc20   93-26959

Published by The Modern Language Association of America
10 Astor Place, New York, New York 10003-6981

Contents

Preface to the Series

The Research and Scholarship in Composition series, developed with the support of the Modern Language Association's Publications Committee, responds to the recent growth of interest in composition and to the remarkable number of publications now devoted to it. We intend the series to provide a carefully coordinated overview of the varied theoretical schools, educational philosophies, institutional groupings, classroom situations, and pedagogical practices that collectively constitute the major areas of inquiry in the field of composition studies.

Each volume combines theory, research, and practice in order to clarify theoretical issues, synthesize research and scholarship, and improve the quality of writing instruction. Further, each volume reviews the most significant issues in a particular area of composition research and instruction; reflects on ways research and teaching inform each other; views composition studies in the larger context of literary, literacy, and cultural studies; and draws conclusions from various scholarly perspectives about what has been done and what yet needs to be done in the field.

We hope this series will serve a wide audience of teachers, scholars, and students who are interested in the teaching of writing, research in composition, and the connections among composition, literature, and other areas of study. These volumes should act as a lively orientation to the field for students and nonspecialists and provide experienced teachers and scholars with useful overviews of research on important questions, with insightful reflections about teaching, and with thoughtful analyses about future developments in composition studies. Each book is a spirited conversation in which you are cordially invited to join.

Series Editors

Introduction

Cynthia L. Selfe and Susan Hilligoss

Computers complicate the teaching of literacy, this volume tells those of us who are engaged in that activity. Technology, along with the issues that surround its use in reading- and writing-intensive classrooms, both physically and intellectually disrupts the ways in which we make meaning—the ways in which we communicate. Computers change the ways in which we read, construct, and interpret texts. In doing so, technology forces us to rethink what it means to be human. We need more problems like this.

The time is past, these essays suggest, for looking at computers as *deus ex machina*, technology removed from our control or from the daily plot of our lives. Rather, as teachers, we have come, sometimes reluctantly, to understand computers as complexly crafted mirrors that we ourselves have shaped, as cultural artifacts that reflect our society and its ideologies, our educational system and its values. Moreover, the influence of technology only *begins* with this process of reflecting our culture. Technology changes us, redirects our thinking about the primary tasks of teaching reading and writing—the tasks of "producing and reproducing as well as transforming" (11) our world, as Biddy Martin explains in her examination of other technologies of power. We need more mirrors like these.

In our classrooms and programs—as the authors note in the following pages—computers and the issues that they raise provide teachers with new, and increasingly uncertain, perspectives: on the existing theoretical problems, on our pedagogical approaches, and on the social systems that influence our instruction. These contributors take us long past the point at which we can be content to see and explain computers as good or evil. They help us understand, as does Michel Foucault in *Discipline and Punish*, that all our explanations of power and the technologies of power are necessarily partial—necessarily composed of contradictions and differences, oppression and resistance, good and bad, productive changes and repressive influences.

1

This rich sense of complication and contradiction will be immediately apparent to readers of this collection—those readers who know little about computers but who have an interest in technology as it relates to literacy programs and classrooms; those who have a great deal of expertise as computer users or computer-using teachers; and those in our profession who are somewhere in between. With this range of people in mind, we have, as a group of writers, attempted to come at *issues of technology* from familiar ground, by starting with *issues of literacy* as we know them. Hence our chapters foreground the political, social, and economic character of literacy education; the roles of authors and of readers; the nature of interpretation and subjectivity; the ways in which humans construct meaning within the web of their own experience and with the help of those around them. It is only within such contexts that we also discuss the issues of technology and how they relate to, reflect, and alter literacy concerns. We have sought to avoid technological jargon in favor of language that teachers share because of their involvement in literacy education.

Structurally, this book comprises four main parts: Changing the Contexts of Literacy Instruction, Extending Literacy through Computer Networks, Expanding the Definitions of Computer-Based Literacy, and Broadening Our Views of Literacy and Computers. Each of the first three sections begins with an overview that articulates the fundamental issues of technology as they grow out of literacy education. In turn, the overviews examine how researchers, scholars, and teachers have understood literacy when computers become part of classrooms; when electronic networks become tools for reading, writing, and interpreting texts; and when a specialized but rapidly expanding genre of computer programs, called hypertext, takes its place beside traditional notions of text. The chapters that follow the overview tie these literacy issues directly to the technological changes we are experiencing in our literacy programs, classrooms, and work environments, among writers and readers at every level of formal schooling. In response entries at the end of each section, teachers and educational critics comment on the understandings and interpretations set forth in the preceding chapters.

Part 1, Changing the Contexts of Literacy Instruction, focuses on the ways that computers, as they move us at least some distance away from the familiar realm of paper, ink, and books, affect the locus of reading, writing, and interpreting texts, and the ways that computers change—or fail to change—our understanding of literate activities in classrooms and schools. Most fundamentally, literacy consists of the actions and transactions of the writer writing and the reader reading.

William Costanzo introduces the section with a discussion of how our profession's thinking about the acts of reading and writing, the roles of readers and authors, are altered in computer-supported environments. While he recognizes the political inertia that can limit the productive use of computers in literacy programs, Costanzo sketches the changes that computers have brought. According to him, "It is not simply that the tools of literacy have changed; the nature of texts, of language, of literacy itself is undergoing crucial transformations."

The everyday site for formal education is the classroom, with a teacher responsible for organizing literate practices among students. The presence of even one computer in this setting can cast light on those practices and the assumptions that accompany them. The three chapters that follow Costanzo's overview discuss both the reflective and the transformational influence of the computer as a literacy technology. In "The Politics of Literacy and Technology in Secondary School Classrooms," Paul J. LeBlanc eloquently articulates the difficulty confronting classroom teachers who use computers to effect positive change within larger educational situations. To that end, LeBlanc suggests ways to link literacy theory and technology. Gail E. Hawisher also indicates, from a historical perspective, just how strongly our educational values and professional vision determine our applications of computers in English classrooms. As evidence of this thesis, Hawisher traces the themes, within the broad field of composition studies, that are played out in descriptions of software and in published accounts of computer use in English classrooms. Ellen L. Barton provides a final reading of the theme of failure to change. While seemingly reformist, the discourses surrounding computer technology, she believes, actually serve the status quo in educational settings, mirroring the cultural assumptions that we build into computers.

Jane Zeni, in her response to this section, summarizes four salient questions that the preceding chapters raise: What does this technology help us do as readers and writers that we could not do with conventional tools? What conceptual framework for literacy, teaching, and learning is implied by software and hardware? How does access to technology reflect differences in gender, race, and class? How does technology shape classroom writing communities? Her comments refine these questions and bring further research, including the experiences of a large metropolitan writing program, to bear on them.

Part 2, Extending Literacy through Computer Networks, considers how the physical linking of computers reorganizes—and does not reorganize—literate activities. Instead of focusing on the actions of a solitary writer and reader and the setting of a single classroom or school, this section concentrates on theories of social construction and collaboration among writers that networked computers make practical, with the problems and issues that result. In their overview, Ann Hill Duin and Craig Hansen use a socially informed model of human communication to illustrate the effects computer networks can have on literate interactions within discourse communities. They discuss the current scholarship on network-based writing in academic settings and several of the important efforts being made to support network-based communication on the job.

The five chapters that follow provide striking examples of how the theory of network-based communication plays out in various literacy programs and settings. The first three of these chapters look at classroom contexts. In "Telecommunications Networks: Expanding the Contexts for Literacy," Betsy A. Bowen discusses the relation between telecommunications and the teaching of reading and writing. While highlighting the successes of literacy teachers who use networks to expand the communities of writers and readers available to their students, Bowen points out that telecommunications projects require additional financing and attention; hence these systems may exacerbate existing inequities in the distribution of resources within a school, literacy program, or classroom. Janis Forman, in her essay on literacy, collaboration, and technology, also identifies the uneven effects that technology can have in programs that focus on reading and writing as ways of solving problems and making meaning. Forman explains what it means for students to be literate in a computer-based communication setting and explores why some students are more successful than others in computer-based collaborative ventures. In "The Effect of Secondary School Structures and Traditions on Computer-Supported Literacy," Gary Graves and Carl Haller speak from the heart about the difficulties teachers can face in integrating computer networks into the life of a school and into the lives of the faculty members who shape its intellectual environment. Theoretically, such efforts represent attempts to open up the sites of literacy education for students and their teachers, to provide alternative forums for learning and communication. Practically, as Graves and Haller point out, computers can overload teachers and programs to the point where both are rendered ineffective.

The final chapters in this section address similar concerns of connection and isolation, resource needs and allocation, preparation and use as they relate to computer-based networks. "Humanist Scholars' Use of Computers in Libraries and Writing," by William Goodrich Jones, explores the ways computer networks can extend access to information and support communities among researchers in the humanities. Cognizant of the limited use that humanist scholars have made of these networks to date, Jones explains why such a situation might exist. Billie J. Wahlstrom suggests how computer use in literacy classrooms could benefit from a critical consciousness of gender and feminist theory. William Wresch, in his response to this section, points out how the issues of connection and isolation, access and privilege touch the lives of teachers and students in ways that affect their worlds and their relations with each other.

Part 3, Expanding the Definitions of Computer-Based Literacy, extends our thinking about computer use in reading- and writing-intensive classrooms by introducing the topic of hypertext. Unlike computers and networks, hypertext is not a physical thing but a sophisticated idea developed in a number of widely available computer programs. Impinging on literacy in the broadest sense, from speculation on critical theory to everyday classroom projects, hypertext engages researchers and teachers of both composition and literature. Beginning with Johndan Johnson-Eilola's overview, this section explores the potential of this new medium to make visible powerful modern theories of reading and writing. Using a concrete example of a hypertext story, Johnson-Eilola defines hypertext and illustrates how readers and writers respond to it. Then, starting from the premise that there is no "natural" technology of literacy, he reviews the tenets of a number of theoretical perspectives—poststructuralist, reader-response, deconstructionist, feminist, critical literacy, and others—to demonstrate how hypertext extends theories of reading, writing, and literacy in key ways.

Stuart Moulthrop and Nancy Kaplan follow the overview with "They Became What They Beheld," a piece that provides a glimpse of the radical visions of the *hyperliteracy* tasks that will soon confront students and teachers. Moulthrop and Kaplan recount how an introductory literature class responded to hypertextual narrative and then interpret the students' experiences in poststructuralist terms. In the next chapter, "The Effect of Hypertext on Processes of Reading and Writing," Davida Charney strikes a more cautious note. Interrogating what she terms the "Romantic" claims about hypertext and its rich associative structures, Charney warns educators about the cognitive difficulties of such texts for readers. Catherine F. Smith presents the intriguing argument that hypertext may offer teachers and students an expansive heuristic for thinking that, in literacy classrooms, can function productively as a teaching and learning aid.

In the first response, L. M. Dryden takes a critical perspective on the themes raised by the previous chapters, flavoring his comments with the experiences of classroom teachers using hypertext and hypermedia tools with their public school students. Dryden describes how student-authored hypermedia can "put technology at the service of students, to encourage their most creative efforts in exploring the connections between literature, history, the arts and sciences, and—most important—their own lives." David N. Dobrin, in the second response, then playfully but seriously challenges the significance of hypertext by extending the philosophical ideas outlined in these essays.

The final part of this collection, Broadening Our Views of Literacy and Computers, represents an attempt to pull together the multiple voices that have contributed to the volume. It begins with Christina Haas and Christine M. Neuwirth's compelling examination of the assumptions on which we, as a community of educators, have built our research-based understanding of technology. The authors encourage researchers to venture beyond the early, and sometimes limited, studies of computers in composition classrooms. Such investigations—exploratory endeavors that lacked standardized research methodology—served to confuse us with their findings even while they informed our thinking. As Haas and Neuwirth note, our profession's increasingly mature understanding of computers demands a research agenda that explores the connections among technology, literacy, and culture. The conclusion to the volume, coauthored by the editors, speaks to the productively complex vision of literacy that these essays on technology have provided us as educators and, we hope, you as readers.

As this brief outline suggests, the issues that link literacy and technology are far from simple. In fact, the more we understand about the social, political, and educational implications of technology, the more complicated our vision of computers becomes, at the same time sustaining our expectations and encouraging our caution. We continue to hope that informed teachers, who think critically about technology, can use computers to initiate and to implement productive reform in literacy programs and classrooms, in individual sites of their own choosing, in ways that support their own carefully articulated goals. We are increasingly cautious, however, as we begin to identify the many cultural, political, and economic forces working against such reform efforts, as we see the lack of support and training that teachers receive in technology, as we trace the ways in which computers can exacerbate the inequities that already characterize our educational system.

This collection—we can only hope with the bone-bred optimism that marks teachers as a collective group—adds twenty-five more voices to the ongoing conversation about computer use. It starts, as well, a thread that we can weave into an understanding of literacy and the technologies that support human communication.

Bringing a book to publication is also a complex act of literacy. As coeditors we wish to acknowledge the generous contributions of those who helped us. Dixie Goswami and Art Young provided the initial encouragement and offered kind words along the way. Anne Ruggles Gere, our contact editor, carefully read the proposal and the manuscript. Her suggestions made us aware of broad issues of audience, and her advice refined the shape of the final work. Joe Gibaldi exercised his tact and judgment at every stage. Without his efforts the project would have languished. Alicia Mahaney Minsky and Adrienne Marie Ward reviewed early drafts, while Rebecca Hunsicker Lanning shepherded the final manuscript through copyediting and production. Our thanks go as well to Beth Lyons, who compiled the bibliography. Finally, we thank our contributors, whose vision of computer-based literacy did not falter even when they had to confront yet another draft.

PART I

Changing the Contexts of Literacy Instruction

Overview

Reading, Writing, and Thinking in an Age of Electronic Literacy

William Costanzo

Literacy seems to have as many definitions these days as there are people to define the word. At the MLA's landmark Right to Literacy Conference in 1988, much of the debate focused on distinctions between functional literacy, cultural literacy, critical literacy, and public literacy, to name but a few robust varieties (Lunsford, Moglen, and Slevin). Why stretch the term still further to include some hybrid electronic species? One reason, amply argued in this book, is that computers are altering the way many of us read, write, and even think. It is not simply that the tools of literacy have changed; the nature of texts, of language, of literacy itself is undergoing crucial transformations. Along with these transformations come shifts in the sites of literacy. From the home and the classroom to the market and the workplace, computers are reshaping the environments in which language is learned, produced, and practiced.

Electronic versus Printed Texts

One of the changing sites of literacy is the computer screen. Anyone who has written with a computer knows that language on the screen seems different from language on the page. It seems more flexible, more fluid, more akin to the flickering of light than to the fixity of print. The effect stems partly from the ease of electronic alterations, the ability to make words dilate, disappear, or dance across the screen. It also results from the multiple identities of electronic texts. A document that is visible on screen may exist, as well, in the computer's temporary memory, in the invisible storage of a floppy disk, or in the printed form of hard copy. In addition to these ontological distinctions, there are differences of textual boundaries, navigation, and portability. Because of the shape and size of a computer screen, fewer words can be seen at a glance. It is harder to visualize our place in an electronic text. Instead of flipping pages, we move through text by pressing keys: line by line or screen by screen. Even the feel of the machine is part of the experience. We cannot easily curl up with a computer, unless we have a laptop.

Much of the challenge in reading electronic prose lies in what Christina Haas calls "getting a sense of the text" ("Seeing It on the Screen" 24). When we read with a purpose—matching assumptions against the content of a document, forecasting what comes next, testing expectations, revising our assumptions—we rely largely on visual information. In print-based reading, we can scan the length of a page or flip through pages to get a feel for what we're reading. We coordinate movements of eye and hand with feats of mind. When our window on the text is limited to the size of a computer screen, and when our movement through the text is controlled digitally, through precise commands from a keyboard, hand and eye work differently. Reading on computers is not less natural, but it may seem so to those of us who have spent a lifetime reading conventional texts. We may forget that even simple habits, like scanning from left to right or taking in large chunks of printed information at a time, had to be learned. For readers who grew up with electronic media, who were weaned from joysticks to keyboards in their early years, control keys may seem as natural as dog-eared pages. To them, a twenty-five-line block of text may be less artificial than the sixty-six-line page breaks that interrupt many word processing screens.

Another distinction lies in the structure of electronic texts. Books are linear because their pages are physically bound in a fixed sequence. For the most part, we read them as a continuous stream of words. By contrast, electronic texts have no set boundaries. Represented in the computer's circuitry as movable bits of electronic data, they can always be expanded, condensed, or reassembled in new configurations. Furthermore, it is as easy to jump between two nonconsecutive pages as it is to move in sequence. This is the concept behind hypertext (see Johnson-Eilola, overview to part 3; Moulthrop and Kaplan, ch. 9; and Charney, ch. 10, in this volume). Readers of hypertext travel along branching lines of narrative within dense networks of interconnected words. They can leave a biography of Lincoln and step into a history of the Civil War, shuttle back to Lincoln's life, and then leap backward to the origins of slavery or forward to the consequences of abolition, all with a few keystrokes. The computer manages the navigation. The process is like moving through a three-dimensional world of language. With hypermedia, this world stretches even further to accommodate the languages of graphics, music, voice, and motion pictures. The sites of literacy expand beyond the flat map of the page.

Reading and Writing Electronic Texts

Do such new forms of text require new reading skills? For years, the great debate among reading specialists has oscillated between two theoretical camps (Costanzo 27–63). One view, represented by Frank Smith in *Understanding Reading*, stresses comprehension. Smith sees reading largely as a matter of constructing meaning, of finding patterns in a text that confirm or contradict the reader's expectations. The other view, articulated by Jeanne Chall, focuses on the importance of decoding. In *Learning to Read* and *Stages of Reading Development*, Chall emphasizes that readers must learn the code by which letters, words, and larger units can be transformed from written symbols into meaningful sounds and thoughts.

Recent work in computer science substantiates Smith's view. For example, Roger Schank's efforts to program a computer to "read" the *New York Times* demonstrates how reading comprehension depends not so much on a complete knowledge of English grammar as on a familiarity with stories and the way they represent the world. Schank's programs scan texts for key words that evoke common news "scripts," such as reports of bank robberies or terrorism; the programs then scan the text for data that will fill in the information expected in those scripts. In effect, the computer learns to recognize patterns, predict outcomes, and validate or revise expectations much as a human reader might.

The progress of computer science also underlines the importance of decoding skills—Chall's point—because computers add new codes to the repertoire of reading. To help readers locate their position within electronic texts, software designers have developed visual maps and color-coded status lines. Thus, to be successful, readers must learn how to interpret the maps and understand the codes. The conventions of printed matter—indentations, margins, titles, page numbers, and the like—are augmented or replaced by new conventions. Cynthia Selfe speaks of "layered literacy," a reference to the additional codes needed for interpreting electronic texts—codes that include computer screens, computer systems, and computer networks. As Selfe says, "We may have to turn to our own students for help, observing the literacy strategies they develop on their own for coping with computer-supported communication environments" ("Redefining Literacy" 12). In chapter 1 of this volume, Paul J. LeBlanc considers the problems we face in enabling teachers to deal with these new literacy techniques.

If computers require students to learn new habits of reading, they also change the way students write and think of writing. Since the early 1970s, composition theory has shifted attention from writing as a product to writing as a process and, more recently, to the social contexts of writing (Faigley, "Competing Theories"). Computers have helped make these evolving views of writing more tangible for students. Word processing has given them a working model of the writing process (or, more accurately, processes), and electronic networks constitute laboratories for testing writing as a social force. Here, too, computers have contributed to the changing sites of literacy. For years, teachers and researchers have debated whether such contributions are largely positive or negative (Collier; Pufahl; Bickel; Rodrigues and Rodrigues; Hawisher, "Effects"). Without rehearsing their arguments, I want to highlight some of the most important differences between traditional writing and writing with computers.

I have already mentioned the fluidity of electronic texts. Some writers wax rhapsodic over the alliance between keyboard and phosphorescent screen that frees their inner speech (Stillman). Not only do computer-generated texts encourage fluency for such writers; they also invite endless alterations. An electronic text always seems open to change. And because no permanent copies need be made of any version, computers blur the boundaries between drafts. Instead of successive generations, there is an almost seamless evolution. Yet other writers note a distancing effect. They emphasize the power of the screen to "decenter" writers from their texts by altering the text's appearance through various formatting or fonts. As Kenneth Fitschen explains, "Decentering is the process of stepping back from one's own writing in order to see it afresh before revision" (105). Pressing a few keystrokes lets the writer view the same words in a new configuration.

Writing that appears on a screen seems more public. In contrast to the privacy of paper documents, the screen displays text for all to see. It's a little like having one's words broadcast on television. In a computer lab, the displayed image invites collaborative writing and peer review. Writing is not so much a solitary act as a gesture of communication. Teachers and researchers alike have commented on the social nature of electronic writing, linking it to the pedagogy of cooperative education (Lindemann and Willert 50; Rodrigues and Rodrigues 43;

Humphrey). Cooperative learning is not automatic, however; it depends on careful training and support, as LeBlanc explains.

The Look of the Text

In an age in which television, films, and magazines are important mediums of language, educators speak of visual literacy as an essential set of skills. They point out that the visual composition of a message, whether a movie or an advertisement, represents a large part of its meaning. Computers seem to reinforce this notion by drawing more attention to the visual aspects of text. Writers tinker with the margins, justify the lines, try centering blocks of information, experiment with spacing. In the course of learning a word-processing program, they discover terms for concepts they may never have thought about before—hanging indents, pitch and font, headers and footers, orphans and widows—all related to the way a text looks on the page. Such preoccupation with format seems to come as naturally as child's play, perhaps because electronic texts are so elastic; but like all play, it deserves close analysis. What does it mean when we spend more time attending to the visual texture of our words than to their content?

The English alphabet has twenty-six letters, but a standard computer keyboard has seventy-two keys, many of them representing manipulations of text. We learn the alphabet in order to record the sounds of English in visible form, as writing; the typewriter keyboard was more or less a tool to mechanize this process. But with word processing, the keyboard becomes something more. Those arrow keys, insert, delete, control, and function keys stand for movements within texts and for textual transformations. One set of keystrokes turns on double spacing; another adjusts the margins. The fact that keystrokes may be embedded in the text as format codes is significant. By giving such codes a symbolic status comparable to that of letters, word-processing programs in effect have extended the alphabet to include visual as well as auditory information. Texts composed on a computer are more than records of spoken language; they are recorded documents, with their own formatting instructions built into the text. The changing sites of literacy entail shifts in the medium of literacy as a visual artifact.

A Sense of Response

If our symbol system is expanding, what is the computer's role in recording and interpreting the system? How does the computer support or contradict current theories of reader response? In one sense, the computer can already "read" letters and embedded format codes by transforming the stream of symbols into an organized display of text. For instance, it interprets a return symbol by skipping to the next line on the screen or printer, or interprets a column code by starting a new vertical row on the page. Such acts of interpretation, though strictly mechanical, often seem uncannily dynamic, so much so that people typically speak of a computer's functions as behavior. When the computer misbehaves and scrambles the text because it's following embedded codes the writer has forgotten, the technology indeed seems to have a mind of its own.

The psychological effect of the machine's behavior on writing can be a hindrance or a boon. To some writers, the computer is a subtle saboteur, subverting their intentions, reconstituting their words in alien configurations, redirecting their attention to the layout of the text. To them, the diversity of format options is a distraction from the central task of writing: to say something meaningful. To others, the computer seems more like a partner in the writing process. The pulsating cursor is a lively invitation to compose, a point of light that gives visible expression to their thoughts, a shuttle for weaving the fabric of their text. The computer's responsiveness, its ability to perform quickly on command, to check spelling or suggest alternatives, to recast whole paragraphs in different arrangements for a fresh perspective—all contribute to the sense of a collaborative presence when one is writing deep into the night.

Perhaps the most fascinating instance of collaboration between the user and the computer is the genre known as *interactive fiction*. Interactive fiction is the textual incarnation of adventure games. Each screen describes part of a story in which the reader is the central character. Whereas traditional fiction is written in the first or third person, interactive fiction is written in the second person singular. Everything depends on the reader. Readers move through the story by typing in commands or questions from the keyboard. In a typical story, they might find themselves in a strange room guarded by an unknown person. They might explore the room, talk to the stranger, or climb out a window, all by typing simple sentences. The computer may respond by describing the room, quoting the stranger, or informing the reader that he or she has just fallen into the shark-infested moat below the window. Much of the appeal of interactive prose lies in readers' learning about their fictional characters, discovering the characters' goals, overcoming conflicts, and exploring imaginary worlds. Typically, readers invest a great deal of themselves in the protagonist; they pay meticulous attention to details of setting, character, plot, and point of view because their literary lives depend on these elements of fiction. Characterization is not something to watch unfold; rather, it is a series of encounters. Dialogue is not a transcript of completed speech but a transaction between character and reader. Setting is more than picturesque description; it is the environment in which the reader must survive. In many respects, then, interactive fiction substantiates theories of reader response. The story is a collaborative creation of the author and the reader. Language, in such texts, is both the territory through which we travel and the instrument by which we find our way (Costanzo, ch. 3).

Interactive fiction is one example of how computers seem to corroborate theories by putting pedagogies into practice. Another example can be found in word-processing software, which supports theories of composition that regard writing as a recursive process of discovery, elaboration, and revision (H. Schwartz, *Interactive Writing*; Moberg; Hult and Harris). Most word-processing programs encourage writers to move back and forth among the stages of generating, developing, organizing, editing, and reconceptualizing texts; some programs explicitly systematize the process by offering menus for each stage. Additional writing aids, such as invention programs and style analyzers, extend the writer's reach by automating prewriting and editing strategies (Burns; Dobrin, "Style Analyzers"; Strickland; McDaniel, "Comparative Study"; Collins). Whereas textbooks may describe the processes and teachers may give demonstrations, computers serve as enactive models. They offer physical analogies to the mental and perceptual activities of writing, giving inexperienced writers access to alternatives that might otherwise remain invisible. With its editing options, spelling checker, thesaurus, and other special functions for manipulating text, the computer visibly reinforces writing as a systematic process.

A third example is the social view of writing, which emphasizes the communal contexts of literacy. Janet Eldred shows how computers have supported the social-minded theories of Lev Vygotsky, Mikhail Bakhtin, and others. Personal computers, in addition to being the private tools they were originally conceived to be, have become instruments for social intercourse. Users look at one another's screens, share databases, and communicate through electronic messages. Computers facilitate group writing, conferencing, and peer review. The quick access computers give to other texts and the ease with which computers merge these texts reinforce principles of intertextuality, confirming how all writing draws on a common reservoir of discourse. Already these features are recognized in composition texts that build on the computer's suitability for fostering communities of writers (Elder et al.). These concurrences of pedagogy and technology are explored more closely in this volume by Gail E. Hawisher (ch. 2); in her essay she relates computer software and the literature on computers to our changing theories about literacy.

Historical Perspectives

Such observations lead to the familiar maxim of media historians that we shape our tools and our tools shape us. Havelock Ellis, Walter Ong, and others have traced what they believe to be the changing qualities of human consciousness to shifts in what might be called the technology of literacy. Ellis describes how the invention of writing came to favor more analytic forms of thinking (*Preface*). Before people had an alphabet to record their speech, language was an evanescent flow of sounds. Writing arrested the stream of words, fixing it visibly in stone or on papyrus. Language thus became, according to Ellis, "an artifact, a thing in itself, an object of its own study" ("Coming" 98). Contrasting the features of oral and literate forms of communication, Ong finds that spoken discourse tends to be more episodic than logical, more formulaic than inventive, and more ceremonial than critical. He stresses, in *Orality and Literacy*, the functional basis of oral rhetoric, noting how the ritualistic formulas of classical, Tudor, or Bantu oratory help speakers and their listeners remember information. Writing frees language from the constraints of human memory, enabling writers to arrange knowledge in new configurations, to follow the thread of an idea beyond conventional wisdom to new depths and complexities of thought. When both writer and reader have unlimited access to the visible text of language, words can be revised and revisited. Written discourse, then, is typically more precise, inventive, abstract, and individualistic than spoken language.

Ong and others use the term *secondary orality* to emphasize resemblances between certain electronic media and speech. Television, for example, with its formulaic programming, ritualistic imagery, noncritical vocabulary, and reliance on collective authorship, has been likened to preliterate forms of communication (Ong, *Orality*; Goethals). But technology keeps evolving. New media shift the patterns of communication and, with them, the course of literacy. If television seems to have revived paradigms of preliterate discourse, computers appear to be tugging in the opposite direction. They have, to a remarkable extent, restored the primacy of writing by making text a central feature of the screen. Executives who formerly dictated their memos now type them on a personal computer. Students who once spent their leisure time in front of a television set now have a computer screen to turn to. True, younger students are likely to use the tube for video games, but there is a difference between passively watching what moves on the screen and controlling the action with a joystick. Today's youngsters are accustomed to being actively involved, and their sense of mastering the medium may well carry over into other text-based activities, when they are reading interactive fiction, traveling through a database, or using a word processor for writing. Increasingly, the sites of literacy have become dynamic centers of engagement.

Questions of Representation

There are questions, here, of power and authority as well as of technology and cognitive abilities—questions related to the key issues of literacy education. Will computers shift control from some external authority to the individual user? Will they help to distribute the instruments of literacy more equitably, or will they function only to buttress a literate elite? If literacy is shaped by new technologies, who is shaping the technologies? What ideological assumptions are being built in, and whose interests do they serve?

Some observers point to developments like desktop publishing as evidence of radical change. Desktop publishing puts an entire system of production at the user's fingertips, enabling one individual to do what formerly required a large staff and considerable money to complete (Sullivan). Moreover, the professional look of a computer-generated document is cited as a further index of authority. To the extent that writers are represented by the weight of their words rather than their titles, electronic conferencing is said to flatten traditional hierarchies. Even in the classroom, computers divert attention and authority away from the teacher to the text.

Of course, these benefits apply only to those who have access to computers. That is why equality of access has become such a serious issue (Gomez). So has the issue of ideology. A growing chorus of scholars has criticized Ong and his followers for neglecting the social and political dimensions of literacy (Daniell, "Situation"; Williams; Kaplan). They argue that machines, and hence whatever influences machines may have on human beings, are determined not so much by impartial technologies as by the ideological climate that produced them. Clearly, we should ask how relations of gender, race, class, and other groupings are represented by computers and how these relations are embedded in the very language we use in talking about computers (see Barton, ch. 3 in this volume).

What are the implications for literacy in an electronic age? When language is experienced increasingly through the medium of computers, it is also filtered through the computer's scheme of internal representation. At some level, language is simulated, systematized, and processed according to programmable rules. Who programs the rules? Who or what directs the programmer? If we are going to read, write, and reason with computers, we ought to know more about the systems by which computers operate as well as the systems that create them. If we are going to adapt ourselves to the behaviors and assumptions of a machine, as history suggests we will, we ought to take a closer look inside. We should also look more broadly beyond the bits and bytes of technology to the social, political, and cultural contexts of literacy education. The next three chapters in this section seek to widen and illuminate the field of view by focusing on three related sites of literacy.

For Paul LeBlanc, in chapter 1, the classroom is a site in which pedagogy often yields to politics, and learning tends to conform to the surrounding social order. He questions the beliefs of parents and of society at large in the prevailing myths of technology, in the view of computers as impartial tools, and in functional models of literacy. Reminding us that technology and literacy are never neutral, he points out the risks of ignoring the ideological agendas they serve. As an example, LeBlanc cites a teacher who is given a computer instead of paper and books but is offered no training, support, or say in selecting her instructional options. What are the consequences of investing in the right technology for the wrong reasons? What are the alternatives? Taking his cue from two recent landmark conferences, LeBlanc argues for a partnership between literacy and technology that is pedagogically sound and socially responsible, as well as personally and politically liberating.

In chapter 2, Gail Hawisher turns our attention to computer software as a conceptual site of literacy. Analyzing several schemes for classifying writing software, she argues that such criteria have restricted our successes with computers by favoring certain theories of composing. In the light of these schemes, Hawisher traces major trends in recent EDUCOM and NCRIPTAL awards and in articles from *Computers and Composition*—evidence that shows how our interests in computers have reflected the changing theoretical frameworks of the profession. Drawing on several categories of learning theory, Hawisher proposes a new method for classifying courseware; she suggests that such a formula need not limit our ability to understand, evaluate, teach, and practice electronic forms of literacy.

Ellen Barton extends the argument by examining the discourses of technology as sites of literacy (ch. 3). Investigating the popular and professional literature on computers as well as everyday speech, she finds two opposing forms of discourse. The dominant one regards progress as inevitable and beneficial; the role of education is to keep pace with a changing world, fostering new literacy skills to serve the economy. The antidominant discourse, forged largely by the cultural Left, offers a critique that reveals how technology supports the status quo by strengthening the privileged class. Barton analyzes these discourse polarities in the research on composition and computers, finding that pro- and antidominant points of view often merge into a single, essentially conservative perspective. She outlines the dangers by which such research may be engulfed by the larger forces of academic politics and thereby rendered powerless. Her conclusions pose a striking, sophisticated challenge to all who would study, teach, or use computers in the classroom.

The sites of literacy are indeed shifting. The spaces in which literacy is acquired and practiced—in classrooms, between people, within texts themselves—are all adjusting to the emerging technologies. The computer is not just a tool; it is an extension of the environment in which we think and communicate. LeBlanc suggests that networking, shared databases, and other electronic options may stretch the ordinary classroom's domains for learning literacy in ways that support Shirley Brice Heath's vision of "ensembled individualism" ("Fourth Vision" 304). Barton points the way toward a more valid discourse of technology that is both more powerful and self-critical than those we have been using. Hawisher's study of software categories as conceptual places of literacy challenges us to extend our thinking as a way of gaining insight into language, learning, and technology. All these sites are focal points of intersecting forces, subject to the magnetic fields of social continuity but responsive to the critical winds of change. These chapters argue that we need to alter our sights as well—to shift carefully between the close-up and the long view—if we are to understand the developments and make them worthwhile.

Chapter 1

The Politics of Literacy
and Technology in
Secondary School Classrooms

Paul J. LeBlanc

At a recent computers and writing workshop for secondary school teachers, a fourth-grade teacher explained that she would soon be getting an Apple IIe for her classroom. No one had asked her whether she wanted a computer or how it might fit into her teaching; she was not offered training, technical support, or release time, nor was she consulted on the software she would eventually be given for use with the machine. Her inquiry "What should I do with the new computer?" reminded me of Pope's cry to his friend Arbuthnot, "Shut, shut the door good John! (fatigued I said), / Tie up the knocker, say I'm sick, I'm dead" (qtd. in Mahoney 46). Surely, if I had applied James Thomas Zebroski's key question "Who may benefit from this [new advance in literacy technology]?" my best answer would have been to box up the Apple, shove it back into the hallway, and lock the classroom door (84).

Such a simple act might be seen as a kind of blasphemy, so invested is our culture in the mythologies created by the media campaigns of Apple and IBM, so weary are our educators from literacy wars for which they receive less and less support and more and more criticism. However, the seemingly benevolent arrival of a computer in a classroom is never a neutral act. As Nancy Kaplan has said, we can no longer "ignore the ways tools implicate and are implicated in power relations, or more broadly the ideologies, permeating reading and writing acts" (4). Technology, as much as literacy, is imbued with ideological conflicts, shaped by forces of economics, history, and politics. Hence technology can be as educationally repressive as it can be liberatory. When computers are used as a tool for literacy education, choices regarding technology can privilege one model of literacy while excluding others. The decision to network, to use drill-and-practice software, to follow a given access policy, to train teachers or give them release time, to spread machines throughout a building or congregate them in one room exerts relentless influence on the success or failure of computers in achieving one's literacy goals. This chapter posits a model of literacy with which to guide technology choices, examines the current use of computer-based literacy efforts through a close examination of one teacher's experiences and the ways in which they are typical of national trends, and then offers suggestions to make computer-based literacy work for teachers, students, and parents.

Defining a Model of Literacy

To realize the potential of technology in literacy education, we must first articulate a model of literacy and its objectives from which we can make decisions about technology. As C. H. Knoblauch points out, any definition of literacy is laden with political, economic, and educational agendas. "Since no definition achieves transcendent authority, their dialectical interaction offers a context of choices within which continually changing educational and other social policies find their justification" (74, 76). As most teachers know, there exists a wide continuum of competing literacy models, ranging from the "vocational matching" model (Kling 25) at one end to the critical literacy of Paulo Freire and his followers (Freire, *Pedagogy*; Giroux, *Theory and Resistance*; Shor; Berlin, "Rhetoric and Ideology"). In this chapter, as I explore computer-based literacy education in the secondary schools, I have chosen as a standard the model of literacy that emerges from the work of two conference groups, the 1987 English Coalition Conference (Lloyd-Jones and Lunsford) and the 1988 Right to Literacy Conference (Lunsford, Moglen, and Slevin). A model sensitive to the politics and ideologies of literacy, it asserts literacy as "democracy through language" (Lloyd-Jones and Lunsford 20) and a right long "denied to an extraordinary number of our citizens" (Lunsford, Moglen, and Slevin 2).

In summing up the work of the Right to Literacy participants, Shirley Brice Heath defines what she calls our new "fourth vision" of literacy, one based on "learners talking and considering together." She articulates three principles for literacy education:

- All of us—children and adults, students and teachers, shop workers and supervisors, clerical workers and managers—learn most successfully with and from each other when we have full access to looking, listening, talking, and taking part in authentic tasks we understand.

- We can complement each other in particular areas of expertise if we learn to communicate our experiences; sharing what we know helps bring the group to higher performance than private reflections of individuals do.

- Humans must move beyond information and skills to meaning and interpretation for learning to take place and to extend itself. So-called at-risk or slow learners frequently have learned in out-of-school experiences a multitude of approaches that allow them to move away from the mere display of learning to the creation of learning. Schools too often demonstrate in their assignments that the meaning is that there is no meaning to be interpreted from self-experiences or comparisons between direct learning and the knowledge found in books. The clear message often seems to be that the meaning lies in the text and not in the active engagement of text and reader together.   ("Fourth Vision" 302)

Heath sees these three points as the underpinnings of an "ensembled individualism" (304), a position complemented by the values articulated in the coalition conference report. The report sees the classroom as a community of learners, embraces interactive and student-centered learning, and includes in its definition of literacy a wide range of genres and functions. It is this model of literacy education that I bring to bear in the following examination of computer-based literacy education in secondary schools.

Computers in the Classroom: Dreams and Nightmares

For four years I have worked with secondary school teachers in summer workshops on computers and writing. Periodic meetings with them, visits to their schools, and transcripts of their group discussions have given me an opportunity to examine the politics of technology and literacy as they occur in those teachers' schools. In at least one school I had a vision of technology's promise—powerful networked computers with videodisc and CD-ROM peripherals, scanners and overhead projection systems, an extensive software library, teachers well trained and assisted by a technical staff. In many more schools I found a stark contrast to the ideal, in scenes such as these:

- a school with a four-year-old Apple on a "crash cart" that is shared among twelve teachers in different disciplines and wheeled from room to room
- a business teacher who dismantles his school's one Digital terminal whenever he's not working with it to teach typing, so that no other class will "use it and break it"
- two brand-new Apple computers sitting in the back of a classroom under dustcovers because the administrator who purchased them did not budget for software or printers
- a school that had no academic computers but whose students collected grocery slips to earn a donated computer (a soon-to-be-discontinued model) for their classroom

Unlike the dazzling simulation and critical skills programs available in expensive and elaborate computer labs, the software available to these students usually consists of drill-and-practice or testing programs. As students vie for snatches of time on the machines, their efforts are often plagued by faulty equipment, incompatible hardware and software, and the underlying institutional problems of tracking, time structures, and class size. Many of the teachers are frustrated by their attempts to use computers in their classrooms, some so disillusioned that they have given up any real effort at curricular integration of the technology. In these schools, which are much more typical than the well-equipped institutions, the integration of computers has been largely ineffective, inequitable, and inadequate in fulfilling our hopes for their use in literacy education and schooling in general.

A Case Study of Computers and Literacy

Indeed, if we return to the fourth-grade teacher whose question opened this essay and examine her situation more closely, we might wonder whether her school and others like it should purchase computers at all. The teacher, Rose, has taught for sixteen years, the last twelve in her current school. She often attends professional conferences, workshops, and the increasingly infrequent in-service training sessions offered by her school district. Such attendance, she believes, is partial compensation for not reading many professional journals or texts, which she has little time to look at. When asked to discuss the reading and writing activities of her class, Rose's comments reflected her concern with basic reading and writing skills, the performance of her students on mandated performance tests, and a sense of isolation from her colleagues in terms of dialogue, goal setting, and control over the curriculum. "We're told what to teach, that our students will be tested on it, and we teachers have no say in that, and we never find time to discuss it," she observed. Excited about a reorganization of the district and a movement to school-based management, Rose hoped to be a member of her school's management team.

Rose teaches at an urban elementary school with a student population that is roughly fifty percent African American, twenty-five percent Puerto Rican, and twenty-five percent white. Those numbers, and her class size (usually 27), fluctuate because many of the students move during the year—a result of several factors, including the availability of low-income housing and work, and changing family relationships. The texts Rose uses in class are seventeen years old on the average, and students are not allowed to take them out of the school building because the text-replacement budget is so low. Rose and other teachers travel to area mills to pick up discarded folders and paper for their students' writing portfolios. Moreover, the city voters' refusal to override a local property tax limit has meant cutbacks in staff and programs. In a situation in which there are so many needs, how did Rose come to get a computer?

Parents and Computer-Based Literacy

Part of the answer to the mystery of Rose's new computer lies with parents, particularly middle-class parents, who are most deeply convinced of the efficacy of computer-based learning. For them the computer has become, for a variety of reasons, the talisman of educational and professional achievement. Chief among the motivators for their faith in technology are their own or their neighbors' displacement, as work becomes transformed by computers; the mythologies of computer-related work (good money, rags-to-riches stories à la Steven Jobs and others, clean office-based work); and the highly effective media campaigns of major computer manufacturers. As Ellen Barton points out in chapter 3 of this volume, the "dominant discourse of technology," which assumes that computer expertise is essential for success, is most pervasive "in the everyday discourse of newspaper articles, popular magazines, advertising, and best-selling books." What results is a widespread belief that "knowing computers," as I have often heard parents say, is the key to their children's future. Paul Olson explains:

> The electronic bogey man is the spectre of the "techno-peasant."
> The fear harks back to an intuitive knowledge of the macro-shifts

which we have alluded to earlier: if work processes are being reorganized around greater efficiencies afforded by computers, then anyone not reskilling will move down and out, not up and in. (194)

As corporate giants Apple and IBM compete for the home computer market, they play on such fears, suggesting that, without a computer, one's children will fall behind their peers. In the words of Richard Ohmann, "This appeal to hope and anxiety calls to mind strongly the pitch of door-to-door encyclopedia salespeople, thirty years ago" (684).

For many parents, grappling with technological change in their own workplaces, the anxiety is indeed real. A grandmother of one of the fourth graders in Rose's class told me that she had retired two years early from her secretary's job because her employer wanted her to learn word processing on the office's new computer. "I'm too old to do that stuff now," she said. "And to tell you the truth, I tried and just couldn't figure it out." The kind of concern that she and others like her feel—that their children or grandchildren should "know computers"— has forced school administrators to play the technology game. In Rose's school district, for example, there is an ongoing attempt to keep middle-class children from leaving the city's schools to attend wealthier suburban or private schools. One way to do so is to appear up-to-date by having computers in the classroom. At a recent public forum, one parent stood up and remarked about a local parochial school, "But they've got a whole room full of computers!" The discussion hinged not on who was doing a better job in educating children but on who had computers and how many. Not long after, Rose and a number of other teachers in the elementary grades were told they would receive computers.

Teacher Training for Computer-Based Literacy

While Rose and her colleagues were grateful and excited to be getting new computers, they were unaware of the impact the machines would have on their work in the coming months. However, they were soon confronted with some of the problems that Andrea Herrmann says are typical of teachers' early experiences with computers:

- administrative problems, including a lack of computer expertise among some administrators that results in their inability and unwillingness to assist teachers;
- teaching problems, including teachers' lack of experience with computers;

■ application problems, even among teachers who are knowledgeable about computers, concerning the pedagogical approaches that are most effective in teaching writing ("Computers in Public Schools" 110).

In an area in which they were woefully unprepared, Rose and the other teachers in her school were left on their own to obtain training (thus Rose's presence in my workshop). Their lack of training mirrors national trends. As the Congressional Office of Technology Assessment reports, when faculty members and student teachers at schools of education were asked to evaluate teachers' readiness in twelve areas that included classroom management, methods, development of material, and dealing with misbehavior, use of computers was rated last (100). Unfortunately, little is being done to support teacher training; in 1988, thirty-four states neither required nor recommended in-service training in technology, while only three states mandated such training (109). The kind of teacher education that Jane Zeni describes in the response to this section—a model program—is indeed rare. For the most part, teachers must train themselves, and when they do, they often become the technical support persons for the whole school (what McDaniel calls the "white coat syndrome" ["Assessing" 90]) and end up doing a good deal more work than they did before the computer arrived in their classroom.

One of my workshop participants, Michelle, reported just such an experience when her school purchased two computers. Before the academic year, she spent hours studying the technology and developing ways to work the computers into her curriculum. A week before school, Michelle learned that her principal had assigned her an additional class "because the computers would save her so much time" (Kelly). She found herself being called into other teachers' classes to help with technical problems, overseeing the logistics of diskette distribution and security, and grappling with the disruption the presence of the computers caused in her own class. Ironically, Michelle's principal did not ask her to sit on the school's technology committee, which was charged with making software and equipment purchases and determining access policies. Even as she worked to make herself a computer specialist, she was excluded from the decision-making process that effectively defined what model of literacy would be served by the technology. Michelle bitterly complained that the software her administrators handed her "had nothing to do with what was going on in the classroom." Her feelings of displacement and exploitation were consistent with Shoshana Zuboff's accounts of worker responses to technological change in nonacademic settings.

Students and Computer-Based Literacy

For the students, in contrast, the addition of a computer to Rose's class seemed a good thing. Her students were excited at the prospect—and one of the few things computer and writing research tells us with some surety is that the machines motivate students (Hawisher, "Studies" and "Effects"; Kurth; Moore; Dalton and Hannafin). Rose too was motivated—the prospect of introducing her students to the computer prompted her to enroll in that summer workshop. She said to another teacher in the workshop, "I could do so much with [the new computer], and the kids' writing will really take off, I think" (Costa). Despite her enthusiasm, however, the project may have been misguided: the money used for her computer might have been spent more effectively on other instructional strategies for Rose's class. Henry Levin and Gail Meister compared the cost effectiveness of four educational strategies: a reduction in class size, the lengthening of the school day, cross-age tutoring, and computer-assisted instruction (CAI). Their results showed that CAI was more cost effective at the elementary level than increasing instructional time was, but reducing class size was more effective than either one, while cross-age tutoring was most effective of all (748). Although the dollars spent on a single computer may not have funded the sorts of approaches examined in the Levin and Meister study, the money certainly would have purchased numerous texts and writing supplies.

The ratio of twenty-seven students to one computer in Rose's class is better than the national average of thirty-one students to each computer. While the 31:1 ratio is a two-thirds improvement on the 1983 ratio of 92:1, it does not reflect inequities in distribution. Studies reveal that minority students have less access to computers than white students do, that black elementary schools are less likely to have computers than white elementary schools are, and that the technology available in poorer school districts is less sophisticated (Congressional Office; Campbell; Olson). The 31:1 ratio means that students spend a meager one hour a week on average in front of a computer in school (Congressional Office 34); but the findings further suggest that many minority students spend even less time than the average, while their wealthier, white suburban peers do considerably better. That indication is borne out in the work of Michael Cole and Peg Griffen, who conclude that "more computers are being placed in the hands of middle and upper class children than poor children" (43).

What did Rose's students do with the one computer at the back of the room? Rose wanted her students to compose narratives on the computer, but because their access time was only about an hour a week, they produced very little by the end of their allotted period. Asking them to compose at home meant that they would spend the whole hour typing their work into the computer (not one of Rose's students had access to a computer at home), with no time for revision. Thus, for writing assignments, the computer merely became a typewriter. With districtwide testing only months away, Rose began to use a number of drill-and-practice software programs, all offering the kind of tasks that could be done in traditional workbooks and assignment sheets, all serving a vocational model of literacy I know to be quite far from Rose's ideal. However, her use of the computer is fairly typical. Drill-and-practice and remedial programs are common in poor and minority schools like Rose's, where students' abilities are often assumed to be inferior. As Mary Louise Gomez points out:

> Students of color and those of low socio-economic status received instruction of a classic compensatory nature, practice in discrete "basic" skills, while their middle- and upper-class white counterparts received instruction in programming and problem-solving that required them to construct, as well as receive, knowledge.
>
> (322)

In his overview to this section, William Costanzo explores three computer-based technologies that have fascinating implications for our understanding of literacy: interactive fiction, word processing, and electronic conferencing. Rose's students partake in none of these, nor do their peers in many of the nation's schools. The Congressional Office of Technology Assessment report indicates that schools have purchased rote drill, skills practice, and tutorial programs in far larger numbers than any other kind of software (132)—even though, as Gail Hawisher points out in chapter 2 of this volume, we seldom "think of literacy in terms of drill and practice."

Schools have invested in such programs not only because they are geared to the performance goals for standardized tests but also because the software industry has been slow to move beyond such limited applications. Apple cofounder Steven Jobs admits that failure:

> I guess we look at the delivery of education on a spectrum from mechanistic (quantitative) to humanistic (qualitative) activities. Examples of this might be a tutor versus drill and practice. Another example might be an essay versus multiple choice. Education is delivered somewhere along this spectrum. What we've seen is that technology applied to higher education has all focused on automating the mechanistic end. I mean, that's what CAI is; everything we've seen is automating the mechanistic side. It's absolutely failed, so we don't want to do that.   (Sprecher 130)

The technology assessment report echoes Jobs's negative evaluation of educational software for the secondary schools market:

> It will be difficult to justify the costs of acquiring and implementing new interactive learning tools unless their software genuinely improves upon conventional learning materials. . . . [Some more creative programs are not chosen by teachers.] Pressured to raise test scores and meet other performance mandates, many teachers prefer software that is closely tied to the curriculum.   (122)

Afflicted by poor computer-to-student ratios, the need to test well, and a lack of quality software, students, especially poor and minority students, often end up isolated at the computer, doing workbook-style exercises and engaged in the least liberatory of applications one might imagine for computer-based learning—a far cry from the "ensembled individualism" affirmed by Heath.

For those who embrace a functionalist or vocational model of literacy, the computer applications I've just described, which are typical of poor and working-class community schools, might not be considered a failure at all. Such software provides students with basic keyboard and hardware familiarity: it serves a product instead of a process model of writing and encourages a pedagogy based on test scores. Knowledge becomes a set of facts and literacy a series of mechanical and rule-bound acts—in total, the computer as tireless "tester" supports what Ohmann calls the "meager literacy" of "subordinate classes" (687). This model of literacy education perhaps prepares students more than adequately for the computer-related jobs that await them. As Ohmann argues, "Graduates of MIT will get the challenging jobs; community college grads will be technicians; those who do no more than acquire basic skills and computer literacy in high school [all the vocational model really aspires to] will probably find their way to electronic workstations in McDonald's" (683). How little literacy such positions demand was made startlingly clear to me recently when I noticed, in a fast-food restaurant, that numbers and codes in the ordering system and cash register had been replaced with large, simple pictures of the items the employee merely punched. This is the level of literacy that the single computer in the back of the room—that seductively technological tool—most often serves. In 1987, Olson wrote, "Will the computer bring the promised benefits for all? I believe that the answer must be a tentative 'no,' *given the configurations and values implicit in current practice*" (201). Even now, we are still far removed from the promise.

Making Computer-Based Literacy Work

According to Gomez, "We can only expect that the use of computers will contribute to students' school achievement, rather than their failure, if the conditions under which technology is used and the assumptions which guide its use are changed" (331). Shifts in the application of technology for literacy education require two things: a clear understanding of the model of literacy one is working toward and a critical perspective of technology and its theoretical implications for classroom use. The effort must begin with the articulation of literacy goals within the community of schools, families, and neighborhoods, and the task is particularly formidable since those most directly invested in students—their parents and teachers—are furthest removed from curricular decision making. Once a model of literacy can be agreed on, it should become the basis on which all technology decisions are made. Such coordination, however, is not always easy to achieve. In Rose's school, for example, language arts teachers essentially taught to the literacy goals implied in and made operational by the district's mandated testing—though, when surveyed, the teachers articulated a diverse set of literacy goals that often stood in stark contrast to the functional standards of the testing program. Because the computers in Rose's school were purchased and installed without consideration for the literacy models (for no *one* model existed) they were intended to serve, their use was ill-fated from the outset. Successful integration of technology in the curriculum starts when communities embrace a model of literacy like that suggested in the synthesis of the Right to Literacy Conference proceedings and the English Coalition Conference report. With an essential curricular vision in hand, teachers and school administrators can then make appropriate choices in the purchase and use of technology.

Making those choices requires, moreover, that everyone involved in literacy efforts, but especially teachers, become technology critics, as Cynthia Selfe would call them ("Preparing English Teachers"). When computer specialists view their work as fitting within the broader framework of literacy theory, they can be instrumental in making that link clear to members of the community and those who fund technology. What legislators, educators, parents, and others need to understand is how technology works and the role it plays in the larger social order for which it is intended. Without that broader critical perspective, there is little hope for curricular change or progress toward an alternative view of computer-based literacy. As Selfe argues:

> When technology, as an artifact of our culture, is employed by teachers who lack a critical understanding of its nature or a conscious plan for its use, and when these teachers must function within an educational system that is itself an artifact of the political, social, economic forces shaping our culture, the natural tendency of instruction is to support the status quo.   (30)

The case of Rose's computer—the reasons it came into her classroom, the evolution of its pedagogical use, and the gap between the vocational model of literacy it served and the progressive model of literacy I knew Rose to hold—illustrates well the need for a critical view of technology-based learning activities.

Reconciling Literacy Goals and Technology

With an agreed-on model of literacy and a critical view of technology's role in achieving literacy goals, teachers and others involved in literacy education can outline their needs and priorities. If we use the "ensembled individualism" model of literacy described earlier, what might our priorities look like? As teachers, we would want our computers to be networked. For example, instead of placing one computer in each of five separate rooms (as happened in Rose's school), we would network them and place them in one room or at least network them in their remote locations if space did not allow for the former configuration. We would then choose software that facilitated group dialogue, a program like the Daedalus Group's *Interchange*, for instance. With a modem on the file server (an investment of less than $150) and an easy-to-use e-mail program like *Contact*, we could hook up to other district schools with similar networks. Because access time is likely to remain a problem, we might invest in an inexpensive hand-held scanner for quick entry of typed papers (a readily available technology). Progress in the scanning of longhand text will probably make quick entry of even handwritten essays feasible in the near future. Although the hardware and software package described here would not cost a great deal more than what was installed in Rose's school, for example, it opens up radically different possibilities for pedagogy and for meeting our goals of ensembled individualism.

If as teachers we could convince our administration to link our computers as outlined here and to provide us with the training we need and some recognition of our time and energy, we could design pedagogical applications in harmony with our model of literacy. Because the scanner would allow quick entry of text written elsewhere, at home or at a conventional desk, more access time could be spent on other writing and reading tasks. Because the computers are networked, students could, for instance, engage in peer discussion of scanner-entered essays. They might collaborate on writing projects, in the spirit of Heath's assertion that "sharing what we know helps bring the group to higher performance." We could create an open access database of student-generated essays, notes, journals, poetry, fiction, and other forms of writing—a type of community-based knowledge making and sharing. We might extend the boundaries of the classroom, via modem, to include other learners, perhaps students in different schools, but also perhaps adult learners and parents and neighbors (see Bowen, ch. 4, and the overview by Duin and Hansen in part 2 of this volume). With such a configuration, we could design assignments that support collaboration and sharing, include diverse genres, and assume interactive forms involving both the computer and other students. In short, this use of hardware and software enables a pedagogy that moves us from the isolated learner engaged in deadening drill-and-practice activities to a community of, in Heath's words, "learners talking and considering together."

Because we have articulated a clear model of literacy and because we function as technology critics, we would avoid some of the awful applications of technology that now take place in many schools. We would not, for example, purchase network control software like Robotel's *Microselect*, which allows the instructor to monitor students' on-line work without the students' knowledge and to appropriate any student's screen. As the company's marketing material attests, computers tend to "interfere with age-old, proven pedagogical approaches." It is just this sort of age-old, authoritarian pedagogy that we, as teacher-technology critics, would avoid. Even if we had only a single computer available to us, we would use it as a device for the creation of community databases and class journals instead of the mere entry of already written text and drill-and-practice assignments.

While the computer applications I have described would not cost much more than the less effective equipment I've witnessed in numerous schools, other emerging technologies are beyond the grasp of many secondary schools. Hypermedia, for example, may allow the creation of instructional software that encourages more innovative problem solving and alternative knowledge-making efforts (see, in this volume, Moulthrop and Kaplan, ch. 9; Charney, ch. 10; and Smith, ch. 11). It requires more expensive hardware, though, than is available in many classrooms, and, at least for now, the programs themselves are more costly. In fact, underlying many of the political issues in computer-based literacy is the question of money. It has become fashionable in some quarters to talk about doing more for less (in keeping with a back-to-basics ideology), and when we describe an alternative use of computers for a school like Rose's, we are clearly engaged in such an exercise. If poor schools are to have access to new technologies, however, the price of such equity will be high, considerably more than the $4 billion it would take to reach the 3:1 student-to-computer ratio many experts agree should be our goal (Congressional Office 8). The cost would include the more expensive hardware needed to run hypertext and hypermedia systems, the assembly of educational databases, the additional hardware for networking and telecommunications, and considerably more teacher training and support.

The event described at the start of this chapter was the simple arrival of a new computer in a fourth-grade classroom. While the decision to place a computer in a classroom often results from chance or coincidence, the issues it raises include our most basic assumptions about literacy, technology, the institutional politics of schools, the influence of corporate marketing on educational policy-making, the displacement of labor in the workplace (and in the classroom, for that matter), and parents' most heartfelt dreams for their children. However, while computer technology effects fundamental changes in our society and what Walter Ong, in *Orality and Literacy*, calls the "noetic economy" of the culture, educational discussions of technology's impact have too often ignored these larger issues, addressing instead more pragmatic pedagogical concerns. Decisions about software and hardware and their use in the classroom are extremely important, but such choices must take place within the framework of a progressive-reformist theory of literacy education, a framework that requires supportive institutional policies and funding. Otherwise, computer specialists, with the best intentions, may end up sustaining the inequities that have thus far characterized computer-based literacy education. Indeed, the risk is that technology will only serve to widen the gap between the privileged and the disenfranchised. In the light of the potential for computers in education, such a reality makes the arrival of new computer a cruel act masquerading as benevolence for Rose's students and others like them.

Chapter 2

Blinding Insights: Classification Schemes and Software for Literacy Instruction

Gail E. Hawisher

> *Categorization is not a matter to be taken lightly. There is nothing more basic than categorization to our thought, perception, action, and speech. . . . Without the ability to categorize we could not function at all, either in the physical world or in our social and intellectual lives. An understanding of how we categorize is central to any understanding of how we think and how we function, and therefore central to an understanding of what makes us human.*
>
> —George Lakoff

Much has been written, in recent years, of paradigms—of conceptual frameworks that mark a particular discipline—in our case, composition studies. Janet Emig describes writing in the schools as "predominantly taught rather than learned" and as "a silent and solitary activity" ("Non-magical Thinking" 140); Maxine Hairston calls on Thomas Kuhn's concept of paradigm to demonstrate the radical shift, from a product to a process approach, in composition teaching; Lester Faigley identifies theories of process as expressive, cognitive, and social; and James Berlin categorizes rhetorics as expressionistic, cognitive, and social epistemic. Each of these writers provides us with frameworks through which we might understand the discipline of composition studies. Literacy studies have been similarly framed by different perspectives, with Walter Ong's well-known terms of orality, literacy, and secondary orality suggesting a historical perspective on the consequences of civilization's progression from a dependence on the spoken and then printed word to a dependence, finally, on electronic words or media. Other views, although not achieving the status of paradigm, include C. H. Knoblauch's terms defining the functional, cultural, liberal, and critical perspectives of literacy.[1] All reflect a particular way of conceiving approaches to language and literacy instruction that have marked the English profession since about 1980 as it has moved steadily toward social constructivist perspectives on language learning. All help literacy educators to understand what we are about as teachers by mediating the perceptions of how we might profitably teach. In John Berger's phrase, they simultaneously enable and constrain "ways of seeing."

By shaping ways of looking at and operating within a particular discipline, these conceptual frameworks sometimes lead to the development of innovative approaches and valuable tools for language and literacy instruction. Moreover, they influence the kinds of materials teachers select, develop, and use for instruction. In the electronic classroom, too, the selection of instructional software reflects current conceptual frameworks that teachers espouse. The classification of this software—how teachers perceive it in relation to theories of literacy learning—is based on the ways in which teachers view composition and literacy studies. Since the categories also influence the same teachers that Paul LeBlanc (ch. 1) and Jane Zeni (response to this section) write about in this volume, they often dictate teachers' software choices. The classification schemes that have been constructed over the past decade are, in fact, barometers of the profession's thinking about computer applications, yielding rich insights into the ways computers are used in the service of literacy education.

To understand how various programs relate to current formulations for literacy instruction, we might chart the profession's use of software over the past several years. One way to do so is to describe the different ways in which scholars and teachers have categorized programs and to survey the software that has been highlighted in *Computers and Composition* since the journal's inception in 1983. A review of the EDUCOM and NCRIPTAL writing instruction awards from the past four years demonstrates how these awards might complement the articles in *Computers and Composition* and documents the kinds of programs for instruction the profession has prized.[2] By examining these classification schemes in the context of journal discussions, we can begin to see how a vision of literacy and language learning directly influences a vision of computer software.

My argument throughout this investigation is two-pronged: first, these categories are useful because they reflect the conceptual schemes through which writing instruction and literacy learning have been viewed over the past decade; second, they are inherently confining in looking to the past rather than to the future. Like textbooks, they often point to notions of what the profession has perceived as important in the past instead of indicating profitable new directions (Kuhn). Literacy educators constantly need to amend the classification schemes to encourage productive applications that stretch the conceptual frameworks on which the schemes are based and that lead to an increased understanding of what we are about as teachers. Scrutinizing how the various programs fit into classification systems and how the profession has incorporated software into its views of literacy as represented by *Computers and Composition* and the EDUCOM and NCRIPTAL awards, this chapter tests recent thinking about teaching, learning, and literacy. In doing so, it attempts to shed light on the thorny issues that accompany a careful analysis of literacy and computers.

Classification Schemes

Before examining how a vision of literacy and language learning influences both classification schemes and software use, I will describe several categories that have evolved since 1980. The classifications themselves emerge from fields that are related yet different and, as such, reflect the dominant theoretical framework of the particular discipline from which they are drawn. These schemes, represented in figure 1,

Robert Taylor (1980)

Tutor	*Tool*	*Tutee*
Drill-and-practice CAI	Word processing	*Logo*
Invention programs	Style checkers	*Hypercard*

Helen Schwartz (1982)

Text feedback	*Drill and practice*	*Simulations*	*Tutorials*
Style checkers	Grammar and punctuation programs	Computerized haiku program	Invention programs

Fred Kemp (1987)

Current-traditional	*Expressive*	*Cognitive*	*Social*
Style checkers	Freewriting	Heuristic programs	*Interchange*
Grammar and punctuation programs	Invisible writing		Electronic bulletin boards

Fig. 1. Software classification schemes

are arranged chronologically, along with a sampling of software corresponding to the categories.

A well-known scholar in the field of instructional computing, Robert Taylor published a classification scheme that provides a helpful perspective on applications for instructional software. His classification emphasizes how the computer itself functions in relation to the student. In his book, Taylor writes of software that uses the computer as a *tutor, tool,* and *tutee.* When writing software is placed into his categories, it becomes apparent that drill-and-practice programs, focusing on the mechanics of writing, function as tutors, while text analysis programs, word-processing packages, and idea processors function as tools. Some software functions as a tutee (i.e., something that student writers teach the computer to do) like *Hypercard* or other hypertext programs. In his original classification, Taylor included *Logo* in this category; in this way, *Hypercard* functions similarly but differently too. Although *Hypercard* can be used to produce diverse types of materials, it is often used to create and link written texts and other media, something that professionals working with programming languages usually do not have as a goal.

Another early construct is the classification Helen Schwartz published in 1982, after studying a year with Thomas Dwyer, a prominent researcher in instructional computing and science education at the University of Pittsburgh. Schwartz was then primarily a literature scholar, but she has subsequently made valuable contributions to composition studies. Her article "Monsters and Mentors: Computer Applications for Humanistic Education," in which she identified the kinds of instruction and learning various software programs promoted, was one of the earliest introductions of computer applications to the college English professional. Borrowing categories from instructional computing, she classified *text feedback* and *drill and practice* as programs for assisting students in mastering skills, *simulations* for leading students to further analysis, and *tutorials* for helping students internalize the process of learning. These categories essentially fall under Taylor's categories of tutor and tool, with the software either delivering or facilitating instruction aimed at individual students.

Yet another scheme for classification was developed by Fred Kemp in a paper he delivered at the Penn State Conference on Rhetoric and Composition in 1987 and further developed in his and Thomas Barker's "Network Theory: A Postmodern Pedagogy for the Writing Classroom." A student of both Faigley and Berlin, and heavily influenced by socially based views of learning and writing, Kemp argues that software programs can be categorized according to the writing theory they reflect.

Text analysis programs, for example, with their emphasis on the "correctness of the product," are intrinsically current-traditional; prewriting programs and the more structured heuristic software conform to expressive and cognitive visions of writing, with the stress on the individual; and networked environments that use electronic conferences and bulletin boards rely on a collaborative model that reflects a social view of writing. It is this last model that he and Barker elaborate on in their network theory for the classroom; each piece of student writing becomes a transaction between students and contributes to group knowledge.

These configurations provide slightly different perspectives on how scholars and teachers have viewed literacy instruction since 1980. Such perspectives have contributed to an understanding of what it means to engage in literacy learning and of how computers can help students in the process. They also reflect the ways in which views of software have changed over the past several years as the profession has moved away from looking at computers as delivery systems for instruction to seeing the user-learner as a more engaged participant. In addition, Taylor's categories of tutor, tool, and tutee suggest that the individual student is the sole recipient of the advantages provided by a computer, as do Schwartz's examples of computer-assisted instructional (CAI) programs that conform to her classification system. Moreover, Schwartz's scheme, with its category of simulations, doesn't quite work with the exercises she assigns to it, in which students are to write poems using templates and prompts. (Simulations often involve students making decisions based on a microcosm of a world presented by a computer.) Without the benefit of recent hypertext applications and multimedia presentations in which scenes from texts might be enacted, the simulation part of her classification seems more appropriate for disciplines outside of English studies. Schwartz's own software, *Seen*, a networked program that creates an electronic bulletin board on which students can share ideas related to a piece of literature, is not really a tutor, tool, or tutee, nor does it fit comfortably with Schwartz's categories of text feedback, drill and practice, simulations, and tutorials. Not until Kemp's scheme did it become clear how computers can be used instructionally by linking writers over a network so that they can communicate with one another. The connected writers can then read and comment on one another's texts, making their writing more public than private, more collaborative than individual. In other words, it was only in 1987 that the social perspectives on literacy instruction began to be reflected in software schemes.

Computers and Composition: A Journal for Teachers of Writing

To illustrate how views of literacy learning intersect with the classification structures developed for software, I turn to the profession's discussions in *Computers and Composition: A Journal for Teachers of Writing*. Because it is the earliest and also the most heavily subscribed-to journal devoted to computers and composition studies, *Computers and Composition* is a good indicator of how the profession has understood the role of technology—both hardware and software—in its teaching over the years. The journal's editorial board consists of members who have been working with computers in literacy classrooms as long as anyone in the field. Each of these scholars plays a significant role in reviewing the articles that the journal publishes, with no fewer than two members judging each submission. In addition to being composed of experienced computer-using teachers, the board itself is reviewed and expanded each year to include newer members who have made their mark on the field. Over the years, members have, furthermore, been drawn from community colleges, four-year institutions, and a pool of teachers working in the corporate sector. Subscribers to the journal, from all fifty states and from overseas, come from elementary, secondary, and college settings. They thus represent a geographically and academically diverse population, a broad readership of scholars and practitioners who often submit manuscripts to the journal as well.

The software review policy of *Computers and Composition*, which contributes to the journal's representativeness in the field, is based on two complementary considerations: that much software can become an effective instructional tool in the hands of good teachers and that the best reviews are prepared by teachers who test the software with students. When we chart the profession's use of software by looking at the programs featured in the journal since 1983, interesting patterns emerge. In 1983 the journal highlighted many different types of programs. Computer-assisted grading and response programs (CARPs), *Writer's Workbench* (Collymore et al.), *Grammatik* (with Barker's *Commentary* to accompany it), Schwartz's *Seen*, fifteen punctuation and usage tutorials from Deborah Holdstein's *Writewell Series*, a sentence-combining program, *Wandah* (the early *HBJ Writer*), templates for writing résumés, and Hugh Burns's *Topoi* made the pages of *Computers and Composition* that first year.

Using the classification systems elaborated here, we can categorize these early programs primarily as tutors and tools (Taylor) and as text feedback, drill and practice, and tutorials (Schwartz). In other words, with Taylor's system of tutor, tool, and tutee, *Writer's Workbench, Grammatik, Commentary*, the *Writewell Series*, sentence-combining programs, and Burns's heuristic *Topoi* fall under the category of tutor, whereas the résumé-producing templates and the integrated word-processing package *Wandah* are tools. Similarly, these programs fit with Schwartz's categories of text feedback (e.g., *Writer's Workbench, Grammatik, Commentary*), while the sentence-combining and the *Writewell Series* fall under drill and practice or tutorials. And the style checkers and heuristic programs, as well as *Wandah*, correspond respectively to Kemp's categories of current traditional, expressive, and cognitive.

The journal discussions of many of these programs also illustrate how both the programs and classification schemes reflect conceptual views of literacy learning. For example, the drill-and-practice programs listed above seem to fit with Knoblauch's definition of functional literacy, which embraces the notion that workers must be prepared for the literacy demands of the workplace, a type of literacy that LeBlanc, in chapter 1 of this volume, refers to as the "vocational model of literacy." According to this concept, students need to acquire an appropriate set of skills, such as spelling, grammar, punctuation, and sentence-level abilities, to succeed in an industrial society. Because they "correct" errors and thus ready text to meet the approval of management, style checkers conform to this view of literacy. Many of the early CAI programs were designed to deliver the skills to promote just this sort of proficiency: the computer could tutor young people so that they might acquire a basic level of literacy that would make them productive students and workers.

Although programs examined in *Computers and Composition* during the next few years were similar to those reviewed in 1983, the value of the computer as a tool gradually became more prominent as word-processing software grew increasingly sophisticated and as process approaches to writing instruction firmly established themselves in literacy classrooms. Still reflecting the view of the computer as a tutor, Mimi Schwartz's *Prewrite*, James Strickland's *Quest* and *Free*, all invention courseware, appeared in its pages in 1984 and 1985. Yet many of the articles also featured word processing.[3] A sampling of titles includes, for example, "The Word-Processor and the Writer," "Word Processing and High School Writing," "Introducing the Word Processor," and "Composition Students Experience Word Processing." At this time professional views of writing embraced such notions as its recursive quality, the importance of prewriting, and the necessity of revision, each of which was thought to be facilitated by word processing. Thus the value of a computer as a tool for writers seemed to take on increasing significance as the applications themselves improved and as the process paradigm became more firmly established in computers and composition studies.

The software described in 1986 and 1987 did not differ substantially from that introduced in the first volume, although it reflected subtle changes in the way the profession viewed literacy instruction. Reviewed in 1987, Nancy Kaplan's program *Prose*, in which instructors can comment on student writing and function in a collaborative relationship with students, suggests a conception of writing at odds with earlier instructor-grading programs in which generic sets of markings such as "agr" or "awk" were deposited on a student's text with the flick of a key in good current-traditional fashion. Unlike the early program that William Marling describes in his 1984 *College English* article, the newer response programs, such as Kaplan's *Prose*, make the term CARP (computer-assisted response program) (Rauch) seem less appropriate. Although Taylor's tutor and Helen Schwartz's tutorial categories are suitable for such response programs, the view of the instructor as collaborator moves the concept of tutor in the direction of a social pedagogy. Thus some CARPs are more than "graders" and derive from more recent investigations in learning: some conform to pedagogical approaches that, instead of viewing the teacher solely as examiner (J. Britton et al. 66), construe the instructor as collaborator and coach, a notion in keeping with Lev Vygotsky's social perspectives on language and his "zone of proximal development," in which the instructor provides scaffolding to lead the student to increased understanding (*Thought and Language*).

New ways of conceiving software, however, are slow in emerging, slower, it would seem, than the development of the programs themselves. As William Costanzo notes in the overview to this section, the visual plays an especially important role when computers enter the literacy arena, a point that the classification systems tend to overlook. The schemes for literacy instruction still do not reflect the graphics capabilities of computers; despite continuous advances in computer applications, such as the drawing and paint programs, it was not until August 1988, with the appearance of John Ruskiewicz's article "Word and Image: The Next Revolution," that the potential of graphics as an aid in writing tasks was discussed in *Computers and Composition*. Ruskiewicz argues that the "imaging of the word" (10) reawakens us to the rhetorical power of the visual elements of text made possible by graphics and desktop publishing software. Although Alan Purves and

William Purves have long noted the importance of a visual understanding of text ("Viewpoints") and Stephen Bernhardt called our attention to the rhetoric of the page in 1986 with his groundbreaking article "Seeing the Text," only recently have the graphics capabilities of computers been mined for literacy instruction. (See Fortune's chapter in *Critical Perspectives on Computers and Composition Instruction* for an excellent discussion of how drawing programs can help students in thinking about their writing. See also Hawisher's "Connecting the Visual and the Verbal.") Certainly developments in desktop publishing, in which writers—not unlike the scribes of the past—control the page have implications for writers and for the teaching of writing (Sullivan). How the visual is incorporated into classification schemes and how writers introduce the visual into texts will influence the ways in which teachers use graphics and video with students. How teachers explain these notions to students will reflect, furthermore, their own understanding of the visual and the way it fits into conceptual frameworks for literacy instruction.

Because of the prominence of the visual in computer technology, it's interesting that, as useful as Taylor's and Schwartz's formulations have been in demonstrating how electronic technology might help literacy teaching, neither accounts for the graphics applications of computers. Nor do the schemes recognize how computers' use as networking tools can enable people to collaborate and create knowledge through discussion. Taylor's and Schwartz's structures look at the interaction of users and computers, neglecting the computer's ability to facilitate interaction among the users—among people themselves. Although electronic bulletin boards have been with us at least as long as the *Plato* system, which goes back to the 1960s with its electronic conferences of *Notesfiles*, the early classifications for instructional applications seem to have ignored this capability. It took Kemp's more recent scheme, and one by a compositionist at that, to value a type of software that links people and hence promotes social approaches to writing instruction. The value of conversation as a way of learning in school—as a means of acquiring literacy—was apparently not firmly established in the frameworks through which, in the early 1980s, the profession understood the use of computers or viewed instruction (Hawisher and Selfe, "Rhetoric").

As the profession has moved increasingly toward social perspectives on learning, articles featuring electronic networking have appeared more frequently in *Computers and Composition*. In the same issue in which Ruskiewicz's discussion of the image appeared, Diane Thompson reintroduced networking as an instructional strategy ("Interactive

Networking"), and Marshall Kremers wrote of his students' mutiny: they took over the electronic network, ousting their instructor as an accepted participant ("Adams Sherman Hill"). Kremers's experience reminds us that classroom uses for technologies require new strategies for working with students—new applications don't always correspond to traditional notions of the American classroom, with the teacher and learner cast into descending hierarchical roles. His article, in a strange way, also foreshadows the move in computers and composition studies toward a politicized vision of literacy, a vision growing out of social perspectives on literacy.

The social-political view of literacy instruction is perhaps best encapsulated in Knoblauch's definition of critical literacy. "Its agenda," argues Knoblauch, "is to identify reading and writing abilities with a critical consciousness of the social conditions in which people find themselves, recognizing the extent to which language practices objectify and rationalize these conditions and the extent to which people with authority to name the world dominate others" (79). Because electronic networks seem to have the potential to encourage egalitarian discourse (Cooper and Selfe), undermining traditional authority structures in American classrooms and society, electronic conferences may be well suited for critical pedagogical approaches. In such approaches, students use the tools of literacy to examine the power structures of society; the goal is to change those structures so that disenfranchised groups might participate in political arenas. As Cynthia Selfe and I have argued elsewhere ("Tradition"), this view of computers and literacy is especially compatible with electronic networking and hypertext programs. Since electronic conferences and hypertexts exist only online in the memory of computers and are without the social cues that moderate face-to-face communication, students often talk more freely, giving teachers an opportunity to explore alternative visions of literacy in which they become active agents for change.

Articles appearing in *Computers and Composition* in 1990 begin to reflect the perspective that computers can help bring about social change in literacy classrooms. Consider, for example, such titles as Marshall Kremers's "Sharing Authority on a Synchronous Network: The Case for Riding the Beast," E. Laurie George's "Taking Women Professors Seriously: Female Authority in the Computerized Classroom," and Charles Moran's "The Computer-Writing Room: Authority and Control." Each of these articles examines the political implications of introducing computers and computer conferences into literacy classrooms and points to dilemmas of authority that the electronic environments may pose. Although none of the classification schemes currently project a politicized view of the literacy classroom, one can imagine the development of certain software programs categorized as promoting "critical pedagogy" in the same way that earlier programs encouraged expressive or cognitive approaches to learning.

During the last few years *Computers and Composition* has published more articles on electronic conferences, and recently it has devoted substantial space to hypertext. Of all the innovations computer technology has brought about, perhaps hypertext is the most revolutionary, for it can exist in electronic form only—it has no counterpart in print. Furthermore, instead of being a kind of software or courseware, it is actually a new medium, as John Slatin has noted ("Reading"), a channel through which many different forms of teaching and learning can occur. By allowing writers and readers to link data online according to their understanding of and experience with the material, hypertexts and hypermedia encourage users to create paths through which they organize large bodies of information. Reflecting recent developments in poststructuralist literary theory, hypertexts also question the roles of authors and readers as knowledge makers and ask us to reconsider matters of interpretation and authorship (Landow, *Hypertext*). The profession has only begun to comprehend the ways in which hypertexts and hypermedia may reshape theories of learning, teaching, and literacy.

In the light of the important role that hypermedia will play in literacy classrooms, it should be noted that in 1990 *Computers and Composition* also featured Jane Yellowlees Douglas's article on hypertext and interactive fiction ("Wandering through the Labyrinth"), as well as Anne DiPardo and Mike DiPardo's *Hypercard*-created instructional program for writing. The first explores the changing roles of readers in hypertext environments; the latter uses hypertext to lead students to a metapersonal essay—that is, an essay that taps the relations between a student's expository and narrative writing by asking the student to make the connections between the two explicit and to create hypertextual links. Both articles examine some of the theoretical and practical implications that hypertexts hold for us as writers, readers, and teachers. Both can be placed somewhat uneasily in Taylor's category of tutee, with the user or student creating conceptual links that program the computer for future encounters with readers and writers. The pieces probably more accurately represent an emerging understanding of literacy that might best fit with notions of intertextuality and thus reflect a social view of instruction. That hypertexts and hypermedia will continue to receive attention became clear, as well, when *Computers and Composition* gave its Ellen Nold Best Article Award for 1991 to

Nancy Kaplan and Stuart Moulthrop's "Something to Imagine: Literature, Composition, and Interactive Fiction." In bringing hypertextual, interactive fiction into the college classroom, the article describes how hypertexts can expand students' experiences with texts and hence their notions of literacy activities.

EDUCOM and NCRIPTAL Awards

Recent EDUCOM and NCRIPTAL software and curriculum innovation awards also demonstrate that the profession's familiarity with computer applications has broadened, as teachers have essentially extended the early schemes to encompass different views of literacy and learning.[4] The award-winning curricula and software for the humanities and for writing pedagogy during the past few years do more than deliver instruction: they engage students in thinking, writing, organizing, and synthesizing material the learners themselves have created. A sampling of the award winners suggests the kinds of materials faculty members in colleges around the country are developing. D. Midian Kurland and his colleagues produced *Wordbench*, an individual writer's tool for taking notes, outlining, brainstorming, writing, and formatting papers; Trent Batson created the Electronic Networks for Interaction (ENFI) project, an environment for teaching that relies on synchronous communication to improve deaf and hearing students' writing; Ann Duin uses an asynchronous networked environment and collaborative writing software for her technical communication classes ("Computer Exercises"); George Landow uses *Intermedia*, a hypertext system that allows students to explore the realm of English literature; and Fred Kemp and his colleagues developed the *Daedalus Integrated Writing Environment* (DIWE), which, again, enables students to use synchronous networking along with other kinds of software to improve their writing. With the exception of *Wordbench*, all these programs reflect social theories of learning. That is to say, the networked and collaborative environments encourage students to generate ideas with the instructor and other students, and hypertext environments underscore the intertextuality of readings that the student explores and then uses in creating a synthesis of his or her various encounters through a series of hypertextual links. Thus students become saturated with others' voices and others' ideas before they move to an individual awareness of their own thinking and knowledge. Recent innovative software and instructional approaches reflect more closely, in other words, Vygotskian rather than Piagetian perspectives.

This cursory review of software programs and awards, categorizations, and journal-based discussions of computers and instruction suggests that views of software development, literacy, and learning have outgrown early classification schemes. As Jane Zeni observes in her response to this section, today's computer-using teachers are not trained to think of literacy in terms of drill and practice, and most regard text feedback programs as having little value for students' writing (Dobrin, *Writing and Technique*). Over the years teachers have construed word processing and, more recently, communication software as corresponding more closely to their theories of learning and, as a result, have used these applications more extensively than other kinds of software designed specifically for writing instruction. Word processing allows students to participate actively in writing in ways that are congruent with process approaches of the expressivist and cognitive rhetorics, and communication software moves the profession more firmly into the realm of social epistemic rhetoric.

It is important, however, to recognize that the progression is not linear—that word processing, communication programs, and theories of literacy and learning do not follow one upon another but rather exist in a dialectical collaboration. Theory and technology are interactively dynamic, with each informing and shaping the development and use of the other. Word processing is probably more prominent in literacy classrooms than ever before, and communication software has been integrated into classes that continue, of course, to use word processing. Early theories that recognize the recursive nature of writing, an activity that loops back on itself, continue to shape the use of computers in literacy classrooms, just as the experience of using the computers, with their capability of underscoring the fluid and ephemeral qualities of text, influences theories of writing.

As Ellen Barton suggests in chapter 3 of this volume, the various discourses that the profession uses to talk about technology and literacy instruction create a complex dynamic in which the discourses and theories often merge, making it difficult to distinguish one discourse, one theory, one application of technology from another. For example, if style checkers are employed in writing classes to emphasize student errors in current-traditional fashion, discussion surrounding their role is likely to disguise the stress on writing as a low-level skill. As LeBlanc's chapter poignantly illustrates, the debate may well focus on the empowerment of students through technology, with style checkers and drill-and-practice software perhaps the primary programs that supposedly will promote educational equity. It should be noted, however, that journals such as *Computers and Composition* are not featuring such software today for instructional purposes, nor is it being showcased through the EDUCOM and NCRIPTAL awards.

Nonetheless, the fact that the profession does not prize these limited applications of software does not prevent teachers from using them with their own students. And, as both LeBlanc and Zeni show, such practices are more likely to develop when teachers are deprived of adequate training in computer use and are forced to forgo important discussion of the issues related to literacy and technology.

As the introduction of authoring software for hypertexts and hypermedia turns the profession's attention once more to software development and new classifications to accompany the creation of multimedia environments, literacy educators must be informed critics of the ways in which media are adapted for classroom use. Hypermedia environments, which rely on a combination of audio, video, and print as instructional tools, again reinforce a social view of writing in which the language the student uses generates knowledge that is the product of his or her interaction with many different kinds of texts and voices. Yet hypermedia environments do not guarantee informed teaching or improved learning—these media can be used just as unimaginatively and with as dire results as earlier drill-and-practice programs. In other words, the new instructional materials can be made to fit into the old classification schemes that the profession has begun to discard. Thus it behooves scholars and teachers to understand the role of new technologies in society at large, so that they may construct expanded visions for software use in literacy classrooms, visions in which students actively participate as critics and learners (Hawisher and Selfe, "Tradition").

Expanded Visions of Software in Literacy Classrooms

There are other ways in which the profession might devise new classifications for software—that is, by looking at how software encapsulates theories of writing instruction, literacy theory, and writing theory and then scrutinizing how these various theories intersect. From the review presented here, Kemp's scheme, perhaps because it grew out of recent writing theory, mirrors most accurately the ways in which software applications are used in writing classes. His formulation also presents a more complete description of software, accounting for communication features, for example, in ways the other systems were unable to do. It would seem, then, that any new formulation must work for writing as a whole, since literacy educators' classification of computer applications will be a feature of whatever writing theory they use. In other words, classroom behavior will reflect an understanding of the way teachers perceive literacy learning and the way they perceive their behavior in the classroom as contributing to it. Thus it makes sense to look at a theory of instruction aimed specifically at literacy activities.

George Hillocks offers a classification system for literacy learning and writing instruction that he has arranged according to what he terms instructional modes: (1) the presentational mode, in which the teacher relays information to students, not unlike Paulo Freire's "banking concept of education" (*Pedagogy* 59; Continuum ed.); (2) the natural process mode, in which students receive little direction from the instructor, relying primarily on their own inclinations and those of their classmates; (3) the individualized mode, in which the instruction is obtained through tutorials or programmed material geared to students' rate of learning; and (4) the environmental mode, in which the instructor selects problems, materials, and activities that lead students, working together and alone, through particular tasks. Because Hillocks derived these categories from his attempt to draw conclusions from writing research and because they were based on his observations of writing classes, they are especially valuable in looking at software in relation to the literacy classroom. Using his categories, along with those of Kemp, encourages teachers to form a more complete description of the way students develop their writing abilities (see fig. 2). For example, the presentational mode becomes problematic if teachers believe that writing is a social act resulting from the participation of a writer with other texts and other voices. (When one is lectured to, there is little opportunity for active participation.) And although the elements of Hillocks's classification don't align perfectly with theories of writing as reflected in Kemp's scheme, the two formulations allow us to see how theories of writing relate to theories of teaching in literacy classrooms. (If I espouse expressionistic rhetoric, for instance, and believe that students can discover meaning through such activities as "freewriting," I

Modes of Instruction	***Theories of Writing***
(Based on George Hillocks's meta-analysis of research in written composition)	(Based on Fred Kemp's classification scheme)
Presentational	Current-traditional
Natural process	Expressive
Individualized	Cognitive
Environmental	Social

Fig. 2. Theories of writing and writing instruction

might enlist the help of prewriting software for a class ostensibly conducted through a natural process mode of instruction.)

While a combination of Kemp's and Hillocks's classifications provides a more comprehensive description of software for literacy classrooms than Taylor's, which is based on the interaction between students and computer (tutor, tool, and tutee), and Schwartz's, which labels the software programs themselves (text feedback, drill and practice, simulations, and tutorials), the combination still fails to account for some types of appropriate software for literacy classrooms (e.g., graphics packages and hypertext programs) and for different modes of teaching (e.g., critical pedagogy) that might be facilitated by networked environments. Thus even the linking of a system of classification that seeks to understand how human beings might learn (Kemp) and how instructors might teach (Hillocks) can't provide adequate theoretical justification for certain software applications.

If we expand our thinking and consider writing and teaching theories in conjunction with literacy theory, we go a step further and contextualize teaching within the culture in which we and our students exist (see fig. 3). Knoblauch's definitions of literacy as functional, cultural, liberal, and critical, for example, enlarge upon current perspectives: they demonstrate how categories, and hence teachers' practices, are tied to society's values. Knoblauch writes, "Literacy never stands alone in these perspectives as a neutral denoting of skills; it is always literacy for something— for professional competence in a technological world, for civic responsibility and the preservation of heritage, for personal growth and self-fulfillment, for social

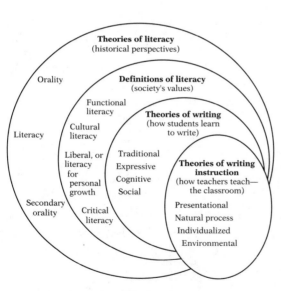

Fig. 3. The dynamic relations among theories of writing, writing instruction, and literacy

and political change" (75–76). Thus, for all the abstractness that definitions and conceptual frameworks appear to convey, they are intimately connected to certain segments of society's values and beliefs, profoundly influencing individuals' teacherly behavior. It seems appropriate, then, to use Knoblauch's categories as a backdrop in thinking about theories of writing and writing instruction. A liberal definition of literacy, for instance, fits with the example above in which freewriting on a computer is used as a strategy to complement a natural process mode of instruction. Thus a view of literacy as a means to self-actualization often accompanies expressivist theories of writing, just as functionalist views accompany current-traditional and presentational approaches to writing and writing instruction.

Ong's conceptions of literacy can also be useful in setting a historical context for thinking about software. Although, as Costanzo has pointed out in his overview to this section, Ong's work has recently been criticized for omitting many of the social and political implications of literacy, his categorization of societies as oral and literate can be useful to the discussion here, especially his notion of "secondary orality." According to Ong, secondary orality occurs in a society that relies less on the sense of sight, as in reading and writing, and more on a combination of senses that includes hearing—senses that human beings use in interacting with multimedia such as videotapes and audiotapes, or an amalgam of media that might be presented through hypermedia. Secondary orality, Ong argues, "like primary orality . . . has generated a strong group sense, for listening to spoken words forms hearers into a group, a true audience just as reading written or printed texts turns individuals in on themselves." Ong goes on to note, however, that electronic technology produces "a sense for groups immeasurably larger than those of primary oral culture—McLuhan's 'global village' " (*Orality and Literacy* 136).

Thus electronic networks and mail systems that rely not only on print but also on voice mail and perhaps on visual enactments to accompany the voice mail take us away from a literacy based primarily in a print culture. Figure 3 depicts the dynamic interaction among historical and cultural perspectives of learning and teaching writing. The figure should really be three-dimensional or hypertextual, with each layer's components seen as influencing the complex history of practices and relations connecting computers and literacy. If we view writing as more than the inscription of print—and place literacy and its instruction in the context of society as a whole—the lenses through which the profession perceives literacy activities become ever wider, pointing to the limitations in classifying software for instruction.

Examining software through theories of writing, writing instruction, and literacy studies, I believe, encourages us to broaden current perspectives on software and to view students' learning as a multidimensional activity that draws on many different sources. That is, through talking, solving problems, thinking, viewing graphic images and animated scenes, writing, reading, assembling materials in hypertext fashion, and critically analyzing the society in which they exist—by using all that the electronic media offer and by constructing meaning for themselves and their teachers—students can become literate in the broadest sense of that term.

Yet classification schemes that grow out of new understandings of writing, writing instruction, and literacy, like the ones cited earlier, remain helpful only so long as they provide insight. In his overview, Costanzo makes the important point that as media introduce new patterns of communication, definitions of literacy and notions of what society expects from the literate also shift. Those who are literate in today's sense of the word may not be literate tomorrow. When whatever schemes scholars and teachers develop to accommodate these new understandings of literacy begin to blind us to other innovative ways of using electronic technology, they must be revised or discarded. Our final challenge as teachers, researchers, and theorists of electronic writing, I believe, is to extend our thinking to reveal ways of learning not yet anticipated—to employ the emerging media not to replicate the past but to create more equitable learning environments for students and teachers. Computer technology offers us the opportunity to rethink our approaches to literacy instruction and to come closer to understanding how the complex activities of reading, writing, and learning define themselves in the electronic age. As literacy educators we must remain active critics in the development and use of electronic technology, for without such critical participation we are likely to construct and adhere to classification schemes that blind us to both its potential and its limitations.[5]

NOTES

[1]According to Knoblauch, functional views of literacy emphasize the need to provide individuals with the requisite skills for daily living; cultural literacy promotes learning that is intended to transmit a nation's heritage; liberal views of literacy extoll the individual and his or her self-actualization through personal growth; and critical views stress reading and writing as a means of raising people's awareness of the social conditions in which they exist, with an eye toward transforming those conditions.

[2] NCRIPTAL stands for the National Center for Research to Improve Postsecondary Teaching and Learning. The EDUCOM and NCRIPTAL Higher Education Software Awards were established in 1987 with the goal of bettering the quality and quantity of instructional software.

[3] See, for example, articles by Moran, Farrell, Roth, Nickell, Waddell, and Brownell, just a few of the pieces in *Computers and Composition* that highlighted word processing.

[4] The EDUCOM and NCRIPTAL awards are themselves classified into two groups that classroom instructors might qualify for: Best Curriculum Innovation and Best Writing Software. The Best Curriculum Innovation Award reflects the idea that the way teachers use software in the literacy classroom can be as innovative as the development of the software itself.

[5] I am grateful to the following people for their helpful commentary and suggestions for this chapter: Ron Fortune, Illinois State University; Paul LeBlanc, Springfield College; Michael Pemberton, University of Illinois, Urbana; Cynthia Selfe, Michigan Technological University; Patricia Sullivan, Purdue University; and an anonymous reader for the MLA. It is a far better chapter because of their participation, and I thank them.

Chapter 3

Interpreting the Discourses
of Technology

Ellen L. Barton

Research in the field of computers and writing has typically framed its discussions within the context of composition, focusing on the ways in which technology interacts with the teaching of writing. This research is also implicitly framed within an even larger context: the interaction of technology and literacy, which is characterized by what I call discourses of technology. These discourses of technology—people discussing, authors describing, and scholars analyzing assumptions and attitudes about technology as expressed in casual conversations, advertising, newspaper articles and best-sellers, educational materials, and scholarly research—have implications for the development of a critical perspective on research in computers and writing. There are two prevailing discourses of technology: one is a dominant discourse characterized by an optimistic interpretation of technology's progress in American culture and by traditional views of the relations between technology, literacy, and education; the other is an antidominant discourse characterized by a skeptical interpretation of technology's integration in contemporary culture and education. Both of these discourses underlie current research on computers and writing: the dominant discourse is the basis for much pedagogical research on the use of computers in the teaching of writing, while the antidominant discourse informs some recent theoretical scholarship analyzing the implications of technology in English studies. In much contemporary research on computers and writing, however, the antidominant discourse merges into the dominant discourse, in effect leaving the field with only one voice, which focuses on the assumed benefits of technology. I suggest that research in computers and writing must be contextualized within the larger framework of discourses of technology and their interaction with literacy to show that the research makes specific contributions to both the dominant and the antidominant discourses of technology.

Dominant and Antidominant Discourses of Technology

The Dominant Discourse

The dominant discourse of technology reflects a tradition of writing about industrialized America. The tone is that of a high school history text; the substance is based on an unquestioned assumption that progress in technology brings a variety of benefits to individuals and society. The dominant discourse takes a variety of forms. One form, for example, is biography. Chroniclers of the industrialization of the United States describe the accomplishments of prominent individuals such as Eli Whitney, Thomas Edison, and Henry Ford; some typical titles of biographies written for children and young adults include *Eli Whitney, Founder of Modern Industry* (Hays), *Thomas Alva Edison, Young Inventor* (Sabin), and *Henry Ford: Automotive Pioneer* (Montgomery). Biographies for adults usually simply name the individual—*Eli Whitney* (Harvard), *Thomas Alva Edison* (Lampton), and *Henry Ford* (Jacqueline Harris)—but one older title captures the celebratory nature of the dominant discourse: *The Amazing Story of Henry Ford, the Ideal American and the World's Most Famous Private Citizen: A Complete and Authentic Account of His Life and Surpassing Achievements* (James Miller). Similarly, chroniclers of the computer age produce laudatory biographies of individuals such as Steven Jobs (Butcher's *Accidental Millionaire: The Rise and Fall of Steve Jobs at Apple Computer*), of computer firms (Kidder's history of the Digital Equipment Company in *The Soul of a New Machine*), and even of particular systems (Pugh's history of the IBM 360, in *Memories That Shaped an Industry*, and Chposky and Leonsis's description of the development of the IBM PC, in *Blue Magic*).

The most pervasive appearance of the dominant discourse extolling the benefits of technology is in the everyday discourse of newspaper articles, popular magazines, advertising, and best-selling books. Newspaper articles describe the latest array of technological products for the workplace and home: in stories arising from the Persian Gulf conflict, for example, the *Detroit Free Press* tells of "high-tech payoffs" (Purdy, Stark, and Weiner) and predicts that "warlike wizardry" might be conducted in suburban garages (Everett). Magazine articles discuss actual and possible changes in American life and work resulting from technology: in its Technoculture column written by Daniel Katz, for example, *Esquire* speculates about the demise of print media ("Are Newspapers Yesterday's News?") and laments the growing separation between those who actually understand computers and those who simply use them ("Don't Be Mean to Your Machine: Have Computers Become Too Complex to Keep Their Users Friendly?"). A growing number of specialized magazines such as *Byte, PC Magazine, PC Computing, MacUser,* and *MacWorld* detail the latest advances in computer hardware and software. And advertisements in all these publications try to convince readers to make these new products part of their lives. In best-sellers these topics of living and working with technology are treated at greater length: Alvin Toffler's *The Third Wave*, for instance, depicts the electronic cottage-workplace of the information age, and Peterson's publishes a guide entitled *Getting a Job in the Computer Age*. Occasionally the dominant discourse cautions against the unbridled use of technology. A writer may issue warnings about the potential of computers for surveillance, as Bart Ziegler does in "Think That Computer Message You Just Sent Is Secret? Think Again"; Peter Gavrilovich's article "Jobs for the '90s" is typical in its prediction of changes to a more competitive job market as a result of advances in technology in a workplace in which, according to Robert Boyd, "data rains and reigns." Best-sellers sometimes present solutions to conflicts arising from technology: in *Megatrends*, for example, John Naisbett argues for his concept of high-tech computerization accompanied by high-touch management; in *Information Anxiety*, Richard Wurman offers his practical approach to dealing with the blizzard of data generated by computers.

Almost all such discourse is based on two assumptions: first, that technology, particularly computer technology, is here to stay; second, that technology ultimately benefits most individuals and all of society. The economist Myron Ross sums up this perspective in a newspaper interview, asserting that technology is a boon to productivity and looking forward to developments in the computer age: "I think we're still in the Model T phase with the computer."

A common theme in the dominant discourse is that the American education system must produce a technologically literate work force; this need generates current definitions of literacy that include reading and writing as well as math and computer skills (cf. Barton and Ray). Most authors make the connection between technology, literacy, and education by arguing for cooperation in improving the literacy of the work force, as, for example, when the Michigan Manufacturers Association publishes a survey criticizing the educational and technological skills of high school graduates (Jackson) or when *Time* predicts a shortage of technologically sophisticated workers in "A Crisis Looms in Science" (Tifft). Educators usually respond courteously: the Carnegie Commission, for instance, has established the goal of rebuilding the educational system to prepare students for "economies based on the use of a wide scale of very highly skilled workers, backed up by the most advanced technologies available" (44). Occasionally, however, the imbalance between the power of industry, with its desire for technologically literate workers, and the powerlessness of education, with its dependence on tax revenue, is set forth more clearly: Gerald Greenwald, former vice chairman of the Chrysler Corporation, warned Michigan officials that no auto company would ever build a facility in inner-city America again if the schools do not produce students familiar with technology ("Get Smart"). Rare instances like this aside, though, the relation between the economy and education is usually assumed to be a joint endeavor, with schools explicitly preparing students for real life in the technological world.

One way in which schools and universities have responded to industry's tacit (and sometimes not so tacit) demands for a technologically literate work force is to add computer courses and similar programs to the curriculum. Echoing the Carnegie Commission, for example, the Council of Independent Colleges urges its members, private liberal arts schools, to include courses in technology. Questioning whether a "liberal arts education as we know it today [is] adequate to provide our young people the requisite skills for life in today's world," the council notes that education must incorporate knowledge about technology if "the United States is to hold its place in an increasingly complex and competitive international world" ("Computer Notes"). Within the liberal arts, such additions to the curriculum often take the form of courses exploring the implications of technology. Not surprisingly, perhaps, a small industry of textbooks for use in these courses has sprung up, and it is in these textbooks that the dominant discourse of technology appears in a particularly influential form.

Consider, for example, Rudi Volti's *Society and Technological Change*, a book that the author suggests would make an excellent choice for courses about the effects of technology (cf. Barton, rev. of Volti). Volti places technology squarely within a social context dating from the industrial revolution, describing advances in machine production, communication, and electronics and arguing that the development of technology is "an inherently dynamic and cumulative process . . . one of continuous improvement" that brings economic benefits to individuals and society. He further characterizes a technologically progressive society as "dynamic and essentially optimistic," implicitly connecting technology to superior moral values. Although Volti notes that "there is no escaping the fact that technological changes that benefit society as a whole may harm individual members of that society"—and points out that individuals and even groups may be displaced as a result of technological advance—he argues that technology creates more than it disrupts, citing the rise in service industries in late-twentieth-century America. In sum, Volti sees the relation between technology, individuals, and society as basically benign and beneficial, "a bargain whereby we consume the fruits of technological advance in return for delegating to others the power to determine the technologies that shape the basic contours of our lives—everything from what we eat, to how we work, to the way we are entertained. Most people seem to believe that this is a fair bargain" (7–8, 11, 19, 259).

The Antidominant Discourse

In counterpoint to the dominant discourse, an antidominant discourse exists as a minority voice, critiquing the assumption that technology always brings progress and pointing out some of its less desirable consequences. As mentioned above, cracks have occasionally appeared in the dominant discourse, usually in response to small problems cropping up during the development of technology. Most often, however, these critical perspectives occur only as a subcomponent within the dominant discourse. Although in the introduction to *Computers in the Human Context*, for example, Thomas Forester identifies as a problem that "the productivity payoff from IT [information technology] is slow in coming," he nevertheless adopts the goals of the dominant discourse, arguing that more attention to the human side of technology will ultimately prove beneficial to individuals and society: "The rationale for getting the human side of automation right is that it is (a) more efficient and therefore more profitable for employers and (b) that it is better for the psychological well-being of the employees involved and by implication, society as a whole" (viii, 13).

In the liberal arts, the antidominant discourse receives its fullest articulation among a certain school of scholars and critics the philosopher Richard Rorty calls "the cultural left" ("Two Cheers" 227) and the literary critic Mary Louise Pratt characterizes as analysts of the ways in which "a narrowly specific cultural capital that will be the normative referent for everyone but will remain the property of a small and powerful caste that is linguistically and ethnically unified" (9). The "cultural capital" Pratt refers to is the traditional canon of Western civilization and literature, that canon promoted as the norm by conservative scholars; the privileged caste she refers to is the European white male, so often the author or explicator of the traditional canon. Most generally defined, the intellectual program of the cultural Left consists in large part of a critique of the canon, as Henry Giroux asserts:

> How we read or define a "canonical" work may not be as important as challenging the overall function and social uses the notion of the canon has served. Within this type of discourse, the canon can be analyzed as part of a wider set of relations that connect the academic disciplines, teaching, and power to considerations defined through broader, intersecting political and cultural concerns such as race, class, gender, ethnicity, and nationalism. What is in question here is not merely a defense of a particular canon, but the issue of struggle and empowerment. In other words, the liberal arts should be defended in the interest of creating critical rather than "good" citizens. The notion of the liberal arts has to be reconstituted around a knowledge-power relationship in which the question of curriculum is seen as a form of cultural and political production grounded in a radical conception of citizenship and public wisdom.
>
> ("Liberal Arts Education" 121)

In English studies, important figures of the cultural Left include such literary theorists as Terry Eagleton and Barbara Herrnstein Smith. In literacy studies, the most prominent figure is Paulo Freire; other scholars are Brian Street, Shirley Brice Heath, Jenny Cook-Gumperz, and Mike Rose. Major proponents in composition studies include James Berlin and Patricia Bizzell. The cultural Left also has been active in developing a critique of the American education system, as exemplified by the work of Giroux and his colleagues.

There is, in fact, somewhat of an intellectual battle being fought between scholars of the cultural Left and neoconservative critics, as discussed by John Searle in the review article "The Storm over the University." The neoconservative defense of the traditional canon in Allan Bloom's *The Closing of the American Mind* and E. D. Hirsch's *Cultural Literacy* has spawned a mini-industry of best-sellers criticizing the American university: titles include *Profscam: Professors and the*

Demise of Higher Education (Sykes); *The Moral Collapse of the University: Professionalism, Purity and Alienation* (Wilshire); *Killing the Spirit: Higher Education in America* (P. Smith); and *Tenured Radicals: How Politics Has Corrupted Our Higher Education* (Kimball). The cultural Left, by and large, has not responded through the medium of best-sellers but has published a number of scholarly works critiquing traditional and neoconservative views of education in America: Stanley Aronowitz and Henry Giroux's *Education under Siege: The Conservative, Liberal, and Radical Debate over Schooling*; Giroux and Peter McLaren's *Critical Pedagogy, the State, and Cultural Struggle*; Darryl Gless and Barbara Herrnstein Smith's *The Politics of Liberal Education*; and Jerry Herron's *Universities and the Myth of Cultural Decline*. To reach the public, the cultural Left occasionally appears in tonier magazines, as, for example, when Gayatri Chakravorty Spivak debated the status of the canon with Hirsch in *Harper's* Forum ("Who Needs the Great Works?"). The debate between the advocates of the cultural Left and the neoconservatives has received coverage in the *Chronicle of Higher Education* and *Academe* (Davidson; S. Dodge; Finn; G. Graff; Heller; Hollander; Mackenzie; Magner; Mooney; Oakley; Ravitch; Stimpson); even more articles and columns have been appearing in general publications such as *Newsweek* and *New York* magazine (Adler; J. Taylor) and in daily newspapers as well (Hinds; Kovanis; Talbert). In these sources, scholars fight the battle of quotes over "political correctness," which Robert Caserio defines in the *Chronicle* as "a prefabricated sense of values, a predetermined set of assumptions about what is good for people and what is bad for them" (qtd. in Heller, "Colleges" A14) and *Newsweek* characterizes as a program whose "goal is to eliminate prejudice, not just of the petty sort that shows up on sophomore dorm walls, but the grand prejudice that has ruled American universities since their founding: that the intellectual tradition of Western Europe occupies the central place in the history of civilization" (Adler 48).

The cultural Left, however, seems to be losing the public relations war, since its proponents tend not to be published in best-selling books, magazines, or newspaper articles (the cultural Left may well respond that to participate in such forums would merely reinforce current political and social inequities). Nevertheless, by appearing as a minority position under attack by the self-proclaimed majority—the neoconservatives—the Left risks seeming to be self-absorbed or incapable of convincing society that its critiques should be taken seriously enough to initiate change in cultural institutions such as education. Of course, the neoconservative movement benefits by presenting itself as the majority view, but the lack of response by the Left also allows neoconservative changes to go unchallenged in the public domain, as, for example, when John Searle minimizes the concerns of the Left as affecting only "a tiny fraction of undergraduate education, usually a single required freshman course in the humanities" (37). Further, the cultural Left is often portrayed as an oppressive force; John Taylor, in *New York* magazine, calls it the "new fundamentalism" and an "intellectual cult . . . demand[ing] intellectual conformity" (34–35), while in *Newsweek*, political correctness is characterized as "a totalitarian philosophy" and its academic practitioners are depicted as vicious campus in-fighters: "they are now gaining access to the conventional weapons of campus politics: social pressure, academic perks (including tenure) and—when they have the administration on their side—outright coercion" (Adler 51, 48). The cultural Left, in fact, is seen as demanding intellectual compliance so fiercely that Lewis Lapham, editor of *Harper's*, paints an ironic picture of the university in which "the range of acceptable intellectual opinion has been reduced to so small a compass as to bear comparison to the wingspan of a moth" (10) and then includes a sarcastic glossary of politically correct and incorrect usage: for instance, "Elitism: admirable only among athletes, surgeons, and divorce lawyers. Otherwise a repulsive proof of chicanery and corruption. Deplore it" (12). In the national press the Left has even assumed cartoon proportions: not long ago the Politically Correct Police showed up in the comic strip "Tank McNamara" (Millar and Hinds).

It seems that every newspaper and magazine recently has run a feature article describing the cultural Left as the malevolent spirit of political correctness (in addition to the references already cited, they include items by Bryden; Hentoff; John Miller; Will; D'Souza's "Illiberal Education" in the *Atlantic*; a spate of articles in *Time*, among them a review of the political correctness issue, "Upside Down in the Groves of Academe" [Henry], a Fourth of July piece on the curriculum entitled "Whose America?" [Gray], and, on a lighter note, Ehrenreich's "Teach Diversity—with a Smile"). Although the lack of response by the Left leaves the impression either that it disdains the general public or that it cannot defend itself, the situation may soon change. An organization called Teachers for a Democratic Culture has been formed as a counterpart to the neoconservative National Association of Scholars (Heller, "Changing Trends" and "Scholars"); one founder, English professor Gerald Graff, claims that an important goal of the organization is to challenge media coverage: "By organizing, the hope is that we can call attention to the side of the story that isn't being told in the popular press" (qtd. in Heller, "Scholars" A19). Whether this group achieves its purpose remains to be seen, but, up to now, the serious goals of the intellectual movement of the cultural Left, especially its emphasis on generating rather than silencing marginalized voices and its efforts to reveal the inherent injustices in the maintenance of social relations and practices of authority, have not been as well articulated in public discourse as have the traditional views of the neoconservative movement.

In both public and scholarly discourse, one crucial issue in the debate between the cultural Left and the neoconservatives concerns the nature of literacy. The traditional view, presented in early work by Jack Goody and Ian Watt, equates literacy with logical cognition, objective history, and the scientific method:

> [Literate societies] are faced with permanently recorded versions of the past and its beliefs; and . . . historical enquiry becomes possible. This in turn encourages scepticism; and scepticism, not only about the legendary past, but about received ideas about the universe as a whole. From here the next step is to see how to build up and to test alternative explanations: and out of this there arose the kind of logical, specialized, and cumulative intellectual tradition of sixth-century Ionia.   (352)

This perspective, which links individual literacy to logical thought and general literacy to social progress, has been critiqued by scholars in history (H. Graff), anthropology (Street), psychology (Scribner and Cole), education (Cook-Gumperz), and English studies (cf. collections edited by Kintgen, Kroll, and Rose; Robinson; Lunsford, Moglen, and Slevin). These scholars present an alternative view of literacy as embedded in a social context, a context that, moreover, privileges "those who use the concept, those who profit from it, and those who have the standing and motivation to enforce it as a social requirement." Thus the cultural Left does not emphasize the progressive nature of literacy but, rather, its oppressive nature, its function to "safeguard the socioeconomic status quo" (Knoblauch 74, 76).

More recently, the neoconservative view of literacy has focused on the definition of the canon as a collective body of knowledge. Hirsch, for example, equates the canon with cultural literacy, "the basic information needed to thrive in the modern world," further characterizing such learning as "the network of information that all competent readers possess. It is the background information, stored in their minds, that enables them to take up a newspaper and read it with an adequate level of comprehension, getting the point, grasping the implications, relating what they read to the unstated context which alone gives meaning to what they read" (xiii, 2). In a step that infuriates the cultural Left, Hirsch undertakes to supply this information in his famous and controversial list, a list that prompts Barbara Herrnstein Smith to respond, first dramatically, "Wild applause; fireworks; music— America the Beautiful; all together, now: Calvin Coolidge, Gunga Din, Peter Pan, spontaneous combustion. Hurrah for America and the national culture! Hurrah!" and then critically, "[The notion of] cultural literacy is promoting a deeply conservative view of American society and culture through a rousing populist rhetoric" ("Cult-Lit" 83, 87). According to Giroux, the Left deplores the definition (or enumeration) of the canon and its perpetuation in education by neoconservatives who are "new elitists rewrit[ing] the past and construct[ing] the present from the perspective of the privileged and the powerful" ("Liberal Arts Education" 119).

In the general debate over literacy, the attention paid to its interaction with technology is limited but predictable. Both traditional and neoconservative scholars tacitly accept the dominant discourse of technology. Traditional scholars such as Walter Ong see technology as a further development of literacy, one that enriches the individual mind and fosters social progress: computers allow human beings to "shape, store, retrieve, and communicate knowledge in new ways . . . enabling the mind to constitute within itself . . . new ways of thinking" (*Interfaces* 44–47). According to neoconservatives, the progress of technology is an appropriate perspective to be included in the background knowledge the canon comprises. Hirsch's list, for example, contains almost all major technological advances and many of the names associated with industrial and computer technology: picking the letter E, for instance, one finds Edison, Einstein, electricity, electron microscope, elementary particles, embryology, the Environmental Protection Agency, enzyme, evolution, and the expanding universe (168–71), concepts whose explanations are usually framed in terms of the progressive development of technology. Clearly, for Hirsch, cultural literacy has a technological component, and the perspective implied is the dominant discourse as articulated more fully by scholars such as Volti.

Critics of the cultural Left, in contrast, present an antidominant discourse, arguing that the integration of technology most often functions to maintain existing lines of power and authority. In the context of the workplace, this critique has been made by Herbert Marcuse; Harry Braverman; James Beniger; Richard Ohmann; Michael Holzman; Shoshana Zuboff; and Marsha Siefert, George Gerbner, and Janice Fisher; computer technology, they assert, often increases the literacy of the privileged managerial and professional class and decreases the literacy of the working class through what Ohmann calls the "deskilling" of labor (683). In the context of education, Aronowitz and Giroux, arguing that the use of technology supports the power structure, caution against looking to technology to solve long-standing problems in American education, an approach that C. A. Bowers calls "technicism" (6) (cf. also the discussions, in this volume, of technology, literacy, and education by Costanzo, in the overview to this section; LeBlanc, ch. 1; Hawisher, ch. 2; and Zeni, in the response to this section). The antidominant discourse of technology in education has been best articulated by the critic C. Paul Olson. After noting that the presence or absence of computers in elementary and high schools generally mirrors the financial condition of the school district, Olson posits that this difference in access to technology reflects the larger difference in society's objectives for educating the privileged and the less privileged: privileged students are schooled to be active problem solvers, while less-advantaged students are educated to be passive rote learners. Moreover, Olson observes, the role of technology in education promotes those larger, diametrically opposed objectives: wealthier students explore the nature and functions of computers by learning to program or to use complex writing and drawing software, while their working-class counterparts experience technology in much more limited ways; they learn nothing about the computers because their encounters are largely restricted to electronic workbook, computer-assisted instruction programs.

Research on Computers and Writing

The Dominant Discourse

In a recent *College Composition and Communication* article, Gail Hawisher and Cynthia Selfe, editors of the journal *Computers and Composition*, called for a reexamination of what they term the rhetoric of technology, characterizing it as "the enthusiastic discourse that has accompanied the introduction of computers into writing classes." What they seek is "a balanced and increasingly critical perspective" on research in the field of computers and writing ("Rhetoric" 56, 62). In attempting to develop such a critical perspective, I argue that both the dominant and the antidominant discourses frame that research. The dominant discourse (equivalent to Hawisher and Selfe's rhetoric of enthusiasm) often appears in pedagogical investigation describing the benefits of technology in the teaching of writing; the antidominant discourse sometimes appears in theoretical research exploring the implications of integrating technology into English studies. Even in this body of research, however, the antidominant discourse is absorbed into the dominant discourse, so that only one informing voice remains. The December 1990 issue of *College English*, which contains three articles on computers and writing, provides the textual evidence for this argument.

Two articles, "Reading Hypertext: Order and Coherence in a New Medium," by John Slatin, and "Teaching Word Processors to Be CAI Programs," by Joel Nydahl, are typical of the pedagogical literature concerning the use of computers in the teaching of writing. Briefly, Slatin argues that the development of hypertext, online databases, represents the first "new medium . . . to emerge from the computer revolution" (870). Contrasting the linear sequence of a conventional text with a nonlinear hypertext program, Slatin then compares the use of hypertext to discontinuous and associative thinking, an interactive and dynamic process whereby a reader actually becomes a coauthor, creating a unique text by following an individual path in the exploration of a hypertext. Slatin's article reflects a common theme in the dominant discourse of technology, that of the creation of new and potentially significant products, products that may, in this case, assist theorists in understanding the associative process of reading and help teachers in developing mature student readers and writers. Although Slatin does not spell out all the implications of hypertext for the teaching of writing, referring the reader to a more pedagogically oriented article entitled "Hypertext and the Teaching of Writing," the consequences of this technology for composition instruction play an implicit role in the article. Slatin relates interactive reading to interactive writing and discusses the most appropriate form of hypertext programs from the perspective of a composition teacher: "The instructor aims at a dynamic process, in which the student moves among three different states: from a user the student becomes a browser (and may then become a user once again); ultimately, he or she becomes fully involved as co-author" (875). In short, Slatin sees hypertext as an important pedagogical tool for students who become engaged in an active process of reading to write.

Nydahl's article on using word processors as CAI tools is more overtly pedagogical than Slatin's. Nydahl characterizes composition teachers as "searching for pedagogically sound ways to use computers in their classes" and suggests innovative ways of using word processing programs, such as interactive grading with notes to students, revision exercises based on scrambled sentences and paragraphs, and invention prompts created by macro functions. According to Nydahl, the potential of word-processing CAI is its development of students' higher-order cognitive skills of analyzing, synthesizing, judging, and evaluating alternatives in their writing; he also sees the capability of CAI to make students more fully experience "writing [as] an act of discovery" (904, 906). Here, Nydahl's perspective on the computer as a teaching tool is exactly the kind of beneficial relation between technology and education assumed in the dominant discourse.

The themes underlying Slatin's and Nydahl's work, the ideas that technology produces revolutionary and innovative products and that it creates pedagogically useful tools, are common ones in the literature on computers and writing. Most of the articles in *Computers and Composition*, for example, offer accounts of individual practice with computers in the teaching of writing: the table of contents for the August 1990 issue, for example, includes the following articles: "Towards the Metapersonal Essay: Exploring the Potential of Hypertext in the Composition Class" (DiPardo and DiPardo), "Annotated Bibliography of Resources in Computer Networking" (Mabrito), and "Electronic Bulletin Boards: A Timeless Place for Collaborative Writing Projects" (D. Thompson). All these articles combine developments in technology— hypertext, networking, bulletin boards—with standard ideas or techniques in composition pedagogy—personal essays and collaborative writing. Improved pedagogy through technology also is the focus of the major collections in the field as well: *Writing On-Line*, for example, is optimistically subtitled *Using Computers in the Teaching of Writing* (Collins and Sommers), and a more soberly titled collection, *Critical Perspectives on Computers and Composition Instruction* (Hawisher and Selfe), includes many essays with the theme of improving the teaching of writing through technology (cf. Spitzer's "Computer Conferencing: An Emerging Technology" and Wahlstrom's "Desktop Publishing: Perspectives, Potentials, and Politics"). In the pedagogical literature, even problems are presented within the perspective of the dominant discourse (cf. the discussion of Forester above). A review comment on the back cover of *Computers and Community* (Handa), for instance, notes that the book is addressed to teachers "who may be skeptical of the role this technology has in a writing classroom," but any problems associated with computers are seen as ultimately solvable: "The contributors aim to answer questions, allay concerns, and make clear the benefits that computers bring to teaching." In sum, even this brief review of the literature shows a clear association between pedagogical research describing the use of computers in the teaching of writing and the dominant discourse, which assumes the advantages of technology in education.

The Merger of Antidominant into Dominant Discourse

The pedagogical research described in the previous section assumes the dominant discourse of technology; this discourse, however, also underlies much theoretical investigation in the field of computers and writing, including scholarship that purports to be structured on an antidominant framework. Consider, for example, the work of Selfe, who has assumed the leading role in advocating that research on computers and writing should seek to articulate theoretical perspectives: "Until we examine the impact of computer technology on language and society from a theoretical perspective . . . we will never glimpse the larger social or educational picture" ("Technology" 119). Selfe has argued extensively that the use of technology in English studies has the potential to contribute to the theoretical debate about the nature of literacy: in "Redefining Literacy," she claims that we are "just beginning to get an idea of how radically our definition of literacy changes when communication activities are mediated by computers." In this article, Selfe seems to assume the dominant discourse of technology, arguing that a view of literacy must "accommodate reading, writing, and technology—our profession can hardly expect to provide students with the skills they need to function as literate members of our technologically supported society." In an especially subtle argument, Selfe suggests that we learn about computer-mediated literacy by turning "to our own students for help, observing the literacy strategies they develop on their own for coping within computer-supported communication environments" (3, 12), because they have more experience with electronic environments than their teachers. This implied praise of a group of sophisticated users of technology often appears as a theme in the dominant discourse, both in its identification of pioneers (recall the biography of Jobs) and in its characterization of the well-trained class of technology workers (recall the newspaper articles about a two-tiered job market, which implicitly represents the technologically literate group as a more privileged one).

Selfe's articulation of the relation between technology and an expanded definition of literacy has been generally adopted in research
on computers and writing: in this volume, for instance, Costanzo's
overview, "Reading, Writing, and Thinking in an Age of Electronic
Literacy," begins by asserting that the field of computers and writing
can confidently view expanded literacy as, in part, technological: "One
reason, amply argued in this book, is that computers are altering the
way many of us read, write, and even think. It is not simply that the
tools of literacy have changed; the nature of texts, of language, of
literacy itself is undergoing crucial transformations." Such claims about
computers and literacy, familiar from the literature (Costanzo quotes
Selfe's "Redefining Literacy" article), implicitly assume the dominant discourse; they are similar to Ong's prediction that computers will change
the way people think and Volti's argument that the connection between
technology and society is progressive and dynamic. This generally accepted characterization of the contributions of technology to an expanded
definition of literacy thus rests on the assumption that the link between
technology, literacy, and education is a beneficial one.

The dominant discourse can thus be seen to underlie much pedagogical and theoretical research in the field of computers and writing, but
the situation becomes even more complicated when research is framed
within the antidominant discourse of technology. Again, the work of
Selfe provides representative examples. In Selfe's more recent work,
she has followed the theoretical drift of the field of English studies,
seeing literacy and its connections to technology increasingly in the
political terms of the cultural Left. In "Technology in the English Classroom" she adopts feminist theory, arguing that female students may
be less advantaged than male students in the academy and suggesting
that technology may be able to privilege this marginalized group
through the anonymity of electronic communication. Here, Selfe sees
the practice of technology in the classroom as an instrument for social
and political change, with change defined according to the agenda of
the cultural Left. Similarly, in their *College English* article "Computer
Conferences and Learning: Authority, Resistance, and Internally Persuasive Discourse" Marilyn Cooper and Selfe explicitly adopt the theoretical framework of the cultural Left and its antidominant discourse:
they begin with a critique of power in the classroom with its "traditional hegemony in which teachers determine appropriate and inappropriate discourse," and then assume a pedagogy of resistance, citing
James Berlin, Patricia Bizzell, Paulo Freire, and Mikhail Bakhtin. Resistance, they argue, "means that individuals challenge and attempt
to change these predetermined roles to produce alternate roles, or

subjectivities, for themselves." These alternatives may result in students' "re-construct[ing] and re-think[ing] existing social structures and visions," the form of intellectual critique and the promise of social action highly valued by the cultural Left. Cooper and Selfe derive their discussion of one specific technology, computer conferencing, from a search for nonhegemonic forums that "encourage students to use language to resist as well as to accommodate"; they argue that the anonymity of a conference held outside the traditional classroom allows students who may be marginalized in the classroom (women, minorities, those with disabilities, the elderly) full authority to contribute to an ongoing electronic discussion. This egalitarian forum, they further assert, "shifts the level of competition from that of personality to that of ideas" (847, 851, 867, 847, 853), enabling a discourse of resistance to emerge.

It is, however, in the goals of conferencing technology that Cooper and Selfe (and Selfe in her earlier article on feminist theory and computer conferences) merge the antidominant discourse into the dominant discourse of improved pedagogy through technology: the use of computers, they claim, gives students the opportunity to create internally persuasive discourse and to "think divergently, to argue from different perspectives, [and] to dissent through discourse." What this opportunity provides in writing classes, Cooper and Selfe sum up, is "an effective learning situation," for several reasons: students "take responsibility for their own learning"; they "learn how discourse leads to the discovery of knowledge"; and this practice "becomes a powerful, generalizable heuristic for them" (851, 866, 856, 857) in their future writing. These aims clearly incorporate the assumption of improved composition pedagogy through technology, exactly the goal of Nydahl, Slatin, and most of the other researchers in the field of computers and writing, and precisely the perspective of the dominant discourse.

This pattern of antidominant merging into dominant occurs frequently in the theoretical literature exploring the implications of technology in English studies. In "Computers, Composition Pedagogy, and the Social View," for example, Janet Eldred adopts the perspective of the cultural Left, which sees texts as reflections of the prevailing social order, when she defines writing as "a social act that helps define an individual's place within a given culture or subculture." After reviewing the theoretical literature on the social view of discourse, however, Eldred argues that the field of composition has used these perspectives to move toward a pedagogy that "recognizes and accommodates the differences in various discourse communities within and outside the university." She also believes that technology can contribute to such a social pedagogy because computers "make tasks more social by inviting in public information, public texts" (201, 208, 209). The conclusion Eldred reaches—that central ideas in composition pedagogy, such as discourse community and collaboration, can be operationalized through technology—suggests, again, an absorption of antidominant into dominant. Similarly, in "Technology and Authority," Ruth Ray and Ellen Barton use the framework of the antidominant discourse to claim that the integration of technology in the workplace and in the university often follows an institutional imperative, in which the making of meaning is subject to the existing lines of authority in a particular context. Their conclusions merge into the dominant discourse, however, when they argue that research and teaching in university English departments could promote an institutional interaction in which the making of meaning is established through the authority of individuals rather than institutions. Here, too, the conjunction of antidominant and dominant centers on the challenge to institutional authority and the establishment of individual control in the making of meaning, a traditional focus of composition pedagogy. And in an argument similar to Slatin's, Richard Lanham, in "The Extraordinary Convergence," argues that a crucially important effect of technology is its ability to "radically democratize [the arts]"; he cites as one example the interactivity of hypertext media. Lanham sees the potential of democratized art, though, primarily in pedagogical terms, noting that "this digital revolution offers the most extraordinary opportunities to teach the arts in new ways, from kindergarten to graduate school" (36). The merger of antidominant into dominant here is in the shift of the domain of radical democraticization squarely into pedagogy, where technology, once again, is depicted as providing products and techniques assumed to be beneficial for education.

Contextualizing the Research

I do not wish to argue that improving writing pedagogy through innovative uses of technology or providing opportunities for students to acquire the technological literacy necessitated by economic conditions are not worthy goals; nor do I wish to argue that innovative applications of theoretical ideas in pedagogy are not worthwhile pursuits in computers and writing. But these goals fall squarely within the dominant discourse of technology, with its assumptions that technology is beneficial and that schools and teachers have a responsibility to create technologically literate student-workers. The field of computers and writing now needs to articulate a more complicated theoretical perspective on its research, a perspective that contextualizes the research by showing that it makes specific contributions to both the dominant and the antidominant discourses of technology: not only does scholarship provide evidence in support of the leading ideas of the dominant discourse—namely, that the use of technology can enhance pedagogy and expand literacy; it also buttresses the major ideas of the antidominant discourse—namely, that the use of technology can contribute to the maintenance of unequal relations of power and authority. The crux of this paradoxical position is in the unequal distribution of technological resources in literacy education.

Most of the research in computers and writing has attempted to furnish evidence, both formal and informal, that technology can improve writing pedagogy (although the quality of this research varies widely, the best evidence tends to be in the form of qualitative descriptions rather than quantitative studies, as discussed by Hawisher in "Research and Recommendations for Computers and Composition" and Herrmann in "Computers and Writing Research"). Nevertheless, the idea of using writing alone or in collaboration to discover self, voice, ideas, authority, meaning, and persuasive discourse, and the argument that technology integrates well with this broader pedagogical goal, has been advanced repeatedly in professional journals and in collections (cf. references I've cited). The research seems to have grown more sophisticated: earlier work simply offered anecdotes as evidence of improved pedagogy, but current scholarship investigates the use of technology in writing pedagogy in more elaborate and subtle ways. An example of such current research is Hawisher's article in this volume (ch. 2). Here Hawisher argues that the way instructors perceive software for writing has evolved from a conception of the computer as a surrogate teacher, exemplified by drill-and-practice programs, through a view of the computer as a tool for developing an effective writing process, exemplified by word-processing software, and finally to a view of the computer, the student, the instructor, and even the writing class as a collaboration in learning and writing, exemplified by network and hypertext software. Hawisher offers a review of the pedagogical literature to show the increasingly sophisticated ways in which instructors discuss software; she also relates this evolution in attitudes to an evolution in views of literacy, from functional literacy, in which students simply receive information (as from drill-and-practice programs), to critical literacy, in which students create and critique knowledge as they collaborate in networked environments. Contextualized within the framework of the discourses of technology as discussed here, Hawisher's piece reflects not a simple acceptance of the beneficial link assumed by the dominant discourse but a more specific argument that certain kinds of technology achieve, and other kinds of technology do not achieve, the goals of improved pedagogy and expanded literacy. This type of research generally supports the primary ideas of the dominant discourse, but it does so by making limited and explicit connections between technology and pedagogy, not by simply assuming that the connection is always beneficial.

As I argued earlier, much of the research in computers and writing that adopts the antidominant discourse actually merges into the dominant discourse in its explicit or implicit focus on pedagogical goals. But research in computers and writing more closely reflects the key ideas of the antidominant discourse when it exposes the unequal distribution of resources across groups using technology in literacy education. In chapter 1 in this volume, Paul LeBlanc is interested in the critique of the cultural Left because it applies to social groups who utilize (and do not utilize) technology in the teaching of writing. He begins with assumptions that technology and literacy are in a political relation and that "technology can be as educationally repressive as it can be liberatory"; both these assumptions are in general agreement with the critique of technology and education offered by culturally Left scholars (cf. the discussion of Olson above). LeBlanc, however, illustrates the politics of technology through ethnographic research in a specific context—the secondary schools:

> Unlike the dazzling simulation and critical skills programs available in expensive and elaborate computer labs, the software available to these students usually consists of drill-and-practice or testing programs. As students vie for snatches of time on the machines, their efforts are often plagued by faulty equipment, incompatible hardware and software, and the underlying institutional problems of tracking, time structures, and class size. Many of the teachers are frustrated by their attempts to use computers in their classrooms, some so disillusioned that they had given up any real effort at curricular integration of the technology. In these schools . . . the integration of computers has been largely ineffective, inequitable, and inadequate in fulfilling our hopes for their use in literacy education and schooling in general.

As Olson would predict and as other ethnographers have found (Herrmann, "Computers in Public Schools"; Gomez), the two situations

LeBlanc describes are characterized by their economic conditions: successful implementation of critical learning on computers takes place in wealthy schools; unsuccessful implementation of rote learning takes place in poorer schools. Contextualized within the framework of the discourses of technology as discussed here, LeBlanc's ethnographic descriptions of the lack of resources in these schools clearly supports the leading tenets of the antidominant discourse: the benefits of technology are not extended equally to all institutions, instructors, and students.

Contextualizing this recent research thus provides a perspective on the specific contributions made by research in computers and writing to both the dominant and antidominant discourses of technology. In support of the dominant discourse, theoretical and pedagogical research suggests that technology has the potential to improve the teaching of writing and expand the concept of literacy. In support of the antidominant discourse, however, ethnographic investigation provides evidence that the distribution of technology may well maintain inequities in education by denying technological learning and literacy to less-privileged students.

Literacy, Technology, and Teacher Education

Jane Zeni

When computers became widespread in the schools, in the mid-1980s, English teachers were sometimes threatened, sometimes bedazzled. Would the computer bring a new kind of writing process, a new kind of text? Now our questions are growing more critical, shifting from What can technology do? to What *should* technology do? We have seen that decisions about tools are linked to bigger issues of literacy and that computers can be empowering—or disempowering—to the learner.

The three essays in this section share a conviction that neither literacy nor technology is a set of neutral skills. As humanists, we should be concerned with the experience of human beings, past and present. As teacher educators, we should seek to develop in the new teacher not a lab management system but an inquiring eye to watch readers and writers learn in complex, multimedia environments. Collectively, the three chapters pose a set of issues we ought to consider when using computers in literacy education.

Paul J. LeBlanc, in chapter 1, starts with a big question: What model of literacy will we adopt to guide a discussion of technology? Drawing his model from the English Coalition and the MLA's Right to Literacy Conferences, LeBlanc tells the story of one inner-city classroom in the year the computers arrived. His case study raises more questions: How does access to new tools reflect differences in gender, race, and class? How does technology change a classroom writing community? These are questions we should address in preservice and in-service courses. LeBlanc speaks for a progressive model of English education; if we classify models of literacy as "functional," "cultural," "liberal-personal," or "critical" (Knoblauch 76–79), most participants in the English Coalition and the Right to Literacy belong in the liberal-personal or critical camps. Yet decisions about technology in elementary and secondary schools tend to reflect a different agenda—the functional or cultural literacy valued by most school administrators and parent-voters. This clash of models sheds light on the dilemma of Rose, in LeBlanc's case study. If, as English educators, we hold a progressive model of literacy, we must learn to communicate with the administrators and parents who subsidize technology in the belief that it supports their own literacy goals.

In the second chapter, Gail E. Hawisher looks further at models to ask critical questions about software design. She first surveys classification schemes for rhetoric (current-traditional, expressive, cognitive, social), for instruction (presentational, natural process, individualized, environmental), for cultures (orality, literacy, secondary orality), and for literacy (functional, cultural, liberal-personal, critical). Using this metascheme, she asks, What conceptual framework for literacy, teaching, and learning does this software imply? Does technology enhance or limit writing instruction in this setting? Hawisher's essay may be read in the context of a position paper by the Fund for Improvement of Postsecondary Education (FIPSE) Technology Study Group.[1] In *Ivory Towers, Silicon Basements* the study group warns that technology, left unexamined and underground, may subvert the intellectual principles of its users. The group urges that academic discourse be expanded to include hardware, software, and a developing pedagogy.

Ellen L. Barton, in chapter 3, calls for a new, progressive discourse of technology and literacy. The "dominant discourse" assumes that technology, like literacy, is fundamentally good for society and for individuals; the "antidominant discourse" of the cultural Left argues that technology, like literacy, may serve to maintain existing social relations and to exclude certain groups from power. Questioning the dichotomy, Barton shows that many who start with an "antidominant" analysis conclude that if certain dangers are avoided, technology will indeed fulfill its promise. Thus the arguments of such critics merge into the dominant discourse. Like Cynthia Selfe, in "Preparing English Teachers for the Virtual Age," Barton sees decisions about technology as inherently political. She challenges the "dominant" enthusiasts and the "antidominant" skeptics to enter into a more critical dialogue.

These "big issues" should become the focus of preservice and inservice programs designed collaboratively by English teachers, administrators, university researchers, and technical specialists. Shirley Brice

Heath finds that "literate behavior" among people engaged in real work is rich in collaborative talk, problem solving, and storytelling as life experience is applied to new tasks ("Fourth Vision"). If our work is teacher education, we should introduce new tools in a social environment fostering literate behavior. Our research should be grounded in classroom experience—ethnographies of writing workshops and computer labs, case studies of writers. These tasks resonate with the agenda of the National Writing Project.[2] Just as teachers of writing must themselves write and reflect on their own process, those who teach with new tools must use technology and also reflect on the experience.

If encouraged to ask the big questions, teachers will provide the sort of critique Barton wants. I write from my own experience as director of a writing project that plans in-service workshops on teaching writing with computers, and as coordinater of a new preservice English education program that uses hypertext software in a campus lab networked to a middle school. In both programs, we must critically hone our vision of technology-supported literacy learning to deal with a set of constraints: a mismatch of authority between computer environments (lab aides, teachers) and computer decisions (district-level technicians, administrators); a shortage of staff development and support for teachers using technology; a gross underestimation of the time needed to learn to teach well amid rapid change.

I will consider four broad questions raised in the three chapters and examine how the issues involved might be the focus of inquiry in English education.

What does this technology help us do as readers and writers that we could not do with conventional tools? Is the new way better or just different?

This question should be central whenever we introduce literacy teachers to electronic tools. At the University of Missouri, Saint Louis, we try to create an immersion experience with computer-supported workshops inspired by the research findings of James Moffett, Nancie Atwell, and Donald Murray. Seasoned teachers demonstrate writing lessons using computers, and their peers respond by analyzing the impact of the technology. After a session in the lab, preservice methods students can be heard to ask, "Couldn't we do that lesson just as well by hand?"

Ideally, in a reading and writing course, the computer is a tool rather than the focus of instruction. But how can a teacher introduce twenty novice users to word processing yet keep the focus on writing? We suggest choosing tasks that highlight the potential of the new tool for the writer, tasks with these features (Zeni 66):

1. They produce short, meaningful pieces of writing.
2. They require revision.
3. They are social or collaborative.
4. They result in quick, informal publication.

But despite our best efforts, the computer, in the early stages of learning, steals center stage from the writing (Flinn and Madigan). It's like bringing an iguana into a fourth-grade classroom. Some kids play, others panic, but nobody is thinking about long division! Yet, in time, the glass tank and its occupant recede, and students can integrate the experience in their own learning.

We can use this foregrounding of the technology to ask teachers how writing with new tools changed their process and how they would introduce computers in their own classrooms. John Dewey sees learning as a continuing process of reflecting on action (*Democracy*). To be literate in an age of electronic tools, learners must act and then reflect: how the writing went; where they got stuck; when their tools helped or impeded the flow; what revisions the text needs; which tools will support the next phase of the process. Through reflection, teachers can bring technology into their conscious repertoire.

What model of literacy will guide our discussion of technology? What conceptual framework for literacy, teaching, and learning does this software (hardware, etc.) imply? Does technology enhance or limit the model of writing instruction in this setting?

LeBlanc, Hawisher, and Barton all speak of the theoretical lenses through which technology and literacy are seen. English educators might help teachers see a conceptual framework by using three levels of interpretation: the tool itself, the learning environment, and the wider political and social environment.

Consider the tool. Suppose that an English curriculum is based on the following conceptual framework: writing as a set of processes; talking, writing, reading as whole language acts; personal construction of meaning; development from self to distant audiences and subjects (Moffett, *Active Voice*); correctness as a function of audience and purpose (Smitherman); social learning in a zone of proximal development (Vygotsky, *Mind in Society*). The main task in choosing computer applications is to see that they fit this paradigm. Preservice and in-service courses should show teachers *how* to evaluate technology. For example, groups of teachers might analyze one word processor or one computer-assisted instruction program. They run the software, skim the documentation, and talk ("That's just like a workbook; I wouldn't let it in my classroom!"). Finally, they collaborate on a list of assumptions about literacy that they infer from the software.

Just as we tell teachers that there isn't one ideal writing process but many individual processes, we can say that there isn't one ideal writing tool. Today's literacy is "layered" (Selfe, "Redefining Literacy"), with shifting conventions for text on screen, for graphics, for hard copy. By asking which tool suits a given task, teachers build a "rhetoric of tools" (Zeni 119–21). They learn how to make wise choices, how to fit their writing tool to audience, purpose, context—and conceptual framework. The basic issues of our craft then guide our thinking, and writers gain power over technology. The tools become socialized, humanized—community property to be discussed as well as used.

But the most flexible software will not transform rigid, formulaic teaching into process pedagogy. Teacher educators must show that even a marvelous tool can be used badly: hypercard stacks for drill and practice; word processing for fancy typing. The teacher's model of literacy and of pedagogy will drive the electronic writing tools. Good teaching is the most powerful program we can run (Zeni 75–95).

Consider the learning environment. A model of literacy can be seen not only in curriculum and methods but also in the physical space for learning. The Gateway Writing Project helps teachers design what we call "Writingland" environments. Analogous to the "Mathland" proposed by Seymour Papert, a Writingland is "a context that supports the learner through relationships with peers and teacher and through electronic as well as conventional writing tools" (Zeni xii). One constraint is that teachers of literacy seldom have the mandate to become "architects of learning spaces" (Selfe, "Preparing English Teachers"). And even if teachers design a superb environment for writers, it may be sabotaged by unsupportive administrators or disgruntled colleagues (as Graves and Haller demonstrate in ch. 6 of this volume).

Our most successful approach to Writinglands has been a one-day seminar that guides teachers, administrators, and others, such as librarians and computer coordinators, through a planning process to form writing improvement teams (WITs). In several Saint Louis–area schools, the team is a recognized decision-making body in charge of writing labs, writing across the curriculum, and the budgets to run these programs. Ironically, after five years of promoting WITs, we have no such team at our own university; the Campus Computing Committee is led by science and business faculty members, more committed to mainframes than to micros. New state-of-the-art labs are designed as electronic lecture halls, not as Writinglands.

One exception is the Christopher Columbus Consortium, which is based on an environment designed by education faculty members. The CCC lab, a Macintosh classroom networked to a middle school shadow lab, is used by methods courses in social studies, English, and math.[3] CCC builds personal as well as electronic links with flexible power relations. Professors visit the school as learners, coaches, and classroom researchers; secondary teachers make guest presentations at the university; methods students observe at the middle school, design interactive lessons, assist in labs, and tutor in English skills; eighth graders send letters of advice to future teachers, coach them in using new equipment, and collaborate in creating multimedia presentations. Still in its infancy, this project connects literacy, technology, and teacher education.

A new hypertext environment, *Storyspace*,[4] supports planning, organizing, and collaborative response to work in progress. Students create writing windows with links to other texts. They play with organization by rearranging these spaces and design paperless essays for readers to navigate. This software has gotten mixed reviews in my English classes. *Storyspace* proved enlightening to theories-of-writing graduate students drowning in case study data; methods students struggled at first but soon could create flexible hypertext lesson plans; a first-year composition class floundered and rebelled when students tried to learn the program with minimal lab assistance. The contrasting experiences of writers working with the same software, setting, and teacher suggest the complex issues in designing a Writingland.

Consider the political and social environment. Often we don't see this level of interpretation unless we compare programs based on differing political assumptions. Consider two centers for teacher education in technology—one in the United States, one in South Africa. The Cape Educational Computer Society is a teacher center run by progressive educators in Cape Town.[5] As a visitor to CECS, I was impressed by the desktop publishing operation. I learned that computers are not valued mainly for supporting writing processes, marketable skills, or pride in authorship. To CECS teachers, computers are tools that empower students to create newsletters, posters, banners, and other forms of political expression. Desktop publishing also enables teachers to design materials outside the control of the apartheid curriculum—for example, by adding black authors to the literature syllabus. At CECS-sponsored computer camps, teachers and secondary students work together with technology available only in white schools. This collaborative learning experience is seen as a prototype for democratic education in South Africa.

Saint Louis's Regional Consortium for Education and Technology might be an American counterpart to CECS, but the consortium's political and social assumptions lead to a different conceptual framework for computers. It trains teachers in a wide range of hardware and software through workshops, guest presentations, and users' groups. The technology can be applied to support whatever goals the teacher and the school curriculum may have. Language arts workshops, often cosponsored by area schools and colleges, help teachers adapt their favorite classroom activities to disk. Consortium courses stress the power of new tools to aid in developing, revising, and publishing text—not the wider political purpose that text may serve.

Borrowing C. H. Knoblauch's definitions (76–79), we can conclude that CECS sees technology in a framework of critical literacy, while RCET uses a framework of functional or personal literacy. To do more than echo the dominant discourse, teacher educators in the United States must take a reflective and cross-cultural stance. "Most practicing and would-be English teachers are encouraged to see their tasks unproblematically, without much sense of dissonance and unaware that they can decide the nature of the reading and writing they profess in classrooms" (Clifford, "Enacting Critical Literacy" 256). By viewing other settings, teachers can see through the high-tech glitter to technology's political underpinnings. As John Clifford might ask, How could a multigrade class in rural Alaska use this software? A writing lab in Harlem with fifteen computers and no lab assistant?

In planning teacher education programs, we should draw on all three levels of interpretation—tool, setting, and society. Through this analysis, we challenge teachers to make conscious their own conceptual frameworks.

How does access to technology reflect differences in gender, race, class?

Literacy is power. It provides access to a community whose members usually surpass, in education, influence, and wealth, those who are not literate. It offers access to what Paulo Freire calls a discourse of political reflection, problematizing, and change (*Pedagogy*). Literacy also serves as a barrier excluding those whose consciousness, if raised, might be troublesome; as Thomas Holt reports, most states forbade teaching slaves to read or write. One of our goals should be to show teachers how literacy can be shared rather than restricted. Shirley

Brice Heath and Leslie Mangiola, for example, developed a cross-age tutoring program pairing at-risk fifth graders with younger nonreaders.

Unlike the orality of preliterate cultures, both literacy and the secondary orality of the media rely on tools—manual, mechanical, or electronic (Ong, *Orality and Literacy*). A clear danger is the unequal distribution of electronic tools, widening the gap between rich and poor, male and female, black and white, urban and suburban. In fact, many studies have shown that access to technology varies by students' race, gender, social class, and language background (Gomez 318; Jessup 336–39).

Yet we cannot assume that all wealthy suburban schools have acquired state-of-the-art labs while inner-city schools are computer wastelands. A 1983 study in California found that ninety-three percent of the computers were purchased with special funds targeting gifted-and-talented, disadvantaged, school-improvement, or desegregation programs (Gomez 322). Through such funding, for instance, the Saint Louis public schools' Division of Technology had installed an IBM lab in every high school by 1985—when many suburban schools were still sharing two computers in the principal's office.

More insidious are the inequities in the *use* of computers by race, gender, and social class, reflecting differing assumptions about learners and their abilities. Numerous studies (see Gomez for a review) have found that low-income and minority students tend to use computers for a remedial curriculum delivered through gamelike software. While the haves are doing word processing and programming (learning to gain power over a computer), the have-nots are doing grammar drills (learning to be programmed). These patterns hold not only from school to school but from room to room within a school. If we believe in affirming the stories, minds, and voices of all our students, then we must resist such impoverished applications.

After hearing about the research on access and equity, several of our teachers decided to give lab priority to their weakest students, those who must learn to draft and proofread many times. One teacher explained, "So many kids labeled 'gifted' just happen to have computers at home. It's the basic writers who need the experience and who really feel the impact of the computer." Some teachers, when they were training lab aides, challenged social expectations by choosing female, nonwhite, low-achieving, or lower-class students. By serving as computer aides, members of marginalized groups can gain access to leadership roles (Zeni 141–42). Mary Louise Gomez argues that equity goes beyond merely treating all students the same: "Equitable teaching with computers means providing some students more than equal time" and opportunities, such as actively recruiting them for computer-based courses and activities (320–21).

How does technology change the social relations in writing and research communities?

Computers reshape the social as well as the individual experience of writing. Computers support revision, collaboration, shared texts, and classroom publishing—themes of process pedagogy. But through awkward arrangements of time, space, and tools, computers can also interfere with the flow of reading and writing activities.

During a time of rapid change, teacher education must avoid the tunnel vision of the software catalogs and instructional managers, to focus on building literate communities. We must work toward a progressive discourse of technology—critical and theoretical as well as practical—even amid pressure to keep abreast of developments.

Such discourse may grow from an interdisciplinary exploration like the Technology Study Group of the Fund for Improvement of Postsecondary Education. We were sixty educators, each immersed in research applying technology to our own field. Our dialogue grew over a three-year period via computer conference, a new medium for most participants. The freedom to test out half-formed ideas on an unseen yet engaged audience helped us break out of habitual roles. As a woman just finishing my dissertation, I found myself moderating an online seminar with senior researchers. Emily Jessup notes that a nonhierarchical dialogue often appears in computer conferences. Unfortunately, when the Technology Study Group's grant ended, so did the subsidy for the computer network. Despite what seemed to be strong professional relationships (several of us had collaborated on papers and presentations), the study group never managed to reorganize on another network. The dialogue nurtured by the computer environment did not outlive its medium.

To continue building a discourse of technology, teachers should become researchers of their own classrooms. In 1984, through a grant from the Fund for Improvement of Postsecondary Education, the Gateway Writing Project began studying how experienced teachers of writing would integrate computers.[6] Our method was collaborative action research (Glaser and Strauss; L. Smith). Ten writing teachers documented their struggles and observations in field note logs. I visited classes, adding my own perspective to triangulate the data. The team met regularly for talk and reflection. Our study found unexpected constraints: weeks of waiting for the electrician to wire the alarm meant weeks of delay in opening a writing lab; a DOS disk that didn't match the word-processing package meant almost a year in which students could type, even print, but not save to disk. We also found unexpected affirmations: the power of the teacher, whose personal style colored even the assignments that had been planned and implemented by a team. But the greatest value of this project was in the experience of classroom research.

Action research by insiders, with a consultant linking them to outside perspectives, is well suited to studies of technology and literacy. For the reflective teacher, action research is a way to solve problems, change patterns, and improve instruction. For the scholar, action research is a way to investigate something that won't sit still long enough for a controlled experiment. For the critical educator, it is a way to put educational decisions in the hands of the teachers and students who will live with them. For the feminist educator, it goes beyond the traditional patriarchal research agenda (Jessup 351–52). Action research suggests a commitment to a more equitable society, to open relationships between researcher and researched, to knowledge that is not simply objective but drawn from human reflection in a specific context.

The discourse of technology grows as we venture out from the university to work with practitioners, from kindergarten through twelfth grade. Teacher educators must study new literacy sites and the teachers who are designing them through a process of trial and error, genius and accident. "Design" is, in fact, an apt metaphor in this collaborative enterprise (Ehrmann and Balestri). Students learn to use new writing tools to design their texts. Teachers learn to design new environments that integrate computers and writing. Watching them, we learn to design new clinical experiences in literacy and technology.

Classroom research brings to English education the wisdom of innovative pedagogy, the vision of humane learning environments, and the exploration of new technological possibilities. Through classroom research, we can develop a rich contextual knowledge base to guide a new generation of literacy teachers.

NOTES

[1] The FIPSE Technology Study Group, chaired by Diane Pelkus Balestri, included about sixty directors of innovative projects in higher education. FTSG met from 1985 through 1988 by computer teleconference (online seminars on such topics as design and equity) and also met in person to draft publications.

[2]The National Writing Project is a network of about 150 sites modeled on the Bay Area Writing Project at the University of California, Berkeley. The Gateway Writing Project, an affiliate of the project, is a joint site with two institutional sponsors, the University of Missouri, Saint Louis, and Harris-Stowe State College.

[3]The Christopher Columbus Consortium, funded by Apple Corporation, is a network of school and university collaborative projects using Macintosh computers. At the University of Missouri, Saint Louis, the CCC project was designed by Donald Greer.

[4]*Storyspace,* developed by Jay David Bolter, Michael Joyce, and John B. Smith, is now commercially available from Eastgate Systems, Box 1307, Cambridge, MA 02238.

[5]The University of Missouri has a faculty exchange program with the University of the Western Cape, a progressive, historically black college in Cape Town, South Africa. Faculty members and students from UWC are involved in the Cape Educational Computer Society, but CECS is an independent organization.

[6]For details, see the final report to FIPSE, *Composing, Computers, and Contexts* (principal investigator, Jane Zeni Flinn), Nov. 1987. #G008440408.

PART II

Extending Literacy through Computer Networks

Overview

Reading and Writing on Computer Networks as Social Construction and Social Interaction

Ann Hill Duin and Craig Hansen

In the last decade many composition instructors have integrated computer networks into their classrooms. We see computer networks as a means for students to acquire literacy; that is, the networks can function as localized forums for acquiring the written literacy of a discourse community. As students write, interpret, and negotiate texts via computer networks, they are participating within a context that promotes active learning. We define the literacy that students experience through this new technology as "situated literacy"—the students' making of meaning as they share and respond to texts is a form of literacy situated within the computer network. Situated literacy is similar to "situated cognition," a term put forth by researchers such as John Seely Brown, Allan Collins, and Paul Duguid. Having examined students' cognition in the culture of learning, they find that students learn best when situating their cognition or their making of meaning in a real-world situation that promotes active participation in the learning process. In short, our approach emphasizes the writing context shaped by a computer network. But we go one step further in this overview: we not only focus on the context of computer networks and their relation to literacy but offer an explanation for how this context works. We find social theory (specifically, social construction and social interaction), discussed in some detail below, to be useful in this regard.

To relate all these elements—computer networks, literacy, social theory—sounds complicated. But we find them to be connected in important and fairly straightforward ways, with significant consequences for students. Computer networks are no more than electronically linked computers through which users can readily share, send, and receive files. Yet they can liberate students, who discover new ways of sharing and receiving information, of reacting and responding to their own texts and those of others. Conversely, networks can repress students' voices, by sustaining existing social and political systems that characterize the dark side of our educational system.

Before we describe how computer networks liberate or repress literacy in writing classrooms and in the workplace, we feel that we must first establish a theoretical framework. Since we view literacy in social terms (as in the essays in Lunsford, Moglen, and Slevin's *The Right to Literacy*), we should provide a theoretical underpinning for our notion of situated literacy. Our first step, then, is to define what we mean by this social perspective. After doing so, we will consider the relation of literacy and computer networks.

A social perspective, which has gained increasing importance in nearly all areas of writing research, can be used to study computer networks. From germinal works in the mid-1980s (Bartholomae; Bizzell, "What Happens"; Odell and Goswami), the social perspective has evolved to highly specialized studies in the 1990s (for just a few examples: social interaction over networks, Hartman et al.; effect of corporate power structure on a collaborative project, Cross; the function of writing in democratic society, G. Clark).

In defining the social perspective, Martin Nystrand draws a useful distinction between social construction and social interaction: the former "concerns itself most immediately with communities of writers and readers," and the latter "concerns itself with the individual interactions of writers and readers." Like different ends of a telescope, "one takes a big view; the other looks up close" (4). We feel that the two comprise a social perspective and that the relation between the two has another important dimension: social interaction can be seen as the mechanism for the process of social construction, the means by which individuals cooperate to construct and interpret reality, and a means by which individuals become literate. However, before we develop this thought any further, we need to consider these two theories in more detail.

Social Construction

The basic idea of social construction is that groups of people, bound by shared experiences or interests, build meaning through an ongoing process of communication, interpretation, and negotiation. Facts, beliefs, truth itself result from a social process of conversation and consensus building. Communication between individuals, however it is carried out, is the central means for creating culture: social construction describes, in essence, an aggregate process.

In his essay reviewing the literature of social construction as it relates to writing research ("Collaborative Learning and the 'Conversation of Mankind' "), Kenneth Bruffee identifies three scholars in different fields who have given shape to the social construction perspective: Clifford Geertz in anthropology, Thomas Kuhn in the sciences, and Richard Rorty in philosophy. Others agree with the centrality of their work (see, for example, G. Clark).

From anthropology, Geertz sees shared experiences, our "local knowledge," as exerting a powerful, even determinant, influence on how we, as individuals, perceive the world around us (*Local Knowledge* 215). Whether we are aware of it or not, we actively collaborate with others to build culture out of agreements that are as complex as codified law and as simple as common sense (*Interpretations* 5–6).

Kuhn also sees culture evolving from agreements or consensus building within the scientific community. In *The Structure of Scientific Revolutions* he asserts that scientific discovery is more than truth revealed through empirical research. Rather, it is a social process in which new information is accepted as verifiably true by gradual consensus building. Scientists become successful through their persuasive ability and a mastery of the community's discourse.

From philosophy we again see culture, literacy, and understanding as evolving from sustained conversation. According to Rorty, philosophy cannot be easily separated from society as a whole. What we say and what we believe are inevitably social products. The goal of philosophy is not an assertion of privileged insight but rather extended conversation, with the philosopher acting as an "intermediary" in a society with multiple discourses (*Philosophy* 318). As portrayed by Gregory Clark, Rorty's focus is similar to that of Kuhn in describing "philosophical notions of truth . . . as socially constructed products of the discourse of a particular community" (6). But in some ways, Rorty's is a wider vision than either Geertz's or Kuhn's, for Rorty sees a constructive process working between communities as well as within.

It is important, especially in the context of literacy studies, to emphasize the dialogic nature of social construction. The individual is not helplessly awash in a storm of social forces but is a contributor, a builder. Likewise, the individual is situated within the active development of literacy; it is a two-way, not one-way, process. As Donald Rubin points out, the writer's text helps to define, even change, the social context (10). How this happens on an individual-by-individual basis is the realm of social interaction.

Social Interaction

Social interaction can be described as an exchange of ideas between individuals in a specific setting, for a specific purpose. It is essential to the idea of social interaction that the number of individuals is limited, but Nystrand's view of "dyadic interactions" (5) seems unnecessarily restrictive. There are many ways to approach a discussion of social interaction: from classical rhetoric, where we might examine the complex relation between rhetor and audience (for interesting readings of classical rhetoric, see Carter, as well as G. Clark, ch. 2); or from the growing body of work on collaborative writing, where we might trace the dynamics of multiple authorship (see, for example, Ede and Lunsford, *Singular Texts/Plural Authors*, particularly ch. 4). But perhaps the most useful approach, again within our context of literacy studies, would be to describe a directly social theory of dialogue, and for this task we will turn to Mikhail Bakhtin.

Bakhtin, in a series of works (although this discussion is drawn chiefly from *Marxism and the Philosophy of Language*, by Bakhtin and Volosinov), articulated a theory of dialogue grounded in a social context. A speaker gives voice to a thought, an *utterance*. This utterance, though representing the ideas of an individual, reflects a social environment that is shared. The listener interprets the utterance in a purposeful, conscious act, in terms of his or her own concept of the social context, in terms of what the words mean to him or her individually. This second step, the *understanding*, completes the dialogic exchange: in other words, utterance and understanding constitute a single unit of communication. For Bakhtin, this theory has all sorts of implications. All dialogue should have the goal of eliciting further dialogue, not shutting it off with pronouncements of truth or other forms of closure. Likewise, all dialogue flows from previous dialogue. And no dialogue has meaning apart from a social context. That is, language is not just a social construct but constructs us socially. V. N. Volosinov, who worked with Bakhtin, puts it this way: "It is not experience that organizes expression, but the other way around—*expression organizes experience*. Expression is what first gives experience its form and specificity of direction" (Bakhtin and Volosinov 85).

Thus the key point of Bakhtin's theory, as it informs social interaction and social construction (and ultimately the creation of literacy), is that communication is an active, deliberate process, where listeners and readers are as fully engaged in meaning making as are speakers and writers and where ongoing dialogue shapes and reshapes the larger social context. Clark relates Bakhtin's theory (and other social theories) to composition studies. What is of special significance here is Clark's emphasis, like Rorty's, on the sustained nature of conversation or dialogue within a community, which is necessary for the community's growth and cohesiveness. He would like to see writing instructors increase student awareness of this process, of their responsibilities as writers and readers within a community, and to encourage texts that seek to sustain dialectic rather than closure (71).

Social interaction, then, cannot really be separated from social construction: it is the mechanism by which social construction takes place. While social construction describes the macro processes by which communities interpret the world around them, social interaction describes how such interpretation results from the micro processes of dialogue and conversation.

A Model of Social Interaction and Social Construction for Literacy Studies

To illustrate how social construction and social interaction define situated literacies, and particularly to show how boundaries affect this process, we have developed the following model (which we will later use when we describe current uses of computer networks). Figure 1 shows the operation of social construction and social interaction in an unconstrained, nonboundaried setting.

The innermost circle contains the individual (*I*), floating, as it were, in the broad social universe. The second circle represents

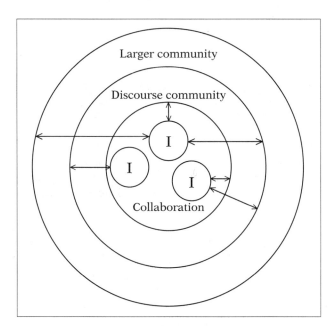

Fig. 1. Individual writers in an unconstrained social construction–social interaction setting

the immediate group with whom the individual collaborates (professional colleagues, a conference group in a writing class, coworkers in a department). We use the term *collaborators* here advisedly: not all communicative acts are formally collaborative (in the same sense as coauthorship), but few are the product of truly isolated, individual activity. Collaboration, in the broad sense here, also includes such factors as input from supervisors, feedback from reviewers, or simply the testing of ideas in informal conversation. Our definition is consistent with the research on collaboration conducted by Lisa Ede and Andrea Lunsford.

The arrows in the diagram represent these social interactions—that is, dialogue or conversation between the individual and the immediate circle of collaborators. Note that the arrows are two-way. The collaboration circle contains few individuals. The next circle represents the "discourse community" (as defined by Faigley, "Nonacademic Writing") of which the individual is part. This circle could have a highly variable number of individuals, depending on the definition (and cohesiveness) of the discourse community. It might be a department within a university or a corporation, or it might be all individuals with a specific common interest, such as lichen collecting. For our purposes, a more cohesive definition makes more sense. In practice, the influence of a discourse community on the utterances and understandings of the individual is potentially large (and essentially sets the parameters for literacy for that community), while the impact of a

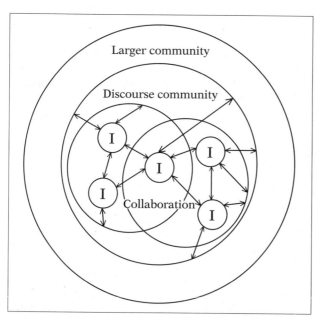

Fig. 2. Collaborative groups in an unconstrained social construction–social interaction setting

specific individual on a discourse community is typically small (although it can be large indeed; e.g., Einstein). How the discourse community is created and maintained by an amalgamation of individual contributions (i.e., social construction) is perhaps better pictured in figure 2.

Figure 2 illustrates the operation of collaborative groups in an unconstrained social setting. Here, multiple *I*'s form a shifting complex of collaborators, of whom only a few are pictured. In other words, the larger circle of the discourse community is "constructed" by multiple collaborative groups; the social interaction between any individual and the community (especially in terms of the individual's shaping the community) is limited because there are so many individuals involved. Yet the effect of the collaborative groups collectively is greater. What further complicates the matter is that any single individual is part of more than one discourse community, with each community, in essence, defining a different literacy.

In both figures 1 and 2, the circle beyond the discourse community represents a larger community. The discourse community might be writing instructors; the larger community might be all teachers. The circles could become broader and broader, including more and more individuals with less and less in common until all of humanity is encompassed, in which case the social interaction of the individual to the community is virtually nonexistent, but the cumulative constructed culture is exceedingly complex.

Figure 3 introduces what we will call boundaries, represented here by the box. Boundaries are im-

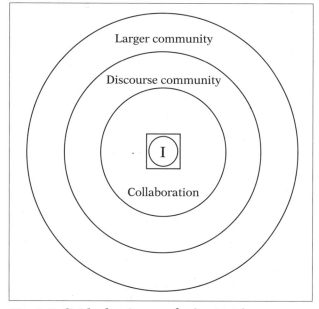

Fig. 3. Individual writer producing text in a contextual vacuum

posed limits on the social interaction between the individual and other circles. Boundaries limit the two-way flow of information, ideas, and influences.

Figure 3 shows a traditional view of the atomistic, lone writer producing text in a contextual vacuum. There is no interaction in terms of dialogue with other individuals. But the figure also shows how difficult it is to imagine the writer isolated from all social input. If the writer reacts to the social context, and the readers interpret the text based on their own perceptions, we have social interaction and the seeds of social construction. In figure 3, then, no literacy is possible, and, according to Bakhtin and others, an impossible situation is represented.

Figure 4 shows the boundary at a different level. The diagram could represent a number of situations, including a writing class in which students write collaboratively in conference groups or by a local-area network.

Notice, however, that the students are cut off from participation in a wider community. In a typical classroom situation, the discourse community is subsumed in the person of the instructor, as assessor and arbiter. The work created in the class does not move to outer circles; the students are not part of a larger dialogue. We view this situation, although it is problematic for most ideas of literacy, as neither good nor bad; as we shall see in some of the studies of computer net-

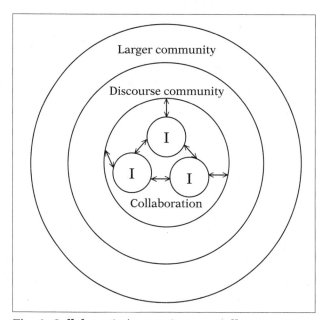

Fig. 4. Collaborative group in a partially constrained social construction–social interaction setting

works, a boundary at this point can be effective pedagogically in a networked environment (and not in opposition to our situated literacy).

If we were to combine figures 2 and 4, we would have multiple collaborative groups with a single boundary around them. This setup could represent several classes collaborating via network. It might also represent an increasingly common network configuration in a large organization, such as a corporation. Groups of departments may be linked by network ("bridged" or "gatewayed" local-area networks), providing a broadly horizontal communications capability (communication between peers), but a narrowly vertical one (communication with higher levels of management). Information then flows freely and informally at a level that often excludes management, a situation that runs directly counter to the hierarchical power structure. In the experience of one of the writers (Hansen), these kind of far-flung horizontal networks often create unexpected cultural tension within corporations.

Social Construction and Social Interaction Caveats

While we think social theory sheds light on the formation of situated literacy, many other factors complicate the apparent simplicity of this model and the entire notion of social construction. First, social construction is, at least in part, a process by which the contributions of individuals gradually build a consensus. There is no reason to believe that consensus per se is a good thing (see, e.g., I. M. Young). The consensus-building process is surely affected by existing power distributions, which may cause it to maintain the status quo and exclude dissenting and marginalized voices. At the level of social interaction, these voices may be strong and eloquent, but they may be filtered by imposed boundaries and the simple cultural inertia of the discourse community.

Second, social interaction, by our Bakhtin model, contains assumptions that probably do not apply in all circumstances. The assertion that social context affects understanding and invention may well be universally applicable, but the concomitant assumption that listeners and readers apply conscious effort in analyzing an utterance, and are determined to contribute to further dialogue, may be reserved for utterances that are judged to have special importance for the individual or that originate within the same specific discourse community. Voices with differing literacies are denied a response. Finally, the structure and use of the networked environment, which is another focus of this essay, may itself have an effect on the type of social interaction that takes place and ultimately the development of literacy.

In the context of social interaction and social construction, literacy can be defined quite simply. An individual who is literate within a discourse community can interact and communicate with other members of that community. The literate individual understands the social context, is privy to the shared beliefs, the unstated meanings. The "illiterate" participant cannot, for a variety of reasons, decode the context. This helps explain the predicament of the student marginalized from mainstream academic culture by race, gender, ethnicity, or other factors. Such a student may be fully literate in one setting (e.g., the family and the workplace, as discussed by S. B. Heath in "Fourth Vision"), actively participating in the creation of meaning, but be sufficiently alienated in the academic environment to be unable to take part in conversation, in dialogue. In short, to be a participant in the constructive processes within a discourse community, an individual has to be "literate" about its social aspects. And to become literate, the individual needs to interact with the community, perhaps be encouraged or welcomed by it. For many individuals, this can quickly become a catch-22 situation: any access depends on initial access.

Therefore, as we apply social construction and social interaction theory to our discussion of studies of computer networks, we focus on the following four areas and related questions:

- *Social construction and interaction*: How does a computer network promote or inhibit the processes of social construction and social interaction? That is, how does it promote or inhibit collaboration and interaction among individuals, collaborators, discourse communities, and the larger community?
- *Situated literacy*: How does a networked environment encourage situated literacy, or the active making of meaning between and within participants? How does a network aid writers in acquiring the literacy of a discourse community? Likewise, how does a network function as a forum for resisting the language of a specific discourse community?
- *Distribution of power*: How do network configurations reflect distributions of power? That is, how do they reinforce or resist existing models of authority?
- *Accessibility*: How do networks allow proximity to others in order to shape a larger view of language and society? Do they allow all participants equal access to the systems?

Next, we present a current, *representative* sample of studies on the use of computer networks in writing classrooms and the workplace, and we interpret the results from these studies in terms of our model and the questions listed here.

Studies on Classroom Computer Networks

Persuaded by the "social linking-together afforded by a network," Geoffrey Sirc and Tom Reynolds implemented a local-area network (LAN) in their first-year and upper-level writing classes. Using the network, students give and receive comments on each other's work during class time, and shared comments appear in a running dialogue on each student's screen. Sirc and Reynolds expected their students to conduct a focused conversation about each writer's audience and purpose for the text. While they indeed found such a dialogue occurring among their upper-level students, their first-year basic writers had collaborative discussions that "seemed more noise than students working in concert toward effective revision" (53, 55). However, they later realized that this "noise" from the younger writers represented an interchange shaped by nonacademic culture rather than academic concerns.

Interpreting Sirc and Reynolds's results in terms of our model, we find that the older students recognized that the instructor was watching; while able to reach beyond this social context, they chose not to for the bulk of their collaborative discussion. They read the social context, and the network became an extension of regular classroom expectations and power relations, albeit a facilitative and convenient extension. In contrast, the younger writers did not recognize the presence of the instructor while they were using the network. The academic experience was likely a new one for them. Because they did not feel any real pressure to accommodate their communication to an academic context, the younger writers centered their dialogue on a struggle for social advantage in the class rather than on the needs of the immediate academic discourse community. Consequently, they were less willing to "risk writing-centered comments," to allow the network to facilitate their entry into the academic discourse community. The younger writers repossessed the network to serve their own ends as they created "a compelling mural of social interaction, a struggle for true power in discourse," whereas the upper-level writers' interaction remained "circumscribed around the limited, formal rules for the successful completion of the assignment, with far more references to the instructor and what he wanted" (66).

In this case, the network was working to promote interaction and collaboration; students easily shared ideas and comments with each other. However, in terms of the distribution of power, the older students acquiesced to established models of authority throughout their use of the network, while the younger writers used the network to negotiate a larger cultural meaning of public stances and identities (67). In a traditional sense of the word, the older students might be recognized as academically *literate*, the younger students less so. But each group saw the network as located in a specific community, requiring a particular style of discourse.

Thus, in terms of our model, the older writers accommodated their discussion to the confines of the academic discourse community. Used during class time and viewed by the teacher, the computer network supported the traditional hegemony in which the teacher imposes the boundaries on interaction within a larger community. The younger writers were as yet unable to adapt their discussion to this boundary; the older writers fully understood the political arrangement of the classroom that discourages such intellectual resistance.

While Sirc and Reynolds investigated a computer network in which students respond and comment on one another's writing, Jerome Bump and his colleagues have used a system called *Interchange* (Bump 52) for class discussion in first-year and senior literature courses and in a graduate humanities class. In this network the instructor does not have the ability to monitor the screens or the conversation, and thus students control the interaction that occurs.

Students used the *Interchange* system to discuss readings for every fourth class meeting, and Bump and his colleagues noted several benefits: it allowed the classes to break down into smaller discussion groups, it enabled instructors to give more individual attention to students, and it improved thinking and creativity. Most important, the system improved accessibility—that is, it appeared to liberate minorities, to restore voices to all students regardless of their sex, race, class, or age. Students who might be dominated by others in a traditional class discussion expressed their views openly via the *Interchange* system.

A key distinction between Bump's application of *Interchange* and the Sirc and Reynolds study is that students in the latter survey discussed their own texts and used the network to give and receive feedback on these texts. In Bump's study, students discussed literary works. When students examine the texts of other writers, they are often more likely to express their opinions, worry less about offending a classmate, and resist a tendency toward silence. Thus, for example, Bump's students could accommodate their computer entries to their literary interpretation rather than adjust their interpretation to requirements of the instructor or of the classroom discourse community.

In terms of our model and the questions stated earlier, we can make two observations. First, in Bump's use of *Interchange*, students' focus on literary works removed some of the complexities of collaborating with other students to negotiate and respond to texts. Second, because Bump worked "to make the controlling instructor obsolete" (56), the ever-present model of authority was absent or the instructor boundary (fig. 4) was eliminated. Here, the network provided a medium for the construction of a limited but useful literacy, as students actively participated in a dialogue and worked toward interpretive consensus.

To promote a forum in which students use language "to resist as well as accommodate" (847), in which students talk and write to each other as well as to the teacher, Marilyn Cooper and Cynthia Selfe have also constructed a network to aid students' discussion of class readings. However, in their case students discuss the readings in computer-based conferences outside of class time. In these conferences students respond to ideas or questions raised in class as well as to their own ideas, problems, or concerns. Moreover, students do not always know each other's identity; they have the option, in some classes, of signing entries with a pseudonym.

Cooper and Selfe found that students in these conferences resisted the roles that academic discourse places on them and instead introduced their own perspectives as they interpreted the readings. Students took on more authoritative roles and became active in their own learning processes. They also discovered that the conferences reduced the dominance of the instructor. Finally, the lack of face-to-face cues eliminated much gender, age, and social status bias. As a result, competition took place "on the level of ideas rather than on the level of personality" (852).

The positive attributes (in terms of social theory) that we identified in Bump's study also apply here. In Cooper and Selfe's use of a network, students can be anonymous, removing (unless they choose not to) some of the immediate social restraints that might limit the participation of all voices in constructing an interpretation of the class texts. However, because students can access this network outside of class time, they are able to read and reflect before contributing to the dialogue. This feature reinforces the network as a site where students can build a peculiarly self-contained discourse community, a situated literacy— limited to text-only participation and assigned class activities but nonetheless facilitating genuine meaning making, where the appropriate literacy is a situated literacy mediated by the participants.

From these studies, one might conclude that networks best promote student-centered literacy and meaning making when they provide a forum for discussing literary texts and when the traditional role of the instructor is reduced or eliminated entirely. However, a study by Karen Hartman and her colleagues found that students who used networks to create, share, and discuss their own texts with other students and with their instructors significantly increased their participation in comparison with student and instructor interaction in nonnetworked sections of a first-year writing course. Students in the networked sections met once a week in a computer laboratory, and they had access to the network from university computer labs at any time during the week. Students used electronic bulletin boards, electronic mail, and two programs, *Comments* (Neuwirth et al., *Comments Program*) and *Talk* (Neuwirth, Palmquist, and Gillespie), to assist them in sending drafts of their papers to each other and to their instructor for feedback.

Studying the patterns of interaction six weeks into the semester as well as at the end of the term, Hartman et al. found that instructors in the networked sections interacted more with their students and, particularly, more with less able students than with better-prepared students. Two results are especially intriguing. First, the researchers observed that students with lower verbal scores on the SAT interacted significantly more with their instructors through the network than did students with higher scores (102). Apparently the network allowed "lower-ability" students an opportunity to access their instructor's knowledge, away from the face-to-face power of the model of authority. Second, the availability of the network substantially boosted student-instructor interaction but did not similarly increase student-student interaction as compared with nonnetworked sections (98). Thus the network made the instructor more accessible to the student; however, perhaps because of the organization of the class and the network, it did not similarly promote collaboration between students.

At the University of Minnesota we have also experimented with computer networks in composition courses, as well as courses in scientific and technical communication (Duin, "Terms and Tools"; Duin, Jorn, and DeBower). Students in these courses meet in a computer laboratory during every class meeting, and a network known as the Appleshare system allows them to collaborate and give and receive feedback during class, as well as outside class, from over one hundred campus locations. Examining students' messages to each other and to instructors via the network (Duin, "Social Construction"), we have found that when they are coauthoring documents, students send most of their messages to students in their collaborative group, and that they use the network as a place to store and share information, to argue and reach consensus on content, tone, style, and direction of a document, and to request feedback from students outside their group as well as from the instructor.

In these examples, networks offer a convenient facility for students and instructors to respond to texts. In particular, those networks that grant students time to reflect before responding give them the chance to contribute to meaning making through written dialogue over a length of time. Networks that provide anonymity allow for greater participation and ultimately greater opportunity for the development of literacy. The key social element, in terms of our model, of all these networks is perhaps not so much the formation of a discrete discourse community but the establishment of a powerful tool for effective interaction and collaboration.

Though these studies primarily show positive effects of computer networks in fostering social interaction and the building of literacy, not all applications work in this fashion. Indeed, however well designed the networks may be (as they were in these studies), they still function in an educational system that essentially preserves the social and political status quo (Lunsford, Moglen, and Slevin). For example, though Sirc and Reynolds's younger students used the network to support the literacy of their nonacademic culture, the older students clearly saw the network in terms of what the academic community expected. Bump's students were granted autonomy through pseudonyms, but they were still bound by the time frame of the traditional classroom (see Lofty's discussion about timescapes). While Cooper and Selfe's use of a computer network outside of class time enabled students to reopen class discussions for their own critique (see Moffett, "Censorship," for an analysis of reopening class discussions and weakening class control), the students were limited to text-only participation and assigned class activities. The structure of the network investigated by Hartman and her colleagues gave students greater proximity to other students and their instructors (see Daniell's discussion, in "Situation," of proximity), yet the students chose to interact most frequently with the instructors or with the established mode of authority. And though Duin's most recent use of a computer network ("Social Construction") allows students to use the network to negotiate and develop collaborative documents, in her earlier studies the majority of messages on the network were, as in the Hartman case, directed mainly to the instructor ("Terms and Tools").

Despite these problems, these networks, for the most part, encouraged an exchange of ideas for cooperative meaning making, involving a wider spectrum of student voices. However, without the benefit of critical perspective and planning, networks can exacerbate the potential to inhibit interaction and collaboration, permit students to avoid active participation and learning, allow only a select few to control the power, and limit accessibility.

Diane Thompson, like Sirc and Reynolds and Bump, used a local-area network during class time to teach basic college writers. When she started, she expected a conversation that would be much like a normal classroom conversation, except for the distinct advantage that students would be writing and that a transcript of the conversation would be produced. Instead, she found that students could not read and write simultaneously, for the longer they wrote, the less time they had for reading; and the slower they read, the less time they had for writing. As students' messages to each other scrolled off the screen, or if a long time passed between messages, students became bored with this kind of collaborative process. Moreover, students who wanted to send private messages to the instructor couldn't, because all messages appeared simultaneously on the shared screen ("Conversational Networking" 194).

Thompson's most striking finding was that she (as the instructor) dominated the conversations. Her analysis of the transcripts from the class sessions revealed that she contributed 40% of the total entries and 60% of the total lines and that her messages became longer and longer throughout each session (196). She states:

> Computer conferencing discourse hinges on the teacher who guides and controls the process. She is responsible for creating multiple dialogues in writing which respond to the needs of each student and to the group as a whole. . . . Whatever the specific content of the lesson, she is at the center of the discourse, organizing and maintaining constant writing to stave off the boredom and rejection which the participants in a computer conference are prone to feel when their comments are not responded to.
>
> (194)

In this case, the lack of private messages and the network itself created a constrained social context (see fig. 3, which depicts a constricted exchange of ideas). For Thompson's students, using the network took more time than did the verbal communication they were accustomed to. As they began to lose interest, it fell to the instructor to keep things rolling: hence, her dominance in messages. These students, in turn, may have felt increasingly constrained by the high visibility of the instructor. They had to compose messages spontaneously that were appropriate for both a peer and an instructor. This network (however unavoidably) was probably not conducive to the "normal" flow of dialogue envisioned by Bakhtin and others and may have seemed like an artificial place to exchange ideas.

Lest we cite only instructor dominance as constraining the social construction of knowledge on a computer network, we note that the collaborators themselves are sometimes to blame. Janis Forman studied the computer-supported group work of MBA students who were both novice strategic report writers and novice users of technology. In this sense, they were much like the first-year students in the studies described earlier—that is, they were newcomers to the discourse expected of them and to the technology. As part of their MBA program, students were required to define and solve a problem for an organization and then present their solutions to their client in a written report. To aid their collaboration, students were provided with computer tools (e.g., word processing, spreadsheets, databases) as well as access to a computer network.

Overall, Forman found that the students had numerous difficulties with the writing task and the technology. They essentially did not use the network (over the course of the project, most students sent only one or two messages over the network, and the largest number of messages sent by any one student was six). In fact, the students saw the network as impeding their interaction. Forman attributes these results to the students' limited commitment toward the new technology, their unwillingness to establish a set of rules for sending and receiving messages, and their conflicting hardware and software preferences. She states that a "full implementation of computer tools to support group writing may require everyone on a student team to regard the tools as direct benefits to doing group writing" ("Novices Work" 69; see also ch. 5 in this volume).

In Forman's case, the limitation on useful interaction and dialogue resulted not from the instructor's behavior or from the technology but from the collaborators' response. Referring to our model, we observe, again, that this study comes close to exemplifying figure 3, in which students erect barriers around themselves and choose not to become part of the discourse community (although they may well be members of other discourse communities that they feel have more to do with their self-interest). When a new network is implemented in the workplace, it is not unusual to see this kind of resistance: some busy employees may not consider it a high priority to change their work habits unless specifically required to do so. This leads us to a discussion of five workplace computer networks.

Studies on Workplace Computer Networks

A great deal of collaboration occurs in the workplace, and while Forman's MBA students perhaps collaborated on the job through other means, they did not transfer such skills to their MBA courses. Because researchers recognize the importance of computer networks in the workplace and are aware of the large amount of collaboration that takes place there, they have begun to develop and study such networks (e.g., see Couture and Rymer; Ede and Lunsford, "Why Write").

Specifically, teams of researchers have worked to develop a set of computer tools to aid collaborative problem solving in face-to-face meetings in the workplace. Mark Stefik and his colleagues developed *Colab*, an experimental meeting room in which collaborators use personal computers on a local-area network (Xerox PARC). Much as the local-area networks described earlier displayed students' comments on a shared part of each student's computer screen (Bump; Sirc and Reynolds; Thompson), *Colab* helps collaborators act simultaneously, write independently, and enter new text into a shared database.

Because there is no formal research on the effects of *Colab* and because the bulk of the collaborative texts developed are confidential, we can only speculate on how this network fits into our model. *Colab* sets up conditions for the interaction that might be useful in building consensus, and the simultaneous entries should encourage equal participation (as well as fast typists). However, like the local-area networks used in writing classes, *Colab* seems better suited to quick decision making and quick responses than to the extended dialogue that characterizes a discourse community and the development of literacy. And the meeting room concept is similar to the writing class networks in another way: while individuals meet and collaboratively problem-solve via *Colab*, their discussion stays within the *Colab* environment. They currently cannot access other networks or other discourse communities. (It is worth noting that, in the early 1990s, there is a definite trend in the corporate workplace toward "open systems networking," a trend well documented in the computer industry trade press. This kind of networking would link disparate computer systems over vast geographical distances. This trend has numerous implications for networking in the workplace.)

Researchers from the Center for Machine Intelligence, strongly influenced by the *Colab* system, built the *Capture Lab*, also a meeting room that provides a local-area network for groups of collaborators (Elwart-Keys and Horton 38). Investigators have studied the *Capture Lab* by videotaping meetings and keeping computer logs of the participants' use of the system. As in the local-area networks used in classrooms, writers can move their text or graphics from their individual machines to the public screen for discussion; however, in this case an individual's text is not public unless the person chooses to make it so. Like *Colab*, one of *Capture Lab*'s goals from our perspective is to create a more socially neutral working environment. In a sense, the collaborators' work is "captured" in the lab, and again we see the network as a boundary to a larger process of interaction and construction. Indeed, Elwart-Keys and Horton state that "Capture Lab users have difficulty coordinating different media and the transitions between group meetings and office work. Some bring paper copies (often printouts of computer-resident information), which cannot be shared or edited during the meeting" (43). Similarly, students who have access only to local-area networks must coordinate work outside of class time with that accomplished in class.

Basically, *Colab* and *Capture Lab* inhibit interaction beyond the "captured" environment; therefore, these networks are accessible only by the chosen few allowed to be part of the group. In addition, when working in these environments, employees are expected to concentrate on the project at hand; such a restriction inhibits semistructured messages that often contain the nuggets of new ideas and directions. By establishing a boundary around the collaborative groups, these networks limit access and the free flow of ideas.

As computer networks proliferate in the workplace, other researchers have developed a system that can help professionals filter, sort, and assign priorities to network messages, much as we filter and sort our junk mail. Thomas Malone and colleagues implemented *Information Lens*, a system that helps workers organize messages that are addressed to them and locate useful messages they would not normally receive (314). Workers can use templates to compose specific types of messages; they can specify rules to filter and classify their incoming messages; they can distribute particular messages to anyone who might be interested; and they can establish rules for messages addressed to anyone who might be interested. To our knowledge, there is no parallel network in writing courses that would allow students to specify rules to filter and classify their incoming and outgoing messages.

As an example of how workers use *Information Lens*, all *New York Times* articles are sent electronically to the system, and because workers have identified information, such as the subjects or authors they are interested in reading, the appropriate articles are automatically sent to them (315). As with most workplace networks, *Information Lens* has not been tested by outside researchers. In regard to our model, part of what this system accomplishes is well represented by figure 2. Individual workers indicate the extent of their involvement with others, not according to the constraints of the network but according to their own interests and specifications. It is a device by which individuals can self-select a community of interest, but it accomplishes little more and thus restricts the development of literacy.

Essentially, unless collaborators know what knowledge (in the form of keywords) to specify, they cannot interact with the group. Likewise, the structuring of message types limits collaborators to the specifications determined by the organization or by certain users. Malone and colleagues state that "individuals who begin using the information sharing system before most other people do can get some immediate benefit from constructing rules" (326); that is, if I get there before you, I set the rules for the communication that follows. We see this system as perpetuating the roles that organizational discourse inscribes for its workers. There is relatively little room for meaningful interaction outside the immediate circles of collaborators. In this system, an individual's established knowledge allows him or her accessibility to more knowledge. Consequently, those with "corporate" literacy can increase their literacy; those without such knowledge regress still further.

Other researchers have studied the use of computer-based tools to support collaboration in the workplace. Bonnie Johnson and her colleagues describe the *Coordinator System*, a computer-conferencing system that helps workers to initiate discussions of possible projects and to set schedules for the projects. Johnson et al., who studied three groups that used the system to aid collaboration, found that the groups did not use the system a great deal at the invention stage of their projects. In contrast, the system helped them handle conflict and gave workers greater access to information.

Others who have used the *Coordinator System* say it fails because it is so explicit about the communication process. Commitments made in the workplace are often ambiguous, and minor deviations from a set schedule are often overlooked. When designing the system, developers eliminated this valuable flexibility of gracefully overlooking deviations from a schedule. Yet another problem is that managers say it deprives them of a critical aspect of their power—that is, since information is available to everyone on the network, the traditional power structure is undermined (T. Erickson 58–59). Thus, because the network does not adequately reflect the social and political realities in the organization, those who traditionally possess power are disturbed by it—just as some composition instructors may be displeased by the redistribution of power that networks offer the writing classroom.

As in the classroom, most linked computer systems in the workplace require writers to compose on a network, and their final products are also used from a network. These networks provide "a writing context in which both process and product are mediated via the computer terminal" (Denise Murray 35). In an eight-month study of the use of such a network by one IBM project manager and his seventy-eight colleagues, Murray worked to identify the cognitive and contextual strategies the writers used to accommodate an environment in which both process and product are mediated through a computer network. Murray found that writers chose to use electronic mail for complex technical descriptions or highly sensitive issues because the computer network allowed them to plan "at the point of utterance" (52). According to Murray,

> computer conversationalists, while adapting their composing processes to the particular task environment, create a new mode of discourse, one that is most appropriate for particular tasks (e.g., brief, nonsensitive), for particular interpersonal relations (e.g., informal, collegial), and for particular modes (e.g., medium distance between participants and topic). (53)

In our model, Murray's findings most closely represent figure 2, with one major qualification. The circles around the collaborators become nearly one with the circle of the discourse community. That is, the network allowed writers to create situated literacy, a new discourse community, one that was appropriate for their tasks and interpersonal needs.

Discussion

Clearly, the relation between a social perspective posited on the processes of social construction and social interaction and computer networks is not simple. But we would like to emphasize a few key points.

First, the terms *social construction* and *social interaction* describe a process of meaning making in our culture: however much they help us understand the way literacies are formed, they are, as descriptive concepts, neither good nor bad, desirable or undesirable. Yet, we feel, when a network mirrors the operation of a larger culture, we have something unique to offer students: the chance to participate in meaning making, in the development of situated literacy(ies), on a comprehendible scale.

Second, networks have an interesting effect on the social dynamics of the classroom and the workplace. In some cases, they simply extend the traditional instructor-based or manager-based hegemony to a new medium. In other cases, the authoritative (and sometimes constraining) presence of the instructor or the manager can be minimized through the use of a network. Networks can encourage students to interact textually, separating classwork (i.e., responses to student or outside texts) from social maneuvering. And, most important, researchers report that networks encourage the participation of voices that may otherwise be marginalized because of race, ethnicity, gender, or other factors. This is, potentially, a profound advantage of networks, both in the classroom and in the workplace.

Technologically, networks can create their own social context and may help create situated forms of literacy. While the studies we have reviewed raise these issues, we have no answers to offer. It appears from the studies that networks that allow students or professionals time to reflect before joining the dialogue have benefits over networks that capture real-time discussion in the classroom or corporate boardroom. Also, we have not dealt at all with issues of physical access, system ease of use, and user technophobia: these factors can have a major impact on how networks are used and who uses them.

Finally, we have seen that computer networks are compatible with models of human communication proposed by theorists. That is, depending on the configuration of the network, people can interact effectively, build on the ideas of others, and work toward consensus in interpreting the world around them. Further, they can form unique, self-contained discourse communities, bounded by common tasks, interests, and technology. Such developments are encouraging for several reasons. First, networks, by reflecting the interaction of communities (or by creating their own), do not have to be a source of cultural tension, an unnatural place to write or do business. Second, it seems likely that some students gain insight from the computer-networked microcosm into the cultural macrocosm in which they read, write, collaborate, and construct. Third, the computer network is a compatible environment for a social concept of literacy, a literacy that is situated in a specific social context. Because networks make possible wider and more flexible participation, literacy on linked computers may have a different look and feel from text-based literacy.

Our discussion of culture and computer networks is far from complete. Fortunately, it is supplemented by the five chapters that follow. Betsy A. Bowen, in "Telecommunications Networks: Expanding the Contexts for Literacy," considers three types of telecommunications networks: those that foster exchanges of students' writing, those that support collaborative projects, and those that encourage communication among teachers. Janis Forman, in "Literacy, Collaboration, and Technology: New Connections and Challenges," explores the confluence of literacy, collaboration, and groupware as she examines what it means to be literate in the computer-supported collaborative class. Gary Graves and Carl Haller, in "The Effect of Secondary School Structures and Traditions on Computer-Supported Literacy" offer ideas about how instructors at the secondary level can establish, maintain, and teach reading and writing in computer-assisted literacy centers. William Goodrich Jones, in "Humanist Scholars' Use of Computers in Libraries and Writing," reports on research on how computers are transforming the ways in which scholars access, retrieve, and use information. And finally, Billie J. Wahlstrom, in "Communication and Technology: Defining a Feminist Presence in Research and Practice," describes current, representative applications of computer technology in literacy programs and suggests how both the research and the pedagogy surrounding these uses could benefit from a critical consciousness of gender.

Readers are encouraged, as they explore the five chapters in this section, to keep in mind the four issues and the questions we raised earlier:

- How does each network or use of computers promote or inhibit social construction and social interaction between individuals, collaborators, discourse communities, and the larger community?
- How does each network or use of computers encourage situated literacy or the active making of meaning between and within participants?
- How does each network's configuration reinforce or resist existing models of authority?
- How accessible is each network?

Harriet Malinowitz, in her article "The Rhetoric of Empowerment in Writing Programs," notes that writing should be seen as part of a larger process, a process of engagement in a dialectic with others. She states that the reorganization of authority in the classroom must consist of more than just the encouragement of students to write, that it must represent a total reordering of the classroom to incorporate collaboration and liberate education:

> To engage in this collaboration sincerely, teachers must be willing to give up some of their own power. To give up power does not mean to make oneself neutral, inconspicuous, ignorant, unavailable, irresponsible, or value-free. Rather, it means to investigate the social foundations and the limits of one's own process of making meaning, recognizing that this construction is political, as well as technical. (155)

Networks provide one means of reorganizing classrooms and workplaces to situate literacy within the control of writers and workers.

Chapter 4

Telecommunications Networks: Expanding the Contexts for Literacy

Betsy A. Bowen

> *Do you have a hunting season? We do. My grandfather got an antelope the first day of hunting season. Me and my dad went hunting and got a buck deer. Do you know what a buck is? A boy deer is a buck. Half of my family calls the antelope a prairie maggot.*

This letter, written by a second-grade student in Wilsall, Montana, to a first grader in Boston, is part of the large volume of correspondence among students using educational telecommunications networks. On these networks students write and read in order to share information about themselves, their communities, and the issues that concern them. During the past ten years, teachers and researchers have used telecommunications networks to create "functional learning environments" (J. Levin et al., "Microcomputer"). This chapter examines the goals that underlie educational telecommunications projects, the design of selected projects, and some of the issues that educational telecomputing raises.

Three kinds of telecommunications networks will be considered here: those that feature exchanges of students' writing in a variety of forms; collaborative projects, usually in the natural or social sciences, in which students at different sites work to solve a shared problem; and those that encourage communication among teachers, not simply to manage the projects in which their students are engaged but also to foster their own professional development. These three kinds of projects remind us that opportunities for literacy are not limited to English

113

classrooms nor reserved only for students. Collaborative science projects require students to write and read as they collect and share their information. Primary and secondary school teachers may find new audiences and purposes for writing as they become members of an invisible professional community created only through reading and writing.

Examining Telecommunications Projects

In the light of the enthusiastic claims sometimes made for educational telecomputing, we should keep in mind several questions as we examine individual telecommunications projects:

1. In what ways and to what extent do telecommunications projects provide contexts for literacy substantially different from those available in most classrooms? What uses do students make of writing, reading, and problem solving?

As with any educational computing project, we need to concentrate on the educational purposes that the technology serves, rather than on the technology itself. Margaret Riel points out that "trying to determine the educational potential of computer networks is a bit like trying to assess the educational potential of a film projector" ("Intercultural" 30). The value of each depends not on the equipment itself but on the uses to which it is put and the educational context created around it. We need to learn more about ways in which telecommunications activities provide, or fail to provide, opportunities for writing, reading, and learning that differ from those we can create without these resources.

In the relatively short history of educational computing, we have repeatedly seen computers themselves become the focus of instruction, rather than the intellectual development that computers can enhance. Such a response is a particular danger with technology as glamorous and expensive as telecommunications. If we do not find imaginative, expansive ways to use this technology, we will shortchange students, fool ourselves about what we are accomplishing, and squander a costly and still-limited resource.

2. What characterizes these projects? What goals do they share? To what extent are they effective in meeting those goals?

The first of these questions calls for careful descriptive research on the design and uses of telecommunications projects. While many anecdotal and loosely descriptive reports have appeared, there has been little systematic description of the uses teachers and students make of telecommunications. In fact, according to *Electronic Learning* (Mageau), no study has been done even of the number of schools involved in telecommunications projects.

This shortage of research is not surprising. Most telecommunications projects are relatively young; many have been funded by short-term grants. Moreover, telecommunications projects are, by nature, labor-intensive, often requiring a year of setup time in which participants learn to use the equipment and integrate the technology into their classrooms. As a result, few projects are well enough established for participants themselves to report on the ways in which students and teachers use telecommunications and the effects of the technology on their reading, writing, and learning. Because of the lack of basic descriptive research, it is difficult to assess the effectiveness of telecommunications projects. We need to learn what effective use of telecommunications looks like, what contexts encourage it, and what conditions discourage participation or lead to exchanges that participants find unsatisfying. As educational telecomputing matures, such assessment will become crucial, if we are to refine our current models of telecomputing and develop more productive ones.

3. In what ways do these projects take into account special issues— such as equitable distribution of resources and sensitivity to cultural differences—that may arise when students communicate across distance and social class?

While the primary educational goal of telecommunications projects may be to improve writing, reading, or problem solving, most projects share an additional goal: to bring together students separated by distance, nationality, or economic status. As a result, projects face two related problems. The more obvious is the potential for misunderstanding or misjudgments when students work with students from schools or backgrounds unlike their own—a problem exacerbated because participants remain, in essence, strangers, seldom meeting face to face.

The second problem is more subtle: in seeking to provide diversity among network participants, organizers must ensure that no participants become the exotic "other." To fail to acknowledge or explore difference among participants means lost opportunities for learning and, possibly, increased risk of misunderstandings. Yet to value some participants—especially those in unfamiliar locations, such as Native American reservations or poor rural areas—largely for their difference, or "otherness," is to risk exploiting them. This problem reveals an inherent tension in educational telecommunications networks: that although they have been described as a "democratic" medium (Stephanie Lynn; Spitzer, "Writing Style"), we can undermine that democracy through inattention or even good intentions gone awry.

How Telecommunications Networks Work

All these projects—writing exchanges, collaborative science projects, and telecommunications networks for teachers—use similar technology to enable participants to exchange messages with one another. A detailed explanation of the technology used in telecommunications networks would be unnecessary, soon obsolete, and, for most readers, dull. The principles of electronic communication, however, are relatively straightforward and helpful in understanding both the nature of telecommunications projects and the difficulties that participants encounter.

Most electronic networks rely on microcomputers, modems, and a host computer (either a mainframe or a microcomputer) to transmit messages through telephone wires. Participants at one site compose messages at a microcomputer that they send to the host computer. There, messages are stored until participants at another site log on and read them. A modem connects the microcomputer to the telephone wires and converts computer signals to ones that can be sent and received through the wires. The host computer, which may be thousands of miles from the participants, stores and organizes messages so that network participants can log on, read, and respond at their convenience.

In addition to this equipment, participants need special software and, generally, a subscription to an information service or utility. Communications software enables the microcomputer to dial and log on to the host computer and then send, receive, and save files. Information utilities or services are commercial firms, such as Unison and Compuserve, that allow participants to reach their host computer by dialing a local telephone number. Because they deal in bulk, these services can generally transmit messages to the host computer at less than the standard cost of a long distance telephone call. Information utilities may provide a variety of other services, such as online help and access to specialized databases. (For further information on telecommunications equipment and services for education, see Clark, Kurshan, and Yoder; Dodge and Dodge; Glossbrenner; Tulonen.)

Telecommunications remains a relatively expensive undertaking for schools, although it is used extensively in business and, increasingly, for recreation. There is not only the initial cost of equipment and software, an outlay that in early projects was often underwritten by grants, but also the incremental costs of telephone charges and information services fees. The latter costs hit rural schools, for whom telecommunications is especially useful, particularly hard. These schools are often remote, even from the local access numbers provided by information services, and may incur long distance charges every time they log on.

Ironically, even the simplest piece of equipment—the telephone jack—sometimes causes problems for teachers. Few teachers have outside lines in their classrooms; many are forced to transmit students' messages from home or the school library. One teacher on Breadnet, a network for writing teachers, reports having to keep the computer and modem on a rolling cart she could wheel to the main office, the site of the school's only outside line (Tulonen).

In general, educational electronic networks offer three kinds of communication: electronic mail, or "e-mail"; electronic bulletin boards; and teleconferencing (Crowley). E-mail is much like ordinary mail. Messages are essentially private, addressed to a single recipient or small group of recipients. Electronic bulletin boards, in contrast, provide more public communication. Most are dedicated to particular topics, with messages posted so that all participants in the conference can read and respond. Both e-mail and electronic bulletin boards provide asynchronous communication—that is, messages can be sent and stored, to be read by other participants later. Teleconferencing, the newest of these three options, provides synchronous, or "real-time," communication. Participants in the teleconference are online at the same time. They "chat" by sending and receiving messages that are transmitted almost instantaneously. The advantage of teleconferencing is its speed and immediacy. It demands, however, considerable planning and coordination of schedules—often difficult in classrooms—to ensure that all participants are ready to communicate at the same time. The inconvenience and expense may make it of limited value for schools.

Writing Exchanges

Telecommunications exchanges of students' writing range from very simple—exchanges of letters between two or three schools—to complex activities, such as responses to drafts, bulletin board discussions of shared readings or special interest topics, and collaborative writing projects.

Several claims have been made about the benefits of telecommunications: that it introduces students to an emergent technology, that it provides purposeful contact among students otherwise separated by distance or circumstance (Schrum), that it increases motivation for learning (J. Levin et al., "Observations"; Mageau; Schrum), and that it helps students develop an ability to anticipate and accommodate the needs of an audience (Cohen and Riel, *Computer Networks* and "Effects of Distant Audiences"; J. Levin et al., "Observations"). While the first three of these putative benefits might apply to telecommunications exchanges of any kind, the last is especially important to teachers of writing.

The development of audience awareness in young writers has been of particular concern in composition studies for the past two decades. Lisa Ede defines audience awareness as "those methods designed to enable speakers and writers to draw inferences about the experiences, beliefs, and attitudes of an audience" (140). Considerable research suggests that the ability to predict and accommodate the needs of one's readers is a hallmark of skilled adult writing (L. Flower, "Writer-Based Prose"; Flower and Hayes; Scardamalia and Bereiter). In their study of "expert" and "novice" adult writers, Linda Flower and John R. Hayes note that both the plans and the texts of skilled writers were substantially more "reader-centered" than those of less-skilled writers. A good writer, they claim, can create "a sophisticated, complex image of a reader" (26). Writers can then use these more fully instantiated images of their readers as they develop and test their plans for texts. Such plans are more rhetorical than those of less-skilled writers; they take into account the task, the *ethos* the writer intends to create, and the effect the writer wants the text to have on the audience.

Young writers, by contrast, often cannot imagine how a reader's knowledge, needs, or beliefs might differ from their own. Without this perception, children are unable to accommodate those differences in their texts. As a result, their writing—particularly school-sponsored writing—is topic-centered, not rhetorically organized. Marlene Scardamalia and Carl Bereiter characterize such writing as "knowledge-telling," because writers simply present information in their texts in the order in which it occurs to them (165). Such compositions are similar, in some ways, to both the "bed to bed" narratives that Donald Graves has observed written by very young children (156) and the "writer-based prose" that Flower has noted among unsophisticated adult writers.

Developing such a sense of audience and an awareness of rhetorical situation is a complex task, influenced by age (Kroll), instruction (J. Britton et al.), and cognitive development (L. Flower, "Writer-Based Prose"; Scardamalia and Bereiter). Recently researchers have begun to examine the nature of reading in schools, particularly the purposes for which students read and the tacit expectations students bring to their tasks (Applebee and Langer; L. Flower, "Construction"). These studies suggest that students develop sophisticated uses of language when they read and write to provide information that other people need, solve shared problems, and reflect on what they know, and that these activities are most likely to happen when students can both learn and teach other students. They suggest, in other words, that we need to expand the contexts for literacy in the classroom.

Telecommunications exchanges of writing may offer one way of doing so. Certainly that premise underlies several of the telecommunications projects designed for English or language arts classrooms. One of the earliest was the Intercultural Learning Network (ICLN), developed by James Levin and colleagues at the Laboratory of Comparative Human Cognition at the University of California, San Diego. Working with researchers at the Center for Cross-Cultural Studies in Fairbanks, Alaska, Levin and his associates initially linked one classroom in San Diego with another in rural Alaska. Throughout the year, students used an electronic network to exchange messages (J. Levin et al., "Microcomputer"; J. Levin et al., "Muktuk"). By 1987, the ICLN had expanded to link schools in the United States, Israel, Mexico, and Japan and had developed larger cooperative research projects. In these, students investigated social and cultural issues such as differences in international news coverage (Cohen and Miyake; Levin, Kim, and Riel) and the relation between social pressure and suicide among Japanese teenagers (Riel, "Intercultural"). In addition, students contributed to an online newspaper, the *Computer Chronicles*, with student-run editorial boards responsible for reading and selecting submissions from contributing schools (P. Horowitz; Riel, "Intercultural"). Since 1987, the ICLN has continued to expand, developing more ambitious projects in language arts and the sciences.

These exchanges, Moshe Cohen and Margaret Riel contend, provide a "functional learning environment [that can] engage students in writing as a communicative act with a real audience." Such exchanges, they continue, provide "an ideal situation" for students to learn to address different audiences, since writing serves as the primary means of communication and differences in students' lives and experience make accommodating the audience both necessary and rewarding (*Computer Networks* 1, 9).

Other telecommunications exchanges of writing have incorporated various features of the ICLN. On Breadnet, sponsored by Middlebury College's Bread Loaf School of English, students have contributed to special-interest bulletin boards and subconferences, consulted with experts from a variety of fields, corresponded with electronic pen pals, and created an annual anthology of student writing, with submissions sent on e-mail and on disk. Other projects also feature exchanges of students' writing. On AT&T's Long Distance Learning Network, for instance, elementary school students in nine classrooms in the United States, Canada, and Australia created round-robin stories (Lake), with students at each school contributing part of a story. Mary Crowley describes exchanges among students at seven schools across Canada and the United States. Like Cohen and Riel, Crowley reports that the geographical and cultural differences among students motivated them, leading these students to produce over one thousand messages in four months.

The Austra-Alaskan Project (Erwin) has sponsored similar exchanges of writing between students throughout Australia and Alaska. Interestingly, Alaska has been the site of considerable telecommunications activity, since the great distances between towns makes enhanced communication desirable and a statewide computer system, based at the University of Alaska, makes telecommunications possible. While this network is used primarily for the "delivery" of college courses, it also provides e-mail and bulletin board services for the state's fifty-six school districts (Seguin). Other notable telecommunications exchanges include Keyboard Connections (Kurshan), which links schools in Australia, the United States, and New Guinea; Apple Computer's ACOT project (A. Erickson); and Fred Mail, a national low-cost educational network, recently used for projects by James Levin and colleagues ("Observations") and by the Kids 2 Kids network (Mageau).

Science Networks

Opportunities for literacy, however, are not limited to English classrooms. Telecommunications projects in the social and natural sciences may also provide students new contexts for writing and reading. In most of these projects, students at a variety of sites collect and analyze data, sharing their results on the network, in order to answer a common question or solve a shared problem. Often experts at universities or other research institutions support the projects by suggesting activities, guiding data collection, and helping with the analysis of findings. As a result, science projects are often more labor-intensive and less self-sustaining than are many of the writing projects in which teachers themselves can organize and coordinate the activities.

Because students in science projects require information from all the other sites to solve a problem, collaborative science projects on electronic networks may provide unique opportunities for collaborative learning. James Levin and his associates contend that, at their best, such projects "can allow us to engage students in the full range of activities of adult scientists (conference presentations, paper submissions, review and publication, scientific debate, etc.) not just as data collectors for some distant expert" ("Observations" 21).

One project that incorporates some of these features is the National Geographic Kids Network, developed by the Technical Educational Research Centers (TERC) with support from the National Science Foundation and the National Geographic Society. In this project, fourth, fifth, and sixth graders at schools across the country have investigated topics such as regional differences in pet ownership and acid rain, creating online databases that they use to generate and test hypotheses (Kurshan; Julyan). With the support of the Department of Education's Star Schools Program, TERC has developed Global Lab, an international environmental studies network for secondary school students (Kapisovsky; Mageau). Students in the United States and the former Soviet Union will establish and monitor outdoor labs, sharing, on the network, the data they collect on environmental conditions.

Other telecommunications projects in the sciences include the Noon Observation Project (J. Levin et al., "Observations") on Fred Mail, in which students at various sites measured shadows to compute the circumference of the earth; AT&T's Long Distance Learning Network, with projects in both natural and social sciences (Mageau); and Bank Street College's Earth Lab Project, in which students in New York City have investigated national weather patterns (Brienne and Goldman; McCarthy).

Teachers' Exchanges

All the projects described so far require communication among participating teachers to arrange and carry out activities. A few networks encourage, in addition, sustained communication among teachers on issues of professional or pedagogical concern. While this article focuses on telecommunications and literacy for students, teachers' use of tele-communications is also of interest because of the relation between teachers' visions of literacy and the contexts for literacy they create in their classrooms.

Considerable research and much anecdotal evidence suggests that teachers often feel isolated from colleagues and professional dialogue. Fragmented school schedules, the scarcity of meaningful in-service programs, limitations on travel to professional conferences, and the lack of reward for professional activity all contribute to the problem. Many teachers, especially good ones, crave the professional support and stimulation that those of us in postsecondary education take for granted. Telecommunications networks may be one means by which teachers can create a supportive professional community for them-selves. Moreover, telecommunications exchanges may provide teachers with a place for purposeful, informal, reflective writing—a valuable addition, since many teachers, even in English, engage in a limited range of writing during the school year. The National Writing Project was among the first to argue that, to teach writing effectively, teachers of writing must see themselves as writers, finding audiences and pur-poses that make their own writing worthwhile.

Telecommunications exchanges, then, seem promising, but only a few projects have viewed teachers' use of electronic networks as an important goal. This omission may be one indication of a tendency to rely on experts and overlook the resources and needs of teachers. One of the projects that has encouraged teachers to participate is the East-ern Navajo Agency Network, which serves six isolated Bureau of Indian Affairs schools in New Mexico. This project has set as one of its four goals the increase in professional communication between teachers throughout the network (Schilling and Gittinger). Breadnet, discussed in the following section, has also sought to promote exchanges between teachers as a way of countering professional isolation, and the lethargy it can cause, and of promoting opportunities for writing not usually found in schools.

Close-up of One Network: Breadnet

A detailed examination of one project may give a better sense of the evolution of telecommunications projects, the kinds of writing that exchanges foster, and problems that remain to be resolved in educational telecomputing. Breadnet, sponsored by Middlebury College's Bread Loaf School of English (with support from Apple Corporate Grants and the Bingham Trust), was established in 1984 to expand students' opportunities for writing and to increase professional contact among teachers. Most of us involved in the project were technological novices when we began. We learned how to set up modems and incorporate telecommunications into our classrooms. We also learned, although more slowly, how to achieve productive exchanges in which telecommunications was essential to, but not the focus of, the project.

Since 1984, Breadnet has expanded from a network linking two or three schools to one that links over one hundred schools across the United States and in foreign countries on several continents. In that time, participating teachers have tried a variety of formats for exchanges, generally moving from small projects linking two or three schools to larger ones involving a greater number of schools for a limited period. This change parallels what James Levin and colleagues described for the Intercultural Learning Network. Teachers' exchanges, however, have remained largely unchanged. They continue to be loosely structured discussions conducted on e-mail and computer conferences.

An early project—a three-way exchange between schools in Sewickley, Pennsylvania; Wilsall, Montana; and the Pine Ridge Reservation in Kyle, South Dakota—exemplifies Breadnet's first years. The teachers in the project had two goals: to provide "real contexts" for student writing (J. Schwartz 16) and to make inquiry the center of the course. To those ends, students wrote and exchanged portraits of themselves and their communities, interviewed students at other sites about their lives and interests, conducted and shared oral histories, and wrote a large number of letters to individual correspondents. Jeffrey Schwartz claims that "as students wrote within a meaningful and purposeful communication context, they learned to test their stereotypes, to expand their skills as writers, and to perceive the computer as an instrument of communication" (24).

In a related project, second graders in Wilsall, a small ranching town, corresponded with first and second graders at a private school in Boston. These young writers exchanged letters, essays on local transportation, and notes about books and birthdays. Initial messages were brief: "I have brown hair and eyes and I am four feet tall," "Do you live in a forest or do you live in a city?" Many of the later messages were considerably longer and showed students trying to make information that was familiar to them clear to distant readers. For example, a student in Wilsall wrote, "A three-wheeler has three wheels. You work on a ranch with it. It is like a motorcycle but it is about middlesized. Its wheels are about two feet wide. You don't even have to balance it." Teachers reported that, for these young students, the speed of telecommunications and intimacy of letters were important in sustaining the exchanges.

While writing exchanges such as these clearly seem to benefit participants, they also have limitations. The first is practical: with only two or three classrooms involved, delays or problems at any site can interfere with the entire project. This drawback is most acute in exchanges of letters, as James Levin and colleagues ("Observations") have noted, since failure to receive a response can undermine a student's commitment to the exchange. The second problem is pedagogical: once students have examined differences in their communities and lives, they need some reason to continue using the network to exchange writing. Since telecommunications is only one way to provide real audiences for student writers, we should ensure, when we use networks, that the scope and rapidity of communication they provide is essential for our purposes.

The larger collaborative exchanges, focused on a particular activity, have attempted to avoid these problems (Durbin and Holvig). Of these, the largest and most enduring has been World Class (Stumbo; W. Wright, "Telecommunications" and "On-line"). For five years, students and teachers in the United States and abroad have examined environmental issues. Each year, students in participating schools have read a shared text—from *National Geographic*, *Newsweek*, or *Time*—as a foundation for their research and discussion. Then they have debated the issues with one another and, in different years, with representatives from the Nature Conservancy and the federal government. Students across the network have commented on local instances of environmental problems: strip mining in Wheelwright, Kentucky; an oil spill near Irvine, California; the increasing demand for water in Deming, New Mexico. Contributions from students in Peru and Indonesia have helped students see the complex relation between environment and economy in developing countries. Typically, students have worked in small groups to prepare messages for the conference. One message, from students in Clarkstown, New York, presented questions that the students in the group had struggled with. It reads, in part:

> Are some of these so-called "global issues" actually local issues? Will our energy and garbage problems, if handled properly, have

any effect on the global problems? Or have things gotten too out of control? Should we start by examining our daily consumption habits or by attacking the corporations and governmental policies that make it all possible and acceptable? (2 May 1989)

In addition to these large projects, Breadnet has developed smaller subconferences, such as Workshop, in which students post drafts for responses from other writers. Perhaps the most interesting of these are NATalk and NA, conferences for Native American students and teachers, respectively. Unlike other Breadnet projects, these conferences are "closed," limited to participants who teach or learn on reservations or nearby communities. Because Bread Loaf has a long-standing commitment to teachers at Native American schools, the subconferences link classrooms in Native American communities from Alaska to Arizona. Furthermore, faculty members at two universities who teach courses on Native American literature participate on the network with their students.

Like other Breadnet projects, these subconferences have two goals: to enable students to correspond electronically, and to allow teachers to talk with one another. Gary Griffith and Lucy Maddox maintain that teachers on NA share a particular set of concerns such as "the relationship of non-Indian teachers to Indian students and parents; drugs and alcohol in the schools; the uses of dialect in teaching writing . . . [and] the problems of professional isolation" (2). Correspondence on both these conferences remains private, in part because of the sensitivity of the subjects and in part because Native American culture has often been casually misappropriated, even by the well-intentioned. One teacher explained that the project had received numerous requests to join the conference from teachers not at Native American schools. Participants, however, have declined the requests, she said, because "you don't want to feel you're performing in front of someone." That privacy and participants' shared concerns seem to have created a special community of trust, one that another participant described as "a family," commenting, "I don't think I could have made it through last year without it."

Teachers' Exchanges on Breadnet

Unlike most other telecommunications projects, Breadnet has, from its inception, seen the reading and writing that teachers do as intimately connected to the opportunities for literacy they provide in their classrooms. Because the medium encourages spontaneity, casualness, even playfulness, telecommunications networks can offer teachers a place for informal but substantive reflection. Teachers' correspondence on Breadnet has included a wide range of issues: censorship, state-mandated testing, impasses in the classroom, the effects of budget cuts, as well as notes on conferences, recommended reading, and personal news.

It has not always been easy to sustain these conversations. In an article about Breadnet teachers' correspondence, Ike Coleman asks, "What is it that encourages people teaching five classes a day, collaborating with students on after-school projects, and reading papers over the weekend to pay to spend their free time writing about education for a fairly small audience—with none of the perks of publishing?" Because the teachers' correspondence is less goal-directed than students' projects are, it is especially vulnerable. It falters, and participants drop out, when a single person or two dominates the conversation or when messages grow so brief or superficial that they stimulate little response. Even when messages are substantive, it can be difficult to follow any single conversation because of the "multiple threads of discourse" (J. Levin et al., "Microcomputer" 33) that characterize electronic exchanges.

At its best, however, the network has offered many Breadnet teachers correspondence they have valued. One commented in an entry:

> I believe that a lot of what Breadnet does for people is invisible. . . . Just knowing that the network is there . . . even on weeks when nothing happens but chit-chat—and little of that—means more to me than I can easily say. I truly believe that isolation is the bane, not just of rural teaching, but of public school teaching in general. And though I'm afraid isolation will always be a problem for teachers, with Breadnet, I don't feel it's possible for a dedicated teacher to feel the degree of isolation I felt teaching in rural Virginia, isolation that drove me from the profession.

Issues to Consider

The previous discussion suggests some of the issues that need to be addressed when we consider using telecommunications in the classroom. Riel reminds us that "new tools alone do not create educational change. . . . The power is not in the tool but in the community that can be brought together and the collective vision that they share for redefining classroom learning" ("Building a New Foundation" 35). As we examine telecommunications projects in schools, we should ask ourselves what kind of "collective vision" these projects embody and in what ways they may redefine educational practice. Without such examination, we are likely to develop uses of technology that reproduce, and reinforce, current practices. If these practices have not, on balance, contributed to the literacy of all our children, then we will be using technology to exclude further those with the greatest needs and, consequently, the greatest claim on our resources.

As we review these uses of technology, two concerns stand out: the equitable distribution and use of resources, and the model of the learning process that these network projects represent. Because telecommunications requires extra resources, it exacerbates a problem computers always present: how to make these special opportunities widely available, among schools and within classrooms. Even now, relatively few schools have telecommunications equipment; even fewer make it available for students of all academic levels. While some poor and rural schools have been supplied with telecommunications equipment through private funding and research grants, such sources are limited and often of short duration. As school budgets are cut and private funding becomes increasingly limited, there is little assurance that we will offer equitable access to these specialized resources for students— regardless of race, sex, or academic track—throughout our schools.

Even when computer resources are available, equitable access to them is not assured. At particular risk for exclusion are girls, and students in lower academic tracks, who tend, disproportionately, to be the poor and minorities. In discussing the gender gap in technology, Sue Jansen points out that "technological designs are also social designs. Cultural values, economic interests, and political decisions are as integral to their composition as mathematical calculations, motors, cams, circuits, and silicon chips" (196). In a longitudinal study of schoolchildren, Kathy Krendl, Mary Broihier, and Cynthia Fleetwood found that girls were "less interested in computers and less confident in their computer skills" (85) even when they had as much experience using computers as boys did. These findings suggest that, to provide female students with truly equal opportunities at the computer, we may have to modify not only classroom practices but also deeply embedded cultural features that contribute to these disparities. (For further discussion of these issues, see "Communication and Technology," by Wahlstrom, in this volume. The chapter provides an extensive critique of current uses of technology as they affect women and reflect cultural assumptions about gender.)

The other group of students likely to be excluded from creative uses of computers are those variously categorized as "low-ability," "low-track," "limited"—in short, those already at a disadvantage in society. One teacher on Breadnet commented on the problem in an entry:

> By miles and miles the biggest problem with electronic mail in the South Carolina project is getting to the computers. And it's not because the schools don't have them. I have yet to visit a secondary school that doesn't have a bank of the machines—but they're reserved for computer instruction. . . . As a result, in too many cases, the only kids who're likely to learn how to use the machines in any real way are those whose parents have computers—and use them—at home. And that means the families who are both literate *and* at least fairly well off financially. . . . I know schools have always discriminated against poor kids. But in the 80's we don't need another way to beat down the poor.
>
> (12 Jan. 1988)

The issue of exclusion is important to examine because networks have frequently been represented as increasing opportunities for vulnerable students. Ann Duin and Craig Hansen, in their overview to this section of the volume, for instance, note claims that networks, which mask users' social status, can encourage participation by students who are otherwise marginalized because of race, ethnicity, or gender. Certainly, many of us working with networks hope that such optimism is justified, but we would do well to keep in mind Billie J. Wahlstrom's warning, in chapter 8, that we may not have done as well as we think in using technology to reduce the social inequalities reflected in our classrooms.

Some of our experiences with Breadnet have made us cautious about claiming that electronic networks can obscure long-standing social inequities and the educational disparities to which they give rise. Teachers on the network have occasionally reported that students remain highly sensitive to differences in ability and even social background of network participants. While networks mask some social cues, they force students to confront differences—in ability, race, or class—that they might not otherwise encounter in relatively homogeneous classrooms. For that reason, we should scrutinize our claims about the democratic potential of telecommunications. Unless we do so, we may mislead teachers into overlooking the mixed effects of networks in their classrooms, and we may fail to learn from teachers who deal with those effects perceptively and creatively.

As Riel points out (*"Computer Chronicles"*), our applications of technology reflect our implicit models of learning. Even now, much computer software in schools is used for computer-assisted instruction, largely "skill-and-drill" programs designed to teach a clearly defined sequence of information or skills. Such uses of the computer, Riel maintains, reflect what Lawrence Kohlberg and R. Mayer describe as the "cultural transmission" model of education. Paolo Freire describes this approach as the "banking concept" of education "in which the students are the depositories and the teacher is the depositor. . . . Knowledge is a gift bestowed by those who consider themselves knowledgeable upon those whom they consider to know nothing." Such an approach, Freire claims, "negates education and knowledge as processes of inquiry" (*Pedagogy* 45–46; Penguin ed.).

Creative uses of technology, with which Riel associates some telecommunications projects, reflect a significantly different model of learning. These projects assume a social model of learning, one in which learners make sense of the world by interaction with others in purposeful activity. Because of its emphasis on both social interaction and inquiry, such a model is associated with Lev Vygotsky's and even Freire's concept of education for critical consciousness.

We clearly need to be careful about appropriating either Vygotsky or Freire without considering the differences between the contexts they described and our own. We also need to realize, as C. H. Knoblauch points out, that we risk misinterpreting or romanticizing Freire's position if we assume that literacy in itself is sufficient to redistribute "prerogatives" in society. Instead, Knoblauch argues, literacy—however it is defined by a society—is the only means that "enables entrance to the arena in which power is contested" (79). Despite these cautions, Riel's discussion of underlying models is significant since it challenges us to scrutinize current uses of technology and to develop new ones that reflect our best beliefs about what education might be.

Chapter 5

Literacy, Collaboration, and Technology: New Connections and Challenges

Janis Forman

This chapter takes its purpose and scope from three research and teaching streams that have begun to converge in composition studies—literacy, collaboration, and technology. Recent literacy studies show that broad cultural, political, and socioeconomic forces influence the ways students learn to read and write and what constitutes that learning (e.g., Lunsford, Moglen, and Slevin). Studies have also shown that such forces influence collaborative learning, reading, and writing (e.g., Clifford, "Toward an Ethical Community"; Gere and Roop; Schilb; Selfe, "Computer-Based Conversations") and have drawn attention to the significance of the group and its practices to collaborative composing (Forman, "Discourse Communities" and "Novices Work"; Karis; Lay, "Interpersonal Conflict" and "Androgynous Collaborator"). At the same time, research in the management of information systems (MIS) stresses the increasing presence of *groupware* (technology to support group work) in business and school settings and its applications to team activities, including collaborative composing (Johansen).

Besides research, our teaching experiences suggest that the collaboratively based classroom is complex and problematic (e.g., Karis; Smit; Stewart; Trimbur). As a microcosm of the broader society, student groups can embody the tensions, born of differences in age, class, gender, and race, that themselves reflect cultural, political, and socioeconomic inequalities. Moreover, student teams can experience difficulties in group dynamics—how, among other things, to determine authority, manage conflict, distribute work, allocate credit, and sort out individual and group goals and methods for achieving those goals.

Once technology is introduced into this environment, the complexity only increases. An "add technology and stir" model does not work. Although some of the rhetoric about technology in collaborative classes suggests that the model is effective, my experiences and those of other instructors belie such claims (Hawisher and Selfe, "Rhetoric"). Unexamined additions of technology to the collaborative classroom can, in fact, intensify the difficulties of teaching and learning.

What happens, then, when literacy issues are intertwined with those of collaboration and a technology that supports collaboration? This chapter explores the confluence of these three issues—literacy, collaboration, and groupware—giving special attention to the third element in relation to the other two. The purpose is to shed light on what it means to be literate in the computer-supported collaborative class; who gets to be literate and why; and what challenges are created by cultural, institutional, political, and socioeconomic forces, group processes, and individuals' preference—all of which can limit or enhance the number of students who join the ranks of computer-supported literacy.

The chapter begins by offering a brief definition of *computer-supported literacy*. Then it discusses how students' computer-supported reading and writing are nested in broader contexts. Third, it considers the immediate context for computer-supported reading and writing— namely, the nature of the small group, particularly in relation to the group task. Fourth, it looks at the role of individual group members and their prior writing and technology experiences as these inform the team's and the individual's adoption, learning, and use of groupware. Finally, it draws out the implications of this discussion for the teaching of composition and literature and suggests topics for future research.

An IBM-sponsored study of computer-supported collaborative writing illustrates some of these issues. Four teams of business students from the University of California, Los Angeles (fifteen participants in all), were observed and interviewed during the course of a six-month consulting project for industry that resulted in a long report. The purpose of the data gathering was to ascertain how and why teams used technology to write their reports. Each team was given a package of computer-based tools to assist members in group writing and project management. The package consisted of portable personal computers with portable printers and modems; an integrated software package with word-processing, spreadsheet, and database capabilities; and a telecommunications package allowing for electronic messaging, electronic file transfer, and electronic filing and bulletin board. In addition, the students had a variety of opportunities to learn how to use this equipment, including training sessions, help from trained assistants, and simplified versions of manuals. Teams were not required to use the technology provided by the study, except to prove competence in its use. Computer-monitored data were collected on the use of the telecommunications package for messaging and document transfer. Although the computer equipment was rather sophisticated for the late 1980s, many schools are now or will soon be incorporating this kind of technology in their basic literacy programs and will expect students to use it routinely for collaborative work.

Computer-Supported Literacy: A Definition

The initial working definition of *computer-supported literacy* presented here is that it consists of a complex set of competencies—the ability to work in groups effectively, to learn collaboratively, to create a high-quality written product, and to make intelligent choices and uses of technology that assist in collaborative composing. But we should recognize that this definition is not value-free. As C. H. Knoblauch has argued, "Definitions of the concept incorporate the social agendas of the definers. . . . Literacy never stands alone as a neutral set of skills; it is always literacy for something" (75). For example, literacy values may include a concern that students have opportunities to identify and debate conflicting ideas and interests, that they value difference, and that they regard their growth as readers and writers in broad cultural and political terms rather than as the acquisition of a narrowly functional competence.

With technology as part of this new equation for literacy, access to groupware becomes essential for enfranchisement. And extrapolating from literacy studies that explore the power of young children's lessons about reading, writing, and listening (e.g., S. B. Heath, *Ways with Words*; Fishman; Lofty), we may infer that the sooner technology is made available to children and the better integrated it is in their school, community, and home lives, the more likely that computing will be useful to them as they read and write collaboratively.

Influence of the Broad Context and the School Environment

Cultural, political, and socioeconomic forces come into play in decisions about who gets access to technology. Although data on access to groupware are not available, marketing analyses indicate that access to computing is dramatically skewed by income and gender. Sixty-three percent of families with incomes of more than $50,000 have at least one member who uses a computer at work, compared with 24% of families with incomes under $35,000; and in 43% of the affluent families, at least one person uses computing at school, compared with 21% in the lower-income households. Primary users are also more likely to be male than female (*Personal Computers*). Access is differentiated, too, by race and language background, with minority students and those with non-English backgrounds having less opportunity to use technology than white students. (See Gomez for further discussion of the inequitable distribution of technology resources and its consequences for literacy.) The absence of technology in poor households and its presence in privileged homes suggest a growing chasm in literacy practices—for instance, in the use and value placed on reading, writing, and listening in conjunction with technology. Also, students who have access to computers in school but not in the home may have more difficulty learning technology than do their classmates with greater exposure to technology.

Thus, cultural, political, and socioeconomic forces promote or inhibit opportunities for students to use technology. But, as my research also indicates, the immediate institutional environment, its technology resources, and its expectations about how technology should be used for reading and writing influence student teams as well. (See Graves and Haller, ch. 6 in this volume, for discussion of two different institutional environments and their impact on the establishment and fortunes of computer-assisted classrooms; see Kling and Scacchi for examination of this issue as it pertains to business settings.) Like students at other research universities supported by corporate funds, the business students at UCLA who participated in the IBM study were a socioeconomically and politically privileged group. One-third of them had home computers, all of them had access to computing at school, and, thanks to the sponsorship of a "literate agent" (Lunsford, Moglen, and Slevin 3) in the form of IBM, they had laptops and groupware as well.

Yet, as may occur in schools where technology is unevenly distributed among students, the UCLA teams never achieved full use of the technology to assist them in collaborative composing. They experimented with group support technology, but, by and large, teams' patterns of computer use—for word processing, graphics, spreadsheet and database management—reflected standard application of technology throughout the program at the time of the study. Interviews with participants revealed that their limited use of technology derived, in part, from institutional expectations about technology use that ran counter to the technology use (such as electronic messaging and document transfer) researchers and vendors had anticipated when the groupware was introduced in the project. Because messaging and document transfer capabilities were not part of students' socialization into the larger school setting—no one else used this technology at that time—participants were not familiar with the technology and had not experienced its utility across a wide range of courses and social activities. As one participant who used technology in limited ways commented, "Telecommunications would be a wonderful thing if everyone at AGSM [the Anderson Graduate School of Management] had it. It would enable us to get rid of the mail and the reminders, and it would be useful for club activities and recruiting." (In discussions of the social perspective for reading and writing on computer networks, Duin and Hansen, in the overview to this section, look at both interaction of specific writers and readers and social construction by larger communities of users. In the UCLA study, limited access to technology in the community—the school—influenced participants' use of technology for their interactions.)

Thus, despite training sessions that directly linked the technology to the students' report-writing assignment, the circumscribed usefulness of the technology—its limitation to the one assignment—diminished its attractiveness to teams. In effect, to the extent that teams used groupware, they represented a "hyperliterate" minority population, able to use more advanced technology than other students but unable to influence or coerce diffusion of the technology into the larger school population.

Although school culture can discourage groupware use in literacy programs and classrooms, it can also foster full and independent choice by students. For instance, the lack of an institutionally prescribed computer package and the variety of hardware and software packages available to the UCLA teams at school (or at home, in the case of the personal computer owners) encouraged freedom of choice in selection of hardware and software. The teams could thus pick and choose among the technology options and piece together a technology package that suited their inclinations rather than matched the ideas of the vendors or research team.

The issue of who gets enfranchised and what form that enfranchisement takes is indeed a complex one. There are, first of all, cultural, political, and socioeconomic factors. The ability of a student's family and school system to purchase equipment separates the haves from the have-nots. But as important is the school culture in its expectations of how technology is to be used.

Influence of the Group

Nested in the school setting and influenced by it and by broad societal forces is the small group, which itself has an effect on technology choice and use for collaborative reading and writing. The nature of student groups and their dynamics contribute to computer-supported literacy.

Unlike most groups in industry, student groups are generally nonhierarchical and immature—that is, team members have, by and large, not worked together before. As a result, many of these groups lack established norms, formal procedures, values, and agendas, and team members are unaware of one another's strengths and weaknesses and level of commitment to a school project. In other words, collaborative writing groups form themselves *as groups*, with all the concomitant strains that accrue from the process, while they are asked to handle a collaborative assignment and to use technology to do so. As illustrated by the four UCLA student groups, the immaturity of teams may intensify three related difficulties that limit the possibilities for computer-supported literacy—the management of group processes, the writing assignment, and the choice and use of technology to accomplish the task. The following sections describe specific difficulties faced by the UCLA teams but are intended to suggest that such difficulties may be representative of what other student teams may encounter as well.

Group Processes

As most instructors who run collaboratively based classes will confirm, the group processes of student teams can be fraught with inefficiencies and unproductive conflict. Group processes, such as conflict management,[1] can be hampered by the immaturity of teams. Undefined and fragmented teams—a characteristic of group immaturity—have been described by the small-group specialist L. Dave Brown as exhibiting "too little conflict . . . unswervingly cooperative action strategies, and collusive harmony and agreement in place of examination of differences" (231). In the UCLA study, three of the four teams (the exception was a mature team, one in which members had worked together on several projects) chose to avoid conflict at great costs. Group invention, the full exploration and debate about ideas, suffered from the teams' conflict avoidance, with teams losing potentially valuable, divergent perspectives of their members. For instance, on team A, two members split off from their teammates, with whom they were experiencing conflict, to decide, on their own, the focus and scope of their report. On team B, the only female member of the group had an unpopular approach to presenting the methodology section of the report—but it was worthy of consideration. Her three teammates dealt with this situation by revising her write-up without consulting her. Equitable division of labor was the victim of the teams' conflict avoidance as well. Two of the teams (A and C) had freeloaders who consistently reneged on assigned tasks; both teams worked around the delinquent students and, as a result, wasted time and took on a disproportionate share of the work. Project management[2] was also hampered by conflict avoidance. For instance, members of team B who each wanted the final say on the report engaged individually in endless editing of their report, without keeping each other abreast of changes and the reasons for them. Partly as a result of group immaturity, both productive debate and the equitable and efficient allocation of tasks among team members may never occur on student teams; the chances for computer-supported literacy, are, therefore, diminished.

The Writing Task

In addition to these challenges of group processes in immature teams, students who have no experience writing collaboratively in an assigned genre may face a variety of writing problems. For the UCLA teams, these difficulties included inefficient division of labor, ignorance of generic requirements for style and presentation of arguments, poor understanding of the rhetorical situation and of the need for multiple revisions, and inadequate decisions about when it was better for all team members to work on the writing as a group and when it was preferable for them to work individually. The novelty of the writing task may, then, complicate the prospects for computer-supported literacy.

Choice and Use of Technology

Along with forming themselves as teams and composing collaboratively in a new genre, student writing teams need to consider how they should use technology to accomplish their writing task. As discussed above, one impediment to optimal use of groupware may be a school culture that does not incorporate the technology throughout the curriculum. But, as researchers in MIS have also shown (see, e.g., Kiesler,

Siegel, and McGuire 1126), groups also have difficulties in using technology because they do not have agreed-on norms and routines for using it. For the UCLA teams, despite early training sessions that stressed exactly how the groupware could assist teams at various stages of writing a long and complex document, no team engaged in sufficient discussion about how groupware should be used. As a result, all the teams created inefficiencies as they attempted to use technology for their writing efforts. For instance, there were time-consuming transfers of texts between different-size disks when teams failed to standardize on hardware (laptop or desk model computer), and text transfer and format changes necessitated by team members' use of different word processing packages. Thus, although technology may ideally serve as a tool for reading and writing collaboratively, student groups may be burdened by the need to learn what technology best serves their purposes and how to use such technology. (Anacona and Caldwell stress the necessary links between purposes and technology in their studies of groups in industry.)

Influence of the Individual

The nature of groupware itself and the conflicting technology preferences of team members can further challenge computer-supported literacy in school settings. Because groupware is, by definition, a highly *interdependent* technology, its effectiveness as a writing and reading tool depends, in part, on the agreement of team members to use a common system. In other words, such technologies cannot be used successfully by individuals alone but need two or more group members (Markus and Forman). Moreover, when student teams are free to choose rather than required to use groupware—as the UCLA teams were—individual preferences can complicate teams' choice and use of technology for writing. In each of the four UCLA teams, students' unique and sometimes conflicting histories in using technology resulted in uneven learning of groupware and commitment to its use. Most notably, students had different tolerances for problems associated with learning new technology. For instance, because of a bad experience he had had learning to program in a college computer course, one student on team B voiced his unwillingness to invest time in learning a telecommunications system that caused him considerable inconvenience. As he reported to the researchers, "I won't subject myself to the indignities of using faulty computer software." But another student on that team exhibited patience for what she perceived to be minor glitches in the system. The first student abandoned both the study-provided word processing and telecommunications, whereas the second wanted to continue using them. On the same team, another member strongly advocated the use of electronic messaging, but he stopped sending messages when his teammates, who did not recognize the benefits of messaging, failed to respond.

Besides varying in their learning of and commitment to groupware, students are likely to disagree in their evaluations of specific word-processing packages and, as a result, to champion different ones. For example, one member of team D condemned as illogical the study-provided software's system of "frames" for inserting graphs and new information into ongoing text. Another team member found it self-evident and efficient. To be fully functional, the team needed to settle on one package.

Further, computer-supported collaborative writing can exemplify what the small-group specialist Joseph McGrath calls a "mixed-motive" task (96)—that is, one in which the interests of the individual may conflict with those of the group as a whole. In particular, students can differ in their willingness to learn a technology they perceive to be helpful to the group as a whole but less beneficial to themselves in their specific roles and responsibilities on the project. For example, on team C, one member refused to learn the spreadsheet package adopted by the others. Since she was responsible only for contributing data analysis to be included in an appendix, she preferred staying with the software she already knew, *Lotus 1-2-3*. As she explained to the researchers, "I know *Lotus* inside and backwards. With the time factor, I didn't have the time or the interest to learn a new spreadsheet." Thus, because of her discrete role in the writing, she opted for giving her own needs precedence over those of her team for coordinating sections of the report, an efficiency that could be achieved only if all team members used the study-provided software.

Ultimately, individuals who emerge as leaders on student collaborative writing teams can decide on the technology package the team adopts, and such leaders may have their individual interests foremost in mind rather than the good of the team as a whole. On the UCLA teams, leaders had the primary role in writing the report, coordinating the discrete writing tasks of others, and handling technology support functions such as archiving, designing formats, and training others. (See Forman, "Leadership Dynamics" for a full discussion of leadership issues.) Teams made different technology choices, but the preferences of the technology leader were the deciding factor. In each instance, the package that leaders chose created a pattern of group writing that best suited their own needs. So, for example, the leader on team A had members work individually on sections of the report and transfer their files to his home computer through the telecommunications package. This procedure was his preferred means of collaboration (and one anticipated by the vendors and researchers), in part because he did not want to work with the group editor, a former friend with whom he had felt increasing conflict during the project. On team B, the leader favored what he called a "party atmosphere" for composing, as he told the researchers. All team members congregated at his apartment and worked in tandem on the laptops or, in his case, on his home computer. The other team members then transferred files from the laptops to his computer by using the leader's two phone lines to upload files from the laptop to the telecommunications system and to download them from the system to his computer, where drafts of the full document were stored. This face-to-face use of document transfer, intended for asynchronous communication,[3] was a technology configuration un-imagined by the vendors and researchers but a comfortable choice for the team leader.

Not surprisingly, because most student teams are immature, they may never adequately identify or negotiate differences in individual preferences and in the emergence of leadership that can determine technology choice and use. Thus significant obstacles to computer-supported literacy may operate beyond the awareness of the very people subjected to their impact.

Implications for Collaborative Reading, Writing, and Literature Classes

References to the four UCLA teams throughout this chapter underscore the significance of submerged issues that nonetheless affected the literacy practices and development of each group and each participant. Students ignored or failed to recognize such matters as individuals' prior use of technology, writing experience, and group experience, as well as processes of the team itself, even though the researchers questioned them about these issues during the project. Perhaps what was at work was a kind of "agnosis," or "not wanting to know," that Andrea Lunsford, Helene Moglen, and James Slevin (5) have identified as the greatest threat to literacy. Certainly, in three of the four teams (all but the mature group), members took pains to avoid conceptual and interpersonal conflict, at great cost. By not looking at these issues, did teams assume that the problems would go away?

From my study of the four teams, I recognized, with some urgency, that the computer-supported collaborative class must bring these issues to light so that students can exercise rational choice in their computer-supported collaborative work, rather than submit unthinkingly to unseen and undebated influences on that work and on themselves. Several formats for raising these issues suggest themselves, such as electronic messaging exchanges, face-to-face talk, group-process essays, and "literacy autobiographies" (self-studies focusing on the environmental and group influences on students' growth as thinkers, listeners, readers, and writers).[4]

On the basis of earlier discussion, students ought to do the following (regardless of format):

- consider the influences of cultural, political, and socioeconomic forces and of the school culture on their attitudes toward and experience in writing, reading, collaboration, and technology
- observe and evaluate their group's development and dynamics, including such issues as conflict management and leadership
- judge the role of individual differences in the way the group manages writing, reading, and the use of technology

These situation-, group-, and self-audits should help students assess the influence of their environment, in the broadest sense of the term, and their own histories as shaped by that environment, on the literacy practices and development of their teams. These audits may also enable students to voice both disagreement and consensus in their collaborative groups on a range of issues and, ideally, may encourage the use of the group as an ethical forum for consideration of literacy practices and values in students' immediate context—the small group itself—and in the larger economic, political, and social structures in which groups are embedded. (See Schilb for a discussion of how collaborative activities can encourage or discourage critical scrutiny of literacy values and practices.) In literature classes that use computer-supported collaborative reading and writing, these audits may help create what Stanley Fish has called an "interpretive community," a group of readers who bring their social and aesthetic values and assumptions about discourse to the study of literary texts.

In the light of the pedagogy recommended here, it is now appropriate to return to the earlier descriptive definition of *computer-supported literacy* and identify the social agendas with which it is and is not aligned. Most obviously, computer-supported literacy should not blindly serve market forces to increase demand for new technology products. (Hawisher and Selfe, in "Rhetoric," warn against the pitfalls of mindlessly endorsing investment in computing.) The audits suggested here are forms of scrutiny with broad latitude—for instance, students can decide that the best technology is a limited set of options or, as with one of the UCLA teams, a configuration unimagined by the research team or vendors.[5] The literacy advocated here is not aimed primarily at achieving the group efficiency and effectiveness—at turning out a competitive product as cheaply as possible, using patterns of hierarchical authority common to industry groups—that concern corporations when they purchase groupware for collaborative writing teams. (See Trimbur and Braun for a discussion of the distinctions between the aims of a literacy pedagogy and the interests of organizations that use collaborative writing.)

The literacy advocated here is, in fact, most closely aligned with Charles Schuster's definition of literacy as "the power to be able to make oneself heard and felt, to signify . . . the way in which we make ourselves meaningful not only to others but through others to ourselves" (227). The audits described above should contribute to such literacy, since they promote class activities focused on literacy issues *as identified, imagined, and debated by students*—issues such as the collaborative group's location in broader institutions and the effect of those institutions on the group, the formation and dynamics of the group, its reading and writing practices, the role of individual preferences, and the place of technology in all these matters. This line of inquiry will help us break from the "short history of educational computing" in which "computers themselves become the focus of instruction, rather than the intellectual development that computers can enhance" (Bowen, ch. 4 in this volume).

Obviously the success of the pedagogy linked to this definition of literacy depends on instructors having value systems compatible with it. And, ideally, instructors' roles and responsibilities would be flexible—at least until there is some evidence of how instructors may best intervene—and might consist of online coaching, leadership of in-class discussions, facilitation of small-group work, and lecturing. Outside specialists might supplement this kind of class: small-group specialists for discussion of group processes, and MIS specialists for discussion of individuals' and groups' choices and uses of technology, and of institutional influences on technology adoption and diffusion. (See works by Dyer and by Shonk on small-group issues and by Galegher, Kraut, and Egido on MIS issues.)

Suggestions for Further Research

The argument raised here for computer-supported literacy suggests a number of questions worthy of further consideration:

- What are the effects of broad societal forces, school cultures, group functions and processes, and individual preferences on such literacy practices?
- How is technology introduced and diffused within a community? Which factors impede and which enhance its use?
- How do instructors' and institutions' definitions of literacy influence the ways that technology is introduced and used?

As the UCLA study indicates, technology use by individuals, groups, and larger communities has broad cultural, political, and social dimensions. This research should encourage more ambitious, broad-based investigation of computer-supported literacy, such as longitudinal studies of the literacy practices of communities with and without access to technology, as well as more limited experimental studies of collaborative reading and writing with and without technology. Findings from a set of systematic studies should ultimately inform our teaching. Further research is mandated, for, as Richard Lanham has argued, "It is becoming increasingly clear that technology will interact with literacy instruction in our democracy in ways not so deterministic as early thinkers predicted. We will have to *decide* how technology can be orchestrated into socially responsible patterns of use" (Foreword xv).

NOTES

[1] In this context, *conflict management* refers to a team's ability to resolve differences among group members, including differences in agendas, styles of work, distribution of labor, and allocation of credit.

[2] In this context, *project management* is a team's handling of all phases of the work effort, including scheduling and subdivisions and allocation of tasks.

[3] *Asynchronous communication* refers to electronic exchanges that occur between terminals at different locations and at different times.

[4] The term *literacy autobiography* is an appropriate replacement for the once popular *composing-process* paper, in which students discussed their cognitive and affective processes in writing, but without reference to social context.

[5] The former (limited set of options) might be the choice if team members prefer face-to-face communication to other patterns for reading and writing together; the latter (novel configuration unanticipated by researchers or vendors) might be selected if team members are sophisticated enough in technology use and well enough aware of their work patterns to design a system tailored to their needs. The freedom of choice in technology use recommended here is indicative of what MIS specialists call a *permissive technology*, one that "does not attempt to constrain or direct the behavior of its human users" (Galegher and Kraut 9), in contrast to a *prescriptive technology*, which is intended to manipulate behavior to achieve specific ends.

Chapter 6

The Effect of Secondary School Structures and Traditions on Computer-Supported Literacy

Gary Graves and Carl Haller

Successful design and operation of a computer-supported writing center depends on close cooperation between the director, teaching staff, and school administration. Although several highly practical, effective guides are available to help schools plan for and establish writing centers (Selfe, "Creating a Computer Lab"; Rodrigues; Bureau), less has been said about how we learn to maintain successful writing centers once they are created. The growth and development of a writing center is only one ingredient in the boiling cauldron, along with other school programs, budget constraints, time limitations, and staff personality conflicts. As a result, literature addressing the planning and establishment stages may not be pertinent to a center's current operations or provide the best strategy for developing and sustaining alternative literacy programs.

This chapter describes the experiences of two computer-supported writing center coordinators: one from a center operating for six years, the other from a two-year-old writing project. We offer ideas and raise questions about success and shortcomings in establishing and advancing reading, writing, listening, and speaking literacies in computer-supported centers. In particular, we examine the effect school structure and tradition (administrative and teacher hierarchies, teacher turfdom, seven-period day, segmented curriculum) may have on secondary literacy programs taking shape in writing centers. This chapter may provide answers to some questions. But another value lies in the questions you may ask as you sense the difficulties and frustrations, as well as the excitement and satisfaction, coming from these two programs.

Frenchtown High School
by Gary Graves

I am not a classroom teacher anymore. My two longtime colleagues in the English department left in 1991; after twenty-one years teaching English at Frenchtown High School (the last six in a computer-supported writing center), I left in 1992. None of us had planned to leave so soon, but a traumatic change in our school caused us to go. Our vision of using computer technology to reform literacy education at Frenchtown has faded.

Frenchtown is a small, rural public high school in the mountains of western Montana. There are 240 students enrolled and a teaching staff of 22. Since 1985, all students at Frenchtown have been using twenty computers in a computer-supported writing center as part of the writing-across-the-curriculum program. The school and community were especially proud when, in 1987, NCTE named Frenchtown a Center of Excellence for its computer-supported, writing-across-the-curriculum program. Because of this designation, hundreds of educators have visited the school's writing center, and Frenchtown teachers have traveled across the country to share the program with others at conferences and in their schools.

But in 1990, the crucial administrative support that had allowed Frenchtown's innovative writing program to flourish eroded, and program maintenance and development atrophied. The reasons behind that declining support are complex, embedded far more in the social and political nature of the school than in professional concerns for good education. Perhaps the best way to convey what happened is to provide a brief history of the program—a history that reveals something about the effect computers can have on a small public school.

In the beginning, active central office support for a computer-supported writing center at Frenchtown didn't exist and wasn't necessary for the establishment of our program. Rather, the keys to the successful initiation and development of the program were the intense determination and preparation of one English teacher and the willingness of our building principal to listen. The teacher was granted a sabbatical to establish a plan for introducing computers into our writing classes. He articulated a proposal for using computers to change the way we taught writing and literature, invited other department members to be a part of the planning team, convinced the building principal of the value of a computer-supported writing center, and then persuaded the school board to fund the program.

Once the program was operating, the administration became very helpful and provided seven critical resources.

1. Two extra periods per day were given for one English language arts teacher to direct the writing center.
2. School in-service time was granted to allow high school teachers to learn about computers and writing instruction and about peer revising and editing.
3. Release time was given for teachers to attend conferences and learn methods of teaching with technology.
4. Teachers were freed from classes twice a year to do direct, holistic assessment of student writing.
5. Money was made available to pay for summer curriculum planning.
6. Writing classes were limited to twenty students.
7. Teachers were given full responsibility for running the program and were held accountable for the results.

Initially we wanted to know whether computers would help us teach writing skills more effectively and develop a more effective writing-across-the-curriculum program. By the end of the first year, the questions were answered. Our holistic writing assessments clearly indicated that writing skills, especially development, organization, and clarity, did improve. And after in-service instruction on computers and the writing process, eleven of our seventeen content teachers began giving new computer-based writing assignments to their classes. As we taught in this new environment, several unexpected positive changes occurred. Two were especially significant: peer revising and editing workshops functioned better, and staff communication was enhanced.

However, the most intriguing surprise was to find that integrating the computer into all stages of the writing process allowed us, even forced us sometimes, to use a more student-centered, collaborative approach to teaching. For example, because we were beginning users ourselves and had no in-house technician to call on when questions about the software or hardware arose, we often relied on students who were more computer-literate than we to solve those problems. They became the experts, instead of the teacher.

Further, since we were novices in the use of computers for writing instruction and didn't always know what we were doing, we grew more open to suggestions from students. We frequently asked them what worked or didn't work in our computer-based lessons. Many of their reactions provided us with insights into how they thought and wrote, both with the computer and without it, and how our computer assignments were aids or barriers to their learning. What began as research and theory leading to our practice shifted to theory stemming from our practice. Increasingly, we questioned our assumptions about writing instruction.

Sometimes students told us what they didn't like even when we didn't ask. And this new environment and our own uncertainty allowed us to listen to their complaints—their resistance—with a more receptive ear than would have been possible had we been more confident about what we were doing. Their unsolicited comments often were as helpful as the opinions we asked for. Maybe if we had been more honest from the beginning about what we didn't know about teaching writing with computers, if we had been less authoritarian in our approach, we would have learned even more, earlier, from our students.

Perhaps the unsureness most of us feel when we begin teaching writing with computers levels the field of literacy between our students and us. This uncertainty seems to create what Suzanne Clark and Lisa Ede call a "resistance to what is already known marking the starting point for collaboration" (283). The students resist what they *think we know* we want them to learn—a computer-based revision skill or an on-screen collaboration activity. But if we acknowledge our ignorance about teaching with technology, they may help us solve our (and their) problem rather than resist our efforts to teach. Such an approach, in turn, makes it easier for us to lighten our control and collaborate with them. I often say, "I don't know how this will work. Nobody else does, either, since we are probably the first to try it. So tell me if what we are doing is helpful or not."

Teachers' increased opportunity and willingness to collaborate with students apparently occurs often in computer writing environments. Carl Haller points out that roles and definitions of roles begin to merge and shift in computer labs. For example, when a student consultant is assigned to supervise the writing center during a drop-in time or even during a class time, who is in the role of "teacher"? Sue Brown, a wise English department chairperson from western Montana, recently observed that talking about an assignment done on computer seems more acceptable to her students than the same assignment done without computer.

This change, this natural blurring of lines between expert and novice, boss and worker, clearly is being demanded of citizens of the next century. Perhaps, in our computer-supported teaching environments, this shift in roles and attitudes represents a new literacy or may lead to new literacies, in addition to those traditionally taught. If this uncertainty reduces the role we, as teachers, play as dispenser of the canon, what is our job? Are we moving toward teaching what C. H. Knoblauch calls "literacy for personal growth" (78)?

Then what happens when more English teachers become literate and competent at using computer technology? At this time it is still relatively acceptable for English teachers not to be experts at teaching writing with computer tools. But will the next generation of teachers, who will have had more experience learning with computers and will have been trained to teach with them, go back to assuming the role of "expert" and take back authority and control, since they are no longer ignorant or, at least, don't want to appear so? Will the innovative and exciting computer-facilitated learning opportunities I have discovered with my students, because I can admit ignorance and be open to their ideas, become less available to future teachers because they have been taught to know better? Twain said, "I never let schooling interfere with my education." The longer I teach with computers, the more I have to remind myself to ask and listen to the writers I teach.

This opening of the classroom and empowerment of students was not the only unexpected benefit we attributed to our computer use. We also sensed that as they collaborated on the computer and in their peer revision and editing groups, students were developing a camaraderie that we had not noticed before. Educators, concerned with the limited opportunities for productive student talk in traditional classrooms, may look to computers as a tool for increasing oral language skills. "Perhaps somewhat paradoxically, in the past decade those occasions of the greatest amount of talk by students interacting with each other have come from the introduction of computers" (S. B. Heath, "Fourth Vision" 293). Our experiences at Frenchtown and McDonogh suggest that informed computer use may encourage more student interaction in classrooms.

Because so many factors came together at the same time—strong leadership, administrative support, staff cooperation, and student ownership—the program became a model of technology used to enhance literacy. Soon, however, the attention devoted to the program, the time given to us for program maintenance, and a change in administration caused some staff jealousy to surface. Misperceptions grew as some staff members complained about inequitable treatment of their programs and an inadequate share of the financial pie.

In the yearly evaluation given by faculty members to administration, in the winter of 1990, the most strident criticism of our building principal was that he favored the English department. The principal subsequently made three changes in the writing-across-the-curriculum program:

1. Eliminating the two planning periods for the writing center director
2. Eliminating the English department staffing of the writing center during the lunch period
3. Eliminating professional leave for the writing center director

These changes stopped even program maintenance. Teaching writing with a computer is more difficult (although more satisfying) and time-intensive than teaching writing with paper and pen. To teach on a computer, we must learn what Cynthia Selfe calls "multi-layered, computer-based literacy" ("Redefining Literacy" 7). The new grammars of the computer screen, the word-processing program, the hardware, and the network are layered upon each other and add significantly to the teaching task. Without support, few teachers will learn this new literacy on their own. If they do learn it but don't practice on computers regularly, they may have difficulty maintaining the literacy. In addition to regular practice, teachers need follow-up training and an opportunity to reflect on their practice with their peers. As new staff members are added, they need time and training to learn the principles, practice, and grammars of computer-mediated writing instruction. The planning and staffing cuts, designed to manage political problems, severely constrained essential skills transfer and interdisciplinary planning. Consequently, at Frenchtown, the program has declined.

What is the status of computers and literacy education at Frenchtown? The school is ahead of where it was before the computer-supported writing center began operating, and growth in other directions is occurring. New desktop publishing equipment was purchased in 1991, students have access for the first time to electronic databases for research, and one writing class has used a computer and modem for an online telewriting project.

However, these opportunities are accessible to relatively few students. And at the moment, a democratic concern to foster literacy for all students, as reflected in our strong writing-across-the-curriculum program, is struggling below the surface of political turmoil. The writing center is now closed part of the day. No longer is there regular, ongoing program assessment or school-wide expectation of writing excellence in all classes. Content-area teachers' use of the writing center has diminished to the point that now only three of these teachers regularly come to the center.

Perhaps schools can do only so much at one time. Perhaps technological change for teachers is especially difficult because of a fear of losing control and status. Better communication with staff and board members during the later years of the program probably would have helped. Whatever the reasons, it has been frustrating and disappointing to see a program with such potential fall short of its promise.

McDonogh School
by Carl Haller

McDonogh School, located on a 750-acre campus in McDonogh, Maryland, has been a part of Baltimore's private school tradition for over 120 years. Established originally as a poor boys' school through funds donated by John D. McDonogh, the institution evolved into a military academy, a boys' college preparatory school, and, finally, in 1975, a co-educational college preparatory school. Tuition, in 1991, was approximately $10,000 per year for upper-school students, grades nine through twelve; boarding, which accounts for only 82 students among the 523 upper-school population, costs an additional $3,060. Although there is competition for quality students in the Baltimore area, McDonogh has a loyal family and community following. It has become increasingly proud of its diversity; at present, the school has a 25% minority population. These facts about McDonogh do not merely provide a setting for the story of computer implementation; they frame an understanding of the varied types of literacy valued in the school. Indeed, it is this diversity of community and the entailing need to create "harmonies of difference" that form the heart of the story (J. Flower 76).

The creation of a computer-supported writing center at McDonogh was similar to what took place in Frenchtown. The English department, the administration, and then the board of trustees agreed in concept to a computer facility that would use word-processing programs for drafting and revising writing. The budget approved by the board of trustees would allow the opening of a renovated wing of a dorm to become the writing center. It would contain twenty-three computers for word processing. During the 1988–89 school year, when I was developing my proposal for the center, I became increasingly aware of the possible effect that teaching with computers could have on our writing program. McDonogh's administration firmly encouraged my investigation of programs in other schools in the Baltimore and Washington area. After also visiting both public and private schools during my trip to the NCTE convention in Saint Louis, I more clearly understood the potential that the new technology, the new literacy, could have for change.

While continuing my full-time teaching position, I became immersed in technological considerations, the design of the renovated room to facilitate comfortable collaboration, and the creation of text files or other methods to involve English teachers in using computers. Planning for the effect that this new technology could have on our conception of literacy remained fuzzy. In fact, our concept of literacy was never really up for consideration. Since we assumed that our goal was to prepare our students for college, our success was measured by the number of students who were accepted at the better universities. Betsy Bowen's notion, discussed in chapter 4 of this volume, of the power of a "collective vision" that enables us to redefine classroom learning was never dealt with. Nevertheless, the computer made an impact.

Within the English department there is a diversification of literacy options. The two that seem dominant are the cultural model and the liberal model. The effect of the cultural model can be seen in the following phenomena: the authoritarian role assumed by certain teachers in the department who adopt primarily a lecturing format interspersed with questions asked by the teacher; the teaching of an approved canon of literature in most required courses, especially honors and advanced placement courses (for the best and the brightest); the weeks spent writing formal research papers during freshman and sophomore years; and the importance of SAT and AP testing scores. At the same time, however, there is a strong liberal argument, represented in the following ways: an emphasis on process writing; teachers who aim for more collaborative learning in classes by using reading journals, conference disks, and other techniques to facilitate student-centered instruction; and creative writing and other electives that stress such content as black literature and the "beats"—offered because of student interest.

During the summer before the opening of the new writing center, I enrolled in a two-week workshop at Michigan Technological University. I developed a three-year training program for teachers, including recommendations for structure, process, and outcomes (I had written this document after reading Dawn Rodrigues's and Edward Bureau's training scenarios). I hoped my proposal would become the basis for negotiating program implementation at McDonogh. The six major stages of development were these:

- Step 1: Finding and mapping our pedagogical roots and goals and then designing our writing center around our goals for writers, writing teachers, and the writing program
- Step 2: Deciding how the writing center would meet program objectives

- Step 3: Obtaining administrative commitment and support for the pedagogical change
- Step 4: Implementing the training. The training program would include: (a) class management strategies, (b) group writing activities, (c) design and use of text files for prewriting and revision, (d) off-machine revision strategies, (e) use of non–word-processing software (e.g., desktop publishing, graphics), (f) review of software for computer-supported instruction
- Step 5: Evaluating the training
- Step 6: Sharing the results of the training

Gary Graves has written about the extensive support needed to train an entire faculty. At McDonogh, a reasonable approach was to begin in the English department by "seeding" computers for home and office use and then discussing how the implementation of computers could fit in with our school's writing program. We agreed on a three-hour workshop with English department members shortly after the writing center would open (Nov. 1989). At this initial workshop, we identified a set of premises and assumptions about writing and the teaching of writing—a first step that I was committed to accomplishing—but our agreements then were necessarily tentative, as the group felt its way through this technology (e.g., assignments should be for a variety of audiences and purposes, final revisions should receive a heavier weight than earlier drafts, and students needed time to develop their drafts). The department had agreed for several years that we would teach the process approach to writing. Beyond this commitment to process, there was no consensus on what we would all strive to achieve with computer-supported writing. Was it a different approach to literacy? We didn't yet know. Because of competing demands on teacher time—most notably, our preparation for the ten-year reaccreditation evaluation—we could not have another department workshop until the end of the school year. During this second workshop we looked at the potential of some computer-supported writing programs and *Hypercard*. Certainly, all the department members who had used the facility (six of the nine English teachers) shared their awareness of the increased peer cooperation in drafting and editing and, as a result, the changing role of teachers in a computer-supported writing center. In addition, two teachers, in explaining the use of conference disks in literature courses, described the potential for disruption of teacher-centered discourse. (A conference disk is a class's asynchronous written discourse about shared readings that is saved on a computer disk or in a network file.)

A further significant political dimension results from a perceived threat to existing hegemonic interests, which James Moffett refers to as "agnosis," self-censorship ("Censorship" 118). It occurs when our own acculturation, or valued literacy, is thought to be threatened by an extension of literacy, such as the computer offers. Moffett compares this state to being under a sort of anesthesia, and, indeed, I have witnessed my own department members and administration glide into this zone when faced with the prospect of training programs to achieve poorly understood change. In fact, my training program became a victim of just such attitudes. And, as a result, at McDonogh change has been slow. The computer is welcome, but only if it assumes the guise of a familiar, older technology, the typewriter. The new literacy that Selfe mentions, in "Redefining Literacy," will have to seep through the cracks created by students and teachers who "will put new creative skills to work quietly in [their] own area of responsibility and [are] willing to share with others who notice and ask about these changes" (S. B. Heath, "Fourth Vision" 301).

Inroads have been made: the administration approved my budget request for 1991; my course load and coaching load have been reduced; with one exception, every teacher in the English department has brought a class into the writing center, either for orientation or for an assignment; the two-week orientation for ninth graders was a success; we are likely to get administrative support for an additional sixteen computers in an adjoining room in the writing center wing; student use has continued to increase on a drop-in basis; and plans are under way for department heads and directors to coordinate the use of computers school-wide.

A big problem in having more teachers involved in the experiment with technology and the move beyond the surface features of writing with the typewriter is the need for more computers, so that classes can follow through the entire process of a writing assignment. The implementation of this technology and the harmonies of literacy it can create are proceeding from the bottom up. Summer workshops are planned to explore how we teach writing and how computers can become an integral part of that process. Meanwhile, in literature classes the potential for disruption from the use of conference disks has been remarkable. Students who have access to an asynchronous public forum (operating either on a network or by the use of designated diskettes) subvert the teacher-centered model by making explicit, in their own increasingly free flow of language, reactions and ideas that are usually perceived only through subtle signals in the classroom. Conference disks also ensure that every voice will be heard. Students at McDonogh have begun their own "private" conference disks, unrelated to any class or adult supervision.

Another opportunity for achieving what Andrew Sledd refers to as "dysfunctional literacy" (497) arrived in 1991, when our school, through participation in the National Association of Independent Schools' Multicultural Assessment Program, began evaluating its racial attitudes. It has been interesting to investigate how an institutional program meant to interrogate social meanings affects the use of such technologies as the writing center. Will our school decide to diversify its literacy options as a result of perceived needs and empowered individual choice?

The implementation of our program is proceeding slowly but surely. The administration has given the English department a great deal of freedom to set a comfortable pace for itself, and other departments have been encouraged to join in with their own writing assignments as they see fit. Already individual members of various departments have made their way to the writing center. Moreover, the lines of communication are open to the administration and the board of trustees. Will the budget support our expansion during the coming year? Perhaps the history or science department will demand its own computer-supported center. At McDonogh, most of what happens is the result of individual investment of time and energy—for example, by the faculty sponsor of the student newspaper who has taught students how to use desktop publishing, or the students who serve as "consultants" to other students and teachers. The psychoanalytic model that, Shoshana Felman has shown, can produce knowledge seems, as well, to reflect the implementation of computer programs at McDonogh: "through breakthroughs, leaps, discontinuities, regressions, and deferred action" (27). Although I am eager to have increased support for the training program, I have accepted the evolutionary process taking place. As a self-contained, independent school, McDonogh operates at its best in this way.

Conclusion

Because of the constraints of time and money, and because of each department's own priorities for program implementation, the administrative assistance for undertaking a computer-supported writing program must be tempered by other demands. The approach that the administration was able to support at Frenchtown for almost six years is indeed remarkable. That all three of the original directors left prematurely is troubling and "traumatic," as Graves says. Perhaps, after a six-year run of successes, it is time to step back and let the next department or program have its turn.

The approaches taken to develop these two programs parallel the types of institutions of which they are a part, but in both cases it is clear that without the dedication of at least one true believer—a person committed to the innovative use of computers to teach writing—these programs never would have been established. However, once the schools' administrations had agreed to commit their time and resources to the implementation of the programs, their continued support became essential. The training programs, release time, funding for directors and teachers to attend conferences and workshops, and the encouragement of other departments to become a part of the effort seem to have been especially important to Frenchtown High School, while in the private school these effects appear less crucial in their initial phases. Five years from now it may be instructive to trace the development of both computer-supported writing programs and their influence on changing models for literacy in these institutions.

These practical experiences have raised issues that are part of a much larger picture—perhaps, even, one day, of the national agenda:

1. As Janis Forman writes, in chapter 5 of this volume, "The issue of who gets enfranchised and what form that enfranchisement takes is a complex one." Although the ratio of computers to student is probably better at Frenchtown than at McDonogh, the private school community most likely has more students who have computers at home or who will be leaving for college with a computer of their own. Certainly, the experience of either of these schools is not similar to that of a public school system in a low socioeconomic area. So now, in addition to distinctions in literacy in traditional methods of instruction, a computer-supported literacy will separate the privileged children from those in the underclass.

2. Even when access is available, integration in a community is not easy. "Collective visions" rarely extend across an entire department, let alone an entire school, and, as was mentioned earlier, "harmonies of differences" may be a more realistic goal. Perhaps the notion that the training of teachers has to precede the training of students should be abandoned. As our experience shows, the students become adept at sharing computer literacy collaboratively with other students. Therefore, the writing center is a place where teachers become radicalized in their role as educators—they learn to share the leadership, to listen. The "collective vision" is best offered by those who learn the power of the new literacy.

3. As William Goodrich Jones points out in chapter 7 in this volume, the modification of work habits and the use of bibliographic databases will take place only when computers offer the same kind of internal,

relational, and contextual information that scholars see among foot-notes and bibliographies in important scholarly works. The ability of networks and computer software to offer this potential, not only for library searches but for all phases of literacy, will most likely increase teachers' demands for access and further training, for themselves and their students. This is just the beginning.

Chapter 7

Humanist Scholars' Use of Computers in Libraries and Writing

William Goodrich Jones

Humanist scholars are among the most skilled users of language. They craft subtle and extended arguments based on evidence from many different kinds of sources—textual, oral, pictorial, and artifactual. They address well-informed audiences that appreciate careful use of language, audiences that can place the humanist's arguments in a context with the arguments of others that address the same topic, audiences that can evaluate the quality of evidence that sustains these arguments. Humanists work within intellectual traditions that have been shaped by generations of scholars and are reshaped in each generation. Like scholars in any field, humanists occasionally reach large generalist audiences of informed laypersons. As humanists pursue their endeavors, new questions about the definition, meaning, and value of literacy, especially literacy as it may be promoted by the application of computers, prompt us to ask how scholars are changing their own behaviors under the growing tendency (and possibly pressure) to use computers.

The essays in this volume are concerned with how literacies are acquired, enhanced, and extended among student populations, particularly with the introduction of computers in the classroom. Their authors explore the multiple relations that arise in the limited environment of the classroom between students, teachers, machines, and software. Definitions of literacy, once limited to acquisition of certain skills, now encompass the questions of reading and writing for what and for whom. In the overview to this section of the volume, Ann Hill Duin and Craig Hansen examine the use of computer networks as forums for enabling students to acquire the written literacy of a discourse community. Betsy A. Bowen devotes a portion of chapter 4 to the need for equitable distribution of resources, noting that one of the most important pieces of equipment (and one of the most difficult to obtain) is the telephone line. Janis Forman, in chapter 5, shows how variable, dynamic, and unpredictable the use of computers in group settings can be. William Wresch, seeing computers as vehicles to provide students with new audiences, prudently observes that the adoption of new technologies requires time as well as money (see his response to this section). But humanist scholars, indeed, are no longer students under the guidance and direction of teachers who have goals and agendas well described in other essays in this volume. Therefore it may be worthwhile to consider how computers affect the professional lives of those who use them in the fulfillment of various career goals.

Shirley Brice Heath develops a broad definition of literacy in the workplace that can usefully be applied to the work of scholars:

> Being literate means "having counsel" for oneself and for others through communicable experience. Being literate means being able to talk and listen with others, to interpret texts, say what they mean, link them to personal experience and with other texts, argue with them and make predictions from them, develop future scenarios, compare and evaluate related situations, and know that the practice of all these literate abilities is practical. Counsel is practical advice, but it is often "less an answer to a question than a proposal concerning the continuation of a story which is just unfolding." Thus, counsel depends on our ability to let ourselves and our situations speak to identify problems, to hypothesize futures, and to compare experiences.   ("Fourth Vision" 298)

Within their world, humanists meet this broadened definition of literacy. Although most humanists claim that they do what they do because they like doing it, it is also the case that their livelihood derives from literacy, from an ability to communicate effectively with influential audiences (their peers, publishers, and editors) as well as informed and influential secondary audiences (administrators, patrons, purchasers of their books). The achievement of high-level literacy significantly enhances the probability that scholars will receive tenure, obtain travel and research funding, have access to privileged sources, and attend conferences and seminars where they will learn of recent thinking in their field. The possibility of applying computers to such practical goals may be attractive to humanists as a means of making themselves better understood by their audiences. Although institutional support for acquisition of computers and training in their use for scholarly purposes varies greatly, access to technology in academic environments is becoming easier and does not hinge on adequacy of personal financial resources. Academic departments offer a variety of subsidies to their members, either through the direct provision of equipment to their faculties or through financial support that permits individual members to purchase equipment of their own choosing. (There are, of course, scholars outside of academic institutions who use computers in their work, but this essay addresses behaviors of those who have formal and sustained affiliations in academe.)

Because humanist scholars are living the lives they have spent years preparing for as students, in which literacy of a particular kind is central (that is, the extensive knowledge of numerous texts and the history of discourse relating to them; the ability to relate theory, data, and arguments to create commentaries about them in books, articles, and reviews), we may with good reason ask whether computers, widely promoted in our society and having a great influence on our economy, advance, retard, or have little or no significance in fostering that literacy, in enhancing the ability of scholars to have "counsel."

In the physical sciences, computers have been used, for many years, to calculate data. Social scientists turned to computers for analysis of survey findings almost as soon as the technology was introduced in the academic environment. Now computers have the potential to transform the work of scholars in two other significant and pervasive ways: to change the methods by which scholars find library materials, and to alter the mechanics by which scholars create their works of scholarship. But scholars' use of computers for locating library materials is limited, while their use of computers for word processing is widespread. Articles encouraging humanists to become more computer-literate in seeking information appear frequently and are often written by librarians. For example, Marilyn Schmitt, program manager in the J. Paul Getty Trust's art history information program, recently urged scholars to learn to search computerized bibliographic databases and to become involved in groups setting standards for "collecting, formatting, and transmitting electronic information in the humanities."

In libraries, the introduction of online public access catalogs (OPACs) is supplanting the older mechanism of access, the card catalog; OPACs are enabling scholars to retrieve bibliographic records from large databases rapidly and, to some degree, precisely. OPACs offer possibilities not only for searching the catalog in conventional ways by author, title, and subject but also for searching elements within the bibliographic record (publisher, year of publication, language of publication) and combinations of elements that could not have been searched in a card catalog. Scholars are increasingly required to use OPACs to gain access to library collections, because that is the way large research libraries are beginning to maintain their catalogs.

Access to general periodical indexes (as well as to some highly specialized indexes) is increasingly available through computers. The ease of use of these indexes continues to improve, although scholars must still understand the basic elements of bibliographic citations (as for paper and printed catalogs) and be willing to read and follow instructions provided on the screen or in supplementary handouts. Scholars can now search the journal literature, either online or with CD-ROM (compact disc–read-only memory) systems, with the same (sometimes superior) retrieval capabilities available in the OPAC. Such access is possible because users may search by keyword or by Boolean operators (finding citation elements in parts of the record other than author and title), examine databases containing not only citations but the full text of the works indexed, look through indexes that have greater depth, and define the elements they want to call up from the bibliographic record. Bibliographic database searching, once available only in libraries and specialized research centers and requiring skilled intermediaries, is now facilitated by end-user systems incorporating so-called user-friendly software, largely eliminating the need for an intermediary.

Through electronic networks, scholars can find materials held by their own libraries and by others. They can do so even when the libraries are not open, retrieving and arranging records to create bibliographic files under their own control. In Illinois, Illinet Online (IO), a large system listing holdings and circulation information for about forty libraries, most of them academic, is accessible from hundreds of terminals in academic libraries and through dial-up ports. Illinet Online is just one example of systems and networks being created throughout the country. Scholars using IO who locate titles in institutions outside their own can borrow them almost as effortlessly as if the titles were held locally. Records for current acquisitions of about three hundred libraries, both academic and public, are gradually being added to this system. State support for reciprocal borrowing makes possible rapid delivery of books and journal articles among participating institutions.

Libraries have also begun to add more than book and journal holdings to their OPACs. CARL-Uncover, an index to current journal contents developed by the Colorado Alliance of Research Libraries, has recently been linked electronically to Illinet Online. The libraries of the two campuses of the University of Illinois have mounted *Current Contents* (an index, published by the Institute for Scientific Information, to contents pages of journals in the sciences, engineering, social sciences, arts, and humanities), ERIC (Educational Resources Information Center) abstracts, and a number of general indexes published by the H. W. Wilson Company (including *Readers' Guide to Periodical Literature*) to their campus data networks. The bibliographic resources included in this system have also been made available to the academic institutions supporting Illinet Online. Fee-based access via password to RLIN (Research Libraries Information Network) enables scholars in many institutions to view the bibliographic holdings of major research libraries, and local mounting of electronic reference sources like the *Oxford English Dictionary* extends the range of databases from bibliographic to full text. these resources are available without restriction and at moderate cost to thousands of scholars and students through telephone lines that link them to personal computers in homes and offices.

These bibliographic resources are convenient for those familiar with automated systems, but they can frustrate the occasional or inexperienced user. Slightly different configurations of keyboards and variations in keyboard labeling, along with ambiguously written instructions, can render the simplest system inaccessible. In addition, local variations require users of a number of different libraries and systems to learn different commands to accomplish the same purposes. Moreover, the same options are not offered in every system, even though the systems may appear identical. Improvements are being made, and some features, like author and title searching, are common to all systems. But some commercially available databases are expensive and require frequent practice and knowledge of the ways they are organized to achieve best results. Although, over time, the importance of these limitations will be reduced, some sophisticated scholars still favor the card catalog over the OPAC. Serious questions continue to be raised about the degree to which scholars have ever relied on the card catalog and its electronic equivalents to uncover resources important in their research (Lancaster; Stoan, "Research and Library Skills").

Other changes are taking place that affect access to sources scholars use. In addition to the long-standing application of computers for statistical analysis, scholars are employing computers in new ways to work with primary texts, to control their data, and to represent their findings. For example, the entire corpus of classical Greek writing (the *Thesaurus Linguae Graecae*, or TLG) is available on CD-ROM. By electronically scanning the file, scholars can pull together all references to particular religious rites and cults in the Peloponnese, or they can review all classical commentaries about customs governing behavior of women in temples. In another case, a scholar engaged in the creation of a critical edition of a major philosopher can use computers to create an index of significant terms in the work. That index will aid the scholar's analysis of those terms each time they occur in the philosopher's opus. An archaeologist can use computer-generated maps to plot the distribution of sherds collected at archaeological sites, and a historian may keep an entire file of notes in a database. Journals like *Computers and the Humanities* publish scholarly papers—some available only in electronic format—that document applications of computers to a wide variety of intellectual problems. Visionaries of universal computer literacy occasionally advocate making the entire system of scholarly publishing accessible in electronic form (E. Smith; Rogers and Hurt).

The ways in which humanists use computers are themselves emerging as topics of investigation. How scholars acquire information that contributes to inquiry has been subject to sporadic study for several decades (Case; Stieg; Stone). Much of this research was undertaken before computers and automated library systems were in widespread use and has emphasized invisible colleges, journal reading, citation tracing, and print indexes and card catalogs. The rapid development of computer systems in libraries and at home, for word processing and control of bibliographic information, is prompting new studies taking account of scholars' use of these machines.

In 1985, when the Office of Scholarly Communication and Technology of the American Council of Learned Societies (ACLS) conducted a survey of members of associations represented in the council, it addressed a number of topics, including use of computers for scholarly work and for library research (Morton and Price). Of 5,000 questionnaires distributed, 3,800 responses were received, 3,000 of them from scholars working in academic settings. The scholarly disciplines represented were literature, classics, philosophy, history, linguistics, political science, and sociology.

The ACLS survey found that scholars use computers as aids to writing and for specialized purposes, including maintenance of note files, text preparation, bibliography compilation, and statistical analysis. The survey also documented the pronounced growth in scholarly use of computers over a five-year period. Where 2% of all respondents owned or had access to a computer in 1980, by 1985 that number had increased to 45%. By 1985, 98% of respondents in research universities had access to computers, while 57% used computers routinely. Of academic respondents who used computers in their work, 95% used them for word processing, but only 17% used computers to access the library's online catalog. According to 59% of respondents in research universities, "part or all" of their library's catalog was computerized, but 38% of the respondents working in research universities who answered a question on computerized catalogs reported never having used the catalog. Only 12% said that computerization had significantly improved access to scholarly material.

Questions in the ACLS survey that related to computerized searches of online databases, such as ERIC, the *MLA Bibliography*, ABC-CLIO (publisher of such electronic databases as *America, History and Life* and *Historical Abstracts*), and *Sociological Abstracts*, revealed that 41% of academic respondents had had searches conducted for them. Of respondents working in research universities, only 22% had had database searches conducted once or twice, and 13% had used this service several times, but only 5% had used it frequently. Another 7% did searches themselves, but only 6% of respondents in research universities said that materials identified through database searches were of great importance to them.

More than 75% of respondents reported that using the computer had improved or greatly improved their writing efficiency, 65% said that it had improved their research productivity, and around 50% noted that it had improved their writing quality. Among academic respondents, 66% thought that computers would have a "positive" or "very positive" impact on the intellectual progress of their discipline in the next five years.

While scholars' use of computerized library catalogs (and probably all uses of computers) in the early 1990s is surely much higher than in 1985, if only because more library catalogs have been computerized, application by scholars of databases is still very limited. A series of interviews conducted by two librarians with three groups of highly productive humanists at the University of Illinois at Chicago's Humanities Institute has produced additional information on scholarly behavior that offers insight into these and other findings of the ACLS survey (Wiberley and Jones).

Beginning in 1987, these librarians, with partial support from the Council on Library Resources, initiated a series of interviews with anthropologists, archaeologists, classicists, historians, literary theorists, political scientists, and sociologists. These scholars participated in year-long seminars as Humanities Institute fellows, devoting most of their time to a major research project and meeting with their institute colleagues from time to time to describe the projects, discuss issues of methodology, and share perspectives on each other's work from their own disciplinary standpoints. At the end of four years, interviews had been held with twenty-eight Humanities Institute fellows. During these interviews, fellows described their experience with library automated systems, their use of personal computers, and their reliance on services offered by the university's mainframe computer through a campus data network, services that included options for word processing and electronic mail.

The Chicago campus has had access to an OPAC in the library and through a campus network since 1985. Although a cumbersome online circulation system that contained elements of an OPAC had been available for some years before that, the OPAC represented a decided improvement in ease of use. Institute fellows acknowledged the advance that it represented, with some using the OPAC from their offices by means of the campus data network or from their homes via dial-up ports. In spite of the OPAC's flexibility for identifying and retrieving bibliographic citations, the librarians were surprised to find that the fellows primarily used the OPAC as an electronic representation of the card catalog, relying on the same author and title approaches they had used with the printed catalogs that preceded the OPAC. Boolean and keyword search capabilities were little utilized. Fellows thought of the OPAC as a device for locating materials they already knew, and they had little incentive or need to conduct searches in other, newly accessible fields in the catalog record (e.g., publisher or year of publication) or even much interest in learning these capabilities. No fellow referred specifically to searching the record in these new ways or to using Boolean logic in developing bibliographic searches; none revealed knowledge of the various options available for limiting the scope of a search, although introductory screens provide basic instruction for such procedures.

Humanities Institute participants' limited reliance on database systems that index the journal literature was comparable to the use reported by ACLS respondents; fellows have little knowledge of the availability of computerized database searching. Those for whom librarians had conducted database searches were not themselves frequent users of those services. Searches, if requested, were often for the purpose of identifying literature in subject areas with which the fellow was unfamiliar and in which he or she might not already have a knowledge of principal bibliographic sources. While database searching occasionally uncovered items of importance, it was one of the least favored ways to gain access to literature on any topic, and certainly not one that fellows turned to regularly.

Some of the searching carried out for fellows came about as a consequence of librarians' involvement in the Humanities Institute. During the years in which interviews were conducted, the campus library underwrote costs of such searches. Although fellows who did enlist the assistance of librarians were generally pleased, the searches sometimes had mixed results, not because the librarians lacked skill but because the structure of the database made it difficult to retrieve citations that fellows needed. For example, a sociologist had a librarian conduct a number of searches to identify authors who were writing in a given subject area in the United States and Canada. The undertaking proved frustrating to both sociologist and librarian, because the database consulted was organized in such a way that it was not possible to identify the institutional affiliations of authors retrieved by the search, information that was essential for the investigation.

The participants in the survey did not make much use of bibliographies that were outside of scholarly publications in their own disciplines. They relied heavily on citations in scholarly articles and books, bibliographic essays in specialized publications, lists in newsletters, publishers' flyers, or even advertisements in the journals they read. The important, comprehensive indexes in the humanities favored by librarians, *Humanities Index* and *Arts and Humanities Citation Index*, were little consulted. Although the humanists who were interviewed, like humanists in general, worked largely by themselves, they frequently depended on a few colleagues with whom they had close professional relationships and who shared an interest in their areas of specialization to tell them of publications they ought to have read (Perrow).

There is growing evidence that informal, but systematic, methods of information gathering based on selective reading, conversation, and referral from other scholars are highly important and that library catalogs and general indexes (automated or not) provide few sources of citations new to scholars (Stoan, "Research and Information"). Informal information sources are valuable to scholars because they offer a context in which to evaluate a citation's probable utility for inquiry, an evaluation that is hard to make for citations embedded in undifferentiated lists generated by searching an OPAC or electronically based index.

The University of Illinois interviews indicate that humanists generally use their campus library to obtain materials they have learned about outside the library and have enough publication information about to identify by author or title. This inference is supported by catalog-use studies showing that, among faculty members, author and title searches predominate (Hufford; Krikelas). Fellows were confident of their knowledge of the important literature and were not very much concerned that they might uncover previously unknown and significant research through subject catalog searches. Nevertheless, they do browse library shelves, and they are aware of the possibilities of discovering useful sources through serendipity. Such purposeful, if unplanned, activity is just one of a number of information-seeking behaviors scholars use in solving the research problems they set for themselves.

For many fellows, particularly historians and others who work with sources kept in specialized archives, a large body of useful material lies outside bibliographic control. The key to access often resides with archivists and in the painstaking inspection of archives' contents. Many fellows create archival files of their own by assembling transcripts of interviews they conduct with subjects, by acquiring materials not yet in archives, and by taking notes and making photocopies from privately held papers. No commercial or scholarly indexing, automated or manual, can trace these elusive sources, and scholars' limited use of library catalogs derives from their knowledge that, of the many kinds of information needed for their work, most catalogs contain only the scholarly monographic literature they already know well. (Also, some scholars maintain large print and photocopy collections of their own, a convenience permitting flexibility in access and in organization of contents, as well as opportunities, not available when working with library materials, for directly annotating texts.)

As noted earlier, only 50% of ACLS scholars believe that computers improve writing quality, but 75% say that the technology contributes to improvement of writing efficiency. For the University of Illinois fellows, as for ACLS scholars, the utility of computers is in word processing. While a few fellows still prefer to inscribe their manuscripts with pen or typewriter, most have taken advantage of opportunities that word processing offers for creating outlines, for writing, and for editing. In addition, many fellows rely on computers for word processing because secretarial support has been withdrawn by their departments. An illuminating discussion of a social scientist's approach to writing (without the use of a computer) may be found in Susan Tax Freeman's "An Anthropologist in Europe: Resources and Problems of Study."

Computers equipped with word-processing software provide a method of writing that offers great flexibility to scholars in creating, rewriting, and editing their texts. First, a standard practice in drafting manuscripts of all kinds is to begin with outlines, once drafted manually and now created with word-processing systems. University of Illinois fellows told us that they usually work from outlines, often highly detailed. One fellow starts his books with an outline that will serve as a statement for a publisher and then returns to it occasionally in the course of writing to see that he is following his original plan. Another creates a rough outline and then develops outlines within that outline. Some fellows conceive of outlines as skeletons to which they gradually attach important organs, heart and lungs, fleshing out the scholarly homunculus. Through word processing, too, textual composition can occur by assembling arguments piecemeal. One scholar observed that "little bits" of text can be written, moved around, and finally brought together to create a sustained argument, a flexibility in manipulating text that earlier generations of scholars did not have. (Before the computer, text could be manipulated manually by cutting and pasting, an exercise requiring a greater investment in time but presumably achieving the same or similar results.) Finally, scholars who use word-processing programs find them especially helpful for revising. Editing programs permit direct revision of text displayed on screens. These scholars read their texts over and over until the words are, as the fellow says, "embedded in their eyeballs," or they may print and edit their texts on paper, return to make changes on the screen, and then print again, and so on until they obtain a version that satisfies them.

If publication is the standard vehicle of scholarly exchange, publication of books is, for the University of Illinois fellows, its highest realization. The magnitude of effort required to write books is measured in years, in thousands of notes, hundreds of citations, and long hours in archives. Fellows often told us of working in distant archives in small towns long after the archival staff had gone home, of spending hours in front of the screens of microfilm readers, of working in rooms filled with disorganized reports, and of laboriously arranging notes and developing arguments. They stressed that books are more than an assembly of individual chapters that first appeared as journal articles. Books represent the realization of a sustained and complex argument, and it is not uncommon for ten years (for some books, twenty years) to elapse from the start of a book to its publication. Word-processing systems lend themselves to the storage of notes and the extensive texts required for book-length manuscripts, for compilation of bibliographies, and for manipulation of data.

Although many ACLS scholars and University of Illinois fellows have discovered the utility of computers for their writing, we now may see why they have not taken them up as enthusiastically for information seeking. Fundamentally, the behaviors that we recognize as scholarly are set down by humanists during their years of graduate training. These behaviors include acquiring general knowledge of a large literature, usually along lines defined by academic departments and disciplines; gaining in-depth knowledge and familiarity with a specialized

literature; and honing the ability to pose questions of scholarly significance and to develop complex arguments that address these questions.
The training, culminating in completion of a dissertation and its eventual publication, is followed by an intense period of testing during
which the scholar demonstrates productivity as a researcher. Habits
of working established in graduate school are refined as the scholar
continues his or her career in the first years of academic appointment.

The invention of machines that make writing easier, especially that
part of writing associated with manipulation of text (addition, deletion,
and rearrangement), offered scholars an appealing way of working,
one that could be used easily at their habitual location. The recent
introduction of laptop computers now permits the storage of notes and
the creation of outlines in remote locations, maximizing use of that
scarcest commodity, time. In contrast, scholars' use of computers to
control and retrieve bibliographic information, a convenience but not a
necessity, still does not offer the same ready opportunity for modifying
working habits that word processing has. Scholars know their bibliographic sources, primary and secondary, and they know how to keep
informed of the publication of new literature. Neither control nor retrieval of bibliographic sources ever required extensive use of the card
catalog, and most humanists have little contact with librarians who
might also serve as guides to information about bibliographic sources.
If anything, fellows are apprehensive that reliance on librarians will
bring them greater numbers of citations than they can efficiently use.
The evidence is that the impact of computers on information seeking
is negligible, in spite of the almost universal tendency of librarians and
many other members of academic communities to declare the changes
revolutionary.

Most fellows had little awareness of the wide range of personal computer hardware available and had few systematic ways of acquiring
that information. They selected computers for purchase by relying on
the advice of one or two knowledgeable people in their departments.
Fellows limited the time they devoted to learning about computers,
resentful of the effort required to set them up and to learn to use them
in their work. One historian—who kept all her research notes stored
in her computer and relied on it heavily—said she had never bothered
to learn how to use the "find" command in her word-processing program, so great was her reluctance to read the accompanying manual
and so little her desire to take advantage of the options for textual
control that the software offered. A friend helped her with any problems she had with its use. Another historian belonged to a users' group
for a time, but he stopped going when he saw that members did not

share his interest in using computers for scholarly purposes. During the year of his leave, he bought another, more powerful computer, foreseeing that the time invested in learning to use it would aid him later on in the preparation of the manuscript for his book. A political scientist asked a friend to help set up her computer, but she complained that getting the printer to work had taken too much time, preventing her from writing that she needed to do.

A few humanists had no interest in computers for any purpose, even for word processing. One historian, who didn't know how to type, wrote all his manuscripts in longhand. Another believed that word processing was a useless, wasteful, and expensive technology. He wrote his texts first by hand, typing the final version; he sometimes drafted his first and only version by typewriter.

For mature scholars, computers are innovations that were introduced after most of them had already received their doctorates and established well-developed methods of working. There is yet no indication that technology has transformed their scholarly procedures, although computers serve useful purposes. Software programs may represent new possibilities for editing and organizing texts, but it is too soon to evaluate fully what the consequences of these changes may be. A basic obstacle to greater use of computers is still the inadequacy of computer resources in academic departments. The array of software and hardware and the varying degrees of support provided by those departments often require scholars to rely on their own ingenuity in choosing among them. But younger scholars are more likely to have used computers for word processing during their graduate and undergraduate training. One of the youngest of the University of Illinois fellows remarked that soon after her appointment, she asked her mother to give her a computer. But wider computer literacy will not be achieved until there is greater compatibility of equipment, standardization in software, and increased accessibility of network services.

The question remains whether humanist scholars fully achieve the kind of literacy envisioned by Heath in the sense of "having counsel" and whether that literacy is enhanced by their use of computers. By most definitions, scholars do attain high degrees of literacy, but it is a literacy that nonetheless operates under the constraints of the particular culture of academe. These limitations derive from the solitary nature of humanities scholarship (most publications in the humanities are singly authored), an academic culture that rewards independent achievement (through promotions, fellowships, sabbaticals) and encourages, like the sciences, primacy of discovery. Many University of Illinois fellows share little information about their work with colleagues and are careful about revealing sources until their own research is in print. Many report that even when they would benefit from informed comment, they have few colleagues with whom they are close enough to ask to read a long manuscript.

Although they know very well the specialized audiences for whom they write, fellows often spoke of a desire to reach larger audiences, ones comprising intelligent laypeople. When asked for whom they wrote, they gave surprising answers, identifying their mothers or other close relatives and noting that they would achieve their goals when they could make their arguments intelligible to an informed readership. They hoped for readers as generous and understanding of their aims as are the close, personal audiences that do read their work. Like students in classrooms, minorities, and the geographically isolated, scholars try to reach beyond those who would read them mechanically and to achieve the kind of literacy described by Charles Schuster: "Literacy is the power to be able to make oneself heard and felt, to signify. Literacy is the way in which we make ourselves meaningful not only to others but through others to ourselves" (227).

Chapter 8

Communication and Technology: Defining a Feminist Presence in Research and Practice

Billie J. Wahlstrom

Rapid developments in technology have overwhelmed both our private and our scholarly lives. As we face incompletely understood change, our personal and professional responses have often been tentative and ineffective. At home we struggle to make wise choices about such seemingly simple things as long distance telephone service. Our households pulsate with the continuous blink of lighted displays on VCRs, flashing *12:00* because we cannot set the clocks or we fail to understand why we should. In this environment, it is not surprising that our ability to engage in the scholarly examination of technology and to ask questions about it and its uses has been slowed.

As Michel Foucault notes, "It is not easy to say something new; it is not enough for us to open our eyes, to pay attention, or to be aware" (*Archaeology* 44–45). One way to formulate questions about the technology we have brought into the writing classroom is to augment existing theoretical perspectives. Feminist theory provides such an augmentation by delineating connections between technology and the cultural hegemony from which it emerges. For instance, a feminist critique can uncover constraints inherent in hardware and software by revealing that technology is gendered. (Other theoretical perspectives expose different sets of constraints on technology and represent additional steps in a full analysis of technology.) Applying feminist theory to technology supports Foucault's claim, in *The Archaeology of Knowledge*, that we must see beyond the traditional ways of organizing knowledge and identify breaks, omissions, and discontinuities in our understanding. Exposing ties between technology and the dominant culture, feminist theory gives us insight into some of the problematic connections we have made as we linked technology to literacy, creating what Janis Forman, in chapter 5 of this volume, calls "computer-supported literacy."

Composition scholars are examining the politics of literacy but have not systematically addressed the politics of the computer in the classroom, especially with respect to gender. The omission is significant because, as Beth Daniell points out, "literacy . . . cannot be separated from the politics of its production and distribution" ("Situation" 205). The few existing feminist analyses of technology are too scattered to support scholars looking at gender and communication technology in the classroom (see Selfe, "Technology"; MacKensie and Wajcman) or to ground discussions of gendered technology and literacy studies.

In their introduction to the 1990 special issue on women and computers in *Signs*, Ruth Perry and Lisa Greber emphasize the need to bring feminist theory to bear on technology as an important first step:

> The relation of gender to technology—the effects of technology on women's and men's lives, the ways in which women and men construct and use technology, the theoretical implications of gender socialization for future needs and developments in technologies—these connections have yet to be made, this story has yet to be written.   (74)

After we have made these connections, we can begin to ask how technology affects computer-supported literacy efforts.

Gendered Technology and the Computer-Writing Classroom

A number of factors have slowed composition scholars' efforts to critique technology. It is a standard approach to say, as does Betsy Bowen in chapter 4 of this volume, that "as with any educational computing project, we need to concentrate on the educational purposes that the technology serves, rather than on the technology itself." This claim misleads, however, by conflating two distinct concepts. It is true, as Bowen asserts, that "in the relatively short history of educational computing, we have repeatedly seen computers themselves become the focus of instruction, rather than the intellectual development that computers can enhance." Enthusiastic rhetoric about computers has diverted us from our educational and intellectual mission, but this focus on technology should not be confused with a necessary critique of the technology itself. Therefore, I dispute her proposition that "the value of [the computer and the film projector] depends not on the equipment itself but on the uses to which it is put and the educational context created around it." Equipment itself constrains the educational purposes that it serves because the process of its creation is political.

A second reason for composition scholars' slowness in approaching technology is one shared with the population at large. Science and technology appear value-neutral, cloaked in an objectivity scholars and teachers are only beginning to question as we come to understand the link between social order and scientific thought (see Keller; Bleier, *Science and Gender*). This objectivity, in itself a fundamental literacy issue, deserves further attention to see how it reinforces culturally privileged definitions of thinking.

In addition, changes in technology appear to have an inevitability that removes them from critical review. Such technological determinism has resulted in the marked "absence of a critical consciousness about gender in discussions of technology" (Jansen 196). For example, a 1987 theoretical analysis, *The Social Construction of Technological Systems* (Bijker, Hughes, and Pinch), completely ignores gender issues except in a brief reference to the development of the bicycle. Feminist theory helps show that social, political, and economic factors combine with currents in science and technology to create new technologies (Perry and Greber 75).

If science reflects cultural values, then the technology that emerges from it shares those social values (see Zimmerman). Ruth Hubbard, in her foreword to Joan Rothschild's collection *Machina ex Dea*, argues that "technology is part of our culture; and, of course, our culture, which is male dominated, has developed technologies that reinforce male supremacy" (vii). Sue Curry Jansen calls the absence of analysis of this hegemony the "socially structured silence" of "phallotechnology" (196).

Although we are researching the effects of networked computers in the writing classroom, composition scholars have not broken this "socially structured silence." We quickly recognized the obvious political potential of computer networks to provide forums for students heretofore excluded, marginalized, or silenced in the traditional classroom (Flores; Cooper and Selfe). Now we need to look at the latent functions computers and computer networks may have on our students, what Ann Hill Duin and Craig Hansen, in the overview to this section of the volume, call the "dark side of our educational system." This hidden aspect can be explored, as Duin and Hansen suggest, by examining existing social and political systems, especially when we extend our inquiry to cover the social values inherent in technology itself.

Feminist Analysis of Technology in the Composition Classroom

Performing a complete feminist analysis of gendered technology in the writing classroom is beyond the scope of this essay. Yet, looking at some common aspects of computer networks and the software they support can lead us to a richer, more political discussion of computer-supported literacy.

The Politics of Networks

Applying feminist theory to technology forces writing teachers to ask questions of the educational system's hidden side: How does the gendered nature of computer technology affect what goes on in the composition classroom? Whom and what interests are we serving when we integrate hardware and software into writing courses? What are the long-range implications, for women and others who lack a voice, of our using computers and other gendered technologies in our writing classrooms? How might what goes on in the classroom differ if the technology were designed and constructed by women? These questions have literacy issues at their heart.

Coming up with answers to all these questions will take time, but by looking at a few of the roles networks are playing in the classroom, we can identify some areas in which further research is necessary. One place to begin is with the teaching of collaboration. The collaborative process, whereby teams of writers, editors, instructional designers, and technical content specialists put together documents, is well established in industry (Faigley and Miller; Ede and Lunsford, "Why Write"; Couture and Rymer). Literacy scholars have identified a cluster of skills involved in collaborative writing as an important component of higher-level literacies (Forman, "Discourse Communities"; Karis; Lay, "Feminist Theory" and "Interpersonal Conflict").

Composition teachers and researchers have developed pedagogical strategies to facilitate collaborative writing by turning to networks. Computers enable teachers to help students create texts in such a way that all (or at least more) of them have access to the text and have equal opportunities for generating and manipulating it (Duin and Hansen, overview to this section; Bowen, ch. 4; Forman, ch. 5; Graves and Haller, ch. 6, in this volume). On linked computers, students from a variety of sites can work together and can do so without all the social and cultural constraints that accompany face-to-face communication.

Applying feminist analysis to the technology itself foregrounds issues different from those raised by an examination of the uses to which technology is put, however. Networks offer an invitation to literate activities—reading, writing, and making sense of texts—to those who traditionally have had difficulty finding access. Although, in the abstract, networks can enfranchise great numbers of people, the question of access to the technology, and therefore access to the teaching of literate practices, has to be considered. Research already provides evidence of "differential access to computer education across racial and gender lines" (Perry and Greber 77). Kathy A. Krendl and her colleagues at Indiana University reported in 1989 that "there is a strong tendency for boys at all ages to respond favorably to computer-based instruction and to pursue outside computer activities; girls, however, appear to be intimidated by the technology and reluctant to make extracurricular use of it" (85).

Thus, although we talk about networks' ability to extend literacy to excluded individuals, the reality is that the more technology is brought into our systems, the more chances exist for financial, cultural, and social exigencies to limit access. And even solving the problem of access may not be enough. Contrary to our expectations, perhaps, simple exposure to and experience with technology does not alter the influence of gender on students' attitudes about computers (Krendl, Broihier, and Fleetwood 90) and, as a consequence, does not automatically result in computer-supported literacy for both men and women in the classroom.

Beyond questions of access, feminist analysis reveals some of the realities associated with how networks are established and what their origins might mean for those who use linked computers. Evidence already indicates that the very fabric of computer system development reflects the dominant cultural values. Joan Greenbaum reminds us that there exist socially constructed differences in women's and men's work, in their attitudes toward their work, and in their concerns. Both the process whereby networks are created and the ways in which they are used reflect these differences. As Greenbaum points out, the "system development process builds on the base of the natural sciences, and in so doing, borrows from the gender-based myths inherent in the sciences." The result of these pressures is the establishment of systems that reflect socially assigned male values:

The systems approach generally defines *information* as identifiable and *quantifiable* data. Systems analysts are trained to define data and follow the flow of documents—the "paper trail" of office procedures. In doing this, the methods focus on procedures and data; concrete "things" that lend themselves to clear-cut descriptions. In an account record-keeping system, for example, data categories like "customer code" and "amount-owed" are the kinds of specific data fields that systems developers are trained to look for.

Consequently, systems developers "leave out the parts of the picture that bring communication and human interaction into focus" (10, 12).

Current systems development focuses on the technical rationality common in good science, privileging the objective, the impersonal, and the quantifiable over the more personal, the more people-oriented, and the less quantifiable (Bjerkness, Ehn, and Kyng). In her review of computer-supported collaborative writing (CSCW), Duin describes various technologies and assesses their strengths and weaknesses. She suggests that consistent flaws in the technology "may be due to the design of the computer systems." Duin cites Jonathan Grundin's list of three "problems that contribute to the failure of CSCW systems":

- the disparity between who does the work and who gets the benefit
- the breakdown of intuitive decision making
- the underestimation of the difficulties in evaluating CSCW applications

In summarizing the second point, Duin says: "Regarding the problem of the breakdown of intuitive decision making, many CSCW systems fail because the thinking behind the design of these systems often seems faulty" ("Computer-Supported Collaborative Writing" 128, 141). Such faulty design may reflect the technical rationality elicited by the pressure of socially assigned male values on systems development. Not surprisingly, gender has not been considered in the analysis of computer networks.

In addition to using networks to support collaborative activities, composition teachers increasingly rely on networks to provide students with access to information in the classroom. Composition specialists often envision networks as expanding the range of information available to students, as opening windows on the world. Many computer writing facilities are connected to wide-area networks (WANs) that permit teachers to introduce students to national services such as BIT-NET and Internet and that allow e-mail and the transfer of files among distant-site users. The language of futurology predicts a world in which information is plentiful and widely available, in which there will be what Wilson Dizard calls a "global knowledge grid" (47). Research on networks being done in the United States, however, suggests that "advanced communications networks are being developed within an existing economic and social context that displays stark geographical inequalities: between, for example, rich and poor nations, central and peripheral regions, cities and rural areas" (Gillespie and Robins 7).

Within the writing classroom, we are likely to find that we have not done as well as we think in providing access to information and to others' opinions. Like larger networks, many of our computer links are structured to perpetuate the very hierarchical, authoritarian principles we have vowed to undo by using the systems in the first place. Instead of expanding literacy, we may be "project[ing] our own experiences, values, and ways of knowing and doing as they relate to literacy on others whose experiences and situations might be different from our own" (Walters 174).

The ENFI (Electronic Network for Interaction) project is a good case in point. ENFI, which is in place in many locations nationally, combines citizens band with a local-area network (LAN), allowing students and teachers to talk with one another on computer screens. Trent Batson, a leader in designing the project, sees ENFI as supplying "the missing link between speaking and writing" and as having "opened up the whole spectrum of social writing" for teachers and students (250). Diane Thompson, who uses ENFI to teach composition, discovered that the system itself had some distinct disadvantages, paramount among them the fact that, because of the way the network was set up, the teacher came to dominate discussions. Looking at transcripts of interactions on the network, Thompson noted that, as the instructor, she had taken 40% of the total turns in the conversations and had produced 60% of the total lines; her messages got longer and longer each session as she tried to keep students interested and interacting ("Conversational Networking" 199).

In the composition classroom, the uses to which networked computers have been put has led to some dissolution of teacher-student hierarchies, with teachers moving into the role of coach instead of evaluator (Selfe and Wahlstrom). Nevertheless, an examination of the network structure itself shows areas, such as file access, that perpetuate hierarchical structures. On some networks, for instance, teachers can read students' files, but students do not have access to teachers' files, except, perhaps, for those marked "handouts." Nor do students have access to one another's files except at the discretion of the instructor. Additionally, networks are sometimes organized so that teachers can read students' unfinished documents, thus removing students' control over their written work. Other systems such as ENFI do not allow for private conversations between teacher and student.

Sound pedagogical and administrative reasons may be offered for such organizational structures, but the political reality of the system itself must be acknowledged. The way networks are structured and the way they are administered can undermine privacy and control by prohibiting writers from sharing their materials with whom they wish and on their own timetables. Thus networks can and sometimes do subvert the literate processes we hope to develop in students.

These issues also affect faculty members who communicate with one another on the same networks their students use. Network managers often set up systems in which faculty members have no access to file servers and never know what options are available for organizing student files or facilitating interactions. Similarly, global passwords that grant general access to the network are often kept by computer specialists who do not allow teachers to "mess up the system" by experimenting with alternative ways of granting access to files. Moreover, faculty members using networks are sometimes subject to the same loss of control over their writing as students experience. At the University of Minnesota recently, for example, a faculty member in the computer science department discovered (in the midst of a heated fight involving the ouster of the chair of the department) that one of her colleagues had accessed her computer files via the network and copied her private memoranda about the conflict. These memoranda were made public and eventually appeared in the student newspaper. Well-founded fears about loss of control of their words and their students' words are a dimension of network design that composition teachers have not fully explored.

Networks established to help us mentor students and aid collaboration can also be employed to monitor students. Many networks support tracking programs originally developed to provide teachers with data on how students use writing tutorial or invention programs. This information is supposed to furnish literacy scholars with cognitive maps of students' explorations of writing software so that the investigators can determine the strategies people employ in writing or researching a topic. Teachers use this ability of the system, however, to observe students for other purposes, verifying or disputing student claims for time spent working on a project. Teachers on the network can enable this data-gathering function directly, and students do not even know that their actions are being monitored, that they are being policed.

Feminist analysis highlights the similarities between the monitoring systems used in the classroom and those used in business to keep track of an operator's keystrokes and the amount of time spent in breaks and away from word processing or data entry. Gender is an issue here because women make up the majority of the clerical employees whose behavior is recorded. Both classroom and workplace monitoring systems grow out of deeply embedded cultural and social realities that place women in secondary roles with respect to authorities—whether bosses at work or teachers in the classroom. One of these realities is the fact that the United States is "both the single largest user and the greatest supporter of the development of computer and telecommunications systems' surveillance capacities" (Gandy 68).

Building the user-monitoring function—as well as other functions—into our networks is not a technological necessity but a cultural choice. As Oscar Gandy points out, "For the most part the 'new' technologies make pursuit of information through surveillance more extensive, more efficient, and less obtrusive than former methods, because advanced electronics allows innovations not originally designed for surveillance to be integrated into the pool of surveillance resources" (62). As we familiarize students with the integrated system of hardware and software that is widespread in the writing environment, we lend tacit support to the cultural hierarchies from which these systems emerge; we also develop citizens who are technologically literate with this equipment. We cannot escape the irony that the electronic forums we use to increase computer-supported literacy also apply the technology designed to monitor and restrict.

The Politics of Software

Networks do not stand alone in the computer-assisted writing classroom. We use them to support a variety of software with which we attempt to foster literate behavior in our students. Word-processing programs, grammar and spelling checkers, invention programs, and the like have received critical attention from composition scholars, seeking to determine their pedagogical soundness. These programs have never been subjected to systematic feminist analysis nor fully explored by literacy researchers, however.

Feminist analysis of grammar checkers, for example, uncovers issues raised by other software commonly supported on our networks. In several articles, David Dobrin has examined what happens when one uses grammar, spelling, and style checkers to study pieces of professional writing. Dobrin ran grammar checkers on a *New York Times* editorial, as well as on other examples of professional writing, in which he identified the number of "errors" he thought the piece contained. In the editorial, Dobrin found that *Correctext* (a grammar checker developed by Houghton-Mifflin) identified errors where both the *New York Times* and most readers would say none existed ("New Grammar Checker" 72–73). In another writing sample, each of three checkers used by Dobrin discovered considerably more "errors" than he had identified, and no checker found all the "errors" he had identified.

The significant point here for a feminist analysis is not the imperfection of grammar checkers but the political agendas built into them. The parsing engines of grammar checkers use artificial intelligence techniques to break sentences down into their constituents so that the error correction element of the software can identify errors and suggest corrections. Each grammar checker deconstructs sentences differently and varies in what it is able to find. Grammar checkers reflect flaws in our understanding of software development and of language as well as the lack of consensus among grammarians, linguists, and writing teachers as to what constitutes an error (Dobrin).

A feminist analysis of this type of software suggests an examination of the nature of "errors." Such analysis requires us to ask who decides what constitutes an "error" and what the authority or warrant is for doing so. There is considerable disagreement among "experts" in grammar as to what represents an error, and a variety of authorities exist (Dobrin). Grammar checkers and style checkers support the political agendas of various "authorities" when it comes to language and language use. The software acts as an agent for those who adhere to particular standards and values.

The implications of giving to one system the imprimatur of the classroom are clear. Supporting one grammar checker (or even two) on a network means accepting its authority on matters of language where there is, in fact, no consensus. For teachers who believe that literacy has something to do with assisting students in finding their authentic voices, such authority issues are problematic. Grammar and style software can be especially detrimental to writers whose prose shows regional, gender, or cultural differences. In many ways such software is incompatible with writing teachers' goal of creating small discourse communities or "literacies" among those students who traditionally find themselves outside the hegemonic structure by virtue of race, class, or gender.

Just as feminist theory encourages analysis of both systems and system development, it encourages analysis of both software and software development. Initial research into software programming suggests that the process of development itself can privilege male and middle-class users. Feminists have argued that artificial intelligence models and current practices for programming favor men and their ways of knowing and undervalue women's ways of knowing (Belenky et al.; Harding and Hintikka; Gilligan). The results have been programs appealing more to men than to women. Additionally, the ways programming skills are currently taught—abstract reasoning and "black-boxing" skills are preferred to styles of *bricolage*[1] and the more concrete reasoning that women seem to favor—means that programs are unlikely to change (Turkle and Papert).

Much more analysis has to be directed at the gendered processes by which software and hardware are created and used in attempts to increase literacy. The development of network systems and of software is highly influenced by cultural factors, including the privileging of socially assigned male ways of thinking. As we rely heavily on technology that we have not subjected to feminist analysis, we let our acceptance of it color our definitions of literacy. As Keith Walters points out in his critique of the ways in which language, logic, and literacy are generally conceived, we run the risk of "select[ing] some subset of our culture's general beliefs about literacy and elevat[ing] them to the status of universally valid truths" (174).

A Literacy That Lingers

Our profession has been enthusiastic about the topic of literacy, and the variety of literacies growing out of the use of computers has been a selling point in our efforts to justify the application of technology in the classroom. What we have been less clear about, I believe, is whom and what computer-supported literacy serves. In chapter 5 of this volume, Janis Forman observes that students in computer-supported collaborative classes may submit "unthinkingly to unseen and undebated influences on that work and on themselves," and she calls, quite rightly, for them to "consider the influences of cultural, political, and socioeconomic forces and of the school culture on their attitudes toward and experience in writing, reading, collaboration, and technology." As teachers, however, we are not fully prepared to assist students in this assessment. Much about the relation of technology and literacy remains obscured by our failure to inquire more persistently into the uses to which computer-supported literacy will be put and whose interests it serves.

Network and Outwork

Currently, many writing classes encourage collaborative activities on the computer, and a variety of collaborative writing software and hardware packages are available for use in both classrooms and the workplace (see Duin, "Computer-Supported Collaborative Writing"). Although this technology facilitates cooperative practices and helps marginalized people find a voice, computer-supported literacy also serves the power structure by preparing students for the society in which female computer professionals are disproportionately concentrated in lower-paid, less prestigious jobs and women and minorities are exploited through outworking programs (Kramer and Lehman 159).

For example, clerical work, increasingly automated and monitored, is moving from the office to the home. *Outworking* and *homeworking* refer to the transfer of clerical tasks to the home. Indicators suggest that homeworking, primarily done by women, encourages salary discrimination. Homeworkers are paid by the piece, and, as a consequence, they often earn lower wages than do people performing comparable work at the office. For example, some Blue Cross–Blue Shield data processors putting in up to fifty-five hours a week make $5,000 less a year than their office counterparts, who work forty hours a week (Perry and Greber 80). In this case, the computer-supported literacy of the classroom serves as preparation for those occupations that keep women second-class wage earners.

Heteroglossia and Loss of Collective Voice

Although computer networks can encourage a multiplicity of voices—a heteroglossia—in the composition classroom, the technology has a reverse side about which we have spoken little. Making students computer-literate on networks may not enable them to find a voice once they leave the classroom. Networks can also prevent the development of discourse communities with multiple voices and foster an isolation that has both social and economic ramifications.

Research by Mary Field Belenky and her colleagues, building on the work of Carol Gilligan, suggests that men and women often interpret their environments differently and that for women "authority or knowing . . . is commonality of experience" (Lay, "Feminist Theory" 363). Mary Lay argues that women and men have different needs in collaborative groups and that they respond to conflict differently. Citing Nancy Chodorow, Lay suggests that women work better when "connected" and men are more comfortable in an environment in which they are "more separate and distinct" (362; see also Kramarae). Indeed, for a variety of cultural and social reasons, dissimilarities exist in the way men and women approach collaboration, consensus, and conflict. Duin points out that computer-supported collaborative writing systems often fail because they don't take into consideration conflict and consensus in group decision making ("Computer-Supported Collaborative Writing" 142). These systems will continue to fall short of our expectations until we design them with an understanding of gender differences, providing for the connectedness that women find essential in the group process and encouraging greater participation by a diverse community.

Networks that do not allow women to establish connectedness put them at an economic disadvantage as well. Homeworkers and outworkers lose individual and collective voice because they interact through networks rather than directly with colleagues in an office or other setting. They have little bargaining power with their employers and fewer employment options; their isolation from one another makes collective action difficult. For these reasons, the AFL-CIO and the organization Nine to Five have called for a federal ban on teleworking for clerical workers (Perry and Greber 80).

Marketing or Empowering

Clearly, we have been putting technology to some good uses. The computer is a boon to the homebound and the elderly (see Breenberger and Puffer; Furlong) and to students who are hospitalized or whose visual disabilities make it difficult or impossible for them to participate fully in writing classes. The Baltimore County public school system, for example, has introduced the computer into its Home and Hospital School for students whose physical and emotional disabilities prevent them from attending the regular schools (Copper). Some universities have official units, like the University of Minnesota's Adaptive Resource Center, that provide, to persons with disabilities, appropriate technology services enabling them to function more productively in the academic community.

In the writing classroom, we hang adaptive technologies on our networks to increase access of those who, because of disabilities, have been unable to participate in the creation of texts and the building of discourse communities. Software programs such as *Outspoken*, which runs on the Macintosh, read text files aloud, allowing students to hear the papers they write and comments made by their instructors and their colleagues in the class.

Despite the success of such programs, we should ask why adaptive software that allows for a variety of learning styles and disabilities has to be added to our systems—why it is not simply developed from the start. What kinds of dependencies are we creating and reinforcing when we teach students with specialized equipment available only at the university? We need to know whether versions of the equipment will be available when these people leave our classrooms—and whether they will be able to afford it in order to continue their learning. As composition teachers, we should make certain that we are not simply expanding a market without forcing real change in the way computer companies envision their roles.

Those of us who rely heavily on the computer in our writing classrooms have been naive to assume the neutrality of the computer or of any techniques we develop for using it. The nature of computer networks and network-supported software, the uses to which we put them, the ways we conceive of their abilities and describe their functions—all show evidence of being part of a gender-coded system less hospitable to women than it should be. Feminist analyses help us foresee possibilities for changing this reality. Such a vision critiques technology and its uses, suggesting alternatives that are democratizing and equalizing. It gives us a glimpse of what technology might be if it were designed for and used in support of women. Because we have other silenced groups in our classes in addition to women, feminist analysis provides a vantage point from which we can imagine applications of technology that enfranchise marginal and oppressed groups.

Teachers in the computer classroom need to "keep human concerns foremost in [their] critique of changing technology" (Perry and Greber 101). Our schools exist within society, and we must remember that technology is not produced in a social or economic vacuum and that what we do with technology in our classroom resonates in the larger context. As we provide opportunities for students to develop the literacies associated with computer-assisted writing laboratories, we run the risk of preparing them to fit into an economic and social structure that will use these skills to exploit them and others. Kathryn Thoms Flannery talks about the "wrenching" reassessment composition teachers must be called on to perform as they realize "the extent to which literacy instruction is likely to be not purely liberatory but in the service of domesticating or hegemonic forces in a given society" (208). When we forget this fact ourselves, we cannot hope to remind our students of it.

We also need to help students understand that literacies can be (and are being) used in support of human concerns. The competencies we assist students to develop and the technology we provide for them to achieve those competencies are mixed blessings. The computer-supported literacy that students develop may prepare them for an exploitative environment rather than protect them from it. Yet this same literacy can enable students to create such networks as Peacenet and Econet, concerned with peace and environmental issues respectively, and to share information with others interested in taking the world in for repairs. John Clifford calls the kind of literacy I am suggesting here "critical literacy," an "alert and critical quality of mind" that is personal rather than culturally decided but "hopes for change, for social justice in a more humane democracy" ("Enacting Critical Literacy" 255).

Technology is not neutral. It is political. Bringing a feminist perspective to bear on technology and the literacy issues associated with it helps us face these politics more squarely. As Perry and Greber suggest:

> We must learn to see computers in their cultural context—to parse the interacting political, economic, social, and technological forces that combine to create and define appropriate use of computers—as part of the process of imagining the kinds of technologies or adaptations of technologies that best reflect the social and political relations that we, as feminists, would like to see.
>
> (83)

Foucault urges us to "question those ready-made syntheses, those groupings that we normally accept before any examination, those links whose validity is recognized from the outset" (*Archaeology* 22). Bringing a feminist perspective to the technologies of the writing classroom prepares us to discover other discontinuities, gaps, and silences. It reminds us that there are no simple answers here.

NOTE

[1] The term *bricolage* originates with Lévi-Strauss, who used it to contrast the analytic approaches of Western science with the concrete approaches of what he called "primitive" societies.

Response

The Challenges of Creating Networked Connections among Teachers and Students

William Wresch

The previous five chapters contain a wealth of information and a wealth of perspectives. It might seem that, because they speak to such divergent issues as discourse communities, feminism, and teachers'-lounge jealousies, little can be said of these articles as a group. But, in fact, a single concern underlies all of them—what Janis Forman refers to in her chapter as "computer-supported literacy." Her label makes a point many try to ignore—that the computer, which has its own "literacy," shapes the reading and writing abilities of those who use it. Several of the authors themselves appear to take contradictory views on this point. For instance, Betsy A. Bowen reinforces the idea by asserting that "we need to concentrate on the educational purposes that the technology serves, rather than on the technology itself." Billie J. Wahlstrom takes an opposing view, principally as a means of critiquing technology as male-dominated.

The role of technology in creating this new literacy is not limited to computer networks, but networks are sufficiently different from former modes of discourse that their impact can more easily be seen. Therefore, the chapters of this section highlight trends that can also be observed in other computer uses, from those as mundane as word processing to those as new as hypermedia.

That technology is shaping discourse is made clear in the discussion of conferencing in the essay by Ann Hill Duin and Craig Hansen. Their examination is an even-handed overview of available conferences, showing where such networks seem to have a positive influence, where they distract from classroom learning, and even where they are

186

ignored. Duin and Hansen begin with the premise that, in current practice, the teacher severely limits classroom communication. They note that, "in a typical classroom situation, the discourse community is subsumed in the person of the instructor, as assessor and arbiter." Such pedagogy is later referred to as the "traditional hegemony." They see networks as a way to break down barriers to communication. Through networks, "students [take] on more authoritative roles and [become] active in their own learning processes." As their description of the University of Minnesota experiment indicates, once the network broke down barriers and students took over communication, they were free to move the topic of conversation to any subject they wanted—regardless of its relevance to the course.

Whether or not the reader supports a classroom environment in which first-year students have equal voice with the professor, it is inevitable that technology will change the roles that participants in education play. In one example of a synchronous network, the teacher assumed a dominating role. In an asynchronous network, the teacher's role was modified. In neither case did the classroom instructor choose the role—it was created by the technology.

To be literate in a computer environment, as Duin and Hansen's overview demonstrates, the individual should have a clear sense of the way in which the communication medium itself is shaping the interaction. The medium is not neutral.

The power of the medium is specifically described in Bowen's chapter on telecommunications networks. Chapter 4 is, first, a marvelous resource on contemporary networks, and I suspect many will use the essay principally for that purpose. But in the process of discussing these networks, Bowen raises a number of issues that lead us toward our definition of *computer-supported literacy*. One of her crucial points is the role of telecommunications networks in providing new audiences. Through linked computers, students can contact young people in other classes and other nations, thus extending their understanding of other cultures and of the complexity of written communication. The need for such experiences for our students is such a commonplace that we can forget what the simple word *audience* means.

Providing an audience can indeed be special. Jeff Golub, a high school teacher in Seattle, has had his classes hooked to the AT&T Long Distance Learning Network for several years. In the fall of 1989, his students were connected to a high school in West Berlin. Each morning the young people heard first-hand how seventeen-year-olds across the globe were reacting to the destruction of the Berlin Wall. In 1991, Golub's students were linked to a high school in Tel Aviv. During the

Persian Gulf crisis, his students rushed to class to see whether their friends in Israel had survived the latest Scud attack. The students asked questions I did not hear asked by professional reporters: "When are you most scared?" The answer? "In the shower." The directness of the questions and the honesty of the replies create a new level of communication. As writing teachers we are accustomed to using such terms as *discourse communities* and *developing audience awareness*. With telecommunications networks these phrases seem trite. We can certainly enlarge discourse communities and develop audience awareness, but we are doing much more than that. We can help students share the joy of newfound freedom and the pain of random death from the sky.

The literacy of these networks is not simple, however. Bowen points out the need for a moderator to prevent the discussion from becoming unfocused and uninteresting. She also points out issues of access. Although telecommunications networks do not require much computing equipment, they do need a phone line—often a significant hurdle. Schools in Alaska are cited as frequent users of telecommunications, but, in fact, for most rural schools telephone communication is irregular—a daily test to see whether the satellite links are correctly aimed and functioning. Telephone access can hardly be assumed. In city schools access requires wiring that older buildings may not have—and money to pay for access fees. As a consequence, telecommunications networks may represent a case of the rich getting richer; those who already have access to a wider discourse community now have the opportunity to reach a larger world. Computer-supported literacy may thus be the understanding of who can participate in a telecommunications network and how the participants shape the conversation. Political literacy might be the understanding of, first, the importance of such networks and, second, of the need to create access for all.

A different approach to computer-supported literacy comes in chapter 5, by Forman. In carefully analyzing why a particular piece of groupware is not used, Forman was able to see an aspect of technology and writing that others have missed.

The use of groupware assumes the presence of teams. Software that makes it easy to share ideas and drafts of a group-written manuscript has value only if participants want to share. The college students in the investigation she reports on didn't. While they had been assigned to a group project, they didn't attack the work as a group. As American college students they were unfamiliar with such projects and unable to function well as a team, and the technology available to them didn't change their lack of commitment to collaborative writing.

In their overview Duin and Hansen refer to this nonuse of conferencing technology and say that "Forman attributes these results to the students' limited commitment toward the new technology." That is probably not a fair interpretation. Forman's point is that conferencing technology assumes a desire to communicate by network. An educational environment that promotes the individual and gives little instruction in group processes produces students who are at odds with this form of technology. The students may like such aspects of technology as word processors and spreadsheets—and the students Forman describes used both widely—but these applications are individual and fully consonant with the social experiences the students have had. In a sense, then, Forman's chapter describes an area of technology that is not acceptable in our culture. She shows the limits of technology. Although groupware offers an interesting new form of computer-supported literacy, our students will apparently keep themselves illiterate for the immediate future.

Wahlstrom's chapter also speaks of limits. According to Wahlstrom, the limits are the result of the exclusion of a feminist perspective in computer system design. Actually, most of her examples speak less of feminism and more of basic human decency. For instance, she describes ways in which computer networks can be used to eavesdrop on private conversations or private files. Such examples are a valuable warning to us all.

In some instances, she says, the misuse of networks to control speech and action is the result of consciously directed efforts to maintain existing hierarchies. Wahlstrom gives some examples of such misuses, but the problem is much better stated in Shoshana Zuboff's *In the Age of the Smart Machine*. Zuboff describes the dangers of electronic surveillance for clerical workers but also depicts the impact such systems have on managers. It is an insightful work that clarifies one aspect of literacy that all of us need to learn about—the loss of privacy possible with these systems.

Although we are all concerned about the larger issue of network misuse often seen in business, we should not overlook the casual misuse often practiced by the best-intentioned teachers. How often do teachers, when taking a class to a networked writing lab, ask for software that will let them see student papers at a "teacher station," allowing them to review student work unseen? They are, in fact, invading students' privacy. The teachers are not being evil—actually, they want to learn about their students in order to help them—but they haven't thought about the consequences of their action.

The problem of damage done by naïveté is an interesting area that

Wahlstrom might have covered better, but she sees conscious evil. For her, grammar checkers have "political agendas" built into them, and all of technology "is not neutral. It is political." While there is no shortage of examples to show that technology has been used for sinister purposes, to dwell on deliberate wrongdoing seems to promote conspiracy theories and to miss that most common of human traits—stumbling affability—the misstep, and damage, resulting from the best of intentions.

Fortunately, the less ambitious, but more personal, chapter by Gary Graves and Carl Haller adds some of this perspective. In their description of their experiences in bringing technology into high schools, they plant our feet firmly on the ground. Frenchtown provides an example of how jealousy on the part of the have-nots—who gained nothing for themselves except the bitter satisfaction of revenge—harmed the haves. It is an important reminder of the politics of the staff lounge and the need to provide equal access to teachers as well as students. The picture portrayed of the McDonogh School is prettier, but that institution offers its own lessons. The slow pace with which teachers accepted the technology, the time constraints that prevent teachers from using important packages such as desktop publishing—these are major barriers to literacy.

These stories remind us of the social context in which we apply technology and develop our expertise. Our efforts are not universally applauded. To some they are another example of privilege—another opportunity restricted to an elite. The experience at Frenchtown tells us what happens when such attitudes are combined with political influence. But even the events at McDonogh convey a message about privilege. The new technology not only costs money but requires time. Not everyone has graduate students or a six-hour teaching load. Even those with the insight to appreciate the value of communications technology may not be able to join us—they may not have enough hours in their day. This observation should remind us that our new literacy is not lightly earned, and may not be widespread.

This message is reinforced by the chapter on libraries, by William Goodrich Jones. While it begins with quotable examples of the technological enhancements coming to every library, much of the survey information Jones presents shows just how many barriers remain to the effective use of this technology. What sense does it make to talk glowingly of the "information age" when, Jones tells us, only 7% of scholars in research universities do online database searches themselves? These are supposedly the best and brightest in our profession, but fewer than 10% can manage an ERIC search without help. Even simple card catalog searches seem beyond much of the professoriate. Jones's statistics showing that 38% of professors at colleges with online catalogs have never used them should shock any librarian (and, of course, the administrators struggling to find the millions of dollars necessary to create these catalogs). Such incredible numbers make us all wonder what "literacy" means when intellectual leaders can be ignorant of a common access point to the most basic information. Something important is missing here, and while Jones may not tell us exactly what it is, at least he helps all of us understand that there is much yet to be done.

So, in sum, what do these chapters say about our computer-supported literacy? They clearly describe the importance of this form of literacy. Synchronous networks simply work differently from anything else we have seen before, while asynchronous networks and telecommunications let us reach out over time and distance. The impact of both types of networks is remarkable, with the power of these resources having a major effect on students.

But this new literacy functions in an existing world, and that world brings its own values and limits. Technology to ease the burden of shared work has no usefulness if no one will share. Technology to improve communication will never fully succeed as long as technology itself is viewed as the privilege of one sex or race or economic class. To those of us who consider ourselves adept at this new literacy, our greatest challenge may be to find ways to bring our facility to all. Surely we want to create a world in which every person can access a computer, and for example, ask friends in a war-torn country, "Are you still alive?" and receive reassurances and understanding in return.

PART III

Expanding the Definitions of Computer-Based Literacy

Overview

Reading and Writing in Hypertext: Vertigo and Euphoria

Johndan Johnson-Eilola

> *We could say that there is no story at all; there are only readings. . . . Or if we say that the story of "Afternoon" is the sum of all its readings, then we must understand the story as a structure that can embrace contradictory outcomes.*
> —Jay David Bolter, *Writing Space*

In 1988, I ran a short hypertext seminar for a group of writing instructors. Teachers worked in pairs reading and responding to "Afternoon: A Story." "Afternoon" is a literary hypertext—a nonlinear, computer-supported text—written by Michael Joyce. Many of the teachers were excited about the changes that hypertext environments introduced into their reading processes. In "Afternoon" readers move from one section of the story to another by clicking a mouse pointer on words in the text; choosing different words yields different paths through the story. The story never comes to a formal conclusion: each reader decides when he or she has read enough. (Intermittently, a reader will cycle through previously read sections of the text, although sometimes the contents of a screen change subtly on rereading.) Individual readings of "Afternoon" develop out of interactions between the multiply structured hypertext and the specific navigational actions of the reader. Users of literary hypertexts can come to realize their power as reader-writers whose actions appear to determine fundamental characteristics of the story. In such a text, the common distinctions between "writer" and "reader" begin to collapse in a way that has long been theorized for print text but not realized in such visible form. For these reasons, hypertexts such as "Afternoon" can give readers a rush of euphoria— or, for the same reasons, a rush of vertigo.

Late in the seminar, toward the back of the room, I heard the rising voices of two instructors engaging in a friendly but heated argument. One of the teachers had become irritated at the lack of a singular, cohesive thread in "Afternoon." Joyce, in his advice on reading the text, warns that there is no "correct" path through the story. But the teacher felt that Joyce had "not done his job" as an author (the assumption being that the author bears sole responsibility for providing a single, linear beginning-middle-end through a published story). "I don't know what this is," she said, "but it's not literature."

This teacher's comment suggests just a few of the pedagogical issues connected with hypertext use. For theorists and teachers, admitting "Afternoon" as literature means redefining what is meant by the terms *literature* and *text*. Such a revision entails fundamental alterations in the roles of the writer, the reader, and the text, as well as that of the teacher and the activity of teaching and learning literacy. In this medium, as Jane Yellowlees Douglas says, we find ourselves moving away from the traditional conceptions of reading and reality as "the great 'either/or' and embracing, instead, the 'and/and/and' " ("Understanding the Act" 125).

Hypertext forefronts the interaction between social and technological issues in a way not normally seen—or not normally discussed—in the use of print-based, linear texts. While the technological, functional aspects of hypertext offer both opportunities and limits to reading and writing, the social and educational aspects of literacy also bring their own sets of opportunities and limits to the processes of reading and writing in hypertext. Neither the technical nor the social elements are completely independent of or dependent on the other—both are semiautonomous, each element opening up and constraining the other.

Highlighting this semiautonomous interaction in hypertext use can make visible the operations and effects of powerful modern theories of reading and writing—postmodernism and poststructuralism, reader-response criticism and critical literacy, and collaborative learning and social construction theory. The parallels between hypertext and contemporary writing and reading theory suggest that the radical alterations in literary theory that hypertext seems to necessitate are not completely new prophecies: these changes were merely predicted in relation to print text. In this essay, I discuss four ways in which hypertext may work to extend, make visible, and challenge key processes associated with current theories and practices: shifting and fusing the roles of the writer and the reader, decentering the subject of discourse, giving voice to those silenced, and constructing knowledge and text in communities.

The Technology of Hypertext

Although I will not devote much space here to specific technical issues, at least a brief functional and historical overview is necessary in order to examine the openings and limitations offered by hypertext in literacy education. The first order of business is to define the term *hypertext,* a task that poses special problems because the differences between hypertext and linear text are deceptively simple (Slatin, "Reading" 870). Hypertext writers and readers depend on a computer-based organizational scheme that allows them to move from one section of text (termed a "node," often the size of a paragraph) to related sections of text quickly and easily.[1] Such a text consists of a network, or web, of multiply connected text segments. Hypertext writers set up multiple connections between nodes of a text, and readers choose which links to follow, which nodes to read, and which nodes to skip.

Figure 1, for example, shows a subsection of a hypertext based on this essay. The background screen in the figure shows a hypertext network of text nodes and links constructed in the program *Storyspace.* The foreground window shows one of the text nodes in the network opened for reading or writing. Links between nodes are expressed not only by the arrows in the network but also by bold words or phrases in the text.

A key difference between hypertext and linear text is the degree to which hypertext readers are allowed to choose from multiple paths through a body of text. A text is hypertextual not because it was written in any specific computer program but because it follows this general theory of textual structure: readers do not read top to bottom across a page and front to back from page to page, but according to a path they navigate through a network of text nodes.

The looseness of the defining characteristics of hypertext allows an extremely broad range of reader and writer options in any specific hypertext. For this reason, the general traits of hypertext organization discussed in this chapter are not necessarily offered in all hypertexts. At one end of the spectrum, a hypertext may be so open—interconnected and reader-controlled—that a reader might be overwhelmed by the sheer number of choices offered by the text.[2] At the other end of the spectrum, a hypertext might be so restrictive that readers find that they have no more—or perhaps less—navigational choice than they would have with a linear version of the text.

"Afternoon" offers a good example of a literary hypertext with a medium-level capacity for reader interaction. The opening screen in "Afternoon" contains the first node of the story (also shown in the upper left of figure 2, along with three of the twenty possible second nodes):

> I try to recall winter. <As if it were yesterday?> she says, but I do not signify one way or another.
>
> By five the sun sets and the afternoon melt freezes again across the blacktop into crystal octopi and palms of ice—rivers and continents beset by fear, and we walk out to the car, the snow

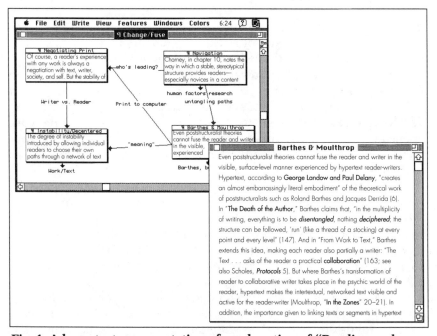

Fig. 1. A hypertext representation of a subsection of "Reading and Writing in Hypertext: Vertigo and Euphoria." Background shows a graphical representation of an interconnected network of text nodes. Foreground window, titled "Barthes & Moulthrop," shows a node from the network open for reading or writing. Hypertext links are indicated by arrows (in the background network) or bold words and phrases (in the opened text node).

moaning beneath our boots and the oaks exploding in series along the fenceline on the horizon, the shrapnel settling like relics, the echoing thundering off far ice. This was the essence of wood, these fragments say. And this darkness is air.

<Poetry> she says, without emotion, one way or another.

Do you want to hear about it?

In this node, there are about twenty "hot" words or phrases that Joyce has constructed as starting points for hypertext links to other nodes in the story. Readers choose paths by selecting words in the text or by typing text into the toolbar at the bottom of each screen (readers' typed responses can be either answers to the narrator's questions or words copied from the text of the story). For example, readers clicking the mouse pointer on the word *octopi* in the first node of "Afternoon" will then see a new node beginning "<We are like that> she says,

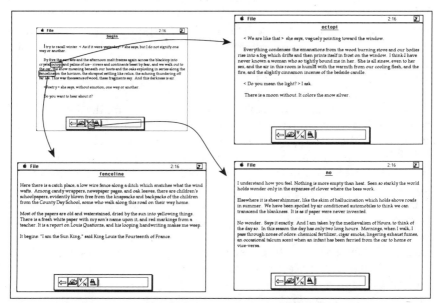

Fig. 2. Beginning of "Afternoon: A Story," by Michael Joyce (Watertown: Eastgate Systems; used by permission). At top left is the opening screen. From there, readers may follow different paths by clicking on words in the text or by selecting options in the toolbar at the bottom of the screen. Three of the twenty possible second screens are shown at top right and bottom.

vaguely pointing toward the window" (see fig. 2). Readers selecting the word *fenceline* would be given a different node, one starting "Here there is a catch place, a low wire fence along a ditch which snatches what the wind wafts." Readers may even respond to the question "Do you want to hear about it?" in the first node by typing *Yes* or *No* into the toolbar; typing *No* yields a node in which Joyce's text begins, "I understand how you feel." Readers selecting or entering a word or phrase that is not specifically tagged as a yielding word move to a default node associated in some general way with the node they just left.[3]

Where in a print version of "Afternoon" Joyce would be forced to offer readers only one of the next twenty possible text segments (although he might suggest other orderings that defy the physical structure of the printed text), in the hypertext environment he can offer twenty possibilities, each of which can be followed with minimal effort. Navigating these threads issuing from the first node (and the multiple threads that issue from each subsequent node) in this interconnected text space represents the basic activity behind reading most forms of hypertext. Although texts such as "Afternoon" are a multidimensional network of segments, the readers' low-level experience of the text unfolds one-dimensionally as readers follow the linear string of words in their movement within and between nodes of text. The developing text differs for each reader on the basis of the specific actions he or she makes in moving from one node to another.

The idea of nonlinear reading and writing—of the reader being given some freedom in determining what and where to read—is not new in technological or literary terms. The precursor to hypertext was theorized in a 1945 essay by Vannevar Bush, director of the Office of Scientific Research and Development under Franklin Roosevelt. Bush called his proposed (but never constructed) device the "memex," a mechanical writing and reading machine that would allow users to map trails within and between documents; these trails could be for personal use or shared with other readers. The mechanical basis of memex, however, made the construction of Bush's machine unfeasible. In the 1960s, hypertext pioneers such as Douglas Englebart and Ted Nelson translated Bush's ideas into computer programs (Englebart and Hooper; Nelson, *Computer Lib* and *Literary Machines*). The hypertext programs developed by Englebart and Nelson allowed readers and writers to establish and explore links among computer-based documents and document sections more easily than in a purely mechanical technology.[4]

Aside from these historical applications, hypertext has a functional equivalent in other, more familiar types of texts. The nonlinear reading that hypertext users do is relatively common in certain print-based texts. Activities such as reading cross-references in encyclopedias, citations and footnotes in scholarly works, and the alphabetized names linked to numbers in a phone book correspond, in a limited way, to the essential idea behind hypertext. (Kalmbach argues, in fact, that defining *hypertext* as a solely computer-supported medium may limit important research in paper-based writing and reading.) Equivalents of functional documents are still the most common kind of hypertext—encyclopedias and dictionaries (Marchionini and Shneiderman; Glushko; Raymond and Tompa), technical manuals (Walker, "Document Examiner"; Remde, Gomez, and Landauer), and online databases (Croft and Turtle; Parsaye et al.). These hypertexts are written for readers who normally have very explicit, concrete goals (see Conklin, *Theory*). For example, a reader of an online hypertext manual for a computer program will probably want to read specific information on a certain command or feature of the program.

More important to the present discussion are texts designed around less easily defined problems or goals. For instance, Christine Neuwirth and David Kaufer have researched the use of hypertext as a way to store external representations of information during writing-from-sources tasks ("Role"). And Joyce, among others, has used *Storyspace* in composition classes ("Siren Shapes"). Other writing and reading instructors have begun exploring the use of hypertext for a variety of student writing and reading tasks (Smith, Weiss, and Ferguson; C. F. Smith et al.; Slatin, "Hypertext and the Teaching of Writing"). Hypertext programs such as *Hypercard* may be designed primarily for business use but, as poet William Dickey points out, such tools might also be used to "create . . . something it was not intended for" (145).

In chapter 9 in this volume, Stuart Moulthrop and Nancy Kaplan discuss the use of hypertext fictions, such as "Afternoon," and hypertext versions of print fiction, such as Jorge Luis Borges's "The Garden of Forking Paths," in an introduction-to-literature class, where students could choose to write their own essays in hypertext. Davida Charney, in chapter 10, provides an important bridge between technical-functional and essay-narrative hypertexts—important because of her objections to rather than her enthusiasm for hypertext. Charney, drawing on cognitive research on reading, contends that hypertext may inhibit rather than promote learning. According to Charney, "Along with greater control . . . comes a greater burden for the readers." And Catherine F. Smith, who argues elsewhere that current conceptions of hypertext are limiting in that they support system-dependent interconnection more easily than social connection ("Reconceiving"), works, in chapter 11, toward defining the domain of hypertext as thinking in general—a social, dynamic, contextualized activity.

A crucial observation in each of these three essays is the difference between how people normally read and how hypertext encourages them to read. Hypertext, in the view of these theorists, is not a medium that can by itself effect great change. As Charney states, "As part of a literate society, we are familiar with traditional text structures. . . . But we lack corresponding theories for how to deal with hypertexts— especially those that push the limits with complex linkages within and between a complex set of texts."

For students, this unfamiliarity can become a site of insurmountable difficulty rather than of empowerment and learning. Charney's analysis echoes the tone of Gail Hawisher and Cynthia Selfe's overview of computers and writing research, in which Hawisher and Selfe warn: "All too often, those who use computers for composition instruction speak and write of 'the effects of technology' in overly positive terms as if computers were good in and of themselves." Hypertext is clearly a technology that should not be blindly applied to writing and reading instruction. As Hawisher and Selfe also point out, "This rhetoric—one of hope, vision, and persuasion—is the primary voice present in much of the work we see coming out of computers-and-composition studies" ("Rhetoric" 56, 57). In her essay Smith takes up a view of what hypertext should but does not do, avoiding Hawisher and Selfe's criticism even as she asserts the potential benefits of hypertext. Smith shows hope and vision, but also pessimism, toward hypertext; she calls for change rather than acceptance. And although Charney thoughtfully points out that hypertext does not fall in line with traditional cognitive views of reading, the goal of what are frequently derided as "romantic" uses of hypertext (Barrett, *Text, Context, Hypertext* xv) is contrary rather than complementary to common reading activities. In addition, the implicit disagreement between Charney and Smith, in terms of the application of cognitive reading theory to hypertext, illustrates the problems with translating one field's research to another: where Charney uses the more traditional macrostructural theory of Teun van Dijk and Walter Kintsch, Smith follows (among other things) more recent work by Kintsch. While many applications of cognitive research (or other external fields) to composition or literature theory often present those external fields as static and univocal, often these fields are in flux and disagreement, just as are composition and literature theory themselves.

The implied debate here about what hypertext should help writers and readers accomplish becomes a primary question for Moulthrop and Kaplan. According to their essay, hypertext use is neither a simple continuation nor a wholesale replacement of normal reading and writing theories and activities but a positive disruption. Using hypertext in the composition or literature classroom may work *against* traditional ways of reading and writing. In some ways, hypertext is useful as a measure of the inadequacies of current pedagogy.

Remapping Literacy: Visible Theory and Practice

In the view of the studies and applications discussed above, hypertext helps us revise theories of reading, writing, and literacy in key ways by making various traits of these theories visible. Despite the linear, fixed, and physical nature of print, literacy theorists in a wide variety of areas have tried to work with nonlinear conceptions of reading and writing to help readers and writers gain a richer sense of text. Poststructuralist, critical-literacy, reader-response, and social construction theories of text, for instance, posit reading and writing as acts that take place to an extent outside the linear structure of the printed text. Although the print text, even in these theories, is still a linear, physical artifact, relative to the print text are many important nonlinear activities—deconstruction, interpretation through personal experience, collaborative work, and so forth.

While such theorists as Walter Ong, Jacques Derrida, Paulo Freire, Stanley Fish, and Kenneth Bruffee assert the necessity for moving beyond the text in one sense or another, they do not call for conceptually linking the social and individual aspects of literacy to its technological aspects; instead, they place primary emphasis on different relations. But overstressing any aspect of such complex phenomena may inhibit analysis—"totalizing," or simplistically summarizing complex situations such as writing or reading, may result in skewed views of these processes. Totalizing writing, for example, in relation to the social situation of the writer tends to collapse all aspects of writing into social relations: the print text and the technology of text production and consumption hold relatively little importance in such theories; strong versions of social construction value group consensus to the exclusion of individual voices (Trimbur) or of the text (Scholes, *Textual Power*). Postmodernism frequently totalizes in terms of a different aspect, reducing everything to text (Poster 140; Haraway 69; Eagleton, *Ideology*); the subject does not only write but is also *written* in discourse.

Such totalizations are problematic because in each case some aspects of writing and reading are considered beyond influence—either all-powerful or completely powerless in determining the nature of writing and reading text. The collapsing of semiautonomous elements, as the technology critic Jennifer Slack writes, "discourages critical analysis of the complex relationships between technology and social structure and practice" (6). Evidence of this occurrence can be seen in the scant attention that traditional and current pedagogical practices pay to, for example, the effects of the typewriter on writing and reading (Braddock, Lloyd-Jones, and Schoer 51).[5] The assumption seems to be that the mechanical, technological aspect of writing is not a fruitful area of speculation (Sullivan)—except in those studies that reverse this pedagogical imbalance in their "technocentrism," examining technological aspects with no sustained consideration of other aspects (Hawisher, "Research and Recommendations"; Kaplan, "Ideology").

More profitable would be the view that various components of writing and reading, as separate elements, may influence each other through intricate connections. John Smith and Catherine Smith, in "Writing, Thinking, Computing," offer a consideration of hypertext as a semiautonomous technology. Noting that "Computerwriting occurs in a mental world at the end of mechanical arms" (133), Smith and Smith begin their analysis of computer-based writing at the juncture of social human and machine (see also Landow, *Hypertext*; Winograd and Flores). Catherine Smith, resuming this study in her contribution to this volume, calls for research on "how . . . people talk as they work in or around the hypertext medium . . . how . . . they talk to the machine, to people in the room, to distant people, even to themselves." Although I cannot undertake here a full examination of the link between the technological and the social sides of hypertext, I want to point out the need for a fuller understanding of the nondeterministic, complex, and interwoven nature of the technological, individual, and social aspects of writing and reading in hypertext.

In observing these imbalances, I am not suggesting a sweeping dismissal. Current composition, literature, and literacy theories provide a rich ground for healthy debate. But disrupting conventional practices by introducing a new literacy technology can force teachers "to rethink and then revise the theoretical and pedagogical premises upon which they base their classes, their research, and their curricula" (Selfe, "English Teachers" 190). Technologies such as hypertext give theorists and teachers the opportunity to remap their conceptions of literacy, to reconsider the complex, interdependent nature of the ties between technology, society, and the individual in the acts of writing, reading, and thinking. Adding the concept of hypertext to theory does not replace other definitions or conceptions of writing and reading; it opens those definitions up to debate and change. As Paul Delany and George Landow somewhat optimistically put it in the foreword to *Hypermedia*,

"The arrival of hypertext causes other occupants of the textual bus to shift position, but no one actually has to get off" (i).

Changing and Fusing the Roles of Writer and Reader

Despite important contributions by theorists in areas such as social construction and reader-response criticism, the actual roles of reader and writer have been largely separate ones—the disjuncture holds most visibly for student writers and readers but the chasm still exists in the barrier (both physical and psychological) between composition and literature departments in the academy. Composition and literature scholars work under an uneasy truce; both profess to study text, but the approaches of the two disciplines to writing and reading differ in both goals and methods. "Reading," in a composition classroom, is often used to help writers revise their texts or suggest revisions to other writers; "writing," in a literature classroom, is usually aimed at helping readers or groups of readers interpret texts. As Anne Ruggles Gere says of the two disciplines, "When asked to select a metaphor that describes their relationship, many of us choose some version of 'bridge,' a metaphor that emphasizes separation and difference" ("Composition" 617) even as it attempts to bring the fields closer together.

If part of the reason for this "separation and difference" lies in the traditionally dissimilar conceptions of writing and reading, hypertext may offer a different cartography, maps that place composition and literature on a connected and overlapping terrain, that problematize, in productive ways, shared and contested ground between the two (Johnson-Eilola, "Trying"). Hypertext may provide a forum in which reading and writing can be reconceived in such a way that these traditionally separate acts begin to partially coalesce (Moulthrop, "Hypertext and 'the Hyperreal'" 266; Johnson-Eilola, "Structure"). In hypertexts, Jay David Bolter explains, "readers cannot avoid writing the text itself, since every choice they make is an act of writing" (144).

Even poststructuralist theories cannot fuse the reader and writer in the visible, surface-level manner experienced by hypertext reader-writers. Hypertext, according to George Landow and Paul Delany, "creates an almost embarrassingly literal embodiment" of the theoretical work of poststructuralists such as Roland Barthes and Jacques Derrida (6). In "The Death of the Author," Barthes claims that, "in the multiplicity of writing, everything is to be *disentangled*, nothing *deciphered*; the structure can be followed, 'run' (like a thread of a stocking) at every point and every level" (147). And in "From Work to Text," Barthes extends this idea, making each reader also partially a writer: "The Text . . . asks of the reader a practical collaboration" (163; see also Scholes,

Protocols 5). But where Barthes's transformation of reader to collaborative writer takes place in the psychic world of the reader, hypertext makes the intertextual, networked text visible and active for the reader-writer (Moulthrop, "In the Zones" 20–21). In addition, the importance given to linking texts or segments in hypertext writing and reading may encourage students to make connections in their own thought processes (Landow and Delany 22), to think in a pluralistic, nonlinear fashion (Beeman et al.).

Using hypertext, people are neither solely readers nor solely writers—users take the two roles simultaneously and visibly. Even nonliterary texts such as corporate memos are not immune to drastic shifts. In hypertexts, Moulthrop asserts,

> any writing can be linked or woven into a de-centered matrix of information, [and] its affiliation with a specific, identifiable speech act comes into question. . . . The changes that have come to the technology of writing take us out of the realm of self-validating truths and decrees and place us instead in a context that requires negotiation, cross-reference, and a constant awareness of diversity.   ("Hypertext and 'the Hyperreal' " 259)

The hypertext not only invites readers to participate in making the text but forces them to do so, requiring both readers and writers to become "co-learners" (Joyce, "Siren Shapes" 12). It is the force inherent in this sudden shift in roles that can give a user varying degrees of either vertigo or euphoria.[6]

The degree of instability introduced by allowing individual readers to choose their own paths through a network of text, an option offered by hypertexts that Joyce terms "exploratory," is only one possible level of decentering the author-text from its traditionally privileged position. Joyce contrasts exploratory hypertexts with "constructive" hypertexts —those that permit readers not only to reorder the text segments but also to add their own text to the network ("Siren Shapes" 11). Catherine Smith offers a similar view of such text, contrasting hypertexts that encourage the construction of "world knowledge" with ones that promote the construction of "personal knowledge" ("Reconceiving").

Of course, a reader's experience with any work is always a negotiation with text, writer, society, and self. But the stability of traditional texts is both physical and psychological; the physical, stable presence of the text denies the intangible, psychological text the reader attempts to construct (Kaplan, *Ideology* 17). As John Slatin points out in his discussion of hypertext, traditional literacy relies heavily on the idea that a printed text should be "stable" ("Reading"; see also Landow and Delany 12–13; Ong, *Rhetoric* 277–78 and *Orality and Literacy* 132–33). Readers can normally count on the fact that a printed text represents the author's final and authoritative words; they can also assume that the printed text (especially a published, canonized text) is a careful ordering of elements that strongly imply the sequence in which the text should be read.

Hypertext challenges, to varying degrees, this idea of stable structure, of careful ordering in a single implied sequence. Because exploratory hypertexts can still preserve much of the original author's node offerings, some sense of stability is preserved: the reader is still only choosing among various options that are inherently in the original text—a path from one node to another exists only because the original writer decided that it should exist. In constructive hypertexts, however, the original author-text's authority begins to evaporate: readers not only choose among the options offered by the original text but may add their own paths or even texts. It is these constructive–personal knowledge hypertexts that most seriously challenge assumptions about the respective positions and functions of student writing and literature in the classroom. Landow and Delany observe that, "from a literary perspective based on book technology, the effects of electronic linking may appear harmful and dangerous" (9). Indeed, Moulthrop and Kaplan, in their contribution to this volume, explore these challenges at length, asking, "If we English teachers embrace this form of text production, do we abandon what we have taken to be central literary values?"

Moulthrop and Kaplan's question about the status of literature in this new medium is a difficult one—and not merely at the level of the current cultural literacy debates. Charney, in chapter 10, notes the way in which a stable, stereotypical structure provides readers—especially novices in a content area[7]—with the ability to judge the importance of information. Although for the most part the cognitive research that Charney reviews is focused on technical-functional texts (both linear and nonlinear), the reader's reliance on a stereotypical, predictable structure holds for literary texts as well. Novels, short stories, and other narratives normally follow a framework of conventional structure that allows readers to judge the significance and purpose of textual elements as they go through the work (Mandler; van Dijk and Kintsch 55–59; de Beaugrande and Dressler; Hobbs). Hypertexts, either exploratory or constructive, emphasize the readers' choice in consciously determining the flow of information (deciding if and when to follow a specific link or read a specific node of text). The cognitive research that Charney discusses, however, raises a perplexing issue: Can readers navigate effectively? Charney's warnings, in addition, reassert the "disruptive" nature of hypertext—if hypertext writing-reading seems valuable (as it does in some of the instances discussed in the chapters in this collection by Smith and by Moulthrop and Kaplan), then hypertext also forefronts puzzling questions about the goals of reading and writing in various areas, of which literature is only one.

Decentering the Subject of Discourse

If the idea that the reader is also the writer is difficult to translate into pedagogy, the decentering of the subject demanded in deconstruction can be even harder for students and teachers to accept. Many teachers are still struggling—or refusing to struggle—with the implications of deconstruction for readers of printed texts (and finding that deconstruction is a tough theory to enact in pedagogical practice). C. Jan Swearingen offers the commonsense reminder that students (and instructors) can see deconstruction as terrifying: "To announce to students that there is no such thing as accurate reference because there is no reality unmediated by language is an arrogant pedagogical act"; such an assertion "cuts off question, discussion, thought itself" (220, 221). With electronic texts we may find, as Mark Poster argues, that the subject is dispersed and "no longer functions as a center in the way it did in pre-electronic writing" (100). Perhaps the visible deconstruction of hypertext writing is even more terrifying than the psychic deconstruction of print texts.

The dispersion of subject and text in hypertext, however, may also uncover deconstructive acts in ways that allow students to find voice and participate in discussion. One of the difficulties in deconstructing print is that the text is *there*: it can be held and pointed to. Applying deconstruction to print text often seems to students like an attempt to negate the text completely: the physical text is *there* but the deconstructed text is *nowhere*, "infinitely open to production, but by definition unable to exist" (Belsey 145). Derrida notes writing's "essential drift" and the consequent state of writing as "cut off from all absolute responsibility, from *consciousness* as the ultimate authority, orphaned and separated at birth" from the writer (181).[8] The contradiction here for readers and writers may be that such a position seems to invalidate, as Swearingen observed, any meaningful action on the part of writers or readers.

A hypertext, because it is electronic, is never completely physically "there," never able to be completely located in physical space because it is simultaneously located in phosphor images on the computer screen;

magnetic configurations of volatile silicon computer memory; more permanent floppy, hard, or optical disk storage; and sometimes electrical impulses in phone lines (Bolter 43; Poster 111). But even in deconstructed form, the hypertext can be seen on the computer screen; the deconstruction of a hypertext can occur visibly, at the surface. Hypertext "accepts as strengths those very qualities—the play of signs, intertextuality, the lack of closure—that deconstruction poses as the ultimate limitations of literature and language" (Bolter 166). In "Afternoon," for example, readers are always conscious that the specific text they are reading is constructed, through their interactions with it, as one instantiation of a seemingly infinite number of possible readings. By seeing the visible effects of deconstruction, students may be led to see deconstruction not as a hopelessly relativistic, paralyzing act (Paine 565–66) but as "a matter of general textual practice" (Moulthrop, "Hypertext and 'the Hyperreal' " 259). Hypertext, in this manner, overcomes the necessity of a deconstructive reading of a linear text existing only as "secondary interpretive layer" that remains "formally distinct from the original discourse" (Moulthrop, "Reading" 123; see also Kaplan 17–18).

But while many experts agree about the potential for overcoming the paralyzing effects of deconstruction, even Bolter and Moulthrop both note that hypertexts can also be bewildering, especially when readers are overwhelmed by confusing screens or text structures. For example, readers of "Afternoon" see only individual text segments, not a graphical representation of the full text and interconnections. A reader trying to envision the structure of "Afternoon," Bolter says, faces a problem "rather like that of a mathematician who attempts to envision a four-dimensional object by looking at several projections in three dimensions" (127). Unlike "Afternoon," which remains comprehensible for most readers through Joyce's careful management of the text, even those hypertexts that provide graphical maps (to aid the reader in visualizing the structure and interconnection of the text) can easily become confusing. For example, in Moulthrop and Kaplan's article in this volume, the diagram of "Karl's Forking Response" offers few clear cues to the general, abstract structure of the text (except to indicate that the text is a complex network).

Karl, the student discussed in Moulthrop and Kaplan, attempts to write his response to Moulthrop's (hypertextual) representation of Borges's text as a resistance to this medium. But his response unintentionally becomes, in Moulthrop and Kaplan's reading, an acceptance of the hypertextual format: Karl's attempts to signal the link between his text and Borges-Moulthrop's text result in a mutated form, a work expressing the symbiotic relation between the writings of Karl and of Borges-Moulthrop. As Charney points out, hypertexts may lack discourse cues that signal the relations among nodes of the text. And as Charney might predict, Karl's attempts at providing discourse cues are overturned, subsumed, against Karl's wishes, back into the voice of the main text. This situation is neither a clear success nor a failure, but a vivid example of the way in which both theorists and teachers must question the redistribution of control in the acts of hypertextual writing and reading.

The problem of "navigation" in a hypertext—readers need to be able to tell which nodes they have read and which node they might want to read next—is one of the most researched and discussed pitfalls in hypertext; nearly every analysis notes the potential difficulty. In hypertexts that make the reader feel "lost," the decentering and confusion— traits that hypertext seems to solve in terms of deconstruction—return with a vengeance. At least with print, readers despairing of their attempts at deconstruction can return to the original, linear text. Many hypertexts offer no such fallback position. In cases where navigation through a hypertext becomes a strain, reading hypertext may lead not to empowerment but to silence for readers and writers.

Aside from the navigation difficulty (which is not an insurmountable problem but a tendency), making deconstruction "visible" and manageable may also lead to loss of identity for writer-readers. Although hypertext threatens the privileged status of canonized works by unfixing them from their physical, unalterable status and placing them in the fluid medium of computer-based text—potentially the same plane and medium in which any writer can work (Nelson, "New Home" 174)— hypertext also unfixes students' writings. *Hamlet* translated into machine-readable form might be only one portion of an immense, multiple hypertext to which students add their own comments, responses, and attempts at script writing—but those student writings are also "only" a portion of that immense network. Hypertexts of this sort encourage readers and writers to make the type of citation and quotation that, in print texts, Derrida claims create "an infinity of new contexts in a manner that is absolutely illimitable. . . . There are only contexts without center or absolute anchoring" (185–86). Hypertexts may challenge the text's canonical status (a move that a number of theorists would applaud); Carolyn Handa warns, however, that the loss of any individual writer's authority can also be intimidating: "From . . . a female point of view . . . authors (no matter whether male or female) are being silenced, while the proponents of hypertext tell them they are being collaborated with by their readers" ("Politics 177; see also Moulthrop, "Writing"; Guyer and Petry). As Moulthrop and Kaplan add, "In the space of hypertextual writing, anything that arises will be merged."

The multiple, contradictory possibilities for deconstructive theory and hypertext obviously require more consideration. In one sense, hypertext brings to the surface the resistance to closure, the infinite deferral of a single, univocal "meaning" in the text, concepts that are sometimes difficult to teach with print texts. At the same time, hypertext's potential resistance and deferral can overwhelm the reader—and even the writer—in an unnavigable tangle of nodes and links (Johnson-Eilola, "Click"). But even if the navigation problem is successfully overcome (as it often is), student writers may discover that their sense of authority over the hypertext is also infinitely deferred, their voices insignificant.

The tendency for deconstructive readings to negate instructors' attempts at empowering student writers and readers is the subject of much debate (Paine; Steven Lynn 262–65; Tompkins). However, as Charles Paine writes, "Just as English studies may be especially guilty of bringing about the ideology of relativism-equals-despair, it also possesses potentially great power for overcoming this ideology" (568).

Teaching deconstruction, for example, can focus students' attention on "what appears to be marginal" and encourage creativity in students (Steven Lynn 263). The problem for some teachers and students is not so much that deconstruction is wrong but that its interpretive processes are too dizzying to cope with on a day-to-day basis (Paine 566). This power, though, does not make the theory useless. After all, deconstruction is meant not to overcome but to open up interpretation. In his overview of critical theory in *College English*, Steven Lynn perceptively recognizes that "deconstruction typically leaves us in uncertainty, but with a richer understanding of the categories we have put in motion" (264). The uncertainty of hypertext is a necessary component of a possibly richer understanding.

Giving Voice to the Silenced

Various theories of literacy attempt to give voice to those whom society has traditionally silenced or disempowered: critical literacy, reader-response criticism, and collaborative learning theory, to name but a few. Critical literacy, for example, encourages a dialogue between teachers and students resulting in "self-realization and self-direction, affecting not only [the students'] relations to school but also their relations to work, family, and community life" (Malinowitz 160–61). Critical literacy is a faculty readers and writers gain in order to "perceive critically *the way they exist* in the world *with which* and *in which* they find themselves . . . without dichotomizing this reflection from action" (Freire, *Pedagogy* 71; Seabury ed.). Literacy, in the critical sense and under a variety of labels, is used by composition and literature instructors in an explicit effort to enfranchise women (Meese; Flynn) and minorities (Dean; Royster; Bogumil and Molino), among others.

In the realm of fixed, linear print, empowerment pedagogies attempt, psychologically, to resist the canonized texts by exposing contradictions, power moves, and multiply constructed positions from which the text may be read (Schweickart 42; Ritchie). In print text, though, the resistance must still work against the visible fact that the writings of "authors" are printed and bound with great expense and care—obviously, someone thinks that the canonized texts are "better" than student writing.

But the text as a site of authority can also become a site of resistance. In hypertext, the disparity in the importance of "student" writing and "author" writing is not necessarily visible. The canon, according to Landow and Delany, "is largely a product of book technology and the economic forces that play upon it" (24). Moulthrop and Kaplan point out that, in hypertext, student texts are no longer so easily subordinated to the bound volumes of revered authors. And Bolter writes encouragingly that the "margins" of a hypertext are no longer necessarily marginalized, that an individual reader's deconstructive moves—attempts to look into the margins—can "serve as a safety valve to prevent the text from disintegrating under the force of a deconstructive reading" (163). Hypertexts do not need to distinguish between margin and center.

The "safety valve" of which Bolter speaks offers one possible solution to Handa's concern that hypertext may co-opt the voice of individuals. In hypertext, according to Terence Harpold, reading and writing subjects can partially cover, or "bandage," the fading of the subject. Harpold characterizes the navigation of a hypertext by individual readers as an instance of the psychoanalytical concept of suture, "a closing of the gap in language by the subject's assumption of the place of the gap." Writer-readers of a hypertext simultaneously "bind the body of the text" and "reveal its erasures and wounds" ("Threnody" 177, 176, 178).[9] Navigating a hypertext might enable students to gain the insight and power of deconstructive interpretation, while the suturing effects of moving in a visibly deconstructed text offer recuperative power to keep students from becoming overwhelmed by the loss of center.

Conceived of in this manner, writer-readers in hypertext may have to give up some of their individual authority, but only some. The constant deferral of meaning occurs not only in the mind of the reader but also visibly, on the computer screen. Although hypertext writer-readers still experience aphanisis, the "fading of the subject" so famous in postmodern and psychoanalytic theories of text (Belsey; Stephen Heath, "On Suture"), they "concretize in social form the significance of the structures of gap and erasure in narrative digression" (Harpold, "Threnody" 178). The same characteristics that can help student writers manage the deconstruction of other writers' texts may allow them to view the deconstruction of their own texts as less terrifying.

The move from writer *or* reader to the writer-reader of hypertext is a negotiation, a redistribution of traditional, hierarchical power arrangements. With the loss of the authoritative, untouchable author's identity comes a new sense of identity as a communicator in dialogue with other texts and other writers (student, teacher, or canonized author).[10]

The possibility of giving a new sense of importance to student writing and the removal of student writing from the margins of the text may also involve the displacement of the teacher from a position of exclusive authority. With print-text-based classes, such a move is sometimes difficult for teachers to make: the teacher is often physically different from students in dress and age; the teacher's voice and physical presence are almost always a reminder of authority in the classroom. At the very least, the always present labels *teacher* and *student* are potentially dominating terms. But in electronic text discussions—even when they are linear—the presence of the teacher diminishes greatly (Cooper and Selfe); in hypertext, dialogues between students, teachers, and canon texts and authors may be even more egalitarian, because, as Moulthrop and Kaplan (this volume) point out, "in this medium, there is no way to resist multiplicity."

Construction of Knowledge and Text in Communities

The decline, in print-based literacy education, of the image of the solitary, isolated author producing the authoritative text has also facilitated the idea of writing and reading as, at least in part, a process of the social construction of knowledge and text (Bruffee, "Some Practical Methods"; Trimbur; Knox-Quinn; Joseph Harris). Social construction, however, is a powerful theory that sometimes does not translate fully into the classroom (Reither and Vipond 855; LeFevre).

One difficulty in this translation relates to the ephemeral nature of speech. In traditional literature classes, the social construction of knowledge in group discussion vanishes if not written down. If discussions are recorded in audiotape, videotape, or writing, they still stand separate—and potentially psychologically inferior to—the printed and bound text of the professional author. In some writing classes, the influence of social construction extends only to early brainstorming and peer-revision group work—the finished artifact is still deemed the product of one person's careful work (LeFevre 49). The social aspects of the construction of knowledge are not always visible to the participants (Ede and Lunsford, *Singular Texts/Plural Authors*; Paradis, Dobrin, and Miller). And even in collaborative settings, individual writers negotiate who speaks and who is silent, opening the linear text to some of the same tendencies toward power imbalance that exist in some participants' lives outside of the classroom. As Greg Myers observes, the "guided consensus" of the classroom "has a power over individuals that a teacher cannot have alone" (159). The types of interaction and discussion that are traditionally asked of students come less easily to already underpowered groups (D. George 6; see also Trimbur 611).

What hypertext might offer in support of John Trimbur's goal of "using consensus as a critical instrument to open gaps in conversation" rather than attempt actually to achieve perfect consensus (614) is the capability of adding and maintaining multiple interpretations and comments between the source text and student writings. A single phrase in a source text could be linked to multiple—and varying—student interpretations; and those interpretations in turn may link to each other in a network of discussion.[11] Slatin theorizes that hypertext offers great potential for student collaborative work, "using hypertext as a means of structuring not only their *individual* access to multiple sources of information, but access by fellow students as well ("Hypertext and the Teaching of Writing" 128).

The linked writings and readings of students that may constitute a hypertext discussion illustrate in a visible way the normally unspoken or unprinted connections that always exist between readers, writers, and texts (Landow, *Hypertext*). A hypertext composed of the individual writings of the members of a group highlights the way in which the individual texts interact. Even collaborative efforts that result in a single-voiced, linear product can still be joined to the large body of individual texts that invariably precede the "final product" (Trigg, Suchman, and Halasz).

In a collaborative hypertext the preservation of multiple voices—especially when *collaborative writing* indicates the maintenance of individual (but internally and externally connected) voices—might be one way in which students can make their own voices part of the conversation (Landow, *Hypertext* 148). In addition, and perhaps more important, the internal and external links might overcome the problem that Elizabeth Ellsworth notes of linear writing or speech when students attempt to speak only in one voice, despite the multiple and sometimes contradictory influences that make up any person's views (312). The type of knowledge embodied in a group hypertext, according to John McDaid,

> exists not as a preconceived truth waiting impatiently to be discovered, but rather as a potential in a Heisenbergian way. Until we create it, link it, write it, recover it—"It" does not exist; the Truth is *our* truth. We create this knowledge contextually and share it electronically not by convincing someone that we are right, but by following their exploration of our links and exploring theirs in order to negotiate our shared and disparate spaces.
>
> (214–15)[12]

In McDaid's perspective, the multiplicity of voices can help individuals recover the responsibility for finding their own truths and for discovering the multiple influences on that "truth." The writings of any individual enter into the text unmarginalized but also open to debate, interpretation, and incorporation into the continually evolving views of all writers. In this way, students may find a voice; they may also be encouraged to find a way out of the difficult problems noted in earlier sections of this essay—particularly the temptation to see, because of decentering and deconstructive processes, their own writings as having a "voice" but only an insignificant one. In hypertext discussions, their voices might take on some authority in speaking—not an *overriding* authority but an egalitarian kind of "authority," a confidence based on an appreciation of intertextuality and social influences in the construction of knowledge and text.

Literacy: Potentials and Traps

I have offered here a broad but incomplete framework for interpreting the role of hypertext in composition and literature instruction. Although popular conceptions of hypertext (especially advertisements) seem to offer this medium as something revolutionary, it would be more fruitful to view the role of hypertext in composition, literature, and literacy theory and practice as simultaneously growing out of, evolving from, and continually articulated and mapped by a variety of modern positions on text: the changing roles of reader and writer, the decentering of the subject in discourse, the attempts to give voice to the silenced in our culture, and the construction of knowledge and text in society.

The concept of hypertext as a revision rather than a displacement of print-based conceptions of literacy is an important one to keep in mind. Hypertextually influenced education might well be disruptive, but therein lies its value: theorists, teachers, and students may take the potentially rupturing influence of hypertext as an opportunity for close consideration of unquestioned assumptions. The euphoria or the vertigo that one experiences in writing and reading hypertext should not be mutually exclusive conditions; challenging long-held assumptions should be both frightening and exhilarating—and, most of all, constructive. As Charles Paine observes, "anxiety is part and parcel of the learning process" (565). One cannot simply (and simplistically) say that hypertext and hypermedia replace linear writing in an evolutionary step toward some perfect communication technology, that the mere act of linking multiple interpretations and voices automatically results in better communication; such a view falls into the trap of technological determinism, in which any notion of human control over technology disappears. To a great extent, hypertext and linear text overlap, but the functions of both are determined neither solely by technology nor solely by society.

The overlap between hypertext and print forms of literacy is evident in this section of the volume. Each essay draws heavily on current print theories of reading, writing, and literacy. This appropriation is a necessary one: although I stated earlier that hypertext is not a completely new concept in theory or practice, hypertext clearly does not have the centuries of research and practice that help us understand print-text theories. Furthermore, elaborating on existing views highlights one of hypertext's important functions—as a medium that forces theorists and teachers to reconsider and revise, not merely to perpetuate or replace, current theories and practices.

Such reconsideration and revision is especially evident in Moulthrop and Kaplan's contribution. In their essay, Moulthrop and Kaplan emphasize the way in which hypertext may enable students to overcome the limiting effects of their notions of literature, often as a "definitive authority." In their study the use of constructive hypertexts allowed some students to become "strong" readers—"responsive and responsible . . . free agents, makers of meaning who . . . [build] *against* (meaning both on and away from) an initial textual foundation." In addition,

Moulthrop and Kaplan observe that the technology of hypertext enforces its own set of limits, ruling out "priority and singularity," a characteristic that may make hypertext "fundamentally at odds with the aims and purposes of conventional literary education."

If Moulthrop and Kaplan admit that hypertext is at variance with the broad goals of literary education, Charney, in the next essay, indicates that hypertext may be contrary to even some general, concrete reading practices. The cognitive theories of writing discussed by Charney emphasize the idea that print-text reading and writing both rely heavily on the schema that people build for these processes over long periods of time—readers and writers base much of their activities on the extensive, often unspoken knowledge of how texts are traditionally structured. Texts violating these assumptions, as hypertexts frequently do, can cause difficulties in comprehension and recall for readers. Even in cognitive studies that show positive effects of hypertext use, Charney notes, the findings are mixed, with some readers benefiting and others suffering.

These two perspectives provide an interesting foundation for Catherine Smith's essay. Smith argues that the node-link conception of hypertext suggests to users a reductive model of thinking. Approaching hypertext use from the dual stances of the philosophy of mind and cognitive theories of reading, Smith provides both a critique of hypertext and a reanalysis of the purpose of hypertext, proposing that the process of *using* a hypertext should reflect dynamic, situated, and contextualized thought and action.

While these chapters stress the tentative nature of any claims that can be made for hypertext, they also affirm the potential value of the technology for encouraging theorists and teachers to review and revise their assumptions about technology. Hypertext has the potential for making visible the goals and processes of current theory; such visibility, in turn, can help theorists and teachers productively articulate concerns within and among writing, reading, and technology. The interpretations I've presented here, as well as those offered by the other contributors to this section, do not portray hypertext as an imminent front that's moving across all sectors of culture; rather, these analyses provide a means for extending theories and practices in which technology is not a component of writing or reading. The number of times I've used the words *can*, *may*, and *possible* to talk about hypertext and literacy illustrate the need for more discussion about the ways in which reading, writing, and technology influence each other. Richard Ohmann warns that the liberating potential of computers "is not a technological question, but a political one" (685). The politics of the issue are often obscured by our culture: Joseph Amato, in a review of Bolter's *Writing Space*, warns that political, economic, and cultural factors may make hypertext a "theme park with no admission" (116)—a place where even those who can afford the computer technologies necessary to write and read hypertext may lose awareness of broader ideological issues, only some of which I've touched on here. In another review of *Writing Space*, Myron Tuman argues that hypertext may in fact encourage isolation and fragmentation in primarily conservative ways (262–63). In using computer technologies such as hypertext, theorists and educators must remain alert to the pitfall that C. H. Knoblauch warns of in his essay on literacy and politics: definitions of literacy "only tell what some person or group—motivated by political commitments—wants or needs literacy to be" (80). We cannot disable or remove the trap when we define and teach literacy—we must acknowledge and integrate it into our definitions as a way of promoting continual self-criticism.[13]

NOTES

[1] The significant difference between *hypertext* and *hypermedia* involves the distinction between textual and nontextual elements: hypermedia incorporates some mixture of text, graphics, sound, or full-motion video. Discussion in this essay, for reasons of space, is limited to those applications that emphasize text (although these programs often incorporate other media in important ways); a full discussion of hypermedia would necessarily include such diverse areas as graphic design, music theory, video production, and more. See, for example, Shirk's "Hypertext and Composition Studies" for a discussion of metaphor theory and hypertext.

[2] See, for example, research reported by Lesk on a hypertext-based, bibliographic-retrieval system containing 800,000 citation nodes. Although the navigation problem is obviously important, I cannot cover here the broad range of cognitive psychology, human factors, ergonomics, and technical communication research necessary to offer a sufficient body of advice for hypertext authors. For an overview of current research in the design of hypertext, see Begoray; Horn; Horton; McAleese. For critiques of current hypertext, see Halasz; Johnson-Eilola, "Structure"; Charney (ch. 10 in this volume); and Smith (ch. 11).

[3] Bolter has commented on the seeming intelligence of such texts by characterizing artificial intelligence programs as complex, dynamic, interactive texts. As Bolter writes, "Almost by accident, artificial intelligence researchers have come upon the central problem of writing: the problem of defining the relationship among author, reader, and text" (190).

[4] For a more complete overview of the history of hypertext, see C. F. Smith; Conklin, "Hypertext"; Begoray. For bibliographies, see Nielsen 208–47; Mitterer, Oland, and Schankula; Berk and Devlin.

[5] Interestingly, despite the influence of theorists such as Ong, mainstream composition theory does not often distinguish between the various technologies of writing and reading. Technologies are deemed roughly equivalent in their effects on the writing and reading processes, and, therefore, the differences between, say, the pen and the computer are not often considered outside the subdiscipline of computers and composition research (Hawisher and Selfe, Letter; Sullivan). For a brief analysis of the semiautonomous interaction between technology and society in literacy, see Tuman ("Words").

[6] See Costanzo (249–50) for an elaboration of the range of reactions to the indeterminacy of media such as hypertext—especially the difference between print-educated adults and cyberspace-savvy teens.

[7] See also Dee-Lucas and Larkin's investigation of the differences between novice and expert readers of physics texts.

[8] But compare Eco's recent distinction between Charles Sanders Peirce's infinite interpretation and Derrida's "drift" (*Limits* 23–43).

[9] Ulmer, however, applies a more cinematic conception of suture to hypertext use: suture, he says, is an "effect binding the spectator to the illusion of a complete reality," a sometimes oppressive act ("Grammatology").

[10] This capability is not a given but a possibility. As Joyce notes in "Mind and History," many current hypertext systems foster the view of the original text as primary and additions to the text as secondary. Translating, for example, the print-text margin comments into small, single-node, "pop-up" windows that exist parasitically on the original author's text still encourages marginalization of student writing.

[11] See Trigg, Suchman, and Halasz; Conklin, *Theory*; Conklin and Begeman; and Greenberg for discussions of the use of hypertext in this manner in corporate and systems design environments.

[12] Like Phelps (131–57), McDaid draws here on modern quantum physics theory, especially the interaction between experiment and observer. The physicist Werner Heisenberg maintained that the measurement of subatomic phenomena cannot ever be completely accurate in a Newtonian sense, that each different individual measurement, in fact, changes the phenomenon itself. What most people would call a "phenomenon" exists only in the act of the experimenter's observation (Zukav 111–14). In hypertext, McDaid asserts, an individual reader comes to realize one personal truth among a number of possible truths. Although hypertexts are well above the subatomic threshold, the philosophical ramifications of quantum mechanics offer an interesting parallel.

[13] The author would like to thank the following people for their valuable comments and engaging discussion on various drafts and portions of this essay: Cindy Selfe, Susan Hilligoss, Marilyn Cooper, Stuart Selber, Jennifer Slack, Michael Joyce, Joe Amato, and two anonymous reviewers at the MLA. The author's work was supported by a fellowship from the Humanities Department of Michigan Technological University and the Ford Motor Company.

Chapter 9

They Became What They Beheld:
The Futility of Resistance
in the Space of Electronic Writing

Stuart Moulthrop and Nancy Kaplan

These last years of the century seem full of flux and controversy, particularly at that interface of culture and technology we call writing. Issues
of interpretation, authority, literacy, and textuality gain salience in a
society driven by transactions in information. The idea of information
itself seems to be shifting, becoming less a matter of content than of
association, less monologic truth than polyvalent discourse. In this
"age of the smart machine," work increasingly focuses both on actual
texts (electronic documents and databases) and on the virtual, social
texts that arise as we organize our work worlds around these acts of
writing (S. B. Heath, "Fourth Vision" 300–01; Zuboff 179). Our tools
for text production change, too, taking us from mixed print and digital
technologies (word processing, desktop publishing), to the paperless
mode that Diane Balestri calls "writing to the screen" ("Softcopy" 17),
and, most recently, to hypertext, or "non-sequential writing" (Nelson,
Computer Lib 29), a kind of discourse that cannot be presented in
definitive, typographic form (see Johnson-Eilola, in the overview to this
section, and also Landow, "Rhetoric"; Slatin, "Reading"; C. F. Smith).

The technology of text construction is, in some respects, nothing
new. It simply extends an approach to reading and writing that has
had broad currency since the 1960s: reader-response theory. What
Wolfgang Iser asserts of conventional writing is fundamentally true of
hypertext—the textual object is "virtual in character, as it cannot be
reduced to the reality of the text [the physical artifact] or to the subjectivity of the reader, and it is from this virtuality that it achieves its

dynamism" (21). Hypertext represents an evolutionary outgrowth of late-modern textuality.

But conventional texts have certain limitations. Print's truest products, as Alvin Kernan recently insisted, are "ordered, controlled, teleological, referential, and autonomously meaningful" (*Death of Literature* 141). When literacy serves the interests of individual authority, monologic discourse, and linear argument, these qualities may be essential; but they have less value as we come to define literacy in terms of communities—positing dynamic, collaborative, and associative forms of writing.

Hypertext differs in important ways from earlier forms of writing. For all its "dynamism," the encounter between text and reader in Iser's theory remains internal and passive: we decode characters and syntax; we match "repertoires" with the text; we construct predications and "passive syntheses" (135). These are all purely mental events. Hypertext includes the same range of internalized responses but adds the mechanism of links, which constitute external or "technologized" conventions. The reader must actively choose among options for proceeding by typing commands, touching a "hot" point on the screen, or finding "words that yield" (Douglas, "Wandering" 95). On one level at least, the transactions of reader with hypertext are physical events.

Of course, some hypertextual constructions, like those Michael Joyce has called "exploratory" ("Siren Shapes" 12), retain much of the passivity of print texts. This category includes most instrumental applications, like technical documentation, training manuals, and kiosk guides, as well as some early academic implementations (see Shneiderman, "User Interface"; Landow, "Rhetoric"). But Joyce also posits a second type, "constructive" hypertext, whose features require "a capability to act: to create, to change, and to recover particular encounters within the developing body of knowledge. These encounters . . . are versions of what they are becoming, a structure for what does not yet exist" (11). Constructive hypertext presumes not just a "virtual" work imaginatively constructed in the "convergence" of reader and text but a formally "open work" (see Eco) that blurs distinctions between reception and production. This more radical form of hypertext holds the greatest potential to transform our reading and writing practices.

What value do these changes have for students and teachers of texts? What might we and our students do with constructive hypertext in the classroom? One obvious application lies in rhetoric and composition studies, where a dynamic, evolving, open-ended text helps students improve their planning and invention (Balestri, "Softcopy" 45; Joyce,

"Siren Shapes" 38). But this sort of pedagogy is not where hypertext is likely to have its most radical or transforming effects.

If we assume that electronic writing belongs exclusively in the composition class, or in the composing process of academic writing generally, we assume a model of writing dominated by definitive, artifactual production. According to this model, the value of texts increases as they become formally fixed and stable. Least valuable are students' essays in process, unvalidated fabrics of experimentation and error. The completed, printed paper has better status, especially if it receives a good mark (the finishing touch, the final letter). But the most highly valued form of writing—in an entirely different category, really—is the text-in-this-class, a work of "literature" or literary criticism. Both a cultural and an economic artifact, it bears the imprimatur of a recognized publishing house and an ever more daunting pricetag. Academic readers get what they pay for: the published work has definitive authority, existing in thousands of copies, identical and apparently univocal. It purveys (and endlessly reiterates) the "last word" on its subject. Thus a kind of capitalist idealism inheres in scholarly texts, a hierarchy of forms running from the momentary, dynamic, and worthless to the timeless, unchanging, and costly.

This hierarchy owes its existence in large part to the cultural impact of the printing press. Our veneration of the author and the definitive text supports a literary value system designed to restrain a technological monster. Unchecked by publishers and critics, the democratic press would presumably churn out an insupportable surplus of print (see Barthes, "From Work"; Foucault, *Archaeology*; Kernan, *Samuel Johnson*). As the conservatives have it, authorship and the text as *eidos*— as absolute and universal form—stand as bulwarks against a cultural deluge. This defense becomes all the more crucial (and futile) as technologies of mass communication and desktop publishing alter the economics of print production.

Constructive hypertext thoroughly negates this ideology and its strategy of containment, insisting instead on plurality and participation—a change that might give us pause. If we English teachers embrace this form of text production, do we abandon what we have taken to be central literary values? If new writing systems threaten the orderly and autonomously meaningful text, maybe we are better off shutting them down in the "silicon basement" (see Fund). But before we reach such damning conclusions, we need to give our textual idealism a closer look. What unvoiced assumptions does it contain, and are they tenable?

Writing as Reading

As a book-learned society, we presumably value the ability to read critically and interpretively—so much so that we regularly agonize over the decline of "literacy" (cultural, multicultural, or simply functional). Our attitudes toward writing are more ambiguous, however. Walter Benjamin observed that, by 1930, any literate European could become an "author," at least to the extent of publishing a letter in the local newspaper (232). But writing never became a truly popular activity, even as the age of mechanical reproduction gave way to the era of desktop publishing. As Anne Ruggles Gere points out, true "authorship" extends only to those with substantial professional or proprietary stake in their work (*Writing Groups* 62). When we refer to "writing" in any context other than pure instrumentality (e.g., business writing or student writing), we invoke a complex system of gates and gatekeepers—the worlds of publishing and academia as we know them (I. L. Horowitz 90).

The gatekeepers behave according to a simple probability judgment: the chances are that any new writing is not worth disseminating. Because productive resources—raw materials, manufacturing time, distribution channels—are scarce and costly (at least if one considers conventional printing), only the most popular or the most highly regarded writing can command them. The default response of publisher and professor must be "not up to our standards" or "this is fine as far as it goes, but. . . ." And, indeed, this principle of conservatism operates retrospectively as well as prospectively. The established canon has its integrity and its prior economic claims, against which any contemporary writing must compete. Unless carefully controlled, expansion means corruption or dilution, so literary gatekeepers attempt to hold authorized production of new texts to a minimum. Thus we might consider *writing* not as a schizoid duality of momentary product versus canonical *eidos* but, rather, in its true economic continuity, as an implicit attempt at competition. Seen in this light, writing is a suspect act, that "perilous" discursive proliferation of which Michel Foucault speaks as threatening to spread out of control (*Archaeology* 216).

Though such assumptions may seem perverse, they are in fact well grounded in economic and social reality. Restrictions on the creation of "authorized" writing produce an economy of scarcity. If only a few texts survive to be disseminated, it is much easier to concentrate and control literary value, and, of course, this economy benefits those who live by study as well as those who live by sales. Among the agents of conservation are academic critics and theorists, who strive to maintain what Paulo Freire called a "banking concept" of education, in which knowledge and cultural value figure as commodities offered in exchange for tuition dollars (*Pedagogy* 59; Continuum ed.). Under this scheme, students become empty receptacles waiting to be filled with intellectual "content," and learning becomes knowledge consumption. As that eminent scholar-banker Allan Bloom has it, education at its best "is merely putting the feast on the table" (51). The rarer the delicacies, the better.

This model of education as commerce and consumption meshes nicely with the idealist hierarchy of text production. The best writings must be definitive and immutable because they will be received as *doxa*, or unquestioned belief, not as *episteme*, or experiential knowledge. Education as banking concentrates on product to the exclusion of process or discursive practice, serving the essentially conservative cultural ends of the system. "The more students work at storing the deposits entrusted to them," Freire writes, "the less they develop the critical consciousness which would result from their intervention in the world as transformers of that world" (*Pedagogy* 60). Lest our students think to change (even) the textual world, we set them to consuming more courses in the canon—even as we endlessly debate its makeup.

According to Freire, Western education suffers from "narration sickness," an obsession with a pedagogic plot directed toward acquisition and accretion (57). But other, more promising and less pathological educational narratives are conceivable. In an imaginative departure from the banking model, Gregory Ulmer introduces surrealism not by referring his students to canonical examples in a surrealist anthology but by constituting his class as a "textshop" charged with creating ready-mades and "automatic" novels. Students are told not to *buy* the text but to produce it—or perhaps to *be* the text themselves. The aim of this radical pedagogy is to "de-program freshmen platonists," dismantling the myth of the textual *eidos*:

> In the textshop, the student has an opportunity to discover the epistemological assumptions at work in culture and in one's own thinking. Textshop is "epic" in that it shares with Brecht's epic theater the desire to show people that culture (or society) is not natural, given, but is made, invented, and hence changeable.

Ulmer's strategy brings into play each student's "mystory," or idiomatic psychic and writerly development, which sets him or her to work in the textual world ("Textshop" 759–60).

Regrettably, the textshop approach does not encourage anyone to change that world. Ulmer seems interested mainly in helping students discover predefined truths, enlisting *episteme* in the reproduction of *doxa*. There is a certain naive historicism in his assumption that any two iterations of the formula will produce identical results: add one part Mallarmé to two parts Breton and, presto, we have *surréalisme*, same as it ever was. But Ulmer's radical pedagogy, despite its limits, demonstrates an important principle: "writing" in a course on literature or aesthetics need not be restricted to the desultory term paper or examination essay. Ulmer treats students' production of texts not as a vice to be regretted (or corrected) but as a source of essential dynamism in the pedagogic process.

Reading as Writing

How might this notion of productive or "constructive" participation be used to engage students in a more open-ended, less constrained encounter with literature? Could constructive hypertext allow a further development of Ulmer's "epic" pedagogy, a way of engaging students in a more extensive transformation of their textual world? How would students define and enact their responses to literary texts when those texts were presented as read-write systems—versions of what they were becoming, structures for what did not yet exist? These were among the instigating questions we brought to a pedagogical experiment with hypertextual narrative in Nancy Kaplan's section of Reading Texts, a one-semester course at Carnegie Mellon University for first-year students, intended both to introduce them to literature and to fulfill a composition requirement.

Our interest in using constructive hypertext was motivated in part by the course's approach, embodied in its primary textbook, Kathleen McCormick, Gary Waller, and Linda Flower's *Reading Texts: Reading, Responding, Writing*. Drawing on response theory (e.g., Bleich, Fish, Iser) and an interpretive model based on cultural criticism (e.g., Eagleton, Jameson, Williams), this book explicitly debunks the "old model" of reading, the naive belief that meaning is "in" the text, waiting for the reader to extract and appropriate it. *Reading Texts* suggests instead that literary encounters require "making sense," a thoughtful engagement with the "repertoire" of codes and references in the text. This encounter consists not of absorption but of interaction, since the reader receives a literary work through the screen of his or her own repertoire of assumptions, beliefs, predispositions, and influential prior texts. Because the nature of this interaction can never be predicted, reading is essentially "polyvalent," a play of differing ideas (3–14).

Though *Reading Texts* (*qua* book) retains the "idealist" model of the text as perfected product, it is reluctant to assign absolute meaning or authority to any artifact—even, presumably, itself. This text argues that a book, play, or poem may be the material outcome of a discursive process but that this process is neither definitive nor foreclosing; literature always instigates later interpretive discourses. Texts are *fabricated* once (in the formal sense only) but are *made* (sense of) again and again as the reader interacts with them to produce what Iser calls "the work."

The introduction of polyvalence to the interpretive scheme provides an opening for resistant readings through critical independence, showing a way past the idealist regression that limits Ulmer's textshop experiment. *Reading Texts* exhorts students to recognize the interpretive framework or ideology inherent in a literary work—in order to resist it, to reject, evade, or revise that ideology. Readers are to develop "strong" readings that emphasize divergence in the interpretive act:

> A strong reading of a text is a clearly articulated reading that self-consciously goes "against the grain" of a text. A strong reading is *not* a misreading. Nor is it perverse or imperceptive. It can only develop if a reader is aware of the dominant text strategies and chooses . . . to read the text differently. . . . A text may want you to respond in a certain manner, but you may *choose* to use your cultural awareness to resist that prescribed way of reading. You become thereby a strong, independent reader.   (28)

Strong readers are responsive and responsible, careful to take into account the agenda of the text before them. But they are also free agents, makers of meaning who resist the text's seductions by building *against* (meaning both on and away from) an initial textual foundation.

Yet however strong, the kind of literary response defined by *Reading Texts* has distinct limits. Though genuinely centered on the reader, this mode of interpretation vectors that reader toward a strictly limited goal—the production of a traditional academic paper. The concentration on process that informs the book's discussion of reading evaporates when the subject of writing comes up, revealing a dominant concern for a particular product. Taking on decidedly instrumental and executive contours, the text invokes "task representation" and cost-benefit analysis: "Let's examine some of the benefits and costs . . . of using the summary plan" (62). The approach to writing here seems less oppositional or critical than pragmatic. Apparently not sharing Ulmer's concern about cultural *doxa*, the authors propose no radical departures from the reading response, the research paper, and other standard assignments. They do not foresee that strong readings may sometimes issue in revisionary poems or fictions, as both Harold Bloom (13) and Ihab Hassan (170) have argued. Nor do they ever suggest that student writing can be placed on the same formal level as "literary" writing or in any way be linked to it except through the standard conventions of quotation and reference.

None of this should surprise us, since *Reading Texts* is, after all, a text*book*, a commercial Gutenberg artifact consisting of a finite discourse fixed in formal borders, a "closed book" that creates a bias toward hegemony and monologue. A textbook may, as *Reading Texts* does, share its discursive space with quoted selections of student prose; but such openings are anomalous and overdetermined, specimen texts offered for examination. (The expropriation of other texts is an inescapable consequence of print. In this essay, which we have written for a book, we too have our mounted specimens.) The textbook maintains its discursive precedence in the history of any writing: first comes the text-in-this-class, then any student's production on, about, or from it. When a textbook embraces a student text, it assimilates that text into its priority. No book can truly open itself to subsequent discourses, which remain dynamic, provisional, and in every sense of the word *imperfect*.

Hypertext challenges this hierarchical, book-centered model of writing and literary response. Being electronic (i.e., defined on the scale of molecules and particles), hypertext knows no real limits on the scope of its discourse. In practical terms, "writing space" may be considered infinitely expansible and thus *promiscuous* (in the root sense of "seeking relations"). Because there is always room for a new link and a new word, no hypertextual discourse is ever formally closed. While one version of the hypertext must always precede another, its precedence is not equal to the formal priority reinforced by printing.

Earlier classroom observations have revealed that hypertextual writings stimulate students to produce their own texts and to accord these texts something better than perfunctory or secondary value (see Joyce, "Siren Shapes"; Moulthrop and Kaplan). Accordingly, we looked to constructive, read-write hypertext as a way of combining the interpretive resistance suggested by *Reading Texts* with the radical writing practice of Ulmer's textshop. We hoped to present a form of literature (or "paraliterature" or "paracriticism") open not only to interpretation but also to expansion and revision. Introducing hypertextual fiction in this way amounted to a strong reading of *Reading Texts* (the course as well as the course text), an attempt to diverge from the standard introduction to literature, to dismantle interpretation as secondary discourse and the textbook as *eidos*. We hoped to engage our students in resistant readings of print-based education.

But a nontraditional approach to literature was not all we expected to instigate. Knowing the nature of resistance, we anticipated that our students might turn against our technocritical agenda as well, pursuing strong readings of our social "text" by offering their own counterresistance. We did not know what interpretive form this reaction might take, nor did we know whether hypertext would help or hinder students in expressing it. But our expectation of resistance in some form was well founded: in at least one instance a student undertook a double reversal—to subvert the very subversiveness of hypertext. In reflecting on this attempt, we have come to realize that our understanding of "resistance" in electronic texts was naive.

Paths of Lost Resistance

For two-thirds of the semester, Kaplan's section proceeded as a conventional introduction to literature: students read canonical poems, stories, and plays and wrote response statements and formal papers. The turning point came when the class encountered Jorge Luis Borges's fiction "The Garden of Forking Paths." The story provides an effective transition between conventional and hypertext writing, since it thematizes the tension between the multiplicity of fictional possibility and the definitiveness of linear narrative.

"The Garden of Forking Paths" is a metaphysical spy story about Yu Tsun, a Chinese agent working undercover in England during World War I. Yu must communicate the location of a British artillery park to his German masters before a British counterspy arrests him. With only a revolver and a single cartridge at his disposal, he forms a desperate plan to murder some person whose last name is also the name of the strategic town of Albert. From newspaper accounts of the murder, Yu's masters will decode the message.

But on arrival at the home of Stephen Albert, his arbitrary victim, Yu discovers that Albert, an eminent Sinologist, holds the key to a mystery from Yu's past. A renowned ancestor, Ts'ui Pên, had undertaken two great but apparently futile projects: an intricate novel and a "strictly infinite" labyrinth. But no trace of the labyrinth was ever found, and the novel exists only as "an indeterminate heap of contradictory drafts" in which the hero dies in one chapter but shows up alive in the next (24–25). Albert has recently solved the riddle of the missing masterpieces: the maze is not lost and the book is complete. Book and labyrinth are one—Ts'ui Pên's *The Garden of Forking Paths* is a narrative labyrinth. Albert explains:

> In all fictional works, each time a man is confronted with several alternatives, he chooses one and eliminates the others; in the fiction of Ts'ui Pên, he chooses—simultaneously—all of them. *He creates*, in this way, diverse futures, diverse times which themselves also proliferate and fork. . . . Sometimes, the paths of this labyrinth converge: for example, you arrive at this house, but in one of the possible pasts you are my enemy, in another, my friend.
>
> (26)

The story's metaphysical tragedy (or surrealist satire) lies in the fact that Ts'ui Pên's theory of time does not hold for Yu Tsun and Stephen Albert, who dwell in *Borges's* "Garden," not Ts'ui Pên's. They have only one past and one future, and in it Yu Tsun must coldbloodedly murder the man who has just restored his cultural patrimony. As he aims his revolver, Yu experiences a momentary "swarming sensation," a blurring copresence of alternate realities. But this hallucination fades and he pulls the trigger, locking in a single, foregone conclusion (the bullet for Albert, the noose for himself).

This outcome can be read as a "deconstruction" of determinism in the detective story (Brooks 319); but this reading assumes that stories, obedient to the limits of print, must always enforce a singular choice of futures. With hypertext the range of options broadens, allowing narratives that at least approximate Yu's vision of infinite pathways (Bolter 137). In fact, if one transfers the text of Borges's story to a hypertext system, it is possible to perform this transformation on "The Garden of Forking Paths" itself. As an exercise in practical paracriticism, Stuart Moulthrop produced a hypertext pastiche of Borges's story, an electronic fiction called "Forking Paths" (see "Reading").

The pastiche contains most but not all of Borges's text, as well as a number of digressions and extensions. For instance, in the original text Yu Tsun is directed to turn always to the left on his way to Stephen Albert's; the pastiche includes the possibility of a turn to the right, an option that leads to an encounter not with Stephen Albert but with a mysterious woman who has her own plot to hatch. Where Borges's story is told mainly in the voice of Yu Tsun, the electronic "Forking Paths" contains a number of voices, some fairly close mimics of Borges's, others transparently metafictional. The hypertext also comprises various endings, realizing alternative resolutions of the Yu-Albert story (e.g., one in which Yu abandons his spy mission and lives out his life as Albert's companion). At least one of these endpoints denies termination:

> The Garden is a place of possibility; it is consecrated to alternatives, choice, and change. It cannot close, but instead OPENS to admit you in the role of co-creator. Come inside. Look . . . learn . . . build for yourself.   (node 84/T)[1]

Our presentation of hypertext fiction in Reading Texts took off from this invitation. Along with "Forking Paths," students encountered "Afternoon: A Story," a multiple fiction by Michael Joyce (see Douglas, "Wandering; see also the overview to this section of the volume) and "Uncle Buddy's Phantom Funhouse," by John McDaid (see Moulthrop, "Toward a Paradigm"). In all these cases, students were faced with narratives that defy closure and encourage highly participatory interactions.

All three hypertexts were also potentially *constructive*, open to revisionary writing as well as exploratory reading. As part of our resistance to the conventional hierarchy of writing, we invited students to realize this possibility—though it was up to the students to decide whether or how to respond. In outline, the hypertext writing assignments resembled those given for conventional texts. Kaplan asked students to move from a subjective, reader-based "response statement" to a more fully articulated piece intended for a broader audience. If they wished, students could write both assignments as conventional essays, treating the hypertexts as occasions for traditional literary analysis. A few writers took this option. Students were also invited to consider working in a hypertext system, either *Storyspace* or *Hypercard*. Doing so posed relatively few problems, since everyone in the course had achieved basic competence with personal computers by taking Carnegie Mellon's required Computer Skills Workshop. Kaplan also offered a brief introduction to authoring in the two hypertext systems and made available online help materials and documentation.

A large majority of the class produced responses to the hypertext fictions as hypertexts. Some created polysequential essays or narratives independent of the prior texts. One student, exploring the relations between compositional and narrative sequence, rearranged the components of Joyce's "Afternoon" in the order they were composed. Others accepted the invitation of the non-ending in "Forking Paths" and built their own extensions of its fictional universe. All these projects represented significant and critical engagements with hypertext fiction. But the most interesting response, from the perspective of our concern about strong readings and resistant writings, was a text that Karl Crary embedded in his copy of "Forking Paths." Crary's writing showed us something about interpretive resistance in hypertext we had not previously considered—quite simply, that it cannot ultimately succeed.

Crary's text comprises seventeen nodes and twenty-seven links created in his copy of the *Storyspace* document (or, in that program's parlance, "space") called "Forking Paths" (see fig. 1). His decision about where his commentary would take place means that "Karl's Forking Response" consists of the nodes and links he wrote *plus* all the nodes and links of the prior text, Moulthrop's "Forking Paths." (In a print environment, the equivalent decision would produce a commentary or reading in which the whole story—the subject of the commentary—is reproduced.) Crary's decision to work within the original text raises interesting questions. How do we identify or affiliate this text? Crary named his work "Karl's Forking Response," but this title is at least as ambiguous as the prior title, "Forking Paths," which deliberately sows confusion between it and the original Borgesian text. Who *is* the author of this writing—Crary? Moulthrop? Borges? Ts'ui Pên? More to the point, why are we asking this question?

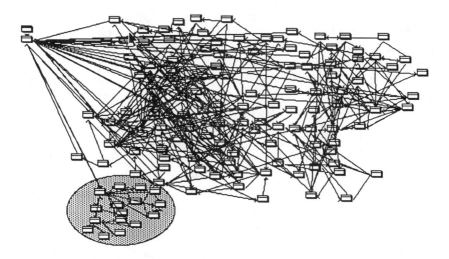

Fig. 1. *Storyspace* structure diagram of "Karl's Forking Response." Boxes are nodes; arrowed lines are links. Structure in shaded oval was added by Karl Crary to the prior text (shading added).

Crary could have avoided these issues by developing his text as a separate hypertext writing or space, in which case his discourse would stand in the same relation to its subject as most student essays or professional articles stand in relation to their subjects, as objects distinct from and outside the physical boundaries of the work they discuss. Instead, he chose to write inside the electronic space of the prior text in order to heighten the question of textual ownership. In a series of nodes, he discusses Moulthrop's appropriation of Borges at length, worrying that publication of the pastiche might violate any copyright held by Borges's heirs and assigns. But he is less certain about property rights in the electronic fiction itself:

> "Forking Paths" is the ultimate realization of the text that Borges wanted to write but wasn't able to. Borges couldn't have written "Forking Paths," and Moulthrop couldn't have written "Forking Paths" if it weren't for Borges. In that sense, "Forking Paths" is a joint work of Borges and Moulthrop.   (node k010)

By his own logic of extension and fulfillment, Crary could name himself in the series of authors. His amplified "Forking Paths" would have been impossible without the print and prior hypertext versions, but those two texts (particularly the second, with its invitation to reader-writerly participation) could not be fully "realized" without his work.

Yet though Crary formally integrates his writing into the structure of the "Forking Paths" pastiche, he does not call himself an author of that text, and this reluctance—or refusal—has great importance. Crary treats "Forking Paths" and its dubious textual genealogy as distinct from his own writing project. After all, even though he decides to write *in* the text, he has been assigned to write *about* the text, and Crary is quite clear about what such assignments involve: "A primary notion in the theory of the Reading Texts class is that of the author-reader interface created by the intersection of the author's and reader's repertoire" (node k008). Reader's text and author's text are different entities, aligned but also separated along an "interface" of repertoires. As a strong reader, Crary realizes that he must come to the text with his own agenda. He has to exercise some form of resistance.

Crary attempts to resist "Forking Paths" by objectifying it, establishing an aloofness from its gregarious metafictional game. Like a good strong reader (and he is a *very* good one), Crary senses what the text "wants" him to do and swerves from that interpretive track. He refuses to invent further variations on pastiched Borges themes. He will be sober and reflective, not fictively playful. His deviation heads him away from the narrative ground of story space, off to the apparently separate realm of commentary, an alternative theory space. "Come inside," the prior text says, "Look . . . learn . . . build for yourself." Though Crary is happy enough to look, learn, and build, he declines the first overture, preferring to hold himself and his writing apart from the earlier texts.

How Does Your Garden Grow?

Thus positioned—theoretically "outside" but formally "inside"—Crary launches into an anatomy of the pastiche, an attempt to classify all its parts according to a comprehensive taxonomy:

> The text in "Forking Paths" can be divided into four types:
>
> 1) original Borges text
> 2) text that sounds like Borges text, but is not
> 3) text that does not sound like Borges text, but is still related to Borges' story
> 4) complete digressions   (node k004)

This formalist theorizing represents Crary's strongest interpretive move against the prior text. The ideological repertoire of "Forking Paths" privileges intertextuality and narrative relativity. Enthusiastically promiscuous, "Forking Paths" interactively "shares" the work of narrative continuity, mixing up receiver and producer. Formally, its links connect its nodes in loops and spirals, defying identification of discrete narrative pathways (see fig. 1). Stylistically, the buccaneering strategy of pastiche plays havoc with what Foucault called the "author-function." To use *Reading Texts*'s language of textual desire, "Forking Paths" "wants" to provoke a general breakdown of distinctions.

Crary wants something else entirely. He wants to draw and enforce distinctions, to restore some rationality and "coherence" to his readerly experience. Insists Crary: "When I read a text, I expect to be able to follow what is going on in the story. One event should flow logically to the next" (node k006). His analytic addition to "Forking Paths" forms a bubble of critical order in the literary chaos of the pastiche. His categorizing imperative helps him swerve from lawlessness to general principles, from confusion to firm conclusions; it is the strong reader's finest hour.

Unfortunately, it is also his last stand. Although Crary attempts to insulate himself from the welter of the pastiche, a touch of self-refer-ence—a fatal flaw—punctures his analytical bubble. In a supremely Borgesian turn, it develops that Crary has encompassed his text in its own taxonomy: all of Crary's nodes fit within his catchall fourth category, "complete digressions" from the stories of Yu Tsun and com-pany. Because of this, his attempt at reader-writerly resistance cannot succeed.

How can this be? Why can't Crary be allowed his independence from the prior text? To echo Borges, "Why does it disturb us that the map be included in the map and the thousand and one nights in the book of the *Thousand and One Nights?*" Our disquiet comes from ontological self-interest: "These inversions suggest that if the characters of a fic-tional work can be readers or spectators, we, its readers or spectators, can be fictitious" ("Partial Magic" 196). Crary's taxonomy may not threaten its readers with fictivity, but it does cast serious doubt on the intratextual "reality" of Karl Crary.

Because Crary's discourse is formally linked to "Forking Paths," a reading of "Karl's Forking Response" is likely to carry the reader from the Borges-Moulthrop fiction into Crary's commentary without signal-ing any intertextual boundary. In this case, the reader might reasonably consider "Karl Crary" (quite contrary) not an external commentator but just another self-conscious *lector in fabula* (see Eco, *Open Work*). As Crary notes, "Forking Paths" already includes several such characters. Crary's fourth category makes as much sense of his own antithetical structure as it does of these previous discursive oddities. Contrary indeed to his textual resistance, Crary's commentary helps the Garden grow.

Becoming by Beholding

Perversely, Crary's failure stems from the very strength of his attempt. He could have written a traditional, printed essay, which would have established a formal boundary between his discourse and that of the fiction, an interface along whose boundaries the play of mutual resis-tance could take place. But this strategy would not have been as strong in its attempted resistance as Crary's decision to build his readerly (and boundary-less) interface inside the hypertext space itself, challenging the medium on its own terms. Crary tries to do strong reading the hard way. Judged on his own terms, he may not have succeeded, but the limits of his achievement are enlightening.

At least as far as constructive, or read-write, hypertext is concerned,

Crary's challenge never stood a chance. In this medium, there is no way to resist multiplicity by imposing a univocal and definitive discourse. Hypertext frustrates this resistance because, paradoxically, it *offers* no resistance to the intrusion. The medium omnivorously assimilates any structure raised within it. Writers can try to build distinctions and hierarchies, but the qualities of hypertext as a writing system ultimately subvert these constructs.

In the space of hypertextual writing, anything that arises will be merged, gathered into the network of polyvalent discourses. Ordering principles imposed on a hypertext remain strictly contingent, open to reinterpretation or circumvention by subsequent writer-readers. Interpreters who enter the labyrinth bent on voyeuristic "objectivity" will inevitably lose their way in the garden. They become what they behold, their efforts at discrimination and definition overrun by the general "swarming" of the text. Any attempt to subvert hypertext from within succumbs to *mimetic collapse*: it becomes the thing it describes.

But perhaps this outcome merely restates the obvious truth that the medium is always the message. Surely "mimetic collapse" is nothing new in literary interpretation. It occurs as a matter of course when we respond to print texts. We regard the print text as an authoritative object, and in our analysis or criticism we imitate that authority. Our interpretive essays are indeed "severe poems" (as Harold Bloom might call them) in the sense that they are distinctive *makings*, powerful and monologic assertions. The point holds even when we espouse intertextuality, polysemy, or difference, for we still expect our disquisitions to keep the reader spellbound through all our dialectical reverses until we have had the last word. What the "strength" in strong reading amounts to, after all, is the ability to compel others to attend to our discourse and admire our cleverness in outwitting the primary text.

We restate the obvious, then. To work in any medium is to express that medium's particular message, whether in conventional writing or hypertext (Kaplan, "Ideology"). But in concentrating on this universal sameness, we risk eliding a critical distinction. As the media differ, so do their messages: the formal, or "mimetic," constraints of hypertext exactly invert those of print. Where a resistant reading of print literature always produces another definitive discourse, the equivalent procedure in hypertext does just the opposite, generating not objective closure but a further range of openings that extend the discursive possibilities of the text for "constructive" transaction. The electronic text becomes a dynamic, expansive system, "a structure for what does not yet exist."

In print's system of textual production and reception, textual fabrication occurs only once for each written artifact. That artifact may subsequently give rise to many remakings (of sense), because each meaning-making act begins with the fixed and stable fabrication that precedes it and that survives the readings and writings perpetrated on and against it. In hypertext's system of textual production and reception, each meaning-making act is potentially, at least, a radical *refabrication*. Because textual fabrication recurs, the hypertextual writing that precedes and gives rise to interpretive reading-writing acts within it does not survive those acts intact.

Every system of textuality imposes conditions on creativity and interpretation. When the defining technology is print, these conditions favor singular and definitive discourse—the production of a literature devoted to property, hierarchy, and a banking model of culture. But in hypertext, very different conditions prevail. Hypertextual writing invalidates priority and singularity. It emphasizes cooperation and community rather than agonistic struggle. Resistance in hypertext is futile; the highest value resides not in contention but in *extension*, not in negation but in collaboration.

What do these theoretical gleanings mean on a more pragmatic level? What relevance do they have for teachers and students in actual classes? It would seem that our conclusions must be negative. If Crary's attempt at creative resistance does not succeed, then our attempt at a technologically radicalized pedagogy must also be counted a failure. In terms of *Reading Texts* and its principles, our experiment appears to offer little. Hypertext does not represent what the computer companies call a "software solution" for courses in reader-based interpretation. It is not merely a more accessible way to introduce or to practice interpretive resistance. Indeed, the more we experiment with hypertext in literature courses, the deeper our conviction grows that this new medium is fundamentally at odds with the aims and purposes of conventional literary education. This conclusion seems particularly true if Shirley Brice Heath is right: that those aims have come to constrain "the full meaning of *responsible*—being able to respond in something other than a prescripted formulaic and almost ritualistic manner" ("Fourth Vision" 303).

But here we, too, like Crary, may succeed by "failing." For if hypertext opens new possibilities for literary culture—even for literacy itself— then the idea of resistance may not have eluded us after all. Perhaps hypertext does not make resistance futile; perhaps it shifts this notion from the neutrality of academic theory onto the livelier and more dangerous ground of social practice. In reading and writing hypertexts, our resistance may come to focus not on prior texts or creative precursors but rather on the literary institutions we have inherited from the history of print—institutions that make reading into a test of strength, authorship into a hierarchic mystery, and texts into closed books. Hypertext may bring many of our basic assumptions about literature in for very hard scrutiny. The subject of our "resistance," in the end, may be print culture itself.

NOTE

[1] Among the other perplexities hypertextual writing brings us, citation conventions are surely one of the most vexing. For the hypertextual fictions "Forking Paths" and "Karl's Forking Response," we have chosen node names because, like page numbers, they can be used for searching and retrieving desired sections of text.

Chapter 10

The Effect of Hypertext on Processes of Reading and Writing

Davida Charney

Texts and Hypertexts

Most people conceive of *text* as a collection of ideas that a writer has carefully selected, framed, and organized into a coherent sequence or pattern in hopes of influencing a reader's knowledge, attitudes, or actions. A key element in this conception of text, from the perspective of both writers and readers, is structure. Linguists and discourse analysts have identified a host of structural patterns that writers work with (and, more frequently, against) at every level of text production, from small units such as sentences and paragraphs all the way to grand structures that describe entire texts, such as sonnets, fairy tales, résumés, or policy arguments (Halliday and Hasan; van Dijk; Fahnestock and Secor). Indeed, readers depend on such patterns to identify a text's genre, anticipate its development, and integrate its parts. Studies of reading comprehension confirm that readers understand and learn most easily from texts with well-defined structures that clearly signal shifts between parts (van Dijk and Kintsch; Kieras, "Initial Mention"; Frase). But apart from any natural disposition we may have to expect structure in text, our conception of text as an orderly succession of ideas is strongly reinforced by the constraints of the standard print medium: texts come to us on printed pages that we generally read in order, from the top down and from left to right.

Today, the constraints of the medium are being lifted by developments in computer technology. Visionaries of information technology foresee a time when most forms of written communication (from books and journals to reference manuals and mail) will be composed and disseminated electronically rather than on paper. And instead of taking the traditional form of linear blocks of prose, such online material will be presented in hypertexts that link together individual bits of text and even whole documents.[1] Thus far, the most common application of hypertext has been for computer manuals, encyclopedias, or guide books, providing readers with immediate access to definitions of key terms, cross-references, graphic illustrations, or commentary from previous readers (Marchionini and Shneiderman; Yankelovich, Meyrowitz, and van Dam). If scholarly journals become routinely published in hypertext, readers may be able to move instantly from a citation in one article to the cited work or to any of the author's earlier or subsequent publications.

The advent of hypertext is a new and exciting development that has important implications for researchers and teachers in English. As Jef Raskin and others have noted, there is as yet a good deal of "hype" in hypertext and its full impact will not be felt in most English departments for a number of years. But the fact remains that sophisticated hypertext systems are increasingly available—commercially as well as within specific academic and nonacademic communities. Hypertext has the potential to change fundamentally how we write, how we read, how we teach these skills, and even how we conceive of text itself.

Hypertext promises to facilitate the writing process in several ways (Pea and Kurland). A writer's invention processes (generating and selecting ideas) may profit from opportunities to freely explore source material presented in a hypertext and make novel associations. The related processes of idea manipulation and organization, such as experimenting with various idea clusters or outlines, may be aided with a system that allows writers to create electronically linked "notecards" that can be sorted and rearranged (Neuwirth et al., "Notes Program"; Neuwirth et al., *Comments;* Trigg and Irish; Smith, Weiss, and Ferguson). Collaborative writing may be fostered by systems that enable peers to annotate each other's drafts or that help writers integrate individually written sections into a coherent draft (Irish and Trigg; Catlin, Bush, and Yankelovich). Hypertext systems may also be designed to meet specific pedagogical goals—for example, guiding novice writers through heuristic activities that support the critical thinking and analysis necessary to writing a policy argument (Neuwirth and Kaufer, "Role").

Apart from serving as a tool for writing, hypertext promises benefits to writers of computer manuals or reference materials. These writers typically face the problem of presenting large amounts of complex information to readers with wide-ranging needs—such as experienced and novice computer users who may seek the same information but have quite different needs with respect to appropriate terminology, format, definitions, examples, and details. The task of these writers is further complicated by its subject matter, usually computer technology that changes even as writers scurry to describe it, so that printed material is outdated even as it is published—the "original sin" of computer documentation. The hypertext solution to these problems would replace printed manuals with an online network of information reflecting various levels of technicality (Robertson, McCracken, and Newell; Walker, "Authoring Tools" and "Document Examiner"). Readers with less technical expertise may choose to follow links to nodes with definitions, examples, explanations, reminders, or advice, which more sophisticated users may bypass completely. Or, instead of leaving the choices to the users themselves, hypertexts may be designed to guide readers on defined paths through the network at the appropriate level for their purpose or level of expertise (Zellweger; Younggren; Carlson, "Way"). A hypertext reference manual would ideally be suitable for all users, from novices to experts (and for novices whose skills develop over time), and for a variety of tasks. Such a system would presumably be easier to update than printed manuals and reduce the high costs of printing and reprinting.

Hypertext thus has a strong pragmatic appeal: to facilitate the efficient creation and dissemination of complex documents and sets of documents of all kinds and to allow people "to access information in the sequence, volume, and format that best suits their needs at the time" (Grice 22). The ultimate goal of these designers is to create a system so tailored to individual preferences and task situations that every user will feel as though entering an "information universe designed specifically for his [or her] needs" (Younggren 85).

In contrast to those who aim to micromanage the presentation of information in a network are the hypertext designers who are attracted to its Romantic side (Herrstrom and Massey). As Edward Barrett notes, "Developers of hypertext systems are inspired by a highly Romantic, Coleridgean concept of writing: an infinitely evolving text that tracks momentary cognitive processes within the individual reader-author" (*Text, Context, and Hypertext* xv). In this information age, hypertext Romantics aspire to a kind of unspoiled landscape of knowledge, dotted with visual and verbal outcroppings captured electronically. They view hypertext as a means to liberate readers (as well as writers) from the constraints of text boundaries, freeing them to wander through an array of connected texts, graphics, and commentary, to explore and create topical paths of associations at will. Such open-ended hypertexts are being used in literature and other humanities courses to give students access to rich networks of cultural and historical material relevant to the primary texts under discussion (Beeman et al.; Dryden, in his response to this section).

Whether pragmatic or Romantic, the potential benefits of hypertext sketched here follow from certain assumptions about how people read or should read. The belief that readers can select for themselves which links in a network to follow rests on the assumption that readers know best what information they need and in what order they should read it. The goal of creating paths for different readers assumes that hypertext designer-writers can predict readers' needs well enough to create the right set of paths and direct each reader onto the appropriate one. The very notion that hypertext designer-writers can create meaningful, useful networks in the first place depends on a whole range of assumptions about how to divide up and relate parts of texts, including which segments of text constitute meaningful nodes, which types of links are meaningful and important, and which types of texts can or ought to be read nonlinearly. In fact, many of these assumptions contradict current thinking in rhetorical theory, cognitive psychology, and document design. The evidence from these fields suggests that, as currently conceived, hypertext may dramatically increase the burdens on both readers and writers. My purpose in this essay is to review relevant educational and psychological research on reading that bears on the problems hypertexts may pose for readers and writers. My goal is not to accept or dismiss hypertext in principle but rather to point to specific aspects of reading and writing processes that hypertext designers must consider if they are to serve readers and writers effectively.

Obviously, readers approach hypertexts for a variety of reasons, from purposively seeking specific facts to browsing out of sheer curiosity (Slatin, "Reading"). I focus here on readers with more complex motives, those who read to learn, to understand and evaluate the ideas and arguments of others, to come to realizations about the subject matter, and to integrate what they have learned with what they already know. These goals will push hypertext to its logical extreme—the rich connection of the parts of a text to each other and to other texts. The hypertexts I have in mind are not so much online reference works or annotations of a single primary text (though the research reviewed here bears on those as well) as a fully interconnected electronic literature. While such hypertexts are, currently, the least well developed, they are also those most likely to influence what we in English studies do as teachers and as scholars.

Thinking, Learning, and the Organization of Memory

Many designers claim that hypertexts will facilitate reading and writing (and even thinking and learning in general) because, unlike linear texts, hypertexts closely resemble the networked, associational organization of information in human memory. This view probably originated with Vannevar Bush, who first conceived of hypertext, and has been carried forward in various forms to the present (Shneiderman, "Reflections"; Carlson, "Way"; Smith, Weiss, and Ferguson; Beeman et al.). While Bush's concept of human memory seems to have been quite advanced for his time, current hypertext proponents tend to misrepresent modern-day cognitive psychological perspectives on information processing.

The idea that hypertext is somehow more "natural" or more "intuitive" than linear text assumes a structural correspondence between networked information in a person's long-term memory and the presentation of information in hypertext network. This assumption contradicts some important, long-standing psychological findings about the organization of information in memory and the process by which new information is acquired.[2] First, although some researchers believe that information in memory is organized in completely amorphous associative networks, a great deal of knowledge seems to be arranged hierarchically and sequentially. Second, there is no evidence that readers can grasp information more easily or more fully when it is presented in a network rather than in hierarchical and linear form. The opposite may, in fact, be true. What people hear and see is not imported wholesale into long-term memory; it must first pass through a constraining "gateway." In particular, the processes of thinking and learning that draw on networks of previous knowledge are crucially constrained by the limitations of working memory (also referred to as *short-term memory* or *focal attention*).

Cognitive theorists posit working memory to account for human beings' inability to attend to more than a small number of things at any one time, regardless of whether these things are ideas recalled from prior knowledge or new information that has just been heard or seen or imagined. Further, what people attend to shifts over time; as they recall other ideas or observe new things, items that had been in focal attention "fade" or become "displaced" or "inactive." The shifting of attention imposes a kind of linearity or seriality on thought processes: since we cannot think about everything at once, we have to focus on a few things at a time in some order. A useful analogy for these ideas in long-term memory might be to imagine an auditorium full of students. A variety of plausible principles might lead them to sit in certain groupings or might cause initially accidental groupings to take on significance over time. But the students did not enter in those configurations—their access to the room from the congestion in the hallway is constrained by a narrow doorway that forces them to enter in some sequence. The most efficient way to create an *intentional* configuration—one that facilitates taking attendance, for example, or that optimizes visibility for the group as a whole—may be to organize the students in advance, while they are out in the hall (as the marshals do at commencement ceremonies). Similarly, the fact that part of human memory may be arranged in associative networks does not mean that the best formats in which to read or write are also associative networks (Neuwirth and Kaufer, "Role"). If the goal is to ensure that readers consider a specific set of associations, then a highly organized text format is more likely to achieve that aim than an amorphous network.

The implications for hypertext can be stated even more directly. Because readers cannot import textual (or hypertextual) structures directly into long-term memory, the putative resemblance of hypertexts to long-term memory is irrelevant. The fact that hypertexts and long-term memory may both have networked structures in no way entails that hypertexts are superior to linear texts for facilitating reading or promoting learning. In fact, the development of linear text forms, with their careful sequencing of ideas, may not reflect constraints of the print medium so much as the needs of readers and writers who depend on the text to help them effectively sequence the flow of ideas through focal attention.[3]

Cognitive Models of Reading

A major premise of most reading theories, consistently supported by empirical studies, is that, as people read, they build a hierarchically structured mental representation of the information in the text (Kintsch and van Dijk; van Dijk and Kintsch; Meyer; Just and Carpenter). As they read successive sentences, they link the ideas or propositions expressed in them to their developing hierarchical representation by means of chains of repeated concepts (or arguments). To the extent that the sentences—or larger units—of the text reuse, develop, elaborate on, and interrelate the same arguments, the text is more cohesive. The more cohesive the text, the easier it is for readers to create a well-structured, meaningful, and useful mental representation (Eylon and Reif). The quality of the representation, and the ease with which it is constructed, crucially depend on the order in which readers encounter the propositions and on the amount of repetition and development of important concepts (or "arguments") in successive portions of the text. It is more difficult to create a mental representation of a disjointed or disorganized text. If readers come to a sentence that seems to contain no previously encountered arguments—that is, has no obvious link to the surrounding sentences—they must either retrieve from memory earlier propositions that contain one or more of the arguments or infer some link between the sentence and some part of their representation of the text. Both retrieval and inferencing are relatively costly processes in terms of time and effort. Working from the assumption that only propositions currently "active" in working memory can be linked, researchers have successfully predicted which kinds of texts are easier to read, understand, and remember than others. Bruce Britton and Sami Gülgöz have recently gone even further, using Walter Kintsch and Teun van Dijk's model to identify sites for textual revisions that resulted in improved comprehension and recall.

As Catherine Smith notes, in chapter 11 of this volume, Kintsch's model has evolved over the years. In its original form (Kintsch and van Dijk), it was fairly rigid and deterministic—allowing little into the mental representation of a text beyond literal decompositions of the sentences and necessary bridging inferences. It did, however, successfully predict what parts of a text are best remembered. In later work (van Dijk and Kintsch), Kintsch fleshed out various parts of the model to account for other kinds of information that readers call on regularly (such as knowledge of genre and situational knowledge). His current position ("Role") extends the model still further, allowing for many more idiosyncratic (and even inappropriate) associations to end up in the mental representation of a text (but also requiring an additional "cleanup" process). This position in no way represents a recantation of his earlier views, as David Dobrin suggests in his response to this section. To the contrary, Kintsch explicitly retains most aspects of his model—and, in particular, the ones relevant here—frequently referring readers to his previous work for elaboration of them (see esp. 166, 167, 168, and 180). In essence, Kintsch's innovations enrich the mental representation or "text base" by allowing more associations to the reader's general knowledge. They do not change the effect of the text itself on the construction of the text base and therefore do not lessen the importance of beginning with a coherent, well-structured text. In Kintsch's "revised" model, as in his original model, the sequence of sentences and sections of a text and the explicitness of their connection to one another largely determine how well and how easily a reader can construct a text base.

Several text features have been identified that consistently make it easier for readers to construct a coherent representation of a text, to reflect on its relation to prior knowledge, and to integrate new ideas and new information with what they already know (Felker et al.; Kieras and Dechert). First, for readers to make appropriate connections between related ideas, the sentences expressing these ideas should appear in close proximity. Thus a text is easier to read if its points are developed in coherent sequences of sentences, paragraphs, and sections and if it contains discourse cues that signal the relations among these ideas (Halliday and Hasan; Fahnestock; Britton and Gülgöz). Second, since readers use high-level ideas to tie portions of the text together, these concepts should be explicitly stated early in the text and should be clearly signaled so that readers can easily recall them as the need arises (Kieras, "Initial Mention" and "Model"). Thus it is easier to read, comprehend, and remember a text if it contains an informative title, headings, overviews, and topic sentences introducing key concepts that are repeated and developed in successive portions of text (Schwarz and Flammer; Glynn and Di Vesta; Mayer, Cook, and Dyck; Wilhite). Reading is also easier when the text reminds readers of relevant points (normally through repetition or reference to the earlier discussion). Finally, while readers are capable of following innovative text structures (especially when the text announces its structure explicitly), the easiest texts to read are those based on a familiar structural pattern or genre (Meyer and Freedle; van Dijk and Kintsch).

The strategies for structuring texts described here are not unfamiliar ones. They are the product of centuries of experimentation by writers striving to make their texts more comprehensible to readers. These strategies, however, place the burden of selecting and arranging information, and providing signals to the arrangement, primarily on the writer. Hypertexts, by shifting a large portion of this burden to the reader, by proliferating the readers' choices about what portions of a text to read and in what order, compound the difficulties of creating a coherent mental representation.[4]

Effects of Text Structure on Reading and Learning

Many reading theorists believe that after reading a number of texts with similar structures, such as a series of fairy tales, newspaper articles, or research reports, people formulate generalized, abstract patterns or frameworks, called "schemas," that they call on as they encounter new texts of the same type. As they realize they are reading a familiar type of text, they invoke their schema for that genre and use it to anticipate what will occur next, to make inferences to fill in implicit or missing elements, and, later, to reconstruct the text from partial memories. People often rely on the structure of the text and the expectations raised by schemas to decide which aspects of the text are most important and, accordingly, where to allocate their time and attention during reading (Just and Carpenter). Further, once a schema is invoked, information in the text that fits the pattern is integrated easily, but information that seems peripheral or incongruous tends to drop out—either it is never linked to the mental representation of the text or, if it is encoded, the link to it is so weak that it effectively is lost (Bartlett).

Schemas have been posited for other cognitive processes besides reading. Many cognitive theories assume that much of the knowledge in long-term memory is organized around such hierarchical frameworks (referred to in various theories as *schemas, frames,* or *scripts*) that capture familiar patterns among elements. There may be schemas for events, for genres of text, for characteristics of a species, for the elements in a system. As Smith points out in chapter 11 of this volume, Kintsch ("Role")—along with other psychologists—has come to reject the schema as a cognitive *mechanism,* that is, as a way to formalize or model the way in which encountering a familiar proposition reliably evokes a pattern of related propositions. Neither Kintsch nor other psychologists, however, will dispute the consistently observed *behaviors* that schemas are meant to capture.[5] Regardless of what cognitive mechanism is ultimately selected as the best formalism for the phenomenon, the concept of a script or schema remains a useful one.

Readers invoke a particular schema in part because of cues provided early in the text, such as the title or the initial sentences. The remainder of the text then may either fulfill the expectations raised by the schema or confound them. When texts set incoherent expectations or fail to confirm expectations they initially raise, they create problems for readers, especially those to whom the subject matter (or "domain of knowledge") is unfamiliar. Bonnie Meyer studied this problem by creating texts that raised expectations for one structure (e.g., problem-solution) but actually developed according to another (e.g., comparison-contrast). She studied how well readers coped with such texts, including both readers who were familiar and readers who were unfamiliar with the subject matter ("domain experts" and "novices"). She found that the novices relied heavily on the text's structure to create their representations and were therefore misled by the opening portions of the text. In contrast, the domain experts were generally able to recover from the textual miscues and construct coherent representations. Experts can draw on their knowledge of the domain's concepts and principles to determine the centrality or novelty of textual information, regardless of where it appears in the text structure.

The structure, or organization, of a text thus signals the relative importance of its various parts, influencing how readers allocate their time and attention and thereby influencing what information they are likeliest to remember. But the way a text is organized can also influence the textual effects that Joseph Grimes has termed "staging"—how easy it is for readers to reflect on the ideas they have read, to juggle and compare them, to see how those ideas relate to one another and to other ideas they have on the subject. We can illustrate the demands that different organizations impose on readers by considering the familiar problem of how to organize a comparison-contrast essay. The two most common strategies, which appear in scores of writing textbooks, are to organize (1) around the objects or alternatives being compared or (2) around the points of comparison—that is, around various aspects of the objects being contrasted or the criteria against which alternatives are judged. In his excellent technical writing textbook, Paul Anderson schematically represents these patterns (266). The first strategy, the "divided pattern," uses the objects as superordinate terms, repeating the criteria (in a consistent sequence) under each object heading. The second strategy, the "alternating pattern," sets up the criteria or aspects as superordinate terms, under which the discussion alternates among the objects under analysis (again in a consistent sequence for each aspect).

The choice between these strategies, of course, has rhetorical implications. For example, an aspectual orientation may be more appropriate for a technical feasibility report whose varied audiences may each have a specific interest in one criterion or another (e.g., cost, efficiency, environmental impact). But the choice also has important implications for readability as well; the two organizations impose different burdens on comprehension processes. Wolfgang Schnotz ("How Do Different Readers Learn" and "Comparative Instructional Text Organization") argues that the aspect-oriented (alternating) organization is the more difficult because readers must switch attention back and forth between different objects; each switch requires reactivation of the reader's prior knowledge and current representation of the object. This switching is especially difficult when the reader is unfamiliar with the topic.

Building on the Kintsch and van Dijk model of reading comprehension, Schnotz maintains that because the two organizations put different propositions into close proximity, readers create different representations of their content in memory. In particular, readers of an object-oriented (divided) organization are more likely to create a well-integrated representation of each object but will find it more difficult to keep track of their similarities and differences. The text itself does little to push the reader to form these interconnections (though the reader is, of course, free to do so). In contrast, readers of an aspect-oriented organization focus on the similarities and differences and as a result are also forced to develop cross-referenced representations of each object (through the costly switching process). Schnotz studied how these organizations influence a reader's ability to recall the overall meaning of the text and make accurate comparisons between the objects. He found, as expected, that aspect-oriented text took longer to read, but readers of these texts remembered more and were better able to make sophisticated discriminations between the objects. Further, the readers' familiarity with the topics significantly affected their ability to cope with the two organizations. Readers with little previous knowledge learned more from the object-oriented texts than aspect-oriented ones, presumably because they could avoid switching. Conversely, readers with more previous knowledge learned more from aspect-oriented text; they were able to take advantage of the close proximity of the comparisons across objects.

These studies highlight the importance of the order in which readers see information. Hypertexts, which proliferate the possible sequences, raise significant issues for both readers and writers. For example, it is easy to imagine a hypertext version of a comparison-contrast essay that allows readers to choose an aspect-oriented or object-oriented organization. What choices will readers make? Will those with little domain knowledge realize that an object-oriented organization will be easier to read? Will they be aware that working through the aspect-oriented organization will be worth the effort for learning careful discriminations?

Implications of Cognitive Models of Reading for Hypertext

Because of the cognitive view of the reading process just described, it is easy to see what potential problems hypertext may raise for readers, for the very reason that hypertext violates standard assumptions of what texts are like. Readers traditionally rely on the writer to select topics, determine their sequence, and signal relations between them by employing conventional discourse cues. The net effect of hypertext systems is to give readers much greater control over the information they read and the sequence in which they read it. Along with greater control, of course, comes a greater burden for the readers, who must now locate the information they need and relate it to other facts in the network, often without the aid of traditional structures or discourse cues.[6]

Many hypertext designers recognize the problems such networks may present, especially for readers who are unfamiliar with the concepts in the text. They report informal evidence that users become overwhelmed by the choices among links and by the difficulties of maneuvering through the networked text structure (Conklin, "Hypertext"). As a result, readers lose track of where they are in the network (and where they have been) and often read a great deal of material that is irrelevant to their purpose (Foss; Yankelovich, Meyrowitz, and van Dam; Whiteside et al.). Technologies related to hypertext have also been shown to pose significant problems for users. Stephen Kerr cites one study on a menu-selection Videotex system in which 28% of users gave up without finding the information they wanted even though they knew that "the information was in there somewhere" (333). Half the users of another menu-driven system had to backtrack at least once before finding the information they sought. While recognizing the navigational difficulties in general terms, hypertext designers have not weighed some of their deeper implications for reading and writing processes.

Consider the hypothetical case of readers using an open-ended hypertext, one without predefined paths, who must choose what links to follow through a set of connected texts (each of which is also represented as a network of nodes). Assume that the goal is not to read everything in the network but instead to gather information relevant to some particular issue. First, since readers must choose what to look at, they may never see all the "right" information, either because they cannot find it or because, for some reason, they fail to select it. Second, even if they do see the "right" information, they may see it at the wrong time. As described above, the timing of seeing a particular bit of information could determine whether readers judge it to be important or whether they see its connection to information they have already read or have yet to read. If they do not see it in conjunction with other relevant information, they may have to expend great effort to integrate it coherently into their mental representations. If they fail to do so, they are likely quite literally to miss the point. Third, readers may see a great deal of intrusive, irrelevant information that may skew their representations. Even if they recognize that some information they have read is irrelevant, there may still be adverse consequences of having spent time reading it. Finally, readers may lose a sense of the integrity of any given text in the network, since they may be unaware of crossing from one text to another. Lacking a sense of textual integrity, they may have difficulty relocating information they have read or attributing the ideas to the correct sources. In short, in addition to suffering the frustrations of disorientation or cognitive overload that hypertext designers already acknowledge, readers may come away with a false or incomplete representation of the texts in the network or even the information relevant to their topics.

The worst-case scenario sketched here is speculative; little research has been conducted of the actual effect of hypertext on reading. However, available research, some using printed texts and some online materials, addresses the specific issues raised in this case. Can readers make appropriate selections of what and how much to read? Can readers create appropriate sequences of textual material? If readers are unable to navigate a hypertext effectively, can hypertext designer-writers reasonably anticipate readers' various needs and create appropriate paths to satisfy them?[7]

Can Readers Select What and How Much to Read?

Many hypertext designers assume that readers know what sequence of information is best for them, that they can tell when they have read enough or judge whether what they are reading is important. However, the evidence suggests that readers are not very good at assessing the adequacy of the information they have encountered and are even worse at anticipating whether important or useful material remains in the portions of text they have not reached.

David Kieras ("Role") found that many readers, left to decide how much to read, stop too soon. In his study, adults with varying technical backgrounds were given online, step-by-step instructions for using a mechanical device. The instructions were presented in a hierarchical network that organized the steps according to major tasks; the bottommost level contained the directives for specific operations, such as turning on a specific switch. At any level of the hierarchy, participants had the option of reading on to a deeper level of detail (using a menu-selection system) or attempting to carry out the steps. Kieras found that the participants tended to stop reading before discovering crucial details—presumably with the impression that they understood what to do—and, as a result, failed to carry out the instructions correctly. In contrast, participants who read and followed the instructions presented in traditional linear order were much more successful at completing the task.

David Reinking and Robert Schreiner also found evidence that readers may fail to take full advantage of useful information available to them in hypertext. In their study, fifth- and sixth-grade students were presented with a set of expository passages annotated with various online aids such as definitions, paraphrases, background information, and distilled main ideas. Students who were allowed to select at will from these aids performed significantly worse on various comprehension tests than did students who were guided through all the aids. In fact, the free-selection group performed more poorly than did students who read the printed version of the linear text without any aids.

While Reinking and Schreiner's results are based on the activities of schoolchildren, they are consistent with Kieras's findings with adults. Taken together, these studies suggest that when readers are responsible for selecting what text to read, they often omit significant information altogether, perhaps because they can't find it, they don't know it's there, or they don't think it's important.

Can Readers Create an Appropriate Reading Order?

The view that readers can select for themselves which links in a hypertext to follow is based on the belief that readers know best what information they need and in what order they should read it. Hypertext designers thus assume that readers can organize information appropriately for their level of knowledge and their purpose in reading. In fact, little research has been conducted on how readers themselves choose to sequence the pieces of a text, whether reader-chosen orders are generally different from those a writer or teacher might create, and what effects these different orders have on what readers learn. As the following discussion indicates, the available evidence is mixed. Overall, it suggests that certain kinds of readers, or readers in certain situations, may benefit from the active effort required to sequence reading material for themselves.

Sequencing an Entire Network

Hans Lodewijks evaluated a variety of text sequencing systems, or "presentation orders," using printed materials. The materials consisted of sixteen passages written for high school students on concepts from electricity (e.g., ampere, conductivity, electron) and presented to different groups of students in different sequences. The "teacher-regulated" sequences were similar to guided paths through a network, giving students little control over the order of the passages. They included a sequence determined intuitively by a group of physics teachers, others based on various logical dependencies or cross-references among the concepts, and an alphabetic sequence based on the concept headings. Two "self-regulated" systems allowed students to choose a concept to study from an alphabetical list, read the passage, and then return to the list to select the next concept. One self-regulated system also provided a structural overview of the relations between the concepts, similar in some ways to the graphical maps (or "browsers") provided in some hypertext systems. In general, the self-regulated sequences (especially self-regulation with a structural overview) led to better recall and better recognition of relations and inferences among the concepts than any of the teacher-provided sequences.

However, not everyone benefited from self-regulation. In particular, Lodewijks found that "field-dependent" learners and low scorers on various logical reasoning tests performed poorly under self-regulation conditions but significantly better with teacher-regulated sequences. The converse was true for "field-independent" learners and high scorers on reasoning tests: they performed significantly better with self-regulated texts than with teacher-regulated ones.[8] Thus the readers' preferred learning strategies (or "cognitive styles") may determine how well they can cope with charting their own path through a hypertext.

Richard Mayer conducted a similar study using instructional materials for writing computer programs, presented as a set of printed cards. He investigated how "experimenter-controlled" and "subject-controlled" card sequences influenced the ability of college students to solve programming problems. In the experimenter-controlled sequence group, students read the cards in either a logical order or a random order. Students in the subject-controlled group were given a table of contents for the cards, in which the topics were listed either in random or in logical order. They used the table of contents to pick which card to read next. Mayer found no overall differences between the sequences. However, he did find differences in the types of problems participants were able to solve. Participants who had chosen their own reading order were significantly better at solving novel, unexpected types of programming problems, while those who had read the text in experimenter-controlled sequences were significantly better at solving problems similar to those in the text. Mayer believes that allowing people to choose their own reading order "may result in deeper, more active encoding, which allowed subjects to struggle harder to relate the text to their own experience rather than memorize the information as presented" (149).

Both Lodewijks and Mayer used printed materials that simulated the conditions of hypertext in many important respects. Two researchers have recently conducted studies of reading in hypertext itself; the results are largely consistent with those based on printed materials.

Sallie Gordon and her colleagues ("Effects of Hypertext") found that reading in hypertext format decreased information retention as compared to studying an online linear presentation. Gordon et al. constructed hypertexts for four expository texts—two on technical topics and two on general-interest topics—each about one thousand words long. In the hypertexts, main ideas were kept on the topmost level and links to elaborative text segments (such as examples, definitions, and noncentral information) were assigned to a second or sometimes a third structural level (about half the text was presented in deeper levels). A highlighted keyword in a main-level segment signaled the presence of deeper information, which readers were free to access by pressing a key. The participants, upper-level college students, were told to use normal, casual reading processes for the general-interest articles but to study the technical texts carefully. After reading both a linear and a nonlinear text, the students were asked to recall as much of both texts as possible, to answer questions about them, and to express their preference for reading format. Gordon et al. found that for both types of texts, students who read in the linear format remembered more of the basic ideas and, for the general-interest articles, assimilated more of the text's macrostructure than after reading in hypertext. Most students also preferred the linear presentation, perceiving it as requiring less mental effort. As a result of finding such negative results for hypertext, Gordon and Vicki Lewis have sought more effective ways to segment material in order to create more easily processed hypertext structures ("Knowledge Engineering" and "Enhancing Hypertext").

Jean-François Rouet ("Interactive Text Processing") found that sixth- and eighth-grade students have difficulty making appropriate sequencing selections with hypertext materials. Rouet constructed hypertexts for four general-knowledge domains. A hypertext consisted of six related thematic units, each containing a title and a fifty- to seventy-word paragraph—representing a "chained list rather than a network" (253). The hypertexts differed in the availability of various cuing aids, such as markers for previously read topics, availability of the topic menu during reading, and explicitness of statements relating one topic to another. Students were asked to read all of a hypertext, selecting the topics in any order and as often as they wished. Then students answered multiple-choice comprehension questions and wrote a summary. Each student read all four hypertexts, two in the first session and two a week later. Rouet computed various measures of selection efficiency, including the number of repeated readings of a topic (indicating global orientation difficulties) and the number of times students picked illogical sequences of topics (indicating local orientation difficulties). Although grade level and some combinations of cuing aids improved performance, Rouet found evidence of global and local disorientation at both grade levels, even with his very simple nonlinear structures. For example, in only 35% of their selections did students pick the topic that was most closely related to the one they had just read. Explicitly marking relations between topics improved students' appropriate selections only to about 50%. Practice at using the system evidently also helped somewhat; the percentage of appropriate selections in the second session increased to 58%. We should not conclude from this study, however, that students can learn to cope with any hypertext with practice. These students may have eventually figured out the simple and consistent structure of these hypertexts, especially when aided by explicit textual cues. Accordingly, these results may just mean that students can improve somewhat at using well-marked and structurally predictable networks.

Obviously, these studies have several important implications. Rouet's study indicates that students may have difficulty making their way through even simple hypertexts. The work of Gordon and her colleagues suggests that reading from hypertext can actually impede a student's comprehension of a text, relative to a linear presentation. However, Lodewijks's and Mayer's investigations hold out the promise that at least some students (those with particular cognitive styles or reasoning ability) may learn more effectively when they choose their own reading order instead of following sequences imposed on them by teachers or writers. Further, self-regulation forces readers to adopt more active reading strategies, which generally lead to better learning.

Several circumstances limit our ability to draw clear-cut conclusions from these studies. First, unlike most hypertext reading situations, participants knew that they had to read the whole text, that everything they needed to learn for the test was in the network, and that they had to learn all of it, to make it all fit together. Second, in all four studies, participants used a finite list to select each successive topic. In the context of reading to understand the network as a whole, the task of ordering the segments reduces to a puzzle: looking at the topics left on the list and guessing which one would be best to read next. This is quite a different task from selectively browsing through a large, messy network. Third, only in the case of Gordon et al. was the text based on an integrated piece of prose; in the other studies, the material was developed from individual modules on fairly discrete concepts. Fourth, neither Lodewijks nor Mayer described the orders students actually devised. Thus, it is unclear whether the benefits of self-selected orders resulted from some feature of the orders per se or from the very fact that the readers were forced to think about how to sequence the text. That is, were the teacher-regulated orders deficient in some way or do learners simply benefit from actively puzzling out how to arrange the text and make sense of it?

Overall, then, these investigations created conditions that encouraged the "self-regulating" students to seek actively for the connections among a finite set of textual elements. Some students in Lodewijks's experiment thrived under these conditions, but not all of them. A task like this may actually encourage students to read more actively (though it's not yet certain that the benefits of these exercises persist). However, for most purposes, readers are unlikely to devote the time and energy necessary to fit all the pieces of a network together, and hypertext designers may not be as fastidious as these researchers about selecting appropriate information to include in the hypertext, to provide explicit relational cues, or to create relatively simple and predictable structures.

Sequencing Selected Information from a Network

Another important situation to consider occurs when readers must select portions instead of having to read the whole text. Carolyn Foss investigated the effects of self-regulation within a large hypertext in which readers controlled both what to read and when to read it. Her participants were asked to compare and analyze information distributed across a hypertext network (Xerox Notecards) to solve a specific problem. The network consisted of encyclopedia entries for a set of ten countries that were not identified by name. Facts about various aspects of each country (population, climate, etc.) were available on "cards" that the user could pull out of a "file," arrange on the screen, or refile. Given a list of the countries' names, the users had to read and compare facts about the countries in order to guess the identity of as many countries as possible within a set time period. These users, then, had to select which cards to read, which ones to leave open, and how to arrange them.

Foss's participants varied greatly in searching skills and the ability to manage the clutter of open entries on the screen. About one-third of them opened very few entries at any one time—and, accordingly, kept their displays rather neat. These users read more total entries than other participants but were unable to make effective comparisons. They identified few countries correctly and took longer to do so. The remaining participants, who kept many entries open at once, were more successful at the task, presumably because they could view more information at the same time. About half of them followed systematic search strategies and used the screen display efficiently. The rest were highly unsystematic, were easily sidetracked, and wasted time revisiting cards and sorting through the cluttered display.[9]

Foss's study reinforces the notion raised earlier that it is crucial for readers to see relevant information in close proximity in order to make appropriate connections. The participants in this study who kept a large number of cards open were more successful at this particular task because they were able to see enough facts at one time to make useful comparisons and notice useful details. The participants who were more worried about keeping neat displays may have read exactly the same cards but failed to make the connections—presumably because they read them at an inopportune time or in fruitless conjunctions.

It follows, as a more important implication of Foss's study, that many people are not very good at regulating their selection and organization of information. Of the participants in the study, fully one-third adopted unproductive "neat-screen" strategies. Another third created wildly messy screens; this strategy seems not to have cost them much in this task but may well create problems in other tasks (just as a neat-screen strategy might be more advantageous in another kind of task). It is unclear, of course, whether people maintain their preferences for neat or messy screens in different task situations, or whether people who use hypertext more often learn strategies appropriate to the task at hand.

In addition to individual preferences for how to manage a display, differences in previous knowledge of the information in a hypertext influences selection strategies. Rouet ("Initial Domain Knowledge") investigated how prior knowledge affected the efficiency of high school students looking for information in a hypertext network in order to answer specific questions. He found that students who were highly knowledgeable about a particular subject area were much more efficient at locating the relevant information than were those with low or moderate knowledge. Furthermore, by showing that students' performance declined when they moved from a familiar to an unfamiliar domain, Rouet demonstrated that the effects resulted from specific domain knowledge and not from general reading ability or practice with the hypertext system. Taken together with the studies by Meyer and Schnotz described earlier in this chapter, Rouet's findings underscore the hardships that face a hypertext user who attempts to learn about an unfamiliar domain.

These studies suggest that the best way to sequence information is not at all obvious to readers. If the goal of hypertext is to allow people "to access information in the sequence, volume, and format that best suits their needs at the time" (Grice 22), the results of these studies indicate that a large proportion of hypertext users will need a good deal of guidance in determining the most appropriate sequence, volume, and format of information.

Can Hypertext Designers Create Appropriate Paths for Readers?

Anticipating that readers will have trouble charting a logical course through a network on their own, some hypertext designers are designing alternative paths through a network to which readers would be directed as appropriate (Younggren; Zellweger). For example, Patricia Carlson ("Way") describes how the reader's task may be used to organize the technical documentation for an airplane into several orders. An alphabetical order would be most appropriate for someone trying to update selected pieces of information. An order based on spatial layout would be suitable for someone who had to work efficiently from one end of the plane to the other, performing a set of repairs. Alternatively, the most efficient order might be to group information according to which tools are needed for maintenance or repair. This solution assumes that designers can anticipate the necessary paths and can reliably determine which readers need which path.

Creating such paths is hardly a straightforward task. Various factors, including the designer's own idiosyncrasies and sensitivity to readers' needs, the type of text being incorporated into the network, and the choices that the hypertext system itself allows, influence what kinds of sequences any given hypertext designer may create. The best evidence of the difficulties involved comes from an attempt, by three leading hypertext designers, to use their own systems to construct hypertexts of one small set of documents, six articles from the proceedings of a hypertext conference. Liora Alschuler carefully analyzed the resulting hypertexts and found vast qualitative and quantitative incongruities in how the articles were segmented and linked, both within any one system and across systems. Alschuler attributed one source of difficulty to the designers' inconsistency and their, perhaps inevitable, subjectivity. However, a second stumbling block was the nature of the hypertext systems themselves, which imposed significant constraints on the kinds of segments and links that were even possible. This uncontrolled variability leads to serious methodological problems for those researching the effect of hypertext on reading and writing: How can one draw generalizations about hypertexts if no two systems produce the same result from a set of source texts and even the texts in any one given system are subject to erratic treatment?

I am skeptical that a hypertext designer, even under ideal conditions, can anticipate all the paths that readers may wish to create within and between texts. As we have seen, a wide range of factors influence the appropriateness of a sequence for a given reader, including the reader's prior knowledge of the domain, the reader's task or purpose for reading, the reader's learning style, and the nature of the information itself. Because of the huge number of possible combinations of such factors, the array of alternative paths that a designer might create becomes a practical impossibility—and there still remains the problem of directing the right readers to the right paths. Obviously, these are issues that only experimentation with hypertexts can resolve; my purpose here is to raise serious concerns that hypertext developers should take into account, not to discourage the development of hypertexts altogether.

Others have raised the issue of what kinds of texts can be or should be integrated into hypertext networks. Many agree that a text with closely interwoven points is not an easy or desirable candidate for conversion to hypertext because "it destroys the subtle interconnections of theme, argument, metaphor, and word choice" (Carlson, "Intelligent Interfaces" 63; Shneiderman, "Reflections"). Darrell Raymond and Frank Tompa note that, because converting a text into hypertext makes implicit structures explicit, "the key question in conversion must be *will explicit structure be as expressive as implicit structure?* When the answer is yes, the document will gain from conversion; otherwise, conversion will degrade the representation of the document" (146). Despite the sense that texts with complex internal structures (including many forms of narrative, expository, and persuasive prose) may suffer from conversion to hypertext, they are the very sorts of texts that many designers want most to include.

Implications of Cognitive Processes for Hypertext Design

The evidence from cognitive psychology reviewed in this essay emphasizes how heavily we rely, in dealing with the world, on systematic patterns of information. Our dependence on predictable patterns creates an enormous tension between the impulse toward creativity, inventiveness, and imagination, and the more conservative, "normalizing" forces that assimilate new information to established and familiar patterns. The cognitive mechanism for encoding information in long-term memory (a process that requires sustained or repeated conscious attention) and the selectivity imposed by schemas (i.e., the loss of things that don't easily fit) are both strongly conservative forces. It seems reasonable that we have mental mechanisms such as these, given the constant barrage of observations and sensations presented to us at every moment from our senses, our emotions, our intellect. Such mechanisms may account for our ability to "make sense," to impose order on the world.

The Romantic view of hypertext that aims at enabling imaginative leaps and connections between disparate texts, facts, and images thus puts enormous technological and creative effort at the service of preserving what might be quite rare and ephemeral associations. Some of these connections, probably a very small proportion, may be of great value and interest to those who initially make them. However, once the insight or connection is made, it is unclear that the thinker needs or wants to store the convoluted trail of associations that led up to them, let alone those that led nowhere. Such trails are probably of even lesser value to subsequent readers. The trails of associations in a hypertext may represent the ultimate in what Linda Flower calls "writer-based prose," prose that reflects the writer's process of coming to terms with a set of ideas but that may bear little relation to his or her final stance and none whatsoever to the readers' needs. Some proponents (e.g., Beeman et al.) claim that allowing students to explore freely in hypertext may foster insights and critical thinking through the creative juxtaposition of ideas from multiple perspectives. However, instead of prompting truly original insights, this process may simply reduce itself to a guessing game, as the user figures out what the hypertext writer (usually the teacher or another student) had in mind when creating a link. As discussed earlier, the nature of the reading process suggests that chance conjunctions and odd juxtapositions tend to be dropped from the reader's mental representation of a text. Thus the most imaginative links that a hypertext writer-designer creates are unlikely to be remembered or to influence the reader's subsequent thinking in any significant way. But, for the reader, the consequences of whimsically following links into disparate texts or text segments may be to obstruct or hinder the more conventional but durable processes of systematically integrating new information with old.[10]

To the extent that readers rely on structure—that they learn by discerning and internalizing the structure of a text (Jaynes)—hypertexts that emphasize free-form browsing may interfere with readers' efforts to make sense of the text and even with more limited and pragmatic efforts to find information relevant to some specific question. A hypertext system that promotes free exploration and browsing, then, may be effective only in certain kinds of situations, such as reading for pleasure but not for scholarship. In contrast, a hypertext system that allows readers to choose only among a fixed set of paths through the network may satisfy particular readers' purposes better—though designers of these systems face significant challenges for creating the right paths and steering the right readers onto them. In these systems, though, the romance of hypertext disappears; the hypertext becomes functionally identical to a set of linear texts.

As part of a literate society, we are familiar with traditional text structures. We have time-tested cognitive and rhetorical theories to bring to bear on describing effective printed texts, and we have derived from these theories a wealth of practical advice to convey to writers—students and professionals alike. But we lack corresponding theories for how to deal with hypertexts—especially those that push the limits with complex linkages within and between a complex set of texts. In this essay, I have sketched the challenges that an effective hypertext would face. Much work remains to fulfill the promise of hypertext for readers and writers.

Some designers are attempting to overcome problems of disorientation and cognitive overload (e.g., Utting and Yankelovich; Rouet, "Interactive Text Processing"; Gordon et al.; Gordon and Lewis), but more research is needed. The critical issues fall into two broad categories: the construction of hypertexts and the effects of hypertext on the reading process. The first order of business may be to create, and to study the creation of, large, complex, sophisticated hypertexts, involving a range of texts. As in Foss's study, some of these hypertexts should contain expository information intended to help people solve research problems. Others should be constructed to explore the effect of hypertext on existing imaginative literature, to supplement the work of "interactive fiction" writers who are designing literary works specifically for the hypertext environment (e.g., Moulthrop, "Hypertext and 'the Hyperreal'"). Finally, in spite of the fact that hypertexts were originally intended as resources for scholars, few complex networks yet exist for scholarly literatures, such as books and journal articles. These studies on the construction of hypertexts should, like Alschuler's, investigate the constraints imposed by different hypertext technologies. Drawing on rhetorical, linguistic, psychological, and literary theories of text structure, these investigations should confront the issue of what kinds of texts can or should be presented in hypertext environments and, for those that are appropriate, should systematically explore different ways to partition and interrelate a set of texts. Formative evaluation of such hypertexts with readers should be ongoing. Research encompassing the full range of factors identified in the research reviewed here must eventually involve readers with different purposes, cognitive styles, amounts of background knowledge. The goal of such research must be to find ways within hypertext to provide appropriate discourse cues, cues that help readers decide what to read, how much to read, and when to read the rich array of information available in the network. These signals may be manifested in hypertext design in a variety of ways—many of which have been inadequately explored in current systems (as discussed by Wright and Lickorish). Hypertexts are here to stay, but it is up to researchers, teachers, and software designers to ensure that these texts promote the work of writers and readers.[11]

NOTES

[1] There is an extensive and growing literature on hypertexts. For a history and overview, see Conklin, "Hypertext." For bibliographies, see Mitterer, Oland, and Schankula; Harpold, "Hypertext."

[2] For a straightforward, general introduction to cognitive psychological perspectives on memory and learning, see Bransford. Many of the issues raised in this chapter are also discussed by Just and Carpenter and by Sanford and Garrod, who all focus on those aspects of cognition that relate to reading. For a brief review of the history of cognitive psychology, see Hayes.

[3] Some hypertext proponents assume that these cognitive limitations somehow result from the limited forms of writing available through print technology. They believe that a revolution in technology will lead to a revolution in cognitive capacity—an analogy with the advances presumed to have taken place when oral cultures became literate. In fact, many researchers have concluded that literacy did not change human cognitive capacity but, rather, the way that capacity is used (for general discussions, see Borland; Rose, "Narrowing the Mind"). In particular, technology is unlikely to influence the way in which we visually process written texts or auditorially process speech, both of which are linear (for reviews of relevant research, see Just and Carpenter). We read in linear sequences of words and sentences. While hypertext may change which sequences are available—and may well impose more frequent decision points for which sequence to follow—it will not change our basic mental architecture.

[4]The shift in burden also has consequences for writers. Carlson ("Way") raises the issue of whether and how writers can create segments of text that will make sense to any reader who encounters them, without knowing what previous segments he or she has read: "Since nodes may be 'threaded' into different paths, they must be reusable, requiring research into the requisites (as well as the effects) of free-standing, rhetorically 'neutral' prose" (96). The concept of "rhetorically 'neutral' prose" is one that many rhetoricians find troubling.

[5]In fact, the mechanism that Kintsch adopts, spreading activation within a network of links of various strengths, in effect functionally reproduces the evocation of a schema. The mechanism works by activating a set of propositions that are most strongly linked to some other proposition—presumably including many previously assumed to reside in a schema—while allowing for the activation of additional, less predictable kinds of knowledge and associations. It is evident from the recent research literature that cognitive psychologists do not take Kintsch's current position as rendering the terms *script* or *schema* meaningless—researchers who cite and build on Kintsch's 1988 article ("Role") continue to explore how schemas and scripts influence learning and memory (e.g., Maki).

[6]A more familiar and analogous case of the increased burdens imposed by technological "liberation" is the advent of desktop publishing. Such systems do indeed free writers to make their own choices concerning details of typography, page layout, graphics, and the like. However, the price of greater control to individual writers is the responsibility (and sometimes the sheer necessity) of acquiring some expertise in effective graphic design and printing.

[7]Some of these problems, of course, apply to conventional printed text too. People don't have to (and don't) obediently read in order (Charney, "Study"). Active readers often break out of a linear sequence to seek an overview of the paper—perhaps by reading the abstract, introduction, and conclusion and then skimming over the headings and looking at diagrams and tables. Depending on their purpose, they may skim for the main points of each paragraph or read only sections relevant to their goal. The point is that hypertext makes the situation much worse. Readers of printed texts can scan the page or thumb through the text to see how much is there, to see whether anything further down the page looks important or useful, or to see how much elaboration the writer considers it worthwhile to include. Obtaining an overview is a lot harder to do in hypertext because readers must consciously choose to look at something (i.e., by clicking a button), because new information may displace other information on the screen, and because making such a choice may make it harder to get back to where the reader started.

[8]*Field dependence* and *field independence* are widely used but little understood characterizations of cognitive style that are based on a person's strategies of visual perception and that purportedly reflect the manner in which the individual attempts to solve problems. Field-independent people are considered to be more individualistic, more self-motivating, and less dependent on external cues

than field-dependent learners. For a review and critique of field dependence and independence, see Rose, "Narrowing the Mind." Such measures of cognitive style may be most reliable, as here, when they are used in conjunction with correlating measures of individual differences.

[9] While Foss examined important issues and reported interesting observations, the available report of her research is frustratingly incomplete in its methodological details and analysis of the results. The number of subjects in the study was small ($n = 10$), and no inferential statistics were reported. It is therefore impossible to tell whether the differences described here were statistically significant.

[10] As the research described here suggests, a reader's (or writer's) tolerance for the confusion engendered by hypertext is clearly situation-specific. Readers' attitudes will vary on the basis of their reasons for reading, their cognitive abilities and familiarity with the content area, their deadlines, the type of texts involved, and so on. Many people enjoy some confusion when they read a modern novel—but not when they read a political treatise or an instruction manual. Hypertext, of course, has effects that go beyond thwarting comprehension on the most basic level. In chapter 9 of this volume, Moulthrop and Kaplan describe other consequences—some positive and some clearly negative—of the deliberate use of hypertext to break down the boundaries between writer and reader, between previously autonomous texts and between texts and interpretations. Their purpose was both playful and didactic—to encourage students to become active, "strong" readers of any text, even those presented in a seemingly closed, authoritative, linear, hardcover publication. As they discovered (and as Johnson-Eilola remarks in the overview of this section), hypertext may subvert even these intentions—silencing where it was intended to give voice.

[11] This essay develops and extends ideas first presented at Hypertext '87 (Charney, "Comprehending Non-linear Text"). The research was generously supported by a Penn State Research Initiation Grant and by Tektronix, Inc. I am grateful to Christine Neuwirth, Rich Carlson, and Mark Detweiler for comments on earlier versions of the manuscript.

Chapter 11

Hypertextual Thinking

Catherine F. Smith

The Issue: Making Meaning

I read: "This is the metaphor of mind for our age: the mind as a network of signs, of which the computer is the embodiment. To understand the mind as a network of signs is also to understand the mind as a text" (Bolter 208).

I react: Is the mind a text? Do I think because I signify, using symbols? Forget, for the moment, quarrels about the effects of using different symbolic modes—either writing, speaking, imaging, or another mode. Focus, instead, on the claim that mind is a text. Does that sound to you like all there is to it? To me, suddenly, it doesn't.

Now, that's interesting—a quick nag, as I read, by a feeling from somewhere that there's more to mind than symbolic functions. Just a flash of . . . doubt? No, more a lightning sense of incompleteness, of having heard half a story.

In the context of this chapter this feeling is interesting, first, because it is a feeling. A felt thought. Susanne Langer (discussed later here) views feeling as the threshold of thought, or the moment when neurophysiological activity is presented to consciousness.

The flash is interesting, too, because it is incomplete. It feels connected to something else, maybe in agreement and maybe not, but, in either case, something just out of view.

Reconstructing here, after the event, I might mumble against Jay Bolter's claim, Well, yes, that's true, just not the whole picture. Then I might look aside from it to wonder, What is making me object to this? (Usually I am persuaded by Bolter's perspectives.) Rather, at this time, this claim seems only partly right. I must have read something else recently that's trying to get through . . . I've got it . . . I recall one of the articles on literacy that I read while writing this chapter . . . Deborah Brandt's, I think, which approaches reading and writing as involvement . . . hmm . . . mind as involvement . . . mind as text . . . alternative ways to frame the issue . . .

The mental events narrated here—feeling dissonance, characterizing it, reflexively initiating a resolution to it through association—illustrate the subject of this chapter: the pragmatics of making meaning. By pragmatics, I mean acts of practical rationality rooted (I tend to agree with Brandt, discussed below) in human involvement and interaction. I am interested in intellectual pragmatics, or moves that minds make in order to form ideas and to understand them.

I explore intellectual pragmatics because I want to use hypertext technology (including hypermedia) for inquiry. I am interested in hypertext as a verb, "to think hypertextually." As a teacher of composition and professional communication, I am motivated to apply hypertext tools in intellectual tasks related to (though not limited to) writing and reading. What I want from hypertext is support for a range of thinking processes that pull concepts and interpretive frameworks into conscious use. The kinds of thought that concern this chapter are, at one edge of a spectrum, less conscious and reflexive actions and, at the other, metacognitive and reflective actions. The emphasis is on less conscious, reflexive thought.

The first question is whether hypertext can support a wide spectrum of thinking activity. Human cognition engages, along with orderly, logical capabilities, other, more anarchistic elements—doubt, contradiction, intuition, recollection, forgetfulness, denial, tacit knowledge, partial awareness—the full, mixed baggage of consciousness. And cognition is embedded in the human condition of plurality. Acts of thinking entail the thinker's multiple physical, social, cultural, and historical life worlds. I characterize this kind of thinking as "thick" cognition, to distinguish it from the more selective "thin" cognition of problem solving. I am asking whether hypertext systems might be designed and used to support the "thicker" kinds of knowing.

Thick cognition, the whole of consciousness and its multiple involvements, challenges current conceptions and implementations of hypertext. Literacy theory may suggest some directions for responding to the challenges. Brandt, for example, argues that literacy involves orientational macroprocesses, not only linguistic microprocesses. Writers compose and readers comprehend, Brandt suggests, less by responding to features in the text than by a

here and now, off the page sense of what is going on. . . . As
process studies have established, the central concern in writing
and reading is not "What does that say?" or "What do I make that
say?" but more broadly "What do I do now?" The work of reading
and writing is not merely and not mostly encoding and decoding
texts or managing semantic meaning. Rather, it is finding and
maintaining the broad conditions that will keep an act of writing
or reading going. . . . The essence of literate orientation is knowing what to do now.   (192)

In literacy studies, generally, intellectual processes and practices are
considered under two large categories, the relation of literacy to the
evolution of consciousness and the relation of literacy to cognition.
Recent collections published by the Modern Language Association,
Literacy for Life (ed. Bailey and Fosheim) and *The Right to Literacy* (ed.
Lunsford, Moglen, and Slevin), sample approaches to the complex
consciousness involved in reading and writing (Becker; Delattre; Salvio) and to the varied conceptual strategies and cognitive activities of
differently literate thinkers (D'Angelo; White; Odell, Goswami, and
Quick; Brandt; Daniell, "Situation"; Flannery; Hull and Rose). This
chapter, in a new MLA collection relating literacy to technology, re-
frames issues of consciousness and cognition in terms of hypertext. It
considers these questions: Can hypertext technology adapt to human
consciousness and support the varied ways that people think? Can
teaching help people use the technology better?

The facets of this chapter reflect the diversity of its intended audience. These days, when you discuss hypertext with people in humanities, language, or literacy fields, you may be talking either with someone
who's designed, built, tested, and applied a system, or with someone
who uses hypertext software for teaching, or with someone who's
played around with the software but not yet used it in the classroom,
or with someone who asks, "Hypertext? What *is* that?" I hope this
chapter speaks to all of them. This complex community—theorists,
designers, researchers, teachers, expert and novice users—represents
the convergence of viewpoints needed to elaborate the future of hypertext.

A thoughtful answer to the question What is hypertext? is given in
Johndan Johnson-Eilola's overview to this section. My chapter adds a
dimension to the definition. In the overview, hypertext is considered
primarily as textual experience related to writing or to reading. Here,
hypertext is thought of as intellectual experience. My focus is on inquiry, including but not limited to the composition and comprehension
of written text. Complementing Stuart Moulthrop and Nancy Kaplan's

chapter discussing hypertext as text in relation to literary theory, this chapter views hypertext as mental activity and examines it in relation to the philosophy of mind, the cognition of comprehension, and the computational modeling of discourse processes.

In the first and second parts of this essay, I speak primarily to people interested in concepts of hypertext and in system design. Building on Davida Charney's review of early research in the cognition of discourse comprehension, the second part takes up recent revisions in comprehension theory and differs with Charney's view of hypertext's potential effects on comprehension. The third part, addressing chiefly those interested in using hypertext in the classroom, agrees with L. M. Dryden that familiar teaching and learning techniques might help students think creatively with an unfamiliar technology. The last part speaks to theorists and researchers wishing to explore the relations between literacy and hypertext, especially relations of orality and hypertext.

Hypertext: The Original Paradigm and Its Limitations

The hypertext vision is worth a try. The demonstrations so far have been tantalizing. It is my guess that the reality will remain tantalizing. . . .

—Jef Raskin

Hypertext, including hypermedia, is a technology for defining meaningful units of information (nodes) and making meaningful connections (links) among them.

Nodes and links are the defining capabilities of hypertext. They distinguish hypertext from other functions that have different defining capabilities—for instance, word processing, with its ability to select, delete, insert, cut and paste. To the basic hypertext capability of nodes and links are sometimes added others intended to provide perspective. For example, sets of linked nodes may be collected in a web or network, to provide an overview. Contexts may be set by partitioning. Linkage may be constrained by attaching conditions or attributes to nodes. These perspectival additions have proved unable to handle much complexity, however.

Uses of hypertext have revealed a number of technical problems related to conceptual limitations in the original nodes-and-links vision. Early hypertext systems made heavy demands on users' memories, could not support many ordinary thinking tasks, and were awkward for extensive tasks such as browsing large databases. An early system designer, Frank Halasz, enumerated major needs requiring better design solutions—the need to navigate in "hyperspace" among proliferating nodes and links, the need to create composite nodes, to tailor the system, to work with large amounts of material, and to collaborate. "The simple nodes and links model is just not rich enough to support the information representation, management, and presentation tasks that . . . users will want to accomplish using their hypermedia system," Halasz concluded in 1987 (363–64).

Other analyses have detailed the implications of Halasz's critique. Studies reconsider the hypertext primitives, the node (what constitutes it? what size is it?), and the link (what motivates a link? what terminates it? how do links aggregate into larger patterns? what are the limits of linking or of aggregating? who decides, the system or the user?). As I see them, such questions represent a struggle with fundamental concerns about cognition as much as with basic problems of technical design. I translate those questions as How does the mind do these things? Until we understand the mind's specifications, we won't get the technology right.

Since 1987, hypertext implementation has seriously, productively addressed the technical issues. Newer systems incorporate direct methods for managing information overload, for allowing composite nodes and "fuzzy" links as well as virtual links, for enabling the user to tailor the system as tasks develop, for handling large-scale tasks, and for fostering collaboration.

Systems are thus becoming more adaptive. The test of adaptiveness—the phenomenology of human users—remains the same, however. Thick cognition, I'm calling it here. If minds and machines are to work together, three major phenomenological conditions on the human side set specifications the technology side must accommodate (C. Smith). The key interdependent conditions are

- consciousness and unconsciousness
- contextualization
- mediation

In other words, when users come to a hypertext system, they bring with them the mixed baggage of consciousness:

- explicit as well as tacit knowledge, interests, and constraints
- particular as well as general needs to know
- symbolized as well as unsymbolized constructions of reality

These human specifications translate into three challenges for the design of hypertext systems and applications:

- knowledge accessibility (the retrieval of content that is partly conscious)
- knowledge involvement (the analysis of content that is always situated)
- knowledge representation (the presentation of discursive, symbolic knowledge structures that may have nondiscursive, nonsymbolic components—e.g., feeling)

It is generally acknowledged that hypertext necessarily relates to human thinking. So far, it might be said, the relation has been implemented in ways that reflect logical positivist, Cartesian views of mind. In those terms, links are positive traces, knowable trails of implication. Objects are defined and manipulated by subjects who are outside them. It's a model that describes well what the early technology could do but not what the user's mind does, or at least not much of what a mind does.

What might hypertext be like if it were reconceived in view of constructivist theories of mind? Two theories, Susanne Langer's philosophy of mind and Walter Kintsch's revised cognitive, psychological model of discourse comprehension, suggest a different conception of hypertext that might support more functions of the constructing mind.

An Alternative View: Hypertext as Living Form and as Cognitive Architecture

A built hypertext (a structural representation of thought by a person using a hypertext system) is a virtuality, a projection of the user's thinking as it progresses through various sources and moments of understanding. The resulting arrangements of nodes and links visually represent current states of knowledge.

As visible thought, hypertexts might be fruitfully analyzed in the terms of Langer's theory of illusion in art presented in *Feeling and Form*. Applicable to hypertext is Langer's "virtual space" (a term she borrowed from physics and applied to visual art), or uses of space in pictures that, like the space "behind" a mirror, reveal an artist's projected symbolic understanding of feeling (72). A rewarding humanities research project would be to apply Langer's aesthetic theory to hypertexts.

More to my purposes here, however, is Langer's elaboration of a general philosophy of mentality, in *Mind: An Essay on Human Feeling*. (To highlight Langer's relevance for hypertext, I have omitted, in the following discussion, many aspects of her extraordinarily suggestive theory of mind unrelated to my purposes.)

Living Form

"Living form" is Langer's characterization for continuous vital process or organic connectivity, both within a single form of existence and across forms of existence. Organic continuity is exemplified in all kinds of existence, whether actual (e.g., a nerve cell) or virtual (e.g., a symbolic expression), and at all levels of existence, from the simplest to the most complex.

The prime example of living form, or organic continuity, is the human mind. Langer theorizes mind as existence that is continuous across biological phases (neural, endocrinal) and psychological phases (sentient, emotive, abstractive). Based on her earlier theory of the relevance of feeling for artistic thinking, Langer logically elaborates a role for feeling in thinking, generally. Feeling is the qualitative difference that in Langer's theory distinguishes human mentality from other kinds, such as animal mentality. Human mind, or "physiological process in its psychical phase" (*Mind* 29), begins with feeling. An instance would be when pain breaks through to awareness.

Langer explains: "Feeling, in the broad sense of whatever is felt in any way, as sensory stimulus or inward tension, pain, emotion, or intent, is the mark of mentality." Feeling arises from and returns to unfelt activities, "millions of processes—the whole dynamic rounds of metabolism, digestion, circulation and endocrine action." The phase of being felt is the crucial qualitative change in the neural economy of an organism that transforms experience to knowledge. To be felt is "to be presented to consciousness." In the phase of feeling its activity, an organism "acquires the capacity to turn around upon its own 'schemata' and to construct them afresh" (*Mind* 4, 22, 5).

What is felt is activity or process, perhaps a complex of actions and processes. To provide a view into living form, Langer isolates a basic unit of analysis, the act (261). Langer's act concept is a formal construct, a theoretical unit for comprehending the working relations of parts and wholes. Because I propose that hypertext might be considered living form in Langer's sense, it is useful to summarize aspects of Langer's act that are most relevant to hypertextual acts. Those aspects are dynamic architecture, origination and effect in a situation, and formative principles of individuation and involvement.

Dynamic architecture. Acts are wholes, "distinguishable centers with labile limits." They "arise where there is already some fairly constant movement going on. They normally show a phase of acceleration, or intensification of a distinguishable dynamic pattern, then reach a point at which the pattern changes, whereupon the movement subsides" in gradients of interaction, abruptly or gradually, isolated or merged. This pattern of incipience, intensification, consummation, and subsidence is the general architecture, the "highly variable, yet fundamentally typical form," of an act (*Mind* 22, 261, 281).

Origination and effect in a situation. An act is motivated by the dynamism of its universe and the permeability of its own envelope. "Every act arises from a situation. The substance of a situation is always the stream of advancing acts which have already arisen from previous situations. . . . All distinguishable acts arise from this matrix, which is their situation." The situation, itself, has agency. The basic causal relation is interaction. Acts, even as they form, permeate other acts. "All vital action, whether of the organism as a whole in its surroundings or of an organ internal to it, is interaction, transaction. Every act of a living unit transforms its situation and necessitates action under the impact of that new development as well as of any fortuitous changes coinciding with it. At the same time, its own state changes" (*Mind* 281, 26–27).

Formative principles of individuation and involvement. Individuation occurs when an act becomes a distinguishable, functioning unit ("a definite center"). But individuation has "labile limits," is always involved—with its own internal subprocesses; with other, external processes; with larger aggregates. Through involvements, an act creates its own ambient in an environment. Through ambience, an act gathers relationships with other acts. The possibilities are so varied as to blur distinctions between kinds of existence, e.g. between organic and inorganic existence (282, 344).

These key elements of Langer's philosophy of mind—conceptualization that is felt, dynamic, differentiated, situated, and involved—yield an organicist, constructivist view of cognition that is relational rather than reductive. It contrasts strongly with a concept of mental life as formally reducible to discrete intellectual objects with connections determined by laws of association, such as the concept underlying the original nodes-and-links vision of hypertext. Toward a different vision of hypertext that is being theorized in this chapter, Langer contributes a notion of mentality that accommodates thick cognition.

To imagine thick cognition in operation (and, then, to see how hypertext might support it), consider Kintsch's revised model of discourse comprehension.

Cognitive Architecture

Kintsch's model focuses on the use of knowledge in discourse comprehension. In the study of language, discourse theory tries to account for language in use. Included within its analysis of language are the circumstantial, rhetorical, and situational contexts that affect and are affected by language activity. Cognitive theory of discourse comprehension attempts to explain how we understand as we read. Kintsch's earlier work on the instrumental role that text features play in shaping a "text base" of propositions, or the mental representation needed for textual understanding, has been central to this cognitive theory (Kintsch and van Dijk; van Dijk and Kintsch; Kintsch, "Text Processing"). Charney reviews this body of theory in chapter 10 of this volume.

In a shift of focus, more recent theory looks at the instrumental role readers' knowledge plays in comprehension. Kintsch's revised comprehension model, for example, looks less at text properties and more closely at mental organization and representation (Kintsch, "Role" and "Representation"; Mannes and Kintsch). Specifically, Kintsch now tries to account for the organization and representation of readers' knowledge in discourse comprehension. "How is it possible," Kintsch asks, "that exactly the right knowledge about a word is activated in the discourse context, and that everything else that we know about it doesn't intrude?" For example, when we read the word *bank*, what triggers the knowledge that a "river bank" and not a "money bank" is intended? "More precisely, there seem to be two questions involved here: what is the knowledge organization that permits this astonishing degree of context sensitivity, and what do we know about the process of knowledge use?" ("Representation" 186).

Summarized, the shifts in comprehension theory most significant for hypertext design and application are as follows. Mental representations of text still are thought to assist comprehension of written text. But the construction of those representations is thought to be less dependent on features in the text and more dependent on knowledge in the reader. Knowledge use is thought to be less influenced by strong, top-down, expectation-based procedures such as frames or schemata. Activations of local relevance by context-sensitive procedures may be more relevant for knowledge use than are large, generic, conceptual frameworks.

It may be helpful to present a condensed description of Kintsch's comprehension model before I show how it might instruct the design of hypertext systems capable of adapting to complexities in consciousness. (I have omitted details unrelated to a potential for hypertext design and discursively paraphrased mathematical aspects of the model.) Briefly, Kintsch's retheorized comprehension process uses "weak," unselective procedures to construct an incoherent mental representation and then, to achieve integrated coherence, uses a connectionist process to pull related and, hence, relevant matters together, dropping the rest.

Comprehension in this revised model has two stages, construction and integration. Construction yields a loosely structured text base, or mental representation of the discourse combining text knowledge and aspects of world knowledge, in the form of propositions. Integration consolidates this mental representation, eliminating unrelated and less applicable propositions to disclose the relevant propositional structure that constitutes comprehension.

Explained in more detail, construction is an iteration process that combines two sources of information: the text itself (linguistic input) and knowledge about language, as well as knowledge about the world. The decoding of words and phrases involves several steps:

> (a) forming concepts and propositions directly corresponding to the linguistic input; (b) elaborating each of these elements by selecting a small number of its most closely associated neighbors from the general knowledge net; (c) inferring certain additional propositions; and (d) specifying interconnections between all these elements. ("Role" 166)

Construction, in Kintsch's revised model, does not rely on "strong" expectation-based procedures or predictive rules such as the elaborate structures required by frame and schema approaches, including Kintsch's own earlier work. This change is an important revision in comprehension theory, highly relevant to hypertext theory. The revision reflects a distinction Kintsch is now making between comprehending text and learning from text.

Instead of depending on structures of expectation such as schemata, Kintsch now proposes, construction of an initial text base occurs by a messy variety of "weak" processes capable of producing a whole set of elements:

- sentence parsing in step (a), forming concepts and propositions
- standard memory cues, such as contiguity, for retrieval in step (b), elaborating text-derived concepts by finding associations
- minimal procedures of bridging inferences and elaborating macro-propositions in step (c), inferring additional propositions
- calibrating strengths of association in general knowledge with the proximity of elements in the text in step (d), assigning connection strength in the text base to pairs of elements (166–67)

The result, Kintsch notes, "is an initial, enriched, but incoherent and possibly contradictory text base" that is largely context-free (166). This constructed output—the initial text base—is an associative network, with propositions as nodes and associations as links. Toward later discussion of this model's relevance for hypertext system design, I might note that the first outcome of comprehension, the initial text base, is structurally analogous to a built hypertext.

Knowledge is engaged early in the construction process. Both knowledge of language and knowledge of the world are required, for example, in parsing a sentence to form a proposition. However, the knowledge that is referenced to produce the initial text base is the comprehender's general knowledge of the world. Coherence requires further, context-sensitive processing, which is the work of Kintsch's integration stage.

Processing works the combined text and knowledge net. This net is a large, incoherent structure containing many propositions and associations that are irrelevant for a given comprehension task. But it also contains, embedded or scattered within it, the meaningful structure that constitutes understanding. The trick is to disembed the meaningful, much as a sculptor liberates a form visualized in stone, or to draw fragments into a pattern, much as a quilter pieces a quilt.

Integration uses spreading activation procedures of the type made familiar in connectionist and neural net research. The process utilizes two components: a matrix representation of the associative (text and knowledge) net, and an "activation vector" that represents the strength of association of each proposition in the net with respect to a given sentence to be understood.

A matrix representation of an associative net consists of a table (columns and rows) of numbers. Each column and each row in the table correspond to a particular node. At the intersection between a given column/node and a given row/node in the table, a number represents the strength of association (weight on the link) between those two nodes in the associative network. For example, in the cell of the table corresponding to the intersection of column 4 and row 3, the number recorded there is the strength of association (weight on the link) between the nodes in the network identified as node 4 and node 3.

The activation vector may be thought of as a stimulus that changes the matrix. The vector is similar to a column or a row of numbers in the table in that its values represent the strength of association between two domains, the words and concepts in a target sentence, and all the nodes in the knowledge net.

The vector and the matrix can be multiplied according to well-established mathematical rules. When this is done, some numbers in the matrix change. If the vector and the new matrix are then multiplied, some numbers again change, but usually not as many. In Kintsch's procedure, this multiplication process is continued until the numbers no longer change or the differences are less than some given value. At that point, the matrix is said to stabilize. These multiplication processes yield valuations of relation. Relations that have high values—versus those with zero or very low values—show meaning comprehended, or meaning represented by the activation vector understood within the context of *relevant* world knowledge.

Applicability to hypertext. Kintsch's knowledge system holds interesting potential for a different concept of hypertext.[1] The conventional view of hypertext as a network of nodes and links is analogous to Kintsch's associative net produced at the end of the construction phase. One early identified problem with nodes-and-links hypertext is that it often appears to the user to have no large-grain structure. All links and nodes seem accessible from any point in the graph and equally relevant. But, of course, this structure is not true for a human user's own particular intellectual mission or intellectual history. From that viewpoint, some links and nodes are probably more relevant than others. However, the system cannot "see" them or help the user "see" where they are. This is the experience of getting lost in hyperspace, even when you know what you are looking for. The representation of "where you are now" (all the links you have followed) or "where you might go" (all the possible links) may look very much like a plate of spaghetti, as system designers ruefully acknowledge. Kintsch's model, in contrast, suggests a way of solving both dilemmas, getting lost in hyperspace and confronting the plate of spaghetti.

To see how Kintsch's model would accomplish this task, imagine the conventional hypertext graph as an associative net, a Kintschian knowledge net. Next, think of an activation vector, perhaps a user's query or a history of the user's recent path through the net. Now, apply the activator to the net and watch what happens. Imagine an activation process, stimulated by the new query or by the history of previous interests, rippling through the net, revealing local "hot spots" of relevance, showing in high relief the portions that pertain. The overall result, through processes of vector-matrix multiplication, shows large-grain patterns of relations elicited by a query or by a continuity of interest. In this way, the user's quest drives the integration instead of getting lost among the possibilities. The system melds the quest with *relevant* material.

The cognitive architecture described by Kintsch's comprehension model paraphrases, for me, the dynamic architecture of Langer's mental act. Kintsch's construction and integration operations that produce meaningful structure are like Langer's individuation and involvement processes that evolve living form. Langer's terms are rooted in biology and Kintsch's in mathematical modeling; nevertheless, they share this implication, that thought is a dynamic system of involvements. A richer concept of hypertext can grow out of this shared implication. Conceptually enriched hypertext systems might be designed that would not disrupt comprehension in ways that Charney, in chapter 10, cautions against in current systems. Rather, systems might accommodate thick cognition, both the messier construction phases and the neater coherence phases.

Such a system will be hard to build, but not impossible. Implementation will probably require integrating hypertext with artificial intelligence methods, particularly connectionist and neural-net activation procedures. Instantiations of this approach already exist; a dynamic medical therapeutics handbook for physicians' use is one example (Frisse; Frisse and Cousins). My primary aim here, however, is not to specify the technical implementation but to bring into view a fresh *concept* of hypertext. As Mark Frisse notes, "How people conceptualize hypertext will affect how they design indexes and information retrieval methods for those systems" (59).

If implemented, the concept of hypertext sketched here could lead to interaction between mind and system that might accommodate thick cognition, or the phenomenology of users, which I have identified as the real-life test of hypertextual capability.

And, it follows, such systems could augment the user's thinking. In the practice of browsing databases, for example, a user could be presented with content and theme links, not only structure or keyword links. Users could teach the system what they want to know, and the system, using context-sensitive procedures, could show users unrecognized as well as anticipated connections and relations. The result would be cooperative inquiry by mind and machine, a coevolution of intellectual possibility.

If reconceived hypertext systems are developed, users may need to develop, too. Some intellectual behaviors may reap more benefits from such systems than others. Education may help users grow in the power to work creatively with hypertext systems.

Implications for Teaching and Learning

> *The greatest need in hypertext today is not for further technical wizardry, but for authors who can exploit the medium successfully.*
>
> —P. J. Brown

Recently, with a group of other composition teachers, I prototyped an individual learning tool that uses *Hypercard* stacks to address styles of punctuation (C. F. Smith et al.). The tool aimed to teach not how to punctuate but why people punctuate as they do. We wanted to stimulate critical, comparative thinking about writing style, even small features of style such as punctuation; we wanted to show that writing styles represent communities and cultures as well as individuals.

On a university campus, for example, a student writing in a composition course and in a mass communications course may be directed to use commas differently in the two settings, because usage handbooks in composition and journalism differ in their prescriptions for separating items in a series. Students function daily and uncritically in this partitioned academic universe, where inconsistency seems normal. We sought to encourage students to question these learning conditions by motivating them, as writers, to think critically across academic disciplines and professions. The kind of thinking we wished to stimulate seemed inherently hypertextual. An individual hypermedia learning tool seemed the right medium.

In our prototype, what the user saw on the screen was a sample of text including marks of punctuation. Selecting any mark automatically introduced a new set of choices. After selecting a particular comma, for example, the user was invited to choose a viewpoint on that comma from among three options: Thought into Language (how syntax structures logic at the selected point in the sample); Convention (how rules and conventions govern the particular comma selected); or Culture (whose rules govern, or how historic and social backgrounds inform language conventions). Icons at the margin of the sample text represented these viewpoints, ready to be chosen as guides to the punctuation mark selected. Users decided whether to select a viewpoint, which one(s), and in what order.

Reflecting later on the world of choice we had built in the prototype, we saw a reductive, Cartesian set of either-or's. Field tests among users showed it to us.

Two effects revealed in user testing are relevant here. The first was some users' reports of getting lost in multiperspectival space. Those users were baffled by being presented with three equally significant options. Worse yet, in the second effect, even more users felt no motivation to choose at all. After selecting a punctuation mark, they wondered, Why do I need all these perspectives on punctuation? Isn't the rule all I need to know?

In short, the hypertextual structure of our tool was predictably confusing and, indeed, not capable of motivating hypertextual thinking. Perhaps we should not have aimed for an individual learning tool intended for independent use. Perhaps classroom teaching would have helped. Must a human teacher accompany educational applications of hypertext if they are to be effective? Does hypertext favor a prepared mind? What kind of preparation is best? One way to consider the question of preparation is to expose the unfamiliar demands made by hypertextual thinking to the light of familiar approaches that may apply. Generative crossover might be the result. As Johnson-Eilola observes in his overview to this section, the new often appropriates the old when it comes to hypertext.

A familiar approach is rhetorical tradition. From the viewpoint of classical rhetoric, hypertextual thinking may be categorized as invention or exploration and discovery. Process theories of rhetoric see invention as, to some degree, conscious, systematic, and teachable. Extending that view to hypertextual thinking seems valid. A writing teacher, for example, will thereby gain familiar tools for encouraging discovery that can be reapplied in situations of hypertext use.

One such traditional tool is the use of heuristics, or exploratory questions and operations to aid thinking about ill-defined problems. An important early-1970s contribution to process theories of rhetoric, *Rhetoric: Discovery and Change*, by Richard Young, Alton Becker, and Kenneth Pike, elaborates three functions of heuristic procedures: to aid recall, to identify needs-to-know, and to prompt intuition toward the formation of an ordering principle or hypothesis (120).

One heuristic for exploratory thinking offered in *Rhetoric* is a three-perspective grid incorporating particle, wave, and field views. The suggested use of the grid is to analyze a unit of experience through each perspective in order to gain alternative views of it. A particle view holds a unit of experience still and looks, as in a still-frame of a moving picture, at its internal components or characteristics. A wave view looks at the same unit in the moving picture, analyzing its dynamic features and its interactions with other units. A field view looks at the same unit as one member of a larger system or as a system itself:

> To take a field perspective on a unit means to focus on the relationships (patterns, structures, organizational principles, networks, systems, functions) that order the parts of the unit and connect it to other units within a larger system. Views of the unit as dynamic, merging and interacting with other units in a constant state of flux (wave), and as a discrete, static entity (particle) are for the moment held at the margin of our attention; ordering principles and relationships (field) are in nuclear focus.   (123)

This procedure, which many writing teachers (myself included) have found to be useful, nevertheless leaves something to be desired, because the strength of the particle, wave, and field grid is also its weakness. The problem is equipotentiality. All the perspectives seem equally important or interesting. Variability prevents closure. In connectionist terms, the grid has nothing to activate it. Nothing leads to the disclosure of large-grain relevance. Multiperspectival thinking of the particle, wave, and field kind is equivalent to the so-called nonlinear thinking of hypertext, an experience that leads to getting lost in hyperspace. The particle, wave, and field grid is shadowed by the same Cartesian model of mind, or the view of an external operator performing operations on free-standing objects of thought, that underlies the original nodes-and-links concept of hypertext.

The limitations of a particular heuristic do not invalidate the general usefulness of heuristics, however. I propose that the teaching of heuristics may aid significantly in preparing students to manage their thinking and their hypertext systems in creative cooperation. This is not to propose that we all teach the same heuristics. Rather, it is to suggest that, if we are going to use hypertext systems in the classroom, perhaps we need also to teach procedures of hypertextual thinking.

What I want in a hypertextual heuristic is openness, with functions for discovering direction. Overall, I find Langer's "act" to have the right characteristics for a heuristic to promote hypertextual thinking. In contrast to particle, wave, and field, the act reflects a relational model of mind, not a reductive one. In Langer's view of acts of thinking, objects are saturated by their relations, grounded in a context; most important, they are motivated by a particular situation. In turn, acts affect these conditions as the act evolves. A new act creates a new ambient, altering as it is altered by its surroundings. An act is reflexive, capable of linking kinds of knowledge or levels of experience in new combinations that still bear kinship with their previous, uncombined differences. Equally important, acts differentiate and develop as organic wholes without forming closed systems. Through their specific involvements, they remain permeable while being distinguishable.

Hypertext, we may increasingly find, favors the prepared mind. Heuristics prepare the human mind to work the gestalts that the hypertext medium makes visible. In his response to this section, L. M. Dryden makes a similar proposal, suggesting that templates, such as teacher-crafted *Hypercard* stacks, can prompt students' creative responses. And while not a template, Moulthrop and Kaplan's teacher-composed interactive fiction seems to have fostered improvisation ("Karl's Forking

Path") intense enough to qualify as Langerian living form, or vital connection between a stimulation and a response.

Engineering instructors concerned with students' problem-solving abilities have long accepted the need for teaching thinking methods directly. In the history of writing and reading instruction, however, preferences for teaching procedure or method directly, for teaching *how to*, wax and wane. Currently, direct methods are out of fashion wherever they are associated with discredited process theories—the "stages" model of composition as prewriting, writing, and rewriting, for example.

Nevertheless, hypertext systems in the classroom force process back into view. Heuristics, templates, and other interventions that encourage thinkers to externalize and manage intellectual processes may be needed, in order to develop human capabilities for designing a conscious intellectual quest (inevitably with some less conscious goals and sources) and for directing the quest in cooperation with an active, facilitative hypertext system.

If hypertextual thinkers develop along with hypertext systems, we will enable as-yet-undefined intellectual experience. Mutually involved minds and machines imply a set of intellectual practices that are different from human practices alone. In his response to this section, David Dobrin, reacting skeptically to the term *hypertextual thinking*, suggests that these practices are "simply a skill in handling certain text structures." I am not so sure. How computer-mediated human thinking differs from other kinds is still very much open to theoretical and research consideration. To help us form the right questions to ask about it, I renew a recommendation made near the beginning of this chapter—that, to identify characteristics of hypertextual thinking, we look to recent redefinitions of literate thinking, especially those that realign literacy's relations to textuality.

Hypertextual Thinking and Orality

Deborah Brandt argues convincingly for uncoupling literacy and textuality. Brandt takes the position that textual knowledge—from possessing the developed skills of decoding and encoding to acquiring objects of information from text sources—is not the whole picture of literacy. "Literate knowledge—that is, knowing how to read and write—is a knowledge embodied in a doing" (193).

For Brandt, qualities of involvement and activation reveal literate knowledge as being closer to orality than to print. In oral language use, knowing what to do next is bound to a present context, to a here and now. I draw on Brandt's argument to suggest that hypertextual thinking, in analogy to Brandt's literate knowledge, is a meaning-making process of practical action carried out in local contexts, a knowing embodied in a doing. Like Brandt on the subject of literate knowledge, I suggest that hypertextual thinking is perhaps more like talk than print, and it may be capable of preserving the connections among context, language, and knowledge that hold in oral language use.

Walter Ong, in *Interfaces of the Word*, set the terms of current debate in literacy studies with his thesis that print technologies restructure consciousness originally framed by oral utterance, thereby profoundly alienating human "noetic" (knowledge) processes from speech and orienting them toward print. I don't want to join controversies engendered by Ong's thesis, but I do want to end this chapter with a call for theory development and research (both observational and experimental) to explore continuities between the oldest representational medium, spoken speech, and the newest, electronic multimedia.

Some early theorists of hypertext saw it as a print form, a new kind of book, that other theorists suggest will bring book culture to an end. To balance book-related theorizing, I would like to see speech-related theorizing of hypertext as a form of talk. To identify fruitful research topics, I suggest attending to the actual talk that accompanies authoring, reception, and use of hypertext systems and products. How do people talk as they work in or around the hypertext medium, either as system designer-developers or as users? How do they talk to the machine, to people in the room, to distant people, even to themselves (as in the mumbles that opened this chapter)?

Talk, theorized as conversation and analyzed as discourse, may provide the models of interaction that we need, in order to improve the design of hypertext systems and to extend the reach of its applications.

NOTE

[1] I am grateful to John B. Smith for pointing out the relevance of Kintsch's revised model for hypertext system design.

Literature, Student-Centered Classrooms, and Hypermedia Environments

L. M. Dryden

The chapters in this section assess hypertext as a tool for engaging in numerous forms of literate behavior and for accommodating (and even simulating) literate thinking. Both Davida Charney and Catherine Smith contemplate the problems of retrieving and manipulating information from hypertext databases, while Johndan Johnson-Eilola joins Stuart Moulthrop and Nancy Kaplan in considering the uses of hypertext fiction in college composition and literature classes. David N. Dobrin, in the second response to this section, casts a dissenting skeptic's eye over the ability of electronic technology to promote literacy.

In the process, the authors examine the phenomenology and epistemology of hypertext and its correspondences with evolving theories of cognitive science, rhetoric and composition studies, and poststructuralist literary criticism; they also consider the political implications of hypertext within the classroom as well as within an academic world that, as Judith Langer notes, is often "schizophrenically" divided. At both public school and college levels, this division occurs between what Sheridan Blau calls "process-oriented" approaches to teaching writing, on the one hand, and "right-answer" approaches to teaching literature, on the other. With one exception, the reflections of the authors in this section suggest that, despite various experimental setbacks, hypertext has the potential to transform the ways in which literacy is understood and the ways in which literate thinking and behavior are taught and practiced in the schools as well as in the larger culture.

All these issues, however, are subsumed by a recurring concern for the promotion of humane and democratic literacy education; many of them recall the notions of literacy as the "active construction of meaning" and of intelligence as "nonlinear" (17) presented in *The English Coalition Conference: Democracy through Language*, edited by Richard Lloyd-Jones and Andrea Lunsford. Implicitly or explicitly, these writers express hope for the attainment of this progressive goal through hypertext's potential to restructure classrooms and, indeed, entire academic institutions. In my own experience and that of my colleagues during the past four years, hypermedia as a tool for students to make their own meaning out of literature (and out of texts in other disciplines across the curriculum) has sparked a powerful synergy. Interactive multimedia reports—the computerized linking of students' notes on the text, scanned graphics, excerpts from films on videodisc and sound on compact disc, even computer-generated animation—provide an electronic platform for the collaborative exploration and interpretation of literary and nonliterary texts. In such an arena, hypermedia unleashes formidable imaginative and creative energy to support literate activities.

Like anything powerful and new, of course, hypermedia also sometimes confounds its users and creates the sense of being "lost in hyperspace" that several contributors in this section have reported. The shock of the new is often just such a mixture of "vertigo and euphoria," the terms Johnson-Eilola adopts in his overview to this section; it provokes both stimulation and exhaustion, buoyant exhilaration and galling frustration. Hypertext is for many a new and sometimes disturbing frontier with no traditional borders. Stephen Marcus expressed hypertext's multivalence in a series of articles aptly entitled "What Are Hypercard?"—deliberately using the "rhetoric of error" to "encourage rethinking about technology and its applications" (1.16); he spoke of its power to make the "strange familiar" and the "familiar strange" (3.24–25). John M. Slatin, in "Reading," described hypertext as "a new medium for thought and expression" (870)—suggesting it was a new technological platform for literacy because it existed only online, in the computer. Comparing the assumptions about readers, reading, and thinking that underlie "conventional text" and hypertext, Slatin explained why hypertext often provokes bipolar responses such as elation and disorientation. Hypertext, which is "discontinuous," "nonlinear," and "associative," allows readers to start at any point they wish. Such freedom can be both liberating and disquieting, for it overturns conventional expectations—in this case, that texts have a beginning, a middle, and an end—along with assumptions that texts are fixed, permanent, and linear (872–74).

Of course, these implications of hypertext are more likely to perplex doggedly Gutenberg text-based scholars and teachers than to bother contemporary teenagers who have grown up with computerized choose-your-own-adventure video games. In responding to the other writers in this section (and, for now, putting aside generational issues), I wish to give testimony concerning the experiences I have shared with my colleagues and our students in California, for these experiences suggest that in collaborative, student-centered classrooms, hypermedia environments can indeed promote the appreciation of literature (and of texts in other disciplines) as they nurture the growth of the learner in intellect and spirit. Moreover, hypermedia has the potential to transform the structure of both classrooms and entire institutions—schools and universities—and to make the teaching and practice of literate thinking and behavior a truly democratic enterprise that respects and serves the needs of both the individual learner and the larger community of learners. As such, hypermedia promises to help in three urgently needed ways: to empower students to become creators of knowledge and constructors of their own meaning; to reintegrate the fragmented, departmentalized vision of knowledge that schools currently offer students; and to heal the cleavage that Theodore Sizer perceives between the academic literacy of the schools and the broader "public literacy" practiced by the rest of society.

Literacy, Hypermedia, and the Universe of Discourse

As it is currently understood, literacy encompasses a good deal more than simply reading and writing (with or without orality and aurality). Literacy is more than formal schooling, correct usage of grammar, or the superficial knowledge of significant names and events in high or popular cultural history. It involves the deep and wide reading not simply of texts but of the world—or, put another way, the reading of texts in relation to the worlds outside and inside the reader. Literacy shows itself in a reader's ability to exploit a text in order to construct his or her own understanding of that text and thereby enlarge both a vision of life and a sense of self. It depends on the complex interaction of the reader's prior knowledge and experience, collaboration with other readers in the discourse community, the texts themselves, and the references in reality to which both readers and texts correspond.

Catherine Smith, in chapter 11 of this volume, affirms such an expanded notion of literacy that is based on a pluralistic understanding of human cognition as "the thinker's multiple physical, social, cultural, and historical life worlds." Moreover, Smith sees in hypertext a model of human cognition and a paradigm for literacy education that reflects and supports an organic view of mind. Conceived in this way, hypertext constitutes an electronic "virtual reality," a simulation that serves as a cognitive model and a heuristic medium that users can interact with and affect, to serve their ongoing explorations of texts—those in books (themselves "virtual thought"), those in the world at large, and those, if you will, in the minds of the readers. In its structure of branching links and nodes, hypertext simulates the mind's associative processes, thereby providing an electronic platform for constructing and recording the reader's literate thinking—the continuously evolving process that Blau calls the "vision and revision" of text by which readers construct meaning.

Hypertext, then, by virtue of its associative, multilinear branching and linking, offers a powerful medium for an expanded notion of literacy. In its polyvalence and its ability to integrate electronically the media of print, video, and sound, hypertext provides structures for a rich interplay of Smith's "multiple . . . life worlds," by facilitating the many intellectual competencies, or "multiple intelligences," identified by Howard Gardner in the course of his work on Project Zero at Harvard University. These intelligences include the conventional triad of linguistic, logical, and intrapersonal skills already valued by the schools, augmented by currently undervalued visual-spatial, interpersonal, musical, and kinesthetic ways of knowing, acting, and solving problems, as explained by Peter Smagorinsky (1–6). While using skills or "intelligences" beyond the linguistic domain in language arts classroom activities is not in itself new, hypertext in the form of interactive multimedia provides a novel and influential format—something like the electronic equivalent of Post-it notes, butcher paper (for hand-drawn graphics), and high-tech bulletin boards through which students explore, record, modify, and publish their literate thinking in linguistic and nonlinguistic media. Marcus presents metaphors for the ways in which hypertext can serve human creativity, noting the characterization of *Hypercard* by its creator, Bill Atkinson, as a "software erector set" that can be used to build many different things. Marcus offers other figurative descriptions of *Hypercard* as a "loom for weaving patterns of the imagination" and the "Swiss Army knife of educational software" (1.16, 18).

It follows, then, that for those of us involved in literacy education, hypertext's polyvalence—its integration of multimedia and its invitation for students to use cognitive skills not traditionally associated with the study of literature—supports an enlarged view of literacy in the worlds inside and outside academia that are becoming, whether we like it or not, simultaneously more diverse and more interdependent. In this regard, hypertext helps us achieve a number of commendable, progressive educational goals. It facilitates the participation in "intellectual tasks related to (though not limited to) writing and reading" that Smith, in chapter 11, claims to be the basis of literacy.

Hypertext also supports a number of student-empowering theories and classroom practices that have evolved in universities and have guided the various curricular reform movements in the public schools of California since the 1970s: the growing influence of reader-response criticism, as well as the emphasis on process writing and the rhetorical tradition—particularly invention—that Smith identifies as a salient feature of hypertext thinking; the expansion of the literary canon and the rise of multicultural and other integrated interdisciplinary curricula; the awareness of the limitations of the lecture method, particularly compared with the power of collaborative learning; the restored reputations of such progressive student-centered thinkers from the 1930s as Louise Rosenblatt, who affirmed the importance of reading the world (including that of students' own experience) through literature (v–xiv), and John Dewey, who favored a project approach to learning in which students made their own discoveries (rather than memorize and recite facts) as a way of developing the intellectual and social skills needed for lifelong learning (*Experience* 51–54).

Not least of these developments has been the increasing application of language-acquisition theory to language arts pedagogy. As Smith observed, hypertext emulates, for writing teachers and students, Lev Vygotsky's "zone of proximal development," offering "real people's ideas progressively disclosed in electronic work/play, and helped by other people and by the medium" (see C. Smith 243; Vygotsky, *Mind* 86–87). Smith predicted that teaching would "necessarily change as the medium of writing and reading moves away from printed pages and toward electronic environments" (243). (Another major trend of the past twenty years, poststructuralist literary criticism, has not so much influenced the pedagogical uses of hypertext as validated it; by the implication that there is no single "correct" interpretation of a text, the diverse schools of postmodern literary thought accord with the polyvalence of hypertext.)

These important trends in literacy education informed the thinking and the choices of the founders and designers of the two institutional affiliations in which I have worked in hypertext. In 1988, the intellectual and pedagogical foundations of the state-funded Model Technology in the Schools project (MTS), for the Alhambra School District in

Alhambra, California, were put in place by professors Cara Garcia, Terence Cannings, and Linda Polin of the Graduate School of Education and Psychology, Pepperdine University, Culver City; they were joined by project coordinators Gary Carnow and Gail Lovley, by curriculum specialists, and by the principals of the high school and the elementary school chosen for the project.

The project was described by Seymour Papert, in his "Background to the Proposal," as an experiment to examine how "technology can support the goals of 'student-centered,' 'humanistic,' 'open' education." It was consciously set in opposition to prevailing uses of technology that had, to that time, supported a curricular-centered model in which the educational process was seen "primarily in terms of conveying information to the learner, developing specific skills, inducing the child into disciplined acceptance of a way of knowing, imposed from the outside." Instead, the MTS project was designed in terms such as "empowerment and development of the individual as an active learner" (i–ii).

MTS recruited—as volunteers—teachers from virtually all departments in the school, trained them in a wide array of Macintosh-based technologies (including *Hypercard*), and encouraged them to find ways to meet the state's new subject-area frameworks through a "cross-curricular" format that addressed the "totality" of a learner's development: "intellectually, linguisitically, physically, socially, and emotionally." The guiding premise for MTS was that a "whole" person would be served not by a "piecemeal" curriculum but by one in which students' learning is "based upon who they themselves are, using and growing from their own lively interests mixed together" (Cannings, Polin, et al. 9–10).

Similar pedagogical goals and values informed the Los Angeles County Macintosh Multimedia Institute (MMI), which I joined in 1989. Like the MTS at Alhambra High, the MMI was designed to explore the ways in which "the creative and responsible use of technology," particularly hypertext, could increase learning in the classroom and give students mastery over their own learning processes. The founders of the MMI were also the directors of the regional branch of the California Literature Project—Lloyd Thomas, Mel Grubb, and Phillip Gonzales. They selected thirty elementary and secondary English and language arts teachers from throughout the county, trained them in *Hypercard*, and obtained the cooperation of Apple Computer, which provided a Macintosh computer for each member to use at home, and the commitment of the teachers' districts to equip the participants' classrooms with full multimedia workstations. The MMI triumvirate then had the teachers meet and work collaboratively once a month for the succeeding years, sharing stacks they and their students had developed on literature.

The MMI project was guided by California's *English–Language Arts Framework*, the source of ultimate authority in the reform of the curriculum, which endorsed the use of technology as a way to "lead students toward better understanding of important literary works by asking interactive questions and developing critical thinking skills through students' responses to reading." The *Framework* encouraged teachers using computers in the classroom to move past the "short-answer workbook stage" of software and into "the more important types of response, analysis, and thought" (20). Deliberately shunning the "electronic worksheet," the MMI and the MTS projects sought to exploit the possibilities of interactive multimedia for students to work with, collaboratively, at high levels of critical thinking. In both projects, the stated goal was to help students use the computer as a "tool" to make their own meaning out of the subjects under study, an aim that meant turning the technology over to the students themselves as quickly as possible.

Five years after my colleagues and I began our work in interactive multimedia, Alhambra High is infused with the very "culture of technology" that Papert envisioned as the natural condition of "schools of the future"—places in which computers would be as common as pencils. Macintoshes, videodisc players, and other peripherals are found throughout the campus—in a full-size multimedia lab, in department offices, in numerous classroom minilabs. My colleagues and I, as well as our students, can carry our work on a floppy disk from office to classroom (then home and back to school the next day) in such an integration of our working life that it is easy for us to forget—even as the dilapidated classrooms housing all this technology literally crumble—that most other public schools are not nearly so privileged.

I have seen my classroom and my role in it thoroughly transformed. The room now contains five Macintoshes, one of which is connected to a full multimedia workstation with a videodisc player, a television monitor, and a liquid-crystal display (LCD) overhead projector. Rather than serve as the manager or, if you will, the intellectual filter of everything that happens in "real time" in the course of a fifty-five-minute class (as I used to attempt), I find myself now as an occasional discussion leader but more often as a facilitator of group activities—with and without the technology. Once students have begun work on their collaborative multimedia projects, my primary job—beyond helping groups with technical or content-related questions—is to stand back and get out of their way. (Last spring the students took over so thoroughly that, for want of anything else to do, I videotaped them at work and used the tape as the basis for conference presentations illustrating the process by which multimedia reports were constructed.)

Those who have never seen a multimedia report might have wondered well before this point in the discussion just what one looks and sounds like. If the current essay were a multimedia presentation, now would be the time to click a video button to activate a section of a videodisc in which readers could view students working in collaborative groups as they negotiate the meaning of literary texts, record their thinking electronically, develop and then present multimedia reports to the rest of the class. Alas, words unassisted by live-action video sequences must suffice here in the current Gutenberg artifact.

The blinds are drawn, the lights lowered to allow the transitional English class to see the LCD projection on the movie screen at the far end of the room. In the semidarkness, Dragana Djukelic reads from the movie screen on which the entire class sees an enlargement of the current *Hypercard* card on the computer—two intersecting circles of a Venn diagram displaying the similarities and differences between the French and Chinese versions of "Cinderella" (chosen from the dozen cross-cultural versions the class has been studying). Dragana and then Ronald Chen stand and extemporize about likenesses (and differences) between such mythic elements as the fairy godmother and the fishbone. They identify cultural matters—for example, the Asian model of filial obedience that runs through these and other versions. While Dragana and Ronald speak, Menh Diep sits at the computer and uses the mouse to highlight each similarity and difference for the class. Menh clicks on pop-up fields that spring open, bearing quotes from texts; these give rise to further comments from the group's rotating speakers.

While they speak, Daniel Valles places a videodisc of Rodgers and Hammerstein's musical version of "Cinderella" into the videodisc player, starts it, then puts it on pause; Menh clicks on the mouse and activates the video button that plays the ending on the television monitor—Cinderella's triumphal transformation, a synthesis of the similarities between the French and the Chinese versions, a promise that dreams and miracles can happen. On another card, pop-up fields are launched, one to offer a cautionary, deliberately anticlimactic statement from Colette Dowling's *The Cinderella Complex*, which has been selected to warn against the legend's implications that women should depend on men to save them; another pop-up field, a dissenting report, suggests that, no, the stories' features of mythic or supernatural assistance merely symbolize the inner strength that the Cinderella figure finds within herself.

In another class period, collaborative groups in senior English use the same equipment for even more elaborate analyses of the relation between Roman Polanski's film of *Macbeth* and Akira Kurosawa's Japanese adaptation, *Throne of Blood*. On the movie screen, larger-than-life images of Macbeth, Banquo, and the witches (scanned from an "illustrated comics" version of the play) glare menacingly at the class, next to the scrolling field bearing passages taken from Shakespeare's text, followed by concise notes for the presentation.

Karyn Yamate, who has remained after school on several days to revise this stack, now reads and enlarges on these notes, then turns the job of analysis over to Jong-Fu Fang. At the given cue, Kenny Vuong clicks the mouse to activate the economically framed thirty-second video sequences involving the witches, first from *Macbeth*, then from *Throne of Blood*, to highlight the different points of emphasis in the two versions—the sense of psychological and moral evil in the former, the feeling of inevitable fate (in the witch's spinning wheel) in the latter. Again, pop-up windows fly open to follow the video clips with the presenters' notes on the group's interpretations of them. With the click of another button, the presentation branches to character analysis cards (or a series of "diary entries," composed by the group to look as if they had been written by the characters in the play) in which the motives, traits, and changes of Lord and Lady Macbeth appear on scrolling text fields, illustrated with more scanned images and appropriate video clips. The students take turns impersonating the characters as they read the imaginary diary entries and comment on the video scenes ostensibly from their lives.

As the presentations proceed, the rest of the students sit at their desks, take notes, and make reflective journal entries by hand (though in some classes taught by my colleagues, their students take such notes with laptop computers). Later, the students will be given credit for these notes, which will serve as the basis for further class discussion and eventually as starting points for the students' individual essays. These are the products that groups have spent weeks on perfecting. What a viewer does not see in this imaginary multimedia "video sequence" could be shown in another sequence activated by a button labeled "Process." It would depict scenes of the long process of collaboration that went into the creation of these student stacks: the group discussions after students had read the text and viewed the videodisc for the first time, and the initial attempts at interpretation; the slow unfolding of trial and error to see whether a thesis can be developed and supported with suitable evidence from the printed text and from the video version; the deliberate tasks—with separate groups clustered about the five Macintoshes distributed around the classroom—of outlining and filling out a multimedia presentation that conveys the group's thinking persuasively in words and images; and the regular, formal self-evaluations and peer evaluations that run throughout the process of creation and follow the final presentation itself.

Interactive multimedia, then, enables students to construct meaning as active, collaborative participants, using a wide array of learning styles and strategies—linguistic, logical, visual-spatial, auditory, interpersonal, and kinesthetic. Engaging the full range of Catherine Smith's "multiple . . . life worlds," interactive multimedia offers avenues of expression and opportunities for success, as Smagorinsky observes, to students whose learning styles tend to be nonlinguistic—that is, the majority of students who have never excelled in the almost exclusively print-based universe of traditional English classes (5–6).

By giving collaborative groups the means to make and record their discoveries about the text and then present their interpretations to the rest of the class in the form of multimedia reports, interactive hypertext facilitates a complete integration of the language arts of reading, writing, speaking, and listening. Moreover, as Smith predicts for hypertext, both the processes and the products of student presentations cross the boundaries between sound and print. Such efforts at "hypertextual thinking" seem to preserve what Smith, in chapter 11 of this volume, calls the "connections among context, language, and knowledge that hold in oral language use." With its revival of orality or, more exactly, its integration of orality and textuality, hypertext in a curious way echoes the customs of earlier cultures with strong oral literary traditions. Perhaps for this reason, a friend of mine, a scholar of classical Greek and Roman civilization, praises interactive multimedia for hearkening back to the pre-Gutenberg age of "the good old tradition" in which texts were scarce and audiences had to apply their attention and their memories to performances or recitations of literary and religious texts accompanied by visual supplements of dramatic paraphernalia or liturgical iconography (Raubitschek). Elements of the orality that predates the printing press may resound when a classroom audience attends respectfully to the spoken word, augmented by imagery from the computer and video monitors and by text from the overhead screen that come together in multimedia presentations by the audience's peers.

There is, of course, a complex dynamic at work in such instances, and it would be difficult to identify the most important element among so many—the mythic power of the spoken word invoked, if you will, around the electronic campfire of an LCD display in a semidarkened room; the well-documented efficacy of collaborative learning and peer instruction; the cognitive and affective appeal of video and computer technology for teenagers in the late twentieth century. For now, it is enough to say that the combination of these elements unleashes a synergistic burst of creative literate behavior and expression that is greater than the sum of the individual parts of the sources.

The Potential of Hypertext Literacy for Restructuring Classrooms, Schools, and Universities

For literacy educators, as Catherine Smith observes, interest in classroom applications might focus either on "passive" hypertext (browsing databases) or on "active" hypertext (authoring one's own stacks). Either type, of course, can support creative thinking, but active hypertext clearly offers greater opportunities for discovering "personal knowledge, constructed by the user" (234–35). The essays by Smith (ch. 11) and others in this section (current volume) offer insights into the most empowering (and least empowering) guiding principles, features, and user options that might be common to both passive and active forms of hypertext—or, in the terms Moulthrop and Kaplan, in chapter 9, borrow from Michael Joyce, "exploratory" and "constructive." Identifying the commonalities that promote (and inhibit) the growth of students as constructors of knowledge would advance the interests of humane, democratic education for literacy; they would help determine how to exploit hypertext's formidable power in order to restructure classrooms and, indeed, entire academic institutions.

Exploratory hypertext tends to be written by professional software designers or college professors; databases on Shakespeare or *Beowulf* and Tennyson's "Ulysses," among many other literary topics, are being released with increasing speed and number. Much of the work is quite impressive and very powerful. The best of such exploratory software has constructive features built into it—that is, it allows students to annotate their readings, keep a record of the hypermedia paths they have been following, and cut and paste elements from the database into their own multimedia reports. Conventional wisdom, however, confirms that often the most interesting hypermedia presentations— and the ones in which the most learning may take place—are those that students create from the ground up, or with minimal start-up templates provided by the teacher. The reason may be simply that the students own their constructive hypertext productions, while they merely rent ones that are professionally designed for exploration.

Such conclusions (and some guiding principles) can be drawn from the experimental failures described in these essays—Smith's hypertext punctuation tutor (ch. 11) and Moulthrop and Kaplan's (ch. 9) invitation to their students to write their responses to hypertext fiction as hypertext. In Smith's account, the tool failed to motivate in the users the kind of thinking that hypertext was capable of supporting; she concluded that the motivation may need to come from outside the tool itself. This form of exploratory hypertext failed, and the users were left floating—lost in hyperspace—because they were not intrinsically motivated to apply the medium as a tool for planning and accomplishing a project of their own selection; the agenda had already been set for them, and their choices were forced, not open. (Such an openness of choice, an invitation to students to think hypertextually on self-selected projects, might be preferable to Smith's recommendation of teaching the methods of hypertext thinking directly; the students learn hypertext thinking best—just as they learn language—by using it as a tool to achieve a self-determined goal within the content area.)

In Moulthrop and Kaplan's account, students did have an opportunity to use the hypertext medium in an open and constructive way but were thwarted by a technological omnivore—hypertext's thoroughly assimilative nature—that absorbed all attempts to subvert it. This failure of resistance, as typified by Karl Crary's ultimately unsuccessful efforts to write resistantly against hypertext within its own environment, suggests—as Smith's account does—that there are definite limits to what students should be asked to do with hypertext. Applying the medium to teach resistant reading apparently lies beyond those limits. Hypertext software or assignments are likely to fail if their hidden agenda is to teach some kind of skill rather than to free students to construct and discover knowledge for themselves.

A more fruitful approach to getting students to think hypertextually (and, to some degree, resistantly) can be found in the software program *Irrawaddy*, a *Hypercard* tool for creating branching stories and simulations. Its author, Bernie Dodge, of the educational technology department of the California State University, San Diego, named *Irrawaddy* after the river in Burma that ends in a delta of spectacularly branching channels (sometimes diverging, at other times converging), much like the activities supported by this software itself. Rather than succumb to "mimetic collapse," as Moulthrop and Kaplan's experiment did, *Irrawaddy* openly imitates—indeed, embraces—the polyvalent nature of hypertext to serve as a platform for students' literate thinking.

Dodge has had students in the San Diego public schools use *Irra-waddy* to create their own choose-your-own-adventure games about characters and readings across the curriculum. The program has motivated students to think hypertextually as they use the medium to explore and even subvert not hypertext itself but the literary and historical texts under discussion. The students' collaborative products are often remarkably complex and witty—the result of an integration of work and play at high levels of cognition. And they show the power of this form of hypertext to achieve Moulthrop and Kaplan's stated goal of "engaging students in a more extensive transformation of their textual world." Finally, students' work exemplifies the essentially positive values of electronic text as identified by the authors—extension, collaboration, and community.

Hypertext, when used to its full potential, not only energizes individual learners and gives them greater control over their literate thinking and behavior; it also holds great promise for redistributing power and authority within classrooms. Student-centered, constructive, meaning-based (and, wherever possible, collaborative) applications of hypertext promote a democratic vision of literacy in a host of ways, according to several of the authors in this section. The issue of students' ownership of texts arises frequently as a salient feature of hypertext literacy.

Along these lines of power and authority in the classroom, Johnson-Eilola (in the overview) considers several related issues—reducing the divisions between composition and literature, strengthening students as writers by elevating the importance of their texts, and promoting collaborative efforts to construct knowledge and understanding of literature. Johnson-Eilola's assertions on the power of hypertext to give "voice to those silenced" are borne out by some of my classroom experiences. Using hypertext as a way for students to explore literature does indeed promote a "dialogue between teachers and students resulting in [students'] 'self-realization and self-direction.' " Quite tangibly, as students enter their responses on templates in teacher-developed stacks or in multimedia reports of their own creation, they cease to be consumers of texts but become producers and consumers simultaneously. As they exploit literary texts to extract and then present their own understanding through interactive multimedia, students become both consumers and producers of *meaning*.

Of course, nonelectronic ways of pursuing such meaning making exist in classes informed by the California Literature Project (collaborative butcher-paper presentations of hand-drawn or hand-written graphic organizers, group enactments, etc.). Nonetheless, hypertext removes student prewriting and writing even further from the margins of the conventional classroom (where work in progress is often confined to pairs or groups, and finished work is seen or heard as the occasional good model of an exceptional essay) and puts it, quite literally, on the center stage of the movie screen and the TV monitor.

These tendencies recall Smith's observation that hypertext thinking can be considered in terms of the rhetorical tradition. Here, such thinking can be likened not only to "invention," as Smith notes, but also to "arrangement" and even to "memory" and "delivery" (and even, ultimately, to "style"), as the groups electronically record their thinking, rework it, and then present it by means of interactive multimedia, explaining it extemporaneously to the rest of the class. Thus hypertext enables students to regain control over the full range of the modes of discourse, reintegrating them after more than a century since their artificial division and distribution among the departments of philosophy, speech, and English.

Another sign of the power shift in the classroom that hypertext makes possible is borne out in Johnson-Eilola's observation that "in electronic text discussions—even when they are linear—the presence of the teacher diminishes greatly." (Earlier in this essay I gave testimony to this development in my own classroom.) With each group's chosen words and images projected electronically in a semidarkened classroom, the voices of many students fill the authority position that the teacher has vacated. Student work in interactive multimedia takes on the authority conferred by the very power of the media. Students can publish their work to the rest of the class in a combination of text and graphics on the big screen through the liquid crystal display, excerpts from filmed scenes on videodisc, and oral commentary by the presenters themselves—in a complete integration of word and image, sight and sound that Sizer considers an "artful, powerful" feature of our public literacy (11). To the extent that "the medium is the message," the technology of our culture's all-pervasive and highly commercial "public literacy" can be harnessed to enfranchise student writers and thereby promote the ends of formal literacy education involving literary texts.

Hypertext's ability to provide an electronic platform for the social construction of knowledge is still another way in which the technology confers increased classroom authority on the learners. Class discussions can be recorded on hypermedia and published instantly on the liquid crystal display. Moreover, the ideas thus made visible also remain fluid; they can be expanded at any time and are preserved for review or further development on subsequent days. Multimedia reports written by groups of students represent yet a further kind of collaboration.

The development of such presentations involves many collective decisions and choices by group participants as they gather evidence from the text and the videodisc for character analysis or locate reference material from which they select information and images for their own multimedia reports on background issues. Individuals or pairs may develop cards that are then merged onto the entire group's master stack for presentation. Through hypertext, such collaborative efforts at exploration and meaning making are made visible. As such, they exemplify John McDaid's view that the knowledge embodied in group hypertext exists not as a "preconceived truth" but as a "potential" in which individual reader-writers share and probe their electronic links to produce a network of their continually evolving views (214).

Redistribution of power in the classroom, of course, is defensible only if it promotes students' growth as learners and thinkers and gives them greater mastery over their subject matter. Moulthrop and Kaplan, in "They Became What They Beheld," pose the central question that must be asked in any pedagogical decision, including interactive multimedia: "How might this notion of productive or 'constructive' participation be used to engage students in a more open-ended, less constrained encounter with literature?"

Charles Dickens's critique of utilitarian education, *Hard Times*, provides the best example of the worst way to answer this question. Mr. Gradgrind's model school—neither constructive nor open-ended nor less constrained—effectively "murdered the innocents" by banishing poetry altogether and cramming its hapless students with facts through the tutelage of the aptly named schoolmaster, Mr. McChoakumchild (11–12). By contrast, what we seek in hypertext is not a knowledge-crammed (if eternally patient) tutor at all but an electronic platform that supports the students' capacity for wonder—the very faculty banished from Gradgrind's experimental (and ultimately disastrous) school.

While Moulthrop and Kaplan reach some somber conclusions about the incompatibility of approaches to *fiction* on hypertext with current literary and composition studies, much of what they say confirms the usefulness that colleagues and I have found in hypertext with *interactive multimedia* as a tool for exploring and interpreting traditional literary texts, or, in their words, "engaging students in a more extensive transformation of their textual world." The writers acknowledge the tendency of electronic media toward open-endedness that extends the possibilities of the text for "constructive" transaction, a dynamic, expansive system that, according to Joyce, provides "a structure for what does not yet exist" ("Siren Shapes" 11). All these tendencies—the constructive, evolving, open-ended, and collaborative potentialities of hypermedia—are conducive to the goals of expanding the authority of students in a classroom community by having them use interactive multimedia to create their own understanding of traditional literary works.

In the late 1970s and early 1980s, Papert foresaw and then pioneered the humanistic, student-centered use of computers with young people. In *Mindstorms*, Papert told how he combined his work in artificial intelligence at MIT with his studies of Piaget's theories of children's cognitive development in order to build a better classroom. Focusing not on the machine but on the mind, seeking to emulate the patterns by which children succeed in learning language and developing as thinkers, Papert designed a computer program that he called *Logo*. As an online learning environment, *Logo* represented an early form of virtual reality, a simulation that the user can interact with and affect. It allowed children to program the computer with simple commands that made a turtle and other graphic images and shapes move on the screen in increasing levels of sophistication. Children using this electronic "erector set" explored and constructed knowledge, essentially of dynamic geometry, while growing as logical thinkers—all as a consequence of what appeared to be simple playing. They learned with *Logo* in the way that children naturally learn language, in the Piagetian sense of "learning without being taught"—that is, as a byproduct of doing something meaningful and engaging, to the point that they forget that they are, in fact, learning (*Mindstorms* 7).

Papert's conclusions in his work with children and *Logo* have some important implications for schools in general. *Logo* showed that computers could support student-centered, meaning-based learning, that computers could provide an alternative to prevailing models of teacher-centered classrooms, which Papert described as "artificial and inefficient." By extension, hypermedia and interactive multimedia, now several generations more advanced than *Logo*, show even further promise of realizing Papert's hopes of better and more successful learning environments for young people. Hypermedia refines and extends Papert's dream of electronic platforms for Piaget's theory of children as "active builders of their own intellectual structures" (*Mindstorms* 8, 19).

Papert was aware that the same technology that supported *Logo* could serve the stultifying interests of latter-day Gradgrinds, and his worries are shared by other contemporary thinkers about the nature and future of computer literacy. Indeed, the lines seem to be drawn, as a number of large educational software publishers have effectively computerized the "nonsense industry" with electronic worksheets that present skills out of context. Many of their ventures into multimedia represent what Polin calls a "canned construction of meaning for students to discover" (33), which in most cases is multimedia CAI (computer-assisted instruction). The online curriculum of "drill and kill" is especially dangerous, according to Frank Smith, because it lends the prestige of technology to a pedagogy that takes the meaning out of literature and the life out of learning and brings on the death of the spirit at an early age. Because these publishers wield enormous influence with school bureaucracies, a fundamental struggle has arisen between the advocates of computerized skills-based instruction and the proponents of humanistic, student-centered uses of interactive multimedia. The outcome of this clash over the future of computers in education is by no means certain (F. Smith, *Insult* 112–20).

As hypertext redistributes classroom authority and energizes its users' imaginations and intellects, it has broad implications for both classrooms and academic institutions. By giving students access to interactive multimedia technology to record and publish their literate thinking, we have created what Moulthrop and Kaplan, in chapter 9, call the "democratic press," which elevates the value of student-produced electronic texts. Since these student texts are essentially interpretations of static texts, they pose no real threat to the "gatekeepers" of traditional literature, while, at the same time, they affirm the "plurality and participation" that are urgently needed in the schools today. And because much of this "writing" remains online, published for a classroom audience by means of the liquid crystal display, one need not worry about a Great Flood of computer printouts glutting the textual market or contributing significantly to global deforestation.

The Freirian "banking concept" also ceases to apply, as the technology, properly used, frees the teacher and the students from a Gradgrindian educational process in which students are considered empty vessels to be filled by the teacher with preconstituted facts. Learning need not be knowledge transfer (and recall on demand) in a mercantilistic scheme (see Freire, *Pedagogy* 57–74 [Continuum ed.]). Instead, it can be an adventure into the unknown, a collaborative enterprise supported by the creativeness of interactive multimedia. Literary encounters, as Moulthrop and Kaplan attribute to *Reading Texts*, the anthology edited by Kathleen McCormick, Gary Waller, and Linda Flower, "require 'making sense,' a thoughtful engagement with the 'repertoire' of codes and references in the text. This encounter consists not of absorption but of interaction, since the reader receives a literary work through the screen of his or her own repertoire of assumptions, beliefs, predispositions, and influential prior texts." Interactive multimedia, holding the potential for a polyvalent and unpredictable play of ideas, can serve as a tool of student-centered literary interpretation—allowing collaborative groups to interact with the text and to create links between it, their prior knowledge and experience, and their ongoing discoveries, unmediated by the teacher as the supposed "central banker."

In my own recent experience with a classroom multimedia minilab, I found myself as a teacher without any banking functions at all, except perhaps the modest role of a teller who distributed and collected the groups' floppy disks each day and who loosely regulated access to the main workstation. Class time was used entirely by collaborative groups to plan and create their multimedia productions and then to present them to each other. With the students' "takeover" of the Freirian bank virtually complete, I was relegated to the margins, where, as noted earlier, I was free to videotape the students at work and advise them as needed.

To those who worry that such a power shift in the classroom might one day make teachers redundant, I would say that good teachers will always be needed to create and maintain student-centered environments, particularly when such environments require current (and operational) software and hardware. Indeed, with the end of the role of the teacher as crowd manager, police officer, or air-traffic controller, the interactions of teachers and students can become more effective and more humane for all involved.

For entire academic institutions, hypertext holds out possibilities for complete restructuring that may be even more dramatic than those already realized in some classrooms. In Catherine Smith's vision of a fully computerized university, outlined in "Reconceiving," students might do all their work online (without paper), reading the text of academic journal articles and then writing their own responses at the computer workstations in dormitories, libraries, and other campus sites. Entire classes could agree to do all their "thinking, reading, writing, and communicating electronically" (244). Through campus e-mail students might send each other frequent and detailed questions and responses concerning readings, prewriting ideas, and drafts.

This model could be extended to include all activities in a university. In the roundtable discussion on multimedia held at the University of California, Los Angeles, in 1990, a gathering of luminaries in the educational and the computer worlds—including James Catterall and Richard Lanham of UCLA, Mark Dillon of GTE ImagiTrek, and Alan C. Kay of the Apple Vivarium Project—speculated (Greenberger) that it may in fact be possible to take the knowledge that is now imparted to students in lecture halls, convert it to interactive multimedia databases, and allow students to browse the data to discover and construct their own understanding of their subjects. Such databases would help students achieve an integrated education that is currently thwarted by the departmentalized and highly specialized organization of the academic world.

Technological innovations of this kind would overturn anachronistic theories and practices and would permit fundamental restructuring of teaching and learning. Kay found that the lecture method is still the prevailing model in North America, essentially unchanged from pre-Gutenberg Oxford in 1190 but badly suited to the age of the book, let alone the era of computer literacy. Catterall looked to computers and multimedia as the "liberating" force that would replace the textbook-based, teacher-centered classroom with a system of education that was individualized and student-centered. Dillon proposed that, in the transformed universities of the future, multimedia would take information currently available in libraries and in classrooms and "shift" it "in time," making it available whenever anyone wanted it. Teachers would have a choice of roles, either as "facilitators" who helped students use the technology or as "interactive designers" who organized and presented information for others to access. In either case, multimedia would increase the quantity and the quality of the interactions between teachers and students (Greenberger 71–72).

The idea of having college professors turn their scholarly production into online hypermedia databases is not as outlandish as it may first sound. As George P. Landow observes in his recent *Hypertext*, there is, in fact, a striking similarity between a scholarly article and a hypertext environment (4–10). The footnote, the scholar's digression of choice, serves as an explicit vehicle for the multisequential reading underlying hypertext; a reader can choose to stay with the text of the article or follow the footnotes. More implicitly, such modern works as James Joyce's *Ulysses* bloom, so to speak, with allusions and references to many other texts or events in a nonelectronic but nonetheless polyvalent environment.

Some working models already exist for the eventual university-wide integration of knowledge bases that currently proliferate but remain, as yet, masses of unlinked nodes. IBM's *Ulysses* is a hypermedia environment in which one can explore text and videodisc readings and interpretations of the Tennyson poem and can browse whole libraries of background information on Homer, the heroic age, and related topics. Robert Winter, at the 1990 UCLA conference, explained that he authored the hypertext software *Ludwig van Beethoven: Sym-*

phony No. 9 CD Companion to recapture online what used to disappear into the air of the lecture room (and to allow the user to repeat the musical sequences or the critical commentary as many times as desired, until the material was fully understood; see Greenberger 19). Putting on the earphones and exploring the multiple paths into the symphony's themes and variations (rendered audibly and visually), and the vast array of musicological and biographical information, one feels drawn inexorably inside the great work itself. It is a most exhilarating experience. Similarly, the Shakespeare Project at Stanford University, a hypermedia endeavor founded by Larry Friedlander, enables students to use an open-ended database of text, graphics, and videodisc images to study the full process of theater by means of easy access to different interpretations of the same character or scene. Users can view, in any order they desire, video sequences of productions in rehearsal or of the same scene played by several different actors. Friedlander devised his hypermedia database for students to explore a vast range of Shakespearean drama not as "a series of right or wrong answers nor a mass of raw data, but [as] a choice of diverse roads into theater" (2). Such hypermedia environments, which in many cases permit users to annotate their reactions and record their path, indicate how the academic universe of discourse might be integrated online for users to explore and make connections among diverse bodies of knowledge.

In the spirit of Polin's earlier admonitions, Davida Charney (ch. 10 in this volume) and Catherine Smith (ch. 11) raise several provocative questions about professionally designed hypertext and students' work in it as well as in their own authoring of stackware. Both Charney and Smith offer persuasive criticism of the burdens that hypertext imposes on readers and writers, particularly the ease with which navigators can get lost in a database. Charney presents a compelling analysis of the ways in which hypertext's associative, free-form browsing structure may interfere with the reader's usual cognitive strategies for making sense of a text. Her caution to professional designers on their choices of "right" paths for the "right readers" is well-founded, and many designers are attempting to produce increasingly user-friendly databases. Several, in fact, are working in the direction of Smith's suggested corrective of an "activation process . . . [showing] large-grain patterns of relations" that highlight portions of an "associative net" relevant to the reader's intellectual quest.

Increasingly, such requirements have been confronted and largely resolved by academic and commercial producers of software stacks that, while configured differently, serve purposes similar to those of the student-centered stacks for meaning making that colleagues and I have been developing. Scholastic's *Interactive Nova* series on science and ecology brilliantly exploits hypermedia's potential for linking, through mnemonic-styled buttons, multiple menus and directories, graphic flow-charted representations (which also serve as buttons) of the structure of each node, and such effective cross-referencing of the nodes that users can explore one node as far as they like and return to the main menu at the click of a single, conveniently located button.

Still another multimedia program, the relational base of Scholastic's United States history package *Point of View*, uses the power of interactive hypertext environment, according to Polin, "to *change the way instruction happens*" (33). Interactive Multimedia (affiliated with Wings for Learning), with its *Literature Navigator* series (Polin), and Intellimation are currently developing *Hypercard* stackware on literary works commonly taught in the public schools and for which film adaptations exist on videodisc. The IMM series, of which I have some experience as a consultant, is expected to meet Polin's ideal of examining literature "within the context of concurrent happenings in politics, economics, science, arts and social events," allowing students to appreciate literature "in its context as well as for its durability and relevance across contexts" (33). In all these projects, students can interact with a database arranged hierarchically by subtopic; they can take notes online as they explore, make connections, and draw conclusions about literary works using text, graphics, and videodisc.

Such professional efforts at interactive multimedia databases, like the student-centered stacks that my colleagues and I have attempted in our own classrooms, are designed to put technology at the service of students, to encourage their most creative efforts in exploring the connections between literature, history, the arts and sciences, and—most important—their own lives. As such, hypertext in the form of interactive multimedia represents a vital and encouraging development in the national debate on the proper classroom use of technology and its influence on the future of literacy education.

Hypermedia and the Future of American Society

The stakes involved in classroom experiments with hypertext are higher than one might imagine. As American schools become culturally diverse and as television and computers promote cultural values focused on the visual rather than on written words, the traditions that define literacy in strictly linguistic and logical terms may cause the schools to fall increasingly out of step with the abilities and interests of students and with developments in the broader culture. In "Public

Literacy," Sizer expresses deep concern over such eventualities by observing that our national culture, purveyed by the communications industry, engages our young people far more intensely than do our educational institutions. "Our public literacy," Sizer writes,

> is pedagogically sophisticated, using understandings about human learning and a range of technologies far beyond the schoolteacher's ken. There are tie-ins—film to video to books to T-shirts. Clustered media characterize this pedagogy, the carefully coordinated use of sight and sound and print in artful, powerful combination. It is tough for your average French teacher to compete with MTV. (11)

Hypertext may help teachers—of French and most other subjects—not merely to compete with MTV but to use its technology and techniques to lessen the rift between the schools and the highly visual and auditory culture in which students are immersed. While Dobrin, in his response to this section, raises some thoughtful doubts about the feasibility of hypermedia to do much to improve education, he has not fully addressed the technological imperatives driving our culture and leaving the schools farther behind. It is too simple to reduce hypertext to some kind of Rube Goldbergesque absurdity, even while acknowledging—however correctly—the fragility and clunkiness of the current technology (which time and market forces will remedy). Television is usually singled out for blame in the technophobic jeremiads of such critics as Neil Postman, whose recent books, *Amusing Ourselves to Death* and *Technopoly*, regard with pessimism the effects of the electronic revolution on public discourse and education. But the development of what Smagorinsky calls "complementary computer technology" will further the trend and create a generation "more attuned to images than to words" (4). Interactive multimedia, which turns students into "directors" rather than simply writers, broadens the range of intelligences that the school culture values and may thereby give students a greater sense of self-worth and potential for success in the age of electronic culture than most students experience in their progress through a system that—nearly a century after Alfred Binet devised a test to predict who would fail in school—still measures literacy and general intelligence narrowly through discrete-point, pencil-and-paper assessment.

Pedagogically exploiting the integrated video and computer technology that has suffused our popular culture might help save the schools from David D. Thornburg's worst fear about education—that the schools will become even more irrelevant to the needs and interests of students (7–11). In the light of dismal statistics that high school drop-out rates exceed forty percent in many districts, experiments with hypertext and interactive multimedia—to include more students in the culture of the schools by promoting collaborativeness and validating multiple intelligences in literacy education and the integration of learning across disciplines—may suggest at least one way out of the continuing crisis in which American education seems to be mired. In 1854, Charles Dickens's *Hard Times* foretold the failure of an industrial model of education, a system that was teacher-centered and essentially hostile to the imagination. With the world economy transforming at an astonishing rate in the late twentieth century, new and better metaphors, models, and media for learning are urgently needed. We live in a postindustrial age, and hypermedia is the literacy of the twenty-first century. The schools, the last institution to technologize, must adopt the dominant forms of contemporary communication, or they, and most teachers, will not survive in any recognizable form. Thornburg argues that those of us who teach have a responsibility to prepare young people for *their* future, not *our* past (73–80). I do not believe he means that schools should discard the history of human achievement; rather, as educators we must learn to use the technology of our age, exploiting its full potential to make the past live for young people and to give them the means to discover and create their own future.

Second Response

Hype and Hypertext

David N. Dobrin

A few readers surely remember the excitement we composition teachers felt when style and grammar checkers first came out. We stood at the dawn of a new era. Never again would lives and years be lost in the drudgery of copyediting. The programs would do it for us. Wouldn't they?

Are we at the dawn of another era, the hypertext era? The papers I am asked to comment on would have it so. Something has happened, they tell us, something big. As a commentator, it is my responsibility to ask, What has happened and how big? After all, the enthusiasm for text analysis programs turned out to be dreadfully wrong, for reasons clearly evident at the time (Dobrin, "Limitation"). If the enthusiasm for hypertext is similarly misplaced, it would be well to say so.

The problem with text analysis programs was that they did not in fact do what the developers claimed they did. This problem was obvious. A developer would say, for instance, that the program checked grammar. When you ran the program, it didn't check grammar; it did something else. Unfortunately, technologically unsophisticated teachers caught up in their enthusiasm chose to overlook the obvious problems, hoping they would go away. Have the authors of these papers made a similar error? Have they given sufficient consideration to how hypertext works?

I speak as someone who has spent ten years working closely with software developers and almost as many years teaching illiterate adults. When I was asked to comment on the articles in this section, whose theme was literacy and hypertext, I assumed that the articles would provide answers to questions like the following: What uses are there for hypertext in the classroom? What kinds of hypertext tools would help people learn to read, and how would the tools work? Would

305

it be a good idea, for instance, to have hypertextual explanations embedded in sample text, where people who had trouble with the original could refer to them easily? Does reading a text presented in hypertext form give people more control over it and thus make them more self-reliant?

I also wondered whether it was now our responsibility to teach people how to read hypertexts. After all, comprised in what we now think of as literacy is the ability to manage with many different kinds of text forms, from encyclopedias to the pages of *LA Style* (a large-format magazine that is deliberately adventurous with layout and typographical conventions). Perhaps people should be taught this new text form? If so, what should be taught, and how?

I never properly appreciated the importance of teaching text forms until I began teaching illiterate adults. Naively, I thought that teaching literacy was mostly a matter of getting the students to associate sounds with letters and then to recognize the words that those sounds made up. But these adults also needed to learn what I want to call, for the purposes of this essay, the conventions of text form. They had, for instance, some difficulty distinguishing between certain advertisements and articles in magazines (because they didn't know layout conventions), and they had trouble figuring out the relation in these same magazines between a sidebar, an italicized introduction, and the text of the article. I'll never forget one student's reading the end of an article and mouthing the author's name as if it were a continuation of a sentence.

Those of us used to reading long, consecutive paragraphs of text do not perhaps realize or remember how complicated, contextualized, and conventionalized texts ranging from handbills and magazines to encyclopedias and telephone books really are. We are able, through long practice, to distinguish the column headings of a dictionary from the dictionary entry, to realize that the incomprehensible abbreviations at the end of the entry are not essential to our understanding. Imagine, though, if we were illiterate or, perhaps more salient, imagine we had learned to read Gutenberg's or Aldus Manutius's books and then were confronted with reading matter like the pages of *LA Style*. We would be confused. We might even fail to understand the magazine, simply because we didn't grasp the conventions. (An eminent computer scientist who was studying fonts once showed me the same letters in two different Chinese fonts. I could not tell—I literally could not—what was similar about them. A Chinese person would literally not be able to understand my confusion.)

What, then, of an inexperienced person confronted with hypertext?

If the conventions are sufficiently new, that person might have to be taught, just as conventions of magazine layout have to be taught. And I wanted from the articles in this section some discussion of this set of questions.

Obviously, the articles do not address either set of questions in any detail. We hear of one application in the classroom, but it is of hypertext experimentally pressed into the service of an ideology, not of a general classroom application. We do not hear anything of hypertextual tools that might be useful in the teaching of literacy. The authors simply assume that we will have to bring hypertext into the curriculum, because they can see that hypertext is important. But there are few details.

The articles are largely about the relation between the authors' theoretical approach to writing, on the one hand, and hypertext, on the other. For Stuart Moulthrop and Nancy Kaplan (ch. 9), the approach is rooted in postmodernist literary criticism; notions like "intertextuality" and "resistance" figure heavily in the article. For Davida Charney (ch. 10) and Catherine F. Smith (ch. 11), the approach is cognitivist, both relying heavily on Walter Kintsch.

Why does each author feel the need to bring a theory to bear? Each considers hypertext to be sui generis, something entirely new that, in Johndan Johnson-Eilola's words, "forces theorists and teachers to reconsider and revise, not merely to perpetuate or replace, current theories and practices." Smith suggests that hypertext is a new form of text; that is what "interests" her in exploring what it is to "think hypertextually." Her focus is not on the thing in the computer but on the "built hypertext" (a structural representation of thought by a person using that thing in the computer). Since she is talking about a "virtuality," she needs a theory in order to describe how the "virtuality" works. The somewhat more skeptical and technically oriented Charney feels no need to describe hypertext as a "living form," but she still says that hypertext "has the potential to change fundamentally how we write, how we read, how we teach these skills, and even how we conceive of text itself." Hypertext, she says, "violates standard assumptions of what texts are like." It is necessary, therefore, to create non-assumptions.

If this assessment of hypertext is correct, then of course the heavily theoretical approach is justified. It would be important to conduct experiments in the classroom and to establish a relation between cognitivist theory and hypertext design. Questions like mine, though significant, would have to await a better understanding of how people deal with this "evolutionary outgrowth of late-modern textuality" (Moulthrop and Kaplan, ch. 9). One should till before one sows.

I happen to think that hypertext is not a new text form. It is not an evolutionary advance. It forces no reconsiderations. It has no potential for fundamental change in how we write or read. Hypertext is simply one text structure among many, made unique by the text conventions it has, conventions that guide the reader's attention and allow him or her to navigate through the text. The conventions are interesting, and a proper understanding of them enables us to answer the questions I have about hypertext. But these conventions are not different in kind from other text conventions. Thus, teaching hypertext is very much like teaching encyclopedias or comic books; you have to teach how the conventions work, and, once you do, you've taught people to be literate in hypertext. "Built hypertext" is no important new category of experience; it is a minor subcategory of "read text," something we all know a great deal about.

I want to be clear about this, because something important hangs on what one takes to be different about hypertext. One's view of hypertext's status relative to other texts sets one's project. I think hypertext is not much different from other text, so my concerns are pragmatic and teaching-oriented. The other authors think that hypertext is fundamentally different, so they wish to reconsider what Michel Foucault, Roland Barthes, Paulo Freire, Walter Ong, Jacques Derrida, or Susanne Langer has to say in the light of discoveries about hypertext.

My objection, moreover, is to the project, not to the philosophers or to the ideas. The issues brought up in these chapters are the most fundamental of all, issues about the mind, about the flow of attention, about the use of guideposts, about politics, about power. My argument is merely that hypertext offers no special excuse for addressing these issues and that consideration of hypertext offers no special insight into them. Foucault's insights about text or Ong's apply equally well to Michael Joyce's work and to the pages of *LA Style*. In all probability, bringing Foucault or Barthes to bear on *LA Style* would be much more interesting. The conventions operating on magazine pages are variations on a theme hundreds of years old, so more people have had an opportunity to be creative with them.

Hypertext as Othertext

Why do the writers in this section think that hypertext is a fundamentally different form of text? The answers take three forms.

1. *Authorship is fundamentally different.* In hypertext, the reader chooses how to navigate through the text; in some hypertexts, the

reader can also choose to add to the text, perhaps in a way that makes his or her additions indistinguishable from the original. This much is incontrovertible.

Both Johnson-Eilola and Moulthrop and Kaplan suggest that the author thereby cedes some degree of control of the text to the reader; the standard relation has changed fundamentally. However, numerous print texts also allow readers to navigate through them at will. (Actually, what print text does not?) There is no "right set of paths" (Charney, ch. 10) through an encyclopedia or through the pages of *LA Style*. Many noncomputer text forms (as Benjamin, cited in Moulthrop and Kaplan, ch. 9, notes) allow people to become authors, and the word processor and desktop publishing have allowed far greater proliferation of "authorized text" than hypertext ever could. When the model of authorship is the academic essay, with an identified writer, a complex gateway system, and fairly strict guidance of the reader, then, yes, hypertext authorship is quite different from academic essay authorship. But much of the difference is merely socioeconomic, not intrinsic (there could, after all, be academic journals in hypertext if people wanted to start them and subscribe to them), and the rest is largely the result of a comparison of apples and oranges.

If "authorship" is nothing new in hypertext, then of course hypertext raises no new conceptual challenges to the theoreticians (Barthes and Foucault, for instance) who spoke of the death of the author, since the problems raised by hypertext are merely those of any heterogeneous texts or unofficial texts, and those texts were well known to Barthes and Foucault. The same applies to related ideas, like "decentering" the subject of the discourse (Johnson-Eilola, overview to this section).

2. *Hypertext operates the way the mind does.* For two of the authors I have been asked to comment on, the operations of hypertext are intimately tied in a unique way to the operations of the mind. Indeed, it is not an exaggeration to say that hypertextual mechanisms are, for each commentator, a reification of the mechanisms identified by the psychology they subscribe to. For Moulthrop and Kaplan, the "formal, or 'mimetic,' constraints" of this new medium "exactly invert those of print." They find this inversion attractive because they object to the "capitalist idealism [that] inheres in scholarly texts," and they hope they have found in hypertext the "potential to transform our reading and writing practices." Because each encounter with a hypertext is "potentially . . . a . . . *refabrication*," hypertext is potentially a site of resistance to authority—resistance created by the intrinsically collaborative act of reading the hypertext.

I may come off in this article as a stolid defender of the academic and the mundane, but I actually sympathize with Moulthrop and Kaplan's goals. My problem is that I don't think that media are where you pin your hopes for social change. People can master any medium—look at Moulthrop and Kaplan's carefully edited, thoroughly definitive, authoritative, and learned essay. The examples of instrumental hypertext that they cite (users' manuals) show how easily these things do fit into an "economy of scarcity." Subversion, after all, was and is possible in print. If you want an example of a modern subversive text, look at *Spare Change*, a Boston newspaper written and produced by the homeless. It challenges the gatekeeper system, upsets assumptions, and raises disturbing questions about ownership in a far more interesting and complex way than anything yet written for the Macintosh.

For Smith, who begins her essay with the question, "Is the mind a text?" the psychologies cited are Langer's and Kintsch's, a yoking of a neo-Kantian and a materialist-cognitivist, which seems to me to be rather unlikely. (Neither would answer in the affirmative.) For Charney, the psychology is also grounded in Kintsch's work, but the work of a younger Kintsch, who has not yet dropped the notion of schema and taken up the terminology of the neural net researchers.

There is a standard reply to anyone who claims that the operations of a machine imitate or replace the operations of the mind, a reply I wish to press on the reader. Even if a machine apparently imitates some operation of the mind, that may not say anything about how the mind works. Take a calculator, for example. It adds and subtracts; so do we. But the way it adds and subtracts tells us nothing whatsoever about how we do so; its internal wiring and input-output strategies are completely different from our own. So even though the machine does what we do, it is of no more interest to a theory of the mind than, say, a hoe, because the way it does what we do differs from the way we do it. A mind may or may not be a text. (I doubt it; the statement confuses kinds.) A print text and hypertext are texts. That's all there is to it.

3. *The medium is the message.* Hypertext runs on a computer. Computers are different from paper. The medium is the message. Different medium, different message. This logic is adumbrated in each of the articles, and it is really at the heart of our disagreement. According to my view, text is text in any medium; what's new and different about hypertext is the navigation conventions. The advantage of the computer is that it seems to make navigation easier; you can press a button and go to some other area of the text. Pressing a button is much easier than, for instance, flipping to an index. The disadvantage is that the follow-up (what happens after you press the button) is frequently disappointing. The author's conception of the connection's relevance is not the reader's, and the reader gets lost. To some extent, both advantage

and disadvantage are artifacts of the computer's ability to store large amounts of information and its inability to display very much of it. But the navigational device itself, which is what's really new, is not actually intrinsic to a computer.

Hoopertext

I want to explore this last statement further, because I think that "the medium is the message" causes many of the confusions in these essays. Despite protestations to the contrary, the commentators know that hypertext runs on a computer, something that hums and whirs and responds smoothly to a mouse. How attractive would their arguments be if this were not the case? Let me propose a thought experiment, one designed to test my statement that there is little intrinsically different (or powerful) about the hypertextual medium.

Imagine that I develop a new text medium, which I will call Hoopertext. I collect a number of hula hoops from the back of my garage, and I mount them on a spoke-and-hub mechanism, perhaps attached to a small motor. I put slots in the sides of the hoops at irregular intervals, and I put index cards with text and pictures on them in the slots. I hook up a set of labeled switches to the hub and engine, and I label the cards, so that pressing a labeled switch brings up the labeled card. On each card, I put recommendations about which card to select next. I also provide the user with long, thin needles, which he or she can poke through several cards at once, so that several of the hoops can be rotated simultaneously. The reader proceeds by looking at the topmost card on the closest hoop but can read any other card that happens to be visible. To make the process simpler, I color-code the cards, to indicate another level of relation between them. All patent rights are reserved.

Hoopertext has every bit as much functionality as hypertext. It permits complex navigation at will; in fact, it has several different layers of connection between cards and several different methods of exploiting those connections. Getting lost, moreover, is much harder, because the user can see many cards at once. The reader, who actually has even more control than the hypertext reader, can even create (with the needles) new patterns of association, unthought of by the author. So many and so various, in fact, are the methods of connection that you couldn't diagram connections, as you can with hypertext. With Hoopertext, however, it is self-evident that the medium is not the message. Hula hoops are the message?

Notice, though, that everything said about hypertext in these articles applies equally well to Hoopertext. Hoopertext reading is nonlinear, and, given the complexity of interaction possible with each card, it is probably a form of "thick cognition." Using it surely "entail[s] the thinker's multiple physical, social, cultural, and historical life worlds" (Smith, ch. 11). Hoopertext, too, is available to anyone; no publishing house imprimatur is required to create, distribute, or alter a Hoopertext stack. To see how well this substitution works, go through the articles and replace the word *hypertext* with the word *Hoopertext*. Much still makes sense. Where it doesn't, when the phrase "Hoopertextual thinking" appears or when Hoopertext becomes an "evolutionary outgrowth" (Smith; Moulthrop and Kaplan, ch. 9), where is the problem?

The term *Hoopertextual thinking* sounds stupid not because special skills are not required in operating Hoopertext; it sounds stupid because Hoopertext is a clunky contraption. What's hard to see about hypertext, contained as it is on those bright, smooth, humming machines, is that it is a contraption, too. Hoopertext is a curiosity, not an evolutionary outgrowth, because it is the product of some mad garage inventor who has little insight into what works for people. But is hypertext much different? The people who developed hypertext were trying to do something cool with the materials at hand, and they succeeded. But being cool and being momentous are two different things.

Hypertext as Contraption

In my opinion, thinking about hypertext as a contraption is probably far more productive than thinking of it as a new medium. Contraptions you can tinker with. No one is afraid to look at the inner workings of a contraption. A similar fearlessness and readiness to tinker ought to be much more a part of our equipment when we confront hypertext. The essential action in reading hypertext, after all, is the perception that a move other than that dictated by the flow of a sentence is possible to the reader. The essential problem is the decision of whether to take advantage of the ability to determine direction. The *essential problem in creating hypertexts*—what ought to be tinkered with—is that, so far, the text itself has a hard time showing readers what will happen after they undertake the move. Existence of another card can easily be signaled; what is hard to signal is whether a shift to that card is appropriate or worth the effort.

Readers unfamiliar with hypertext may not appreciate how obvious and intractable this problem is. So let me propose a quick experiment. Say you discovered that, in the previous paragraph, what I had meant by highlighting the words *essential problem in creating hypertexts* was that an entire disquisition on the subject was available in the appendix. Would you have turned to this disquisition? Why? Why not? The problem, put this way, ought to be familiar, since it is the problem of whether to read the endnote, something we all have solved unsuccessfully. What, after all, would be in that appendix? a definition? an expansion of the point made in the paragraph? a bibliography? a collection of references to other works of mine? Even if you knew, would you want to go?

The problem is not new. Frank Halasz (qtd. in Smith) saw it long ago, and he realized (as Smith does not) that technical improvements would be massively difficult. The way to solve the problem, rather, is to be more inventive, to create other ways of establishing connections and telling the reader, quickly and easily, whether changing the flow of attention is worthwhile. In magazines and encyclopedias, we have a whole array of conventions. In hypertext, we don't have many at all; even Hoopertext seems to have as many. We're not likely to be inventive, however, if we don't start seeing hypertext as a rather weak text form that needs to be nurtured and if we don't see the hypertext forms created thus far as temporary solutions that need far more work.

Last Controversies

In a way, then, I am saying that we need to assert ourselves when it comes to creating hypertexts and hypertext tools. But we are not likely to do so if we continue to see hypertext as some sort of shared medium, in which the reader becomes author and the author dies. Thus I'd like to close by once again looking at the question of authorship in hypertext.

In my view, remember, hypertext is simply the same old text with somewhat different navigational conventions. If so, then authorship of hypertext is just the same old authorship, with slightly different use of those conventions. The audience of hypertext is certainly given more choice about where to go than the audience of an academic essay is, but the audience is probably given less choice than the audience of a magazine is given. In either case, the degree of choice and the kind of choice are made available to the audience by an author (or editor). Authorship does not change, even if the hypertext produced by that author is exploratory.

To see why, imagine that I have been entrusted with the task of designing a path through an area of ground. I am the author of that path. I can choose to create a regular, ordinary path that guides the person taking it down only one route. Or I can create a maze, where there are many guided routes. Or I can take down all the trees and bushes and leave people to find their own way. In all cases, I am the author; what is different is the relationship that my pathtakers have with me.

Now, of course, it might be that one or more of the choices I make is interesting, revolutionary, a work of art, the focus of numerous academic articles—not because the notion of authorship has changed but because the relationship I have with my pathtaker is worthy of some attention. I might also do a bad job and produce nothing but chaos, in which case it would behoove academic commentators to note the result. Chaos is something we want to be suspicious of.

When we look critically at Joyce's "Afternoon: A Story," we should ask the same questions we ask about my garden. Is it original? brilliant? chaotic? We should not be cowed by what is, after all, a gimmick and announce that it is a new form of participatory literature. What Joyce did is not much different from what Cortázar did in *Hopscotch*.

Whenever somebody invents a form of narrative structure, it takes a long time to develop conventions for the new genre. Take movies, for instance. Attempts at narrative in movies were made almost as soon as cinematographs were invented. But anyone who has seen Méliés's *A Trip to the Moon* would scarcely accuse the early efforts of producing lithe, graceful, or sophisticated films. Not until some narrative meaning could be attached to technical devices like the cut, the dissolve, and the face shot could the power of the form be felt.

Hypertext narrative may also develop conventions, as soon as more work is done on letting people know what will happen when you zap. But in the meantime, I can only sympathize with Karl Crary's response to the hypertext "Forking Paths" (see Moulthrop and Kaplan's chapter). Is he undercut by the medium? Not at all. He perceives that the conventions are in their infancy.

While these conventions remain undeveloped, readers who don't know them or can't use them effectively or want more from them will be dissatisfied and uncertain. The people participating in the experiments that Charney cites are in that situation. Their failure is not grounded in the way the mind works. It's just the natural groping behavior of the neophyte. Their minds might work quite differently if good hypertext conventions existed and they knew how to use them. Why, in other words, does the phrase *hoopertextual thinking* make *hypertextual thinking* absurd? It is because we are then forced to accept such arcana as *dictionary thinking, comic book thinking,* and *encyclopedia thinking.* Hypertext thinking is simply a skill in handling certain text structures, not a form of being that will succeed orality and textuality.

Skill in handling text structures is what teaching literacy attempts to impart. With hypertext, we have yet to determine precisely what skills are needed or how they can be taught, mostly because hypertext structures themselves are not well developed and the technical capabilities of the machines are not well established. It may perhaps be that some part of the skill in handling hypertext is easily transferred to other text, in which case hypertext ought to be used in the classroom. But it could also be that in ten years, hypertext will be almost forgotten. Some years ago, the 3-D movie process was invented, and, for a time, audiences would shriek as the ground dropped out from under them or a knife was thrown straight at them. Pretty soon, however, everybody got used to what 3-D movies could do and got tired of wearing funny little glasses. Hypertext skills could end up like 3-D movie skills, something terribly exciting for a little while and then a bore.

PART IV

Broadening
Our Views
of Literacy and
Computers

Chapter 12

Writing the Technology That Writes Us: Research on Literacy and the Shape of Technology

Christina Haas and Christine M. Neuwirth

In "Literacy in Three Metaphors," Sylvia Scribner describes three ways of seeing literacy—as adaptation, as a state of grace, and as power. She argues that in fact all three views contribute—but each only partially—to understanding literacy, its nature and its implications. Scribner was one of the first scholars to bring to discussions of literacy an articulation of the many, often conflicting, definitions of the term and an awareness that the controversies in definition had, as she put it, "more than academic significance" (6). Cautioning against assumptions that literacy, or literacies, are straightforward and unproblematic, she instead demonstrates that differing views of literacy carry with them complex value systems and inherently competing agendas for action. And Scribner's cautions about oversimplifying literacy are ones those interested in computers and literacy might well take to heart. In this essay we put forth a caveat similar to Scribner's: researchers, teachers, and scholars in the field of English studies should not assume that literacy *technologies* are either straightforward or unproblematic. Views of computers, like views of literacy, are value-laden. Conceptions about what technology *is*, and how it comes to be, profoundly shape specific acts of computer-based reading and writing; they influence as well the construction of our individual and collective selves in *relation* to that technology.

The ultimate aim of this chapter is to argue for a new, more complicated approach to research on computers and literacy. The initial efforts at understanding and implementing computers in writing classrooms were full of enthusiasm, as English teachers and scholars began to recognize the new ways of writing and thinking that computers seemed to invite. This early work sought to document what many teachers and scholars felt intuitively: that writing with computers was more enjoyable, more efficient, yes, even "better." As Cynthia Selfe and Susan Hilligoss discuss in the introduction to this volume, however, these investigations were not simply guided by our enthusiasm; they were often derailed by it, as hastily and sometimes poorly designed studies yielded results that were difficult to interpret and less than conclusive.

A new, more mature research agenda will aid us in understanding how computer technologies, literacy, thinking, and culture are connected. Such research is crucial for informing the design of curricula for teaching writing and can guide the wise use of technology in writing. But an even more critical (and, to our minds, heretofore unacknowledged) justification for such research is that it can help authorize our voices not just in the proper *use* of computer technologies for literacy but in the very *shape* such technologies should take. A critical reason for conducting research, then, is to help us give shape to the technologies that, in turn, shape our literacy acts—to "write" the technology that "writes" us.

Prerequisite to this goal, however, is a need to adjust current thinking about technology. We begin this essay by critiquing three assumptions about computer technology that stand as serious personal, institutional, and cultural obstacles to research and, ultimately, to our free and critical authoring of technology for literacy. These assumptions place us in a subordinate position to technology and, in effect, silence us in the shaping of it. They take us out of the realm of technology development and critique and set us in positions to be merely receivers of technology.

The three assumptions are closely related: the first two assert that technology is either "transparent" or "all-powerful"; while seemingly disparate, these two assumptions actually share an "instrumental" view of technology. That is, they view technology as a means to produce reading and writing, which are somehow imagined to exist independently of and uninfluenced by that means. These two assumptions echo two of the metaphors Scribner discusses. Like literacy as adaptation, the "technology is transparent" assumption appeals to pragmatic values (e.g., increased efficiency) and has a certain commonsense appeal. Like literacy as a state of grace, the "technology is all-powerful" assumption grants certain privileges or virtues to technology and to those who possess or understand it.

These two assumptions are inherently bound to a third: an instrumental view of technology can lead us to forget that literacy is constituted by technology and to leave the work of technology to others. And a belief that "computers are not our job" means that the power (Scribner's third metaphor) to shape technology is by default left to others, to those unnamed "others" whose job it is to "do" computers. Together, these three assumptions negatively affect our understanding of the relation between technologies, individuals, and cultures; limit our power in the conduct of research; and, ultimately, impede our active authoring of technologies for literacy.

Technology Is Transparent

The assumption that technology is transparent is a belief that technologies for reading and writing are a distortionless window, through which we can see essential acts of thinking. In this view, "writing is writing is writing" (or "reading is reading is reading"), unchanged and unaffected by the mode of production and presentation. The essential processes of reading and writing are universal and unchanging: writers and readers simply exchange their pens and books for word processors, replace their face-to-face conversations with computer conferences, and continue to produce texts and construct meanings in the ways they always have.

The assumption that computers are transparent is evident in certain approaches to research and teaching and in most current theories of writing. The assumption is operating when teachers simply transfer "what works" in a traditional pen-and-book classroom to computer-based settings and assume that writing and learning will continue as usual. It is operating when researchers do not attend to the medium with which writers compose and ignore how processes and products may be influenced by various media. And it is operating when theorists attempt to explain composing and its myriad manifestations without examining, or at least acknowledging, the impact that technologies may have.[1]

A variant of the transparent technology assumption acknowledges that writing is *different* with computers—but limits the difference to an increase in efficiency. According to this aspect of the assumption, we can compose, revise, edit, and produce texts more quickly and with less effort with computers; therefore, using computers increases our efficiency as writers but makes no profound difference in *how* reading and writing get done. The belief that technology is a "win" because it increases our efficiency is open to critique: the very metaphor of "efficiency" equates literacy acts with production acts—a somewhat problematic equation (Olson).

Historical studies have documented the problems with the assumption that literacy technologies are transparent. For example, Elizabeth Eisenstein argues that the printing press was a revolutionary agent of change in medieval Europe—a chief contributor if not a prime cause of the rise of science, the growth of Protestantism, and the emergence of the middle class. While critiques of Eisenstein have also tended to act as a corrective on her sometimes overstated claims[2] (Grafton), the power of the printing press in shaping Western history is widely understood. Although the effects of new communication technologies on individuals and cultures are complex, multifaceted, and far from unitary, and while historians may argue about specific claims of degree or direction of such effects, the powerful shaping force of technologies on thinking and culture seems clear.

While it is too early for historical studies on the scale of Eisenstein's to examine the effects of computer technology on reading and writing, ample evidence shows that computer technology is not transparent; rather it can be a contributing agent to changes in both cognitive and social processes. In some of our own research, for instance, we found that writers may move away from note making and other planning activities more quickly when they use word processing (Haas, "Composing in Technological Contexts"). The writers we studied tended to begin production of sustained, connected discourse sooner than they did with pen and paper. The implications of this finding are troubling for teachers who wish to *delay* students' writing until exploration of the problem has been attempted, especially in the light of research results that show a link between initial planning and writing quality (Glynn et al.). And in a study of writing classrooms that use computer networks in addition to traditional modes of communication (face-to-face, paper, phone), we found a significant change in patterns of social interaction about writing, with teachers and students in the networked section interacting more than those in the traditional classroom, and teachers interacting more with less able students (Hartman et al.). These studies are important as a first step in understanding the dynamic relation between technologies and literacy. They also suggest that writing research that examines composing with traditional technologies may not be generalizable to those situations in which writers use computers. At the very least, we need to understand how writing and reading differ in different technological contexts, so that we can interpret research findings accordingly.

The most serious drawback to the transparent technology assumption, however, is that it invites a wholehearted acceptance of computer technology without any accompanying examination of its effects: the transparency myth (wrongly) precludes there *being* any interesting effects. Acceptance of this assumption leads to a belief that writers can *use* computer technology without being shaped by it; it discourages any examination of how computers shape discourse and, consequently, does not authorize us to take an active role in shaping technology. In adopting the transparent technology assumption, those of us in English studies put ourselves in a position to be influenced by technology but not to understand or control that influence.

Technology Is All-Powerful

The counterpart to the transparent technology myth is the assumption that computers are all-powerful. This assumption sees technology as an instrument that is self-determining. In this view, computer technologies will have far-reaching and profound—but essentially one-way—effects. The new technologies for literacy are such a powerful force that simply introducing them to writers or in writing classrooms will change writing and reading for the better, supplanting completely the old pen-and-book technologies. Although the "technology is transparent" and "technology is all-powerful" assumptions appear to be diametrically opposed—characterizing technology as either "all" or "nothing"—they both are based on an instrumental conception of technology, reducing and simplifying its nature and its effects.

An adherence to the "technology is all-powerful" assumption is evident when teachers assume that what they have known about language learning is now outmoded—the "rules" (i.e., our theories and our pedagogy) must be rewritten to accommodate computer technology, which is essentially a brand-new ball game. The assumption is also apparent when teachers expect benefits of technology to accrue similarly for all students and across contexts—as if the power of computers will overshadow or make irrelevant important differences between writers, tasks, contexts. In reality, a writer's particular background, skills, goals, and expectations will strongly determine the way the writer uses computers, as will the particular cultural, social, and educational setting within which he or she works. (Wahlstrom, ch. 8, and Moulthrop and

Kaplan, ch. 9, discuss these issues in this volume.) Teachers should be aware of—and should help students become aware of—how individual, task, and situational differences help to determine the use, and usefulness, of various computer technologies.

Adherence to the "technology is all-powerful" stance is evident, too, when researchers and theorists assume that what we need to know about literacy will have to be rebuilt from the ground up—our old theories will be unable to account for literacy in the age of computers; they are not even useful starting points. Research influenced by the assumption looks for strong, unitary, one-way, and often only positive effects of technology. Under this assumption, research about computers and writing is not a way to determine how best to *use* technologies but simply a way to examine their effects. Studies become a justification *for* computers, rather than critical inquiry *about* computers.

One corrective to this assumption is to apply our current theories to think seriously about consequences of technology, both positive and negative. Davida Charney (ch. 10 of this volume) attempts such a corrective to this assumption, especially as it is manifested in much current thinking about hypertexts, when she examines the predictions that existing theories and research about reading would lead us to make concerning the impact of hypertexts. Another corrective is to realize that the effects of any technology are the result of certain cultural and cognitive ways of reasoning about and using that technology (Rubin and Bruce). That is, in a very real way, technologies are "made" through our thinking and talking about them. Consequently, technologies are continually evolving; they are not static but shaped subtly and constantly by the uses to which they are put and by the discourse that accompanies those uses. For example, any effect of computer networks on writing processes stems from a complex interaction between the technology itself and the teachers and students using the networks to achieve their goals (Neuwirth et al., "Why Write—Together").

The "technology is all-powerful" assumption also ignores the dynamic and complex relation between old and new technologies. Again, historical analyses of other literacy technologies provide illumination. Tony Lentz, in a recent study of orality and literacy in ancient Greece, shows compellingly how the "old" technology of orality and the "new" literacy actually existed side by side, in a symbiotic relation, each technology enriching the other. Another well-worn example is the computerized office that uses more paper than it did before the purchase of computers—to the chagrin of the office manager, who had justified the purchase of the machines by claiming that paper expenses would decrease.

In effect, this assumption errs by placing individual uses and motives, and cultural habits and beliefs, in a subordinate position to technology, which "determines" its own uses and effects. Like the "technology is transparent" stance, this one essentially remains noncritical and nonparticipatory; adherents believe (again incorrectly) that profound effects will accrue from technology but that we cannot control, predict, or even understand them. The assumption is detrimental to the conduct of literacy research because, while profound technology-based changes in literacy activity are expected to occur, researchers are not encouraged to ask questions or posit theories about how to account for these changes. The belief that technology "determines" itself removes, in effect, the space where critique of technology takes place and silences us in the conversations that *do* determine the shape of technology.

Paradoxically, while human purposes and cultural contexts shape technologies, those same technologies exert a powerful influence on cultures and on individuals. The relation, then, between technologies, cultures, and individuals is a complex, multifaceted, and symbiotic one, with influence passing in all directions. Unless we recognize and are willing to explore this dynamic relation, we cannot be part of the dialogue that shapes technologies for literacies.

Computers Are "Not Our Job"

The final assumption may most directly and seriously stand in the way of our empowerment as shapers of technologies for literacy. The assertion that "computers are not our job" distances us from technology by invoking a division of labor: the study of English is our job; the study of computers is the work of others. The assumption has several manifestations, depending, in part, on the various, contested definitions of English studies. The narrowest traditional definition of the English profession is that the proper object of study in English is the preservation and interpretation of the best of our culture's literature, with "best" and "our culture" construed more or less broadly. The methods associated with this definition are primarily text-based analyses of written artifacts. This narrow definition, of course, affects far more than just studies of literacy and computers, since it excludes from sanctioned inquiry many objects having to do with literacy itself. Adherence to such a limited perspective results in the inadequate training of students to address objects beyond literary texts, including texts produced by students or in nonliterary settings, readers' responses to

texts, the situations that give rise to texts and other utterances, and—
of primary concern here—the media that shape those utterances.

Popularly associated with this narrow definition of the proper object
of English studies is an anticomputer stance. Everyone (including
those outside English studies) is familiar with the stereotypical image
of the English professor as resistance fighter, a last bastion of human-
ism, refusing to have truck with the "tool of the devil"—that is, the
latest innovation in computer technology, be it the word processing of
a few years past or today's voice-annotated mail. To the extent that this
antitechnological stance has any actuality, one of the forces that may
be operating to produce it is the division of labor itself. As Richard
Emerson notes, people often attempt to remain independent of what
they do not control (e.g., computers), either by reducing investment in
goals mediated by others (e.g., the production of manuscripts) or by
maintaining alternatives for achieving those goals (e.g., pen and paper).

An anticomputer approach, however, is not a necessary concomitant
of the narrow definition of English studies. A second, somewhat more
sympathetic stance toward technology, but one that still holds to a
traditional view of the proper province of English studies, is witnessed
by professors of literature who have learned how to "message" on
Humannet and by scholarly articles, such as Richard Lanham's "The
Electronic Word: Literary Study and the Digital Revolution," that fore-
cast a brave new world of electronic texts and counsel colleagues to
embrace it or, at the least, brace for it. While the antitechnology stance
tends to vilify technology and those who develop it, this second stance
tends to revere it, even worship it: "The electronic word stands on our
side in this endeavor [literary studies] and for that we should return
thanks" (288).

But what unites these seemingly diametrically opposed stances is an
instrumental view of technology, a view that technology is merely and
simply a tool. This instrumental view is implied by the underlying
shared assumption of the division of labor: we either choose (or are
forced) to use computer technology, or we choose not to. But we do
not contribute to its development. The social actors, the agents of
development, are in some unspecified way the technology itself, evi-
denced in statements like "electronic 'texts' will redefine the writing,
reading, and professing of literature" (Lanham, "Electronic Word"
265), a circumlocutory discourse that avoids facing the possibly painful
thought that other people are redefining reading and writing, while
humanists maintain the speculative high ground, remaining above the
fray and remote from those actually involved in the process of shaping
technology. In this view, technology may merit our attention because

it is revolutionizing the study of books, but there is no suggestion that humanists should or even could participate in that revolution as social agents. Just as it is the job of creative writers to produce texts and the job of English scholars to critique them, according to the instrumental view of technology it is the technologists' job to create technology and the job of the cultural critic or teacher to interpret it and use it.

The division of labor and its attendant decisions about what to know and how knowledge of technology is to be formed limits the options available to members of a discipline who inherit it. The point is not that members are *forced* to conform but that the ways in which they are able to depart are restricted (Shumway). The restriction stems in part from members' education, which influences patterns of knowledge acquisition and discursive practices and, perhaps, in part from the ways in which specialization tends to produce, in those occupying a particular role, points of view and beliefs that are consistent with that role (Dearborn and Simon; Lieberman). Even those in English studies who see themselves as directly opposed to the traditional definition of English studies may in fact (perhaps because of background and training similar to their more traditional colleagues or because of the reward systems within traditional English departments) take the speculative high ground with regard to technology. These members of the discipline—whom we call composition scholars for ease of reference— operate from a somewhat broader definition of English studies, a definition that includes questions about the ways in which people interpret and produce texts as proper objects of study. These members often come from educational backgrounds appropriate to their less narrow definition of the field (with graduate work in rhetoric, education, or linguistics, for instance). Frequently these composition scholars run, or are closely tied to, writing programs; their research may center on the acquisition and use of discourse in varied settings; and, while their own departments may not widely share an interest in technology, groups such as the Fifth C (a special-interest group of the Conference on College Composition and Communication) and the spring Computers and Writing conference (held in 1991 in Biloxi, in 1992 in Indianapolis, and in 1993 in Ann Arbor) provide a community for scholars involved in teaching or using technology.

However, even these composition scholars may adhere to the "it's not our job" assumption, although it is often manifest in different ways. Because the assumption conditions attempts to understand technology in that members of this group may see themselves as users, but not as shapers, of technology, research in this community tends to pursue certain questions but not others. Researchers may ask, "Does computer technology improve writing quality?" and "How do computers affect the process of composing?" but too often avoid any inquiries concerning what shape computer-based literacy tools should take. These studies simply are not designed to produce knowledge about the shape of technology. For example, pretest-posttest designs with "the computer" as an undifferentiated treatment condition do not create knowledge that can shape technology, since they explain little about what characteristics of a particular technology are most salient or influential. Not surprisingly, implications are seldom drawn about specific features that are useful, or options that are needed for readers and writers.

Thus studies need not openly express the cultural dominant "computers are not our job" to support that dominant. Research that is concerned with literacy and computers but remains unconcerned with shaping that technology can have the same impact. Although few researchers doing investigations in literacy and computers would actively endorse the "computers are not our job" assumption, much of the work fails to provide grounds for opposition. Such opposition could come, for instance, from work that attend directly to the features of word processors that seem to be most valuable for various kinds of writing tasks or to ways in which groups of writers manage the conventions and procedures of computer mail in their collaborations.

This unwillingness, or inability, to address the issues surrounding technology's shape helps to explain recent exhortations to move beyond so-called basic questions concerning the relation of computers to writing processes and quality, to accept computer technology as a "given" and to go from there. Those exhortations depend on our belief that, because we have already chosen to use computers for writing and teaching and because "the computer" is given to us, complete and already formed, our inquiry should focus on how to use computers to meet such goals as "positive social and political change in our writing classrooms and our educational system" (Bridwell-Bowles 88). Such a stance implores teachers to "make a difference" in their classrooms—and, by implication, *only* in classrooms, since influence would not extend beyond that sphere. To hold to such a stance, one must ignore the critical role of technology in shaping response. In fact, the very shape of the technology used in the classroom, whether word processors, networks, or video displays, conditions the kinds of social and political change that can and will take place in classrooms.

The "computers are not our job" assumption is faulty for two major reasons. First, it ignores the fact that computer technologies—like other tools—are created by humans, usually with particular uses in mind. While tools are not always used as they were intended to be, those who fund, design, and build computer tools exert a powerful control over what kinds of activities those tools facilitate. As Richard Ohmann has pointed out, computers are developed "within particular social relations, and responsive to the needs of those with the power to direct [their] evolution" (680). A great deal of current scholarship acknowledges that theories of literacy shape literate practice. Similarly, computer scientists, actively working on the literacy tools of the future, are operating with their *own* theories of reading and writing, theories that may, in our estimation, be quite different from our own (see Charney, ch. 10 in this volume, for extended discussion of this issue). It is not the case that these developers will necessarily design and implement the same tools and features that researchers or teachers of literacy would. For instance, although writers may see a need for word processors that provide a margin in which collaborators can annotate texts, the technology itself simply does not have such a feature. Moreover, the feature is not going to be developed to be consistent with what researchers in English know about writing and reading processes without the hard work, planning, and execution by those with the technical skills (and resources) to make it happen (Neuwirth et al., "Issues in the Design"). It is, in fact, the skills, desires, and resources of those in a position to effect such decisions that has profound (if indirect) effects on literacy—not the technology itself.

Second, the "computers are not our job" assumption ignores the fact that decisions concerning technology are not infinitely retractable. It seldom suffices to criticize computers after the fact of their development. The QWERTY keyboard persists, although more effective keyboard layouts have been solidly demonstrated. Like the contents of Pandora's box, the QWERTY keyboard, once unleashed, cannot be recalled, despite known limitations. Thus interaction between those who know about literacy and those who know about computers, not after the artifact but during its shaping, is central to the development of the field of literacy and computers.

Research and the Future of Literacy Studies

At this point, it is tempting to see the division of labor as arbitrary and invidious, but such a view would be a mistake. Divisions of labor play important roles in our departments and in other cultural institutions as well. Divisions of labor, for instance, permit specialization by members of a discipline and allow for various economies of expertise. Further, such divisions can aid in overcoming the inherently limited knowledge and information-processing capacities of individual members of a group (J. D. Thompson).

It would be foolish, then, to do away entirely with divisions of labor and the rich range of perspectives and goal orientations they engender. But the failure to see task interdependencies between the goals we have and the goals of those in computer science and related fields has led to a territorialization and parochialism in research on literacy and computers that needs to be overcome. While it is not necessary for scholars of English studies to become computer scientists, cross-disciplinary inquiry on computers and literacy is necessary. It is not necessary to abandon our differences (in training, expertise, and goals), but it will be necessary to achieve more integration. To do so, we need to complicate our research to take into account a conception of computer technology that includes more than a simple instrumental view of technology—as either transparent or as all-powerful. Martin Heidegger, in *The Question concerning Technology*, expressed it thus:

> The manufacture and utilization of equipment, tools, and machines, the manufactured and used things themselves, and the needs and ends that they serve, all belong to what technology is. The whole complex of these contrivances is technology.   (288)

As we have argued, certain ways of thinking about technology and about our relation to it stand in the way of research that can authorize those in English studies to become active shapers of technologies for literacy. Discarding these assumptions means acknowledging that it *is* our job to reason about computer technology, to engage in the discourses that constitute that technology, and to bring our knowledge about literacy to bear on the design of tools for literacy. Further, it means acknowledging that individuals, cultures, and technologies exist in a complex and symbiotic relation, a relation that is still too little understood.

Those with a knowledge of literacy, its myriad manifestations and its ramifications, must become actively involved in shaping the complex of technology that, in turn, shapes our literacy, our cultures, and ourselves. We (and our students) are "written" by the technologies we use, or, more accurately, those with the knowledge, power, and desire shape the technologies that in turn shape us. We are advocating here that those in literacy studies take greater responsibility in "authoring" technology—that is, engaging in sustained and critical dialogue about technology, both its shape and its uses. (In this volume Hawisher, ch. 2, and Barton, ch. 3, take a first step in this direction in critiquing the habits of mind that underlie discussions of technology, both inside and outside English studies. However, neither author extends the argument to show how such critiques might usefully lead to our own involvement in critically authoring literacy technologies.)

Such authoring requires a change in numerous social and political values and institutional practices that work against the broadening of our authority. First, we need to alter our perceptions of ourselves and of one another: understanding computers and literacy is a task not for "individual" researchers but for research communities, whose members' often diverse ways of forming knowledge about computers and writing can, indeed must, be integrated. Members of the computers and literacy community certainly represent diverse methodologies, ask different kinds of questions, advocate differing solutions to common problems. However, we need to learn more about our colleagues' methods, questions, solutions, and problems. Common sense, if not humility, forces us to acknowledge that understanding the multifaceted relation between technologies, cultures, and individuals requires *all* of what we know—much more than any one of us can know.

Second, we need to support more contact across disciplinary boundaries. Certainly cross-disciplinary work will entail a great deal of effort and require a great deal of open-mindedness. Different groups may have different goals explicitly provided as a part of their task assignment. These goals may inherently conflict, as in the case of a computer scientist wanting to maximize functionality (i.e., by increasing the number of separate functions that a given computer feature might possess) and an English professor wanting to maximize learnability (by "keeping it simple"). Similarly, different groups have different areas of expertise: computer scientists know things about search and redisplay algorithms; English professors know things about reading and writing processes. Initiating and sustaining conversations in the face of such differences will be intimidating but crucial.

Finally, and perhaps most important in the long run, we must reduce the homogeneity of orientation and background of our students. We should introduce them to the varied ways of thinking and reasoning about technology (historical, cognitive, sociological), ways that may not always be our own. We must prepare them to traverse disciplinary and subdisciplinary boundaries. One way to accomplish this would be to recruit students who themselves have different disciplinary training and encourage them to work together on common problems. Another would be through the example of the discipline's rewards systems: policies should be established that credit publications about writing in journals of computer science, educational technology, and human factors, as well as in English journals, for hiring, promotion, and tenure.

Modifying our assumptions about technology and reconceiving the boundaries between our own work and those of our colleagues inside and outside our discipline is a first step. We must also embark on a research agenda that will authorize our voices in the dialogues that shape technology. Of course, these goals can and should be pursued concurrently. We cannot realistically expect to change institutional, educational, and cultural configurations and procedures before we begin our research. Indeed, our research ideally will contribute to such changes.

The general goals of such a research agenda would include increasing our knowledge of the relation between individuals and cultures, their literacies and their technologies for literacy. Discourse is inherently social but finds its voice through individuals within cultures. Research should tell us more about how literacy, and specifically literacy constituted by computer technology, mediates the relation between social and cultural groups and individual thinking. In general, then, research should ultimately contribute to a broader understanding of the complex interdependencies of literacy and technologies as they are manifested in cultures and in individuals.

A new research agenda would also have the more specific aim of increasing knowledge about computer features and configurations of uses that help or hinder literacy acts. As teachers, we want to contribute to an understanding of how computers can expand our students' use and knowledge of discourse. As researchers, we want to speak to the design and implementation, not merely the use, of computer technologies to support our pedagogical goals. Our aims, then, must include a consideration of how computer technologies should be implemented (the nuts and bolts of how computers get used in our classrooms) as well as how computer tools for literacy should be designed (software and hardware features that facilitate literacy acts). For instance, classroom-based questions might include the following: Which configuration of machines and software is best suited to particular writing tasks (individual or collaborative, short-term or long-term, routine or novel)? Which is best suited to specific pedagogical goals, such as extended development of ideas, coherent organization and fluid style, or the fruitful sharing of ideas by multiple writers? A question suggested by Betsy A. Bowen's essay in this volume (ch. 4) is, How might the *potential* for democratization inherent in computer networks be brought to fruition? What specific features should such technologies have? For example, Marlene Scardamalia et al. are working to shape a computer system in addition to examining its effects in classrooms. Such questions imply, of course, that researchers of technology and literacy must go beyond speculation and attend to actual classrooms, actual writers, and actual technology in use.

Classroom experiences are closely tied to a second goal: increasing our knowledge of specific hardware and software features that facilitate particular literacy acts. One way to pursue such a goal is to examine problem areas, mismatches between existing technology and writers' needs, goals, and prior experiences. For instance, our previous work on writers' reading from computer displays (Haas and Hayes) began, in a classroom, with complaints from freshman writing students about the lack of printing facilities available to them. This complaint, in turn, pointed to their continued use of hard copy throughout composing (see also Haas, "Seeing It on the Screen"). Systematic examination of their hard copy use eventually suggested the benefits of large-screen, high-resolution displays for complex literacy acts like composing and reading extended texts (Haas and Hayes; Haas, "Does the Medium Make a Difference?"; further corroboration is provided by Gould and Grischkowsky).

Such goals for research, of course, rest on theories of literacy—implicit or explicit. Consequently, clear articulation of theory must accompany any research agenda. Research should be driven by a theory of how literacy works, why and when people engage in literacy acts, how cultures and literacies constitute one another. For instance, the research on writers reading from computer displays described above rests on a particular theory of mind and human action suggesting that when writers have problems with computers—when they encounter mismatches between their practices of literacy and the available technologies—the writers are not simply "in error," do not merely need to be "weaned" to the new technology. Rather, they are demonstrating their cognizance of their own needs as literate agents, needs shaped by the literacy practice of their culture. An effective research agenda will include clear articulation of how specific theories of writing undergird research, justify questions, and help determine the interpretation of results. Further, results of research should explicitly feed back into theory—informing, testing, and enriching it. Research, then, becomes a way not simply to answer questions but also to open them up—a heuristic for inquiry.

A pluralistic variety of methods will be necessary to examine the symbiotic relation between technologies, cultures, and individuals. While no one study can address all aspects of this relation, collectively our methods should ultimately invite integration. And while no one researcher need be, or even can be, adept at all approaches, we should strive to understand the methodologies our colleagues use. The benefit of any one method is less important than rich and theory-driven questions, and rather than advocate techniques, we would advocate attention to the way specific questions call for particular methods. In general, we should apply methods that allow us to take both a "fine-grained" and a "wide-angle" view. Fine-grained research would examine individual writers and groups of writers, in detail and in situ, and might employ a range of observational methods (e.g., participant-observer research, interviews conducted over time) as well as more controlled studies of larger groups of writers and readers (Neuwirth and Kaufer, "Computers and Composition Studies"). New methods may also prove necessary and useful. A wide-angle view, drawing on clearly articulated theories and clearly specified research designs, would link disparate studies and examine issues that stretch across methods, across time, and across field of inquiry. Both approaches must be tied to research goals and should be theoretically grounded. A third view, one that might metaphorically be characterized as an "elapsed-time" view, would look at historical changes in literacy and technology and help ground all our research.

A final critical need is to expand the range of audiences to whom we speak. By looking within our own institution, we will undoubtedly find colleagues—in education, psychology, even in business and engineering—who are interested in decisions about the shape and implementation of technologies for literacy. Of course, in dialogues with these colleagues, we may find initial difficulties with terminology: where we would refer to "literacy acts," our colleagues may use different terms—"discourse production" and "comprehension" in psychology or education, for example; "information structuring" and "information management" in business. Such variations in terminology certainly imply some differences in theoretical perspectives and worldviews, but fruitful exchanges of ideas will still be possible and valuable. In addition, we should make our research accessible to designers involved in computer development, both hardware and software. Such cooperation may mean sitting on university task forces with our colleagues from computer science, publishing our results in journals read by computer scientists, attending conferences (like those sponsored by the Association for Computing Machinery) with developers and other computer professionals interested in education issues.

We can also expand our audience by making our research relevant and important to the work of our field generally. To do so, we might challenge our colleagues—who may themselves suffer from faulty assumptions like "computers are not my job"—to recognize what is at stake as literacies for technology evolve. As the new perspectives on literacy in this volume make clear, what is at stake is our active voice in the development of tools for literacy; indeed, what is at stake may be the very shape of literacy itself.[3]

NOTES

[1] Hayes has recently proposed an adaptation of the 1981 Hayes and Flower process model of composing that recognizes the role technologies may play in writing, although his new model does not account for precisely *how* technology affects composing (Personal communication). Neuwirth and Kaufer offer one account of the role external representations can play in composing ("Role").

[2] Kaestle believes that this overstatement was deliberate—an attempt to disrupt the status quo assumptions about the presumably inconsequential effects of the rise of print.

[3] The authors would like to thank David Shumway, Nancy Kaplan, David Kaufer, Alan Kennedy, and Cheryl Geisler, who offered thoughtful comments on earlier drafts of this essay.

Conclusion

Studying Literacy with Computers

Susan Hilligoss and Cynthia L. Selfe

In tracing how one society gradually invested meaning in written documents, the historian M. T. Clanchy describes the development of medieval English wills and other conveyances of property (202–08). A number of objects, mainly knives, survive along with written conveyances. The knives were part of spoken, face-to-face ceremonies, in which the giver transferred a personal object symbolizing the gift of land to the recipient. For witnesses to hear the donor speak the words of the grant and see the object given made the gift valid. Over two centuries, written charters gradually accompanied, then superseded, these objects. In an analysis of the complex relation between the written and the spoken word, Clanchy demonstrates that for a long period, the charter was more a visual symbol than a practical device and the inscribed words' value as evidence was ambiguous, even to the writers themselves. However, once documents began to be systematically preserved, archivists threw the knives away unless they were inscribed or had inscribed parchment labels (207). For them these artifacts were not "text" and so had nothing to do with the documents. Though nontextual practices like affixing seals still validate texts, the archivists, like most of us who call ourselves literate, could not connect objects that bore no writing with those that did.

Clanchy's description bears on the essays in this volume. For scholars and researchers of composition, computers have been something like those knives to historians of literacy. Neither knives nor computers are themselves strange, but it has taken hard work to admit these items as intimately connected with literacy. Literate practices go on without either one, and so, when we define literacy, we seek a definition that transcends these "local, specific, and necessarily temporary" circumstances (Flannery 210). But like the knives to historians of literacy, computers' sheer physical presence reminds us anew of the sensory, kinetic, and cognitive features, the local settings, the social contexts, and the power relations through which we read and write. They remind us that our literacy is not transparent, that literate knowledge is not the same as textual knowledge (Brandt), and that literate behaviors, in Shirley Brice Heath's terms, are where we find them; they are not bound by our notions of text or our disciplinary city limits.

Through observing, enacting, and speculating about computer-supported writing practices, contributors to this volume have questioned our definitions of text, literacy, literature, even the distinction between reading and writing. With computers as a starting point, the writers have made these concepts problematic. They have amplified Cynthia Selfe's 1989 argument that "the real work of developing computers as aids to literacy has just begun" into theoretical as well as practical realms ("Redefining Literacy" 3). A theme rung throughout the volume is the many ways that computers reflect us. The writers here do not agree on particulars of that reflection or on the degree to which we can and should hold the mirror differently to get different views of ourselves. Some, like Stuart Moulthrop, Nancy Kaplan, and L. M. Dryden, have examined how computers might alter the prestige of one or another aspect of literacy. With our current assumptions, for example, it is difficult to think of, let alone present, literary texts in a way that does not privilege them over composition studies or student texts (Scholes, *Textual Power* 5). Hypertext offers one means of so doing, although it too carries its hidden authors and repressions. With hypertext, teachers and researchers have also blurred the boundaries between writing and reading, something that can hardly be experienced without this system and, no less, the thoughtful application of it. The very notion of "classroom" is extended in Betsy A. Bowen's essay on Breadnet and other discussions of conferencing. However, technology only complicates rather than offers directions for addressing other deep cultural terms and assumptions, such as Billie Wahlstrom's feminist critique has illustrated. And the perspectives that cross-cultural studies might bring to studies of literacy and computers have barely begun to emerge.

This seesawing of views recurs across sections. Several contributors, William Costanzo, Ann Hill Duin and Craig Hansen, Johndan Johnson-Eilola, and Catherine Smith among them, have sketched new metaphors, practices, and ways of thinking wrought by our experience with computers. But the volume also sounds warning notes. In particular, William Wresch, David Dobrin, and Christina Haas and Christine Neuwirth voice dissent as well as hope, offering hard thinking and encouraging diverse ways of seeing computers and literacy.

With different, problematic definitions of literacy in mind, contributors have observed practices, especially classroom practices, for reading and writing with computers. The authors document enthusiasm and success but also the beneficial failure that prompts closer questions about our practices and assumptions—including our acceptance of *success* and *failure* to describe learning. In assessing what we know—the research—writers have also described a wealth of good, thoughtful teaching. In one or two cases, teachers have shared with their students the controversies that engage them. In Gerald Graff's view, that, too, is salutary (*Professing Literature* 251–52).

Writers here are well aware that students and teachers who use computers are part of larger social groups. To mention individual contributors here scarcely does justice to the rich insights throughout the essays. Paul J. LeBlanc, and Gary Graves and Carl Haller, demonstrate how computers become entangled with program conflicts and wasted human as well as material resources. As professionals with our own schooling now internalized as trusted, semiautomatic practices, we are selective in using computers even in the familiar area of bibliographic searching, as William Goodrich Jones describes. Gail E. Hawisher, in her essay on software, undertakes the beginning of a history of this field, separate from computer science. Her narrative also removes software from the domain of hobbyists, their magazines, and the commercial publications and advertisements that have fueled many humanists' and composition scholars' early interests in computers. These affiliations still represent a major source of our literate practices with computers—and, as several here have noted, a major source of conflicts. Ellen L. Barton, for one, examines the dominant metaphors of technology in both the public discourse and the more specialized discourse of this field.

These essays explore issues so that teachers can decide how to use (and not use) technology for writing and reading. Many of the chapters, such as Davida Charney's, also address the interpretation of technological change as it bears on discourse practices. As a whole, they lay a foundation of current issues from which future research may proceed. Above all, these investigators are integrating computers into our thinking about literacy in its many forms, whether writing and reading practices in various settings or theories about discourse.

In this admittedly emerging field, with what should teachers, scholars, and researchers concern themselves? With the "fine-grained" view and the "wide-angle" view that Haas and Neuwirth describe, looking for that broader understanding that can comprehend the intricate relations of "literacy and technologies as they are manifested in cultures and in individuals." The answer implied by the title of this volume is to study literacy, not just computers. For the efforts in teaching, action research, and scholarship described in these pages, *study* means not only "read and write" but also *attend to, absorb, observe, enact*. And literacy encompasses the many meanings that play throughout this volume, taking in a wealth of practices and the theoretical stances that grow from and, in turn, nourish these practices. Shirley Brice Heath summarizes these from an ethnographic perspective:

> Being literate means being able to talk with and listen with others to interpret texts, say what they mean, link them to personal experience and with other texts, argue with them and make predictions from them, develop future scenarios, compare and evaluate related situations, and know that the practice of all these literate abilities is practical. ("Fourth Vision" 298)

With this theme, studying literacy with computers, as peroration, we will close. As teachers and researchers, we need to study literacy, with computers as an important feature of the setting and the means, a feature that changes literate practices and our understanding of them but neither wholly sustains nor destroys any given literacy. "What sustains literacy isn't a what but a who," concludes Deborah Brandt (194). If we have wrongly identified text with literate knowledge, the next fallacy may be "computer knowledge," in which the computer—even a certain kind of computer—becomes the new picture of literate orientation. This is a real possibility. As Haas and Neuwirth note, we must be wary of research designs that assume that any one technology, any one text, or any one practice is all (Halio; Levy; Kaplan and Moulthrop, "Other Ways").

Therefore, study literacy with computers as people's practices and behaviors, and know, as Janis Forman and Bill Jones have shown here, that such practices are specific, often well suited to the purpose, and reliable. People do not change practices simply because a technology is introduced, and they will suit the technology to their needs. Study literacy, not as textuality or its computer-screen equivalent, nor as something opposed to speech and social interaction, because the latter are essential in being literate. In addition to direct research in writing and reading with computers, do as these writers have done and study theory of literature and discourse. Study the literate practices of software designers. Study, too, the many histories and ethnographic narratives of literacy that immerse themselves in the stories, documents, crafts, and practices of small groups, rather than technological explanations of human progress or decline (Daniell, "Against the Great Leap Theory" 189). Study the power relations of literacy in homes, schools, workplaces, and public sites where computers are present (Siefert, Gerbner, and Fisher 5). The diffusion of relations within our societies, heightened by telecommunications, makes this study challenging. As Haas and Neuwirth conclude, studying power means trying to empower our students, but also ourselves as members of a widely connected discipline, with a past, affiliations, conflicts, and responsibilities.

These exhortations make the future sound sure and this field, literacy and computers, a real thing. That is not the case. Naming literacy and computers together in this publication and iterating the connections through its pages has been a means to an end, a way of seeing for a while—maybe quite a while. However, this field may never emerge at all but submerge, dissipate, into other kinds of knowledge about discourse. Applying Michel Foucault's ideas, Kathryn Thoms Flannery has celebrated the failures that even thoughtfully researched approaches to literacy have suffered. If this yoking of concerns proves ephemeral, Foucault might say, so be it. The terms of debate will change rapidly; that is certain. Some of our literate behaviors with computers, novel now, will become tacit. Many already have. Within a decade, some language for talking about word processing has become "naive" or "subjugated" knowledge, difficult to recover except by novices who have little voice (Flannery 211). Another possibility—implied in some of these pages—is more speculative. As computers and electronic multimedia are more and more a component of our literate behaviors, they may cease to be a distinctive part of literary or composition studies. If so, the picture of literate knowledge may not simply be "computer knowledge," in Brandt's sense. But it is possible to imagine that *computers* (or some related word like *hypermedia*) may become a linguistically "unmarked" term for devices of reading and writing, even for text, as paper, pen, and type have been. That eventuality is to be neither desired nor avoided. What we have here named as knowledge will evaporate into the tacit practices of any number of fields, with both losses and gains for us and, more important, for those who come after us. No matter. We constantly find ourselves in the position not of the archivists but of their predecessors, the givers and inscribers of knives. We can never inscribe all we do with these knives, nor can we control the knowledges of those who follow, but, with effort, part of what we learn they may know.

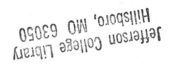

Notes on Contributors

Ellen L. Barton is associate professor in the Department of English at Wayne State University, where she teaches in the linguistics and composition programs; she was coordinator of the computers and writing program from 1985 to 1991. Her research interests are in syntax, pragmatics, discourse analysis, and composition theory, and her work has appeared in *College Composition and Communication, Journal of Teaching Writing,* and *Computers and Composition,* and in *Evolving Perspectives on Computers and Composition Studies,* edited by Gail E. Hawisher and Cynthia Selfe.

Betsy A. Bowen is associate professor of English and director of composition at Fairfield University. She is coauthor, with John Elder, Dixie Goswami, and Jeffrey Schwartz, of *Word Processing in a Community of Writers.* Her work with educational technology began at Carnegie Mellon University and the Bread Loaf School of English, where she served as director of the Computer Center.

Davida Charney is associate professor of English at Penn State University, University Park, where she teaches technical and business writing, advanced expository writing, research methods, and rhetorical theory. Her research focuses on document design, reading and writing processes, and the rhetoric of science. Charney's work has appeared in *Research in the Teaching of English, Memory and Cognition, Human Computer Interaction, Cognition and Instruction, Journal of Business and Technical Communication,* and *Technical Communication Quarterly.* With Marie Secor, she edited the volume *Constructing Rhetorical Education.*

William Costanzo is professor of English at Westchester Community College, New York, where he has taught courses in writing, literature, and film for more than twenty years. His publications include *Double Exposure: Composing through Writing and Film, The Electronic Text,* and *Reading the Movies.* He has received state and national awards for teaching, scholarship, and educational software. Active in NCTE, Costanzo has chaired the Commission on Media, the Committee on Film Study, and the Assembly on Media Arts. He lectures widely on the educational uses of technology and has led workshops on media and English throughout the country.

David N. Dobrin is a consultant to the software industry on writing matters. Formerly on the writing faculty at the Massachusetts Institute of Technology, he has been a principal at Lexicom, in Cambridge, since 1985. He has published many articles on subjects ranging from warning labels to desktop publishing; his book *Writing and Technique* appeared in 1989.

L. M. Dryden has taught high school and college English since 1974. He has authored his own *Hypercard* stackware for students, has served as a content-area consultant to multimedia software publishers, and has written and carried out grants to establish multimedia minilabs for English and career education projects. Dryden will become, in 1994, associate professor of English at Nagoya University of Foreign Studies in Nagoya, Japan, where he will help design and then teach in an interactive multimedia learning center for the study of international relations.

Ann Hill Duin is associate professor in the Department of Rhetoric at the University of Minnesota, where she teaches and conducts research in the undergraduate and graduate scientific and technical communications programs. Her research interests include computers and collaboration, the construction of online information, and mentoring by means of telecommunications and multimedia. With Craig Hansen, Duin is coediting the text *Challenging the Boundaries: Multidisciplinary Research in Nonacademic Writing*.

Janis Forman is director of management communication and adjunct associate professor of management at the Anderson Graduate School of Management at the University of California, Los Angeles. She has published widely on computing and collaborative writing, in such publications as the *Journal of Business Communication*. She also edited *New Visions of Collaborative Writing*, a collection that brings together scholarship from several disciplines on the topic of collaboration. Her current projects include studies on cross-disciplinary collaborative research and on the application of composition theory to research in business communication.

Gary Graves taught English language arts and science in Montana for twenty-four years. He is now a full-time consultant to education and business in "curriculum, computers, and change." Graves lives in Missoula, Montana.

Christina Haas is assistant professor of English at Penn State University, University Park. In addition to technology studies, her interests include technical discourse, reading and writing processes, and learning in the disciplines.

Carl Haller received his BA in English and his MA in community development from the University of Michigan. He has taught in public and private schools for over two decades. Currently, he is a teacher at McDonogh School in Owings Mills, Maryland, and the director of the school's computer-assisted writing center.

Craig Hansen, a lecturer in the Department of Rhetoric at the University of Minnesota, has worked in the computer industry in a variety of technical and managerial positions. His research interests include the study of contextual factors in writing and the role of emerging communication technologies in the workplace. Hansen and Ann Hill Duin are coediting a text, *Challenging the Boundaries: Multidisciplinary Research in Nonacademic Writing.*

Gail E. Hawisher is associate professor of English and director of the Center for Writing Studies at the University of Illinois, Urbana. She serves on the NCTE College Editorial Board and also chairs NCTE's Instructional Technology Committee. She has published widely in computers and composition studies, and her most recent book is *Re-imagining Computers and Composition: Teaching and Research in the Virtual Age,* which she coedited with Paul LeBlanc. With Cynthia Selfe, she edits the *CCCC Bibliography of Composition and Rhetoric* and *Computers and Composition,* a journal that examines issues related to writing, writing instruction, and the new technologies. She is currently at work on a book with Cynthia Selfe, Paul LeBlanc, and Charles Moran on the history of computers and composition studies.

Susan Hilligoss, assistant professor of English at Clemson University, has served as associate editor for the MLA series Research and Scholarship in Composition. She has given papers on the history and technology of literacy, as well as on the social processes of electronic conferencing. Currently Hilligoss is finishing a book on the psychiatrist Robert Coles.

Johndan Johnson-Eilola is completing his dissertation, "Nostalgic Angels: Re-articulating Hypertext Writing," at Michigan Technological University. His work on hypertext and other literacy technologies has appeared in the *Journal of Advanced Composition, Computers and Composition, Writing on the Edge, Collegiate Microcomputer,* and several edited collections. He has recently joined the technical communications program at the New Mexico Institute of Mining and Technology.

William Goodrich Jones is assistant university librarian, Collections Development and Information Services, and associate professor of library administration at the University of Illinois, Chicago. He has also served as head of the Seeley G. Mudd Library for Science and Engineering at Northwestern University and as librarian for the University of Michigan's Institute for Social Research. Jones received his AB from Princeton University and his AMLS from the University of Michigan.

Nancy Kaplan, who teaches at the University of Texas, Dallas, is a hypermedia educator. She is codeveloper of *PROSE* (*Prompted Revision of Student Essays*), writing software published by McGraw-Hill. In 1987 *PROSE* won the EDU-COM/NCRIPTAL Higher Education Software Award; "Something to Imagine: Literature, Composition, and Interactive Fiction," by Kaplan and Stuart Moulthrop, received the 1991 Ellen Nold Award for best article on computers and writing.

Paul J. LeBlanc is associate professor and chair of the Department of Humanities at Springfield College. He is the software review editor for *Computers and Composition* and heads the software subcommittee of NCTE's Instructional

Technology Committee. With Gail Hawisher he coedited *Re-imagining Comput-ers and Composition: Teaching and Research in the Virtual Age*, and he is the author of *Writing Teachers Writing Software: Finding Our Voice in the Electronic Age*. LeBlanc has written articles and presented and conducted workshops on technology and writing; he currently directs the Hypermedia Project at Springfield College.

Stuart Moulthrop, a hypermedia educator, teaches at the Georgia Institute of Technology. He is the author of several articles on hypertext as well as of *Victory Garden*, a hypertext fiction published by Eastgate Systems. For their essay "Something to Imagine: Literature, Composition, and Interactive Fic-tion" Moulthrop and his coauthor, Nancy Kaplan, won the 1991 Ellen Nold Award for best article on computers and writing.

Christine M. Neuwirth is associate professor in the Department of English and the School of Computer Science at Carnegie Mellon University. She has authored numerous articles and book chapters on computers and writing, including works on the design of user message systems, intelligent tutoring, and hypertext tools for writers. Neuwirth has also designed and tested comput-er-based tools to support writing and collaborative writing.

Cynthia L. Selfe, professor of composition and communication and head of the Department of Humanities at Michigan Technological University, founded the journal *Computers and Composition* with Kathleen Kiefer and currently coedits the *CCCC Bibliography of Composition and Rhetoric* with Gail E. Haw-isher. She has coedited *Critical Perspectives on Computers and Composition Instruction* and *Evolving Perspectives on Computers and Composition Studies: Questions for the 1990s* (both with Gail E. Hawisher), as well as the MLA volume *Computers and Writing: Theory, Research, Practice* (with Deborah H. Holdstein).

Catherine F. Smith teaches in the Syracuse University Writing Program and consults in government and industry in the fields of composition, computer applications, and professional writing and speaking. Her essays include "Writ-ing, Thinking, Computing" (with John B. Smith) and "Reconceiving Hyper-text." Currently she is writing about public discourse in governmental hearings and applying hypertext theory to the cognition of witnessing.

Billie J. Wahlstrom is professor in, and head of, the Department of Rhetoric at the University of Minnesota. Her primary areas of research are the effect of technologies on communication practices and the role of gender in communi-cation. Her work has appeared in several publications, including *Computers and Composition, Journal of Business and Technical Communication*, and *Colle-giate Microcomputer*, and in 1991 her book, *Perspectives on Human Communica-tion*, was published. Wahlstrom has been a consultant to Paramount Pictures in Hollywood, Toin Corporation in Tokyo, and other businesses.

William Wresch chairs the Department of Mathematics and Computing at the University of Wisconsin, Stevens Point. He also heads NCTE's Assembly on

Computers in English. He is the author or editor of four books on computers and writing, including *The English Classroom in the Computer Age*, and the author of *Writer's Helper*, named best writing software in the 1988 EDUCOM software initiative.

Jane Zeni is associate professor of English and educational studies at the University of Missouri, Saint Louis. As director of the Gateway Writing Project, she assists experienced teachers in staff development and action research (see her *Writinglands*). Zeni is involved in a university-wide project linking methods courses by computer network with classrooms at an area middle school. Since 1987, she has worked with an action research team of teachers in Webster Groves, Missouri, to develop culturally sensitive writing classrooms. Zeni has published in *Computers and Composition, English Education, Educational Leadership*, the National Writing Project *Quarterly*, and *Writing Program Administration Journal* (formerly under the name Jane Zeni Flinn).

Works Cited

Books and Articles

Adler, Jerry. "Taking Offense." *Newsweek* 24 Dec. 1990: 48–54.

Alschuler, Liora. "Handcrafted Hypertext: Lessons from the ACM Experiment." Barrett, *Society of Text* 343–61.

Amato, Joseph. Rev. of *Writing Space*, by Jay David Bolter. *Computers and Composition* 9.1 (1991): 111–17.

Anacona, Deborah G., and David F. Caldwell. "Information Technology and Work Groups: The Case of New Product Teams." Galegher, Kraut, and Egido 173–90.

Anderson, Paul. *Technical Writing: A Reader-Centered Approach.* 2nd ed. San Diego: Harcourt, 1991.

Applebee, Arthur, and Judith Langer. *How Writing Shapes Thinking: A Study of Teaching and Learning.* Research rept. 23. Urbana: NCTE, 1987.

Aronowitz, Stanley, and Henry Giroux. *Education under Siege: The Conservative, Liberal, and Radical Debate over Schooling.* South Hadley: Bergin, 1985.

Atwell, Nancie. *In the Middle: Writing, Reading, and Learning with Adolescents.* Portsmouth: Boynton/Cook, 1987.

Bailey, Richard W., and Robin Melanie Fosheim, eds. *Literacy for Life: The Demand for Reading and Writing.* New York: MLA, 1983.

Bakhtin, Mikhail. *The Dialogic Imagination.* Ed. Michael Holquist. Trans. Caryl Emerson and Michael Holquist. Austin: U of Texas P, 1981.

Bakhtin, Mikhail, and V. N. Volosinov. *Marxism and the Philosophy of Language.* 1929. Trans. L. Matejka and I. Titunik. Cambridge: Harvard UP, 1986.

Balestri, Diane Pelkus. "Softcopy and Hard: Wordprocessing and Writing Process." *Academic Computing* Feb. 1988: 14 + .

Barker, Thomas T., and Fred O. Kemp. "Network Theory: A Postmodern Pedagogy for the Writing Classroom." Handa, *Computers and Community* 1–27.

Barrett, Edward, ed. *The Society of Text: Hypertext, Hypermedia, and the Social Construction of Information.* Cambridge: MIT P, 1989.

———, ed. *Text, Context, and Hypertext: Writing with and for the Computer.* Cambridge: MIT P, 1988.

Barthes, Roland. "The Death of the Author." Stephen Heath, *Image-Music-Text* 142–48.

—————. "From Work to Text." Stephen Heath, *Image-Music-Text* 155–64. Rpt. in *Textual Strategies*. Ed. Josué Harari. Ithaca: Cornell UP, 1979. 73–81.

Bartholomae, David. "Inventing the University." *Journal of Basic Writing* 5.1 (1986): 4–23.

Bartlett, F. C. *Remembering.* Cambridge: Cambridge UP, 1932.

Barton, Ellen. Rev. of *Society and Technological Change*, by Rudi Volti. *Computers and Composition* 7.3 (1990): 129–37.

Barton, Ellen, and Ruth Ray. "Developing Connections: Computers and Literacy." *Computers and Composition* 6.3 (1989): 35–45.

Batson, Trent. "Teaching in Networked Classrooms." Selfe, Rodrigues, and Oates 247–55.

Becker, A. L. "Literacy and Cultural Change: Some Experiences." Bailey and Fosheim 45–51.

Beeman, William, et al. "Hypertext and Pluralism: From Lineal to Non-lineal Thinking." J. B. Smith et al. 67–88.

Begoray, John A. "An Introduction to Hypermedia Issues, Systems, and Applications Areas." *International Journal of Man-Machine Studies* 33 (1990): 121–47.

Belenky, Mary Field, et al. *Women's Ways of Knowing: The Development of Self, Voice, and Mind.* New York: Basic, 1986.

Belsey, Catherine. *Critical Practice.* London: Metheun, 1980.

Beniger, James. *The Control Revolution: Technological and Economic Origins of the Information Society.* Cambridge: Harvard UP, 1986.

Benjamin, Walter. *Illuminations.* Ed. Hannah Arendt. New York: Schocken, 1969.

Berger, John. "Ways of Seeing." *Ways of Reading: An Anthology for Writers.* Ed. David Bartholomae and Anthony Petrosky. New York: St. Martin's, 1987. 47–71.

Berk, Emily, and Joseph Devlin, eds. *The Hypertext/Hypermedia Handbook.* New York: McGraw, 1991.

Berlin, James. "Contemporary Composition: The Major Pedagogical Theories." *College English* 44 (1982): 766–77.

—————. "Rhetoric and Ideology in the Writing Class." *College English* 50 (1988): 477–94.

—————. *Rhetoric and Reality: Writing Instruction in American Colleges, 1900–1985.* Carbondale: Southern Illinois UP, 1984.

Bernhardt, Stephen A. "Seeing the Text." *College Composition and Communication* 37 (1986): 66–78.

Bickel, Linda. "Word Processing and the Integration of Reading and Writing Instruction." Collins and Sommers 39–46.

Bijker, Wiebe E., Thomas P. Hughes, and Trevor Pinch, eds. *The Social Construction of Technological Systems.* Cambridge: MIT P, 1987.

Bizzell, Patricia. "Arguing about Literacy." *College English* 50 (1988): 141–53.

—————. "Beyond Anti-foundationalism to Rhetorical Authority: Problems Defining 'Cultural Literacy.'" *College English* 52 (1990): 661–75.

—————. "Cognition, Convention, and Certainty." *PreText* 3 (1982): 213–43.

──. "What Happens When Basic Writers Come to College?" *College Composition and Communication* 37 (1986): 294–301.

Bjerkness, Gro, Pelle Ehn, and Morton Kyng. *Computers and Democracy: A Scandinavian Challenge*. London: Gower, 1987.

Blau, Sheridan. "Transactions between Theory and Practice in the Teaching of Literature: A Professional Development Model." *Research in Theory, Practice, and Policy in the Teaching of Literature*. Ed. Judith Langer and James Flood. Urbana: NCTE, forthcoming.

Bleier, Ruth. *Feminist Approaches to Science*. New York: Pergamon, 1986.

──. *Science and Gender: A Critique of Biology and Its Theories of Women*. New York: Pergamon, 1984.

Bloom, Allan. *The Closing of the American Mind*. New York: Simon, 1987.

Bloom, Harold. *The Anxiety of Influence: A Theory of Poetry*. New York: Oxford UP, 1973.

Bogumil, Mary L., and Michael R. Molino. "Pretext, Context, Subtext: Textual Power in the Writing of Langston Hughes, Richard Wright, and Martin Luther King, Jr." *College English* 52 (1990): 800–11.

Bolter, Jay David. *Writing Space: The Computer, Hypertext, and the History of Writing*. Hillsdale: Erlbaum, 1990.

Borges, Jorge Luis. "The Garden of Forking Paths." *Labyrinths* 19–29.

──. *Labyrinths*. Trans. Donald A. Yates. New York: New Directions, 1962.

──. "Partial Magic in the *Quixote*." *Labyrinths* 193–96.

Borland, Katherine. "Orality and Literacy: Thoughts about the Evolution of Consciousness." Secor and Charney 43–62.

Bowers, C. A. *The Cultural Dimensions of Educational Computing: Understanding the Non-neutrality of Technology*. New York: Teachers Coll. P, 1988.

Boyd, Robert. "When Data Rains and Reigns." *Detroit Free Press* 19 Feb. 1989: 1B+.

Braddock, Richard, Richard Lloyd-Jones, and Lowell Schoer. *Research in Written Composition*. Champaign: NCTE, 1963.

Brandt, Deborah. "Literacy and Knowledge." Lunsford, Moglen, and Slevin 189–96.

Bransford, John. *Human Cognition: Learning, Understanding and Remembering*. Belmont: Wadsworth, 1979.

Braverman, Harry. *Labor and Monopoly Capital: The Degradation of Work in the Twentieth Century*. New York: Monthly Review, 1974.

Breenberger, Martin, and James C. Puffer. "Telemedicine: Toward Better Health Care for the Elderly." *Journal of Communication* 39.3 (1989): 137–44.

Bridwell-Bowles, Lillian. "Designing Research on Computer-Assisted Writing." *Computers and Composition* 7 (1988): 79–91.

Brienne, Deborah, and Shelley Goldman. "Networking: How It Has Enhanced Science Classes in New York Schools . . . and How It Can Enhance Classes in Your School Too." *Classroom Computer Learning* 9.7 (1989): 44–53.

Britton, Bruce, and Sami Gülgöz. "Using Kintsch's Computational Model to Improve Instructional Text: Effects of Repairing Inference Calls on Recall and Cognitive Structures." *Journal of Educational Psychology* 83 (1991): 329–45.

Britton, James, et al. *The Development of Writing Abilities (11–18)*. London: Macmillan, 1975.

Brooks, Peter. *Reading for the Plot: Design and Intention in Narrative*. New York: Random, 1984.

Brown, John Seely, Allan Collins, and Paul Duguid. "Situated Cognition and the Culture of Learning." *Educational Researcher* 18.1 (1989): 32–42.

Brown, L. Dave. "Managing Conflict among Groups." *Organizational Psychology: Readings in Human Behavior in Organizations*. Ed. Irwin M. Rubin and James M. McIntyre. Englewood Cliffs: Prentice, 1984. 225–37.

Brown, P. J. "Assessing the Quality of Hypertext Documents." Streitz, Rizk, and André 1–12.

Brownell, Thomas. "Planning and Implementing the Right Word Processing System." *Computers and Composition* 2 (1985): 3–5.

Bruffee, Kenneth A. "Collaborative Learning and the 'Conversation of Mankind.'" *College English* 46 (1984): 635–52.

———. "Collaborative Learning: Some Practical Methods." *College English* 34 (1973): 634–43.

Bryden, David. "Debate Not What's Studied, But How It's Taught." *Detroit News* 2 Feb. 1991: 3B.

Bump, Jerome. "Radical Changes in Class Discussion Using Networked Computers." *Computers and the Humanities* 24 (1990): 49–65.

Bureau, W. E. "Computers: Catalysts for Change at Springfield High School." Selfe, Rodrigues, and Oates 97–110.

Burns, Hugh. "Recollections of First-Generation Computer-Assisted Prewriting." *The Computer in Composition Instruction: A Writer's Tool*. Ed. William Wresch. Urbana: NCTE, 1984. 15–33.

Bush, Vannevar. "As We May Think." *Atlantic* July 1945: 101–08. Rpt. in Nelson, *Literary Machines* 1.39–54.

Butcher, Lee. *Accidental Millionaire: The Rise and Fall of Steve Jobs at Apple Computer*. New York: Paragon, 1987.

Campbell, Paul. "Computers in Education: A Question of Access." Annual Meeting of the American Educational Research Association. Apr. 1983.

Cannings, T. R., L. G. Polin, et al. *Technical Report TR88-1 Project Overview, Approach and Rationale*. Alhambra: Alhambra Model Technology Schools Project Office, 1988.

Carlson, Patricia A. "Hypertext: A Way of Incorporating User Feedback into Online Documentation." Barrett, *Text, Context, and Hypertext* 93–110.

———. "Hypertext and Intelligent Interfaces for Text Retrieval." Barrett, *Society of Text* 59–76.

Carnegie Commission. "A Nation Prepared: Teachers for the Twenty-first Century." Excerpts from *Report by the Carnegie Forum's Task Force on Teaching as a Profession*. *Chronicle of Higher Education* 21 May 1986: A43–55.

Carter, Michael. "*Stasis* and *Kairos*: Principles of Social Construction in Classical Rhetoric." *Rhetoric Review* 7 (1988): 97–112.

Case, Donald Owen. "The Collection and Use of Information by Some American Historians: A Study of Motives and Methods." *Library Quarterly* 61 (1991): 61–82.

Catlin, Timothy, Paulette Bush, and Nicole Yankelovich. "Internote: Extending a Hypermedia Framework to Support Annotative Collaboration." Meyrowitz 365–78.

Chall, Jeanne. *Learning to Read: The Great Debate*. New York: McGraw, 1967.

———. *Stages of Reading Development*. New York: McGraw, 1983.

Charney, Davida. "Comprehending Non-linear Text: The Role of Discourse Cues and Reading Strategies." J. B. Smith et al. 109–20.

———. "A Study in Rhetorical Reading: How Evolutionists Read 'The Spandrels of San Marco.' " *Understanding Scientific Prose*. Ed. Jack Selzer. Madison: U of Wisconsin P, forthcoming.

Chodorow, Nancy. *The Reproduction of Mothering: Psychoanalysis and the Sociology of Gender*. Berkeley: U of California P, 1978.

Chposky, Jim, and Ted Leonsis. *Blue Magic: The People, Power, and Politics behind the IBM Personal Computer*. New York: Facts on File, 1988.

Clanchy, M. T. *From Memory to Written Record: England, 1066–1307*. Cambridge: Harvard UP, 1979.

Clark, Chris, Barbara Kurshan, and Sharon Yoder. *Telecommunications in the Classroom*. Palo Alto: Computer Learning Foundation–ISTE, 1989.

Clark, Gregory. *Dialogue, Dialectic, and Conversation: A Social Perspective on the Function of Writing*. Carbondale: Southern Illinois UP, 1990.

Clark, Suzanne, and Lisa Ede. "Collaboration, Resistance, and the Teaching of Writing." Lunsford, Moglen, and Slevin 276–85.

Clifford, John. "Enacting Critical Literacy." Lunsford, Moglen, and Slevin 255–61.

———. "Toward an Ethical Community of Writers." Forman, *New Visions* 170–97.

Cohen, Moshe, and Naomi Miyake. "A Worldwide Intercultural Network: Exploring Electronic Messaging for Instruction." *Instructional Science* 15 (1986): 257–73.

Cohen, Moshe, and Margaret Riel. *Computer Networks: Creating Real Audiences for Students' Writing*. Tech. Rept. 15. La Jolla: Center for Human Information Processing, U of California, San Diego, 1986.

———. "The Effects of Distant Audiences on Students' Writing." *American Educational Research Journal* 26.2 (1989): 143–59.

Cole, M., and P. Griffen. "Contextual Factors in Education: Improving Science and Mathematics Education for Minorities and Women." Madison: Wisconsin Center for Educ. Research, 1987.

Coleman, Ike. "An Online Community." *Bread Loaf News* (Summer 1990): 26.

Collier, Richard. "The Word-Processor and Revision Strategies." *College Composition and Communication* 34 (1983): 149–55.

Collins, James. "Computerized Text Analysis and the Teaching of Writing." Hawisher and Selfe, *Critical Perspectives* 16–29.

Collins, James, and Elizabeth Sommers, eds. *Writing On-line: Using Computers in the Teaching of Writing*. Upper Montclair: Boynton/Cook, 1985.

"Computer Notes." *Chronicle of Higher Education* 17 Jan. 1990: A24.

Congressional Office of Technology Assessment. *Power On! New Tools for Teaching and Learning*. Washington: GPO, 1988.

Conklin, Jeff. "Hypertext: An Introduction and Survey." *IEEE Computer* 20.9 (1987): 17–41.

———. *A Theory and Tool for Coordination of Design Conversations*. MCTC Tech. Rept. STP-236-86. Austin: Microelectronics and Computer Technology Corp., 1986.

Conklin, Jeff, and Michael L. Begeman. "gIBIS: A Hypertext Tool for Team Design Deliberation." J. B. Smith et al. 247–52.

Cook-Gumperz, Jenny, ed. *The Social Construction of Literacy*. Cambridge: Cambridge UP, 1986.

Cooper, Marilyn M., and Cynthia L. Selfe. "Computer Conferences and Learning: Authority, Resistance, and Internally Persuasive Discourse." *College English* 52 (1990): 847–69.

Copper, Linda R. "CAI with Home-Bound Students Proves Successful in Model Program." *T.H.E. Journal* 18.6 (1991): 68–69.

Costa, Rose. Interview. Springfield, MA, 1988.

Costanzo, William. *The Electronic Text: Learning to Write, Read, and Reason with Computers*. Englewood Cliffs: Educational Technology, 1989.

Couture, Barbara, and Jone Rymer. "Interactive Writing on the Job: Definitions and Implications of Collaboration." *Writing in the Business Professions*. Ed. Myra Kogen. Urbana: NCTE, 1989. 73–93.

Crary, Karl. "Karl's Forking Response." Unpublished hypertext, 1989.

Croft, W. Bruce, and Howard Turtle. "A Retrieval Model for Incorporating Hypertext Links." Meyrowitz 213–24.

Cross, Geoffrey. "A Bakhtian Exploration of Factors Affecting the Collaborative Writing of an Executive Letter of an Annual Report." *Research in the Teaching of English* 24. 2 (1990): 173–202.

Crowley, Mary. "Organizing for Electronic Messaging in the Schools." *Computing Teacher* Apr. 1989: 23–26.

Dalton, D. W., and M. J. Hannafin. "The Effects of Word Processing on Written Composition." *Journal of Educational Research* 20 (1987): 338–42.

D'Angelo, Frank. "Literacy and Cognition: A Developmental Perspective." Bailey and Fosheim 97–114.

Daniell, Beth. "Against the Great Leap Theory of Literacy." *PrelText* 7 (1986): 181–93.

———. "The Situation of Literacy and Cognition: What We Can Learn from the Uzbek Experiment." Lunsford, Moglen, and Slevin 197–207.

Davidson, Cathy. " 'PH' Stands for Political Hypocrisy." *Academe* Sept.–Oct. 1991: 8–14.

Dean, Terry. "Multicultural Classrooms, Monocultural Teachers." *College Composition and Communication* 40 (1989): 23–37.

Dearborn, Dewitt C., and Herbert A. Simon. "Selective Perception." *Sociometry* 21 (1958): 140–43.

deBeaugrande, Robert, and Wolfgang Dressler. *Introduction to Text Linguistics*. New York: Longman, 1981.

Dee-Lucas, Diane, and Jill H. Larkin. "Novice Strategies for Processing Scientific Texts." *Discourse Processes* 9 (1986): 329–54.

Delany, Paul, and George P. Landow. Foreword. Delany and Landow, *Hypermedia* i–ii.

———, eds. *Hypermedia and Literary Studies*. Cambridge: MIT P, 1990.

Delattre, Edwin J. "The Insiders." Bailey and Fosheim 52–63.

Derrida, Jacques. "Signature Event Context." *Glyph* 1 (1977): 172–97.

Dewey, John. *Democracy in Education*. 1916. New York: Free, 1967.

———. *Experience and Education*. New York: Collier, 1974.

Dickens, Charles. *Hard Times*. New York: NAL, 1961.

Dickey, William. "Poem Descending a Staircase: Hypertext and the Simultaneity of Experience." Delany and Landow, *Hypermedia* 143–52.

DiPardo, Anne, and Mike DiPardo. "Towards the Metapersonal Essay: Exploring the Potential of Hypertext in the Composition Class." *Computers and Composition* 7.3 (1990): 7–22.

Dizard, Wilson P. *The Coming Information Age*. London: Longman, 1982.

Dobrin, David N. "A Limitation on the Use of Computers in Composition." Holdstein and Selfe 40–57.

———. "A New Grammar Checker." *Computers and the Humanities* 24 (1990): 67–80.

———. "Style Analyzers Once More." *Computers and Composition* 3 (1986): 22–32.

———. "Style Checkers for English." MLA Convention. Chicago, 28 Dec. 1990.

———. *Writing and Technique*. Urbana: NCTE, 1989.

Dodge, Bernie, and June Dodge. "Selecting Telecommunications Software for Educational Settings." *Computing Teacher* Apr. 1987: 10–14.

Dodge, Susan. "Few Colleges Have Had 'Political Correctness' Controversies, Study Finds." *Chronicle of Higher Education* 7 Aug. 1991: A23–24.

Douglas, Jane Yellowlees. "Understanding the Act of Reading: The *WOE* Beginner's Guide to Dissection." *Writing on the Edge* 2.2 (1991): 112–25.

———. "Wandering through the Labyrinth: Encountering Interactive Fiction." *Computers and Composition* 6 (1990): 93–103.

Dowling, Colette. *The Cinderella Complex: Women's Hidden Fear of Independence*. New York: Pocket, 1982.

D'Souza, Dinesh. "Illiberal Education." *Atlantic* Mar. 1991: 51–79.

Duin, Ann Hill. "Computer Exercises to Encourage Rethinking and Revision." *Computers and Composition* 4.2 (1987): 66–105.

———. "Computer-Supported Collaborative Writing: The Workplace and the Writing Classroom." *Journal of Business and Technical Communication* 5.2 (1991): 123–50.

———. "Social Construction and Interaction: The Making of Collaborative Meaning via Computer Networks." Forthcoming.

———. "Terms and Tools: A Theory- and Research-Based Approach to Collaborative Writing." *Bulletin of the Association of Business Communication* 53.2 (1990): 45–50.

Duin, Ann Hill, Linda Jorn, and Mark DeBower. "Courseware for Collaborative Writing." *Collaborative Writing in Industry: Investigations in Theory and*

Practice. Ed. Mary M. Lay and William M. Karis. Farmingdale: Baywood, 1991. 146–69.

Durbin, Bill, and Ken Holvig. "Beyond Pen Pals." *Bread Loaf and the Schools* Fall–Winter 1988: 22–23.

Dyer, William G. *Team Building Issues and Alternatives.* Reading: Addison, 1977.

Eagleton, Terry. *Ideology: An Introduction.* London: Verso, 1991.

———. *Literary Theory: An Introduction.* Minneapolis: U of Minnesota P, 1983.

Eco, Umberto. *The Limits of Interpretation.* Bloomington: Indiana UP, 1990.

———. *The Open Work.* Trans. Anna Cancogni. Cambridge: Harvard UP, 1989.

Ede, Lisa. "Audience: An Introduction to Research." *College Composition and Communication* 35 (1984): 140–54.

Ede, Lisa, and Andrea Lunsford. *Singular Texts/Plural Authors: Perspectives on Collaborative Writing.* Carbondale: Southern Illinois UP, 1990.

———. "Why Write . . . Together: A Research Update." *Rhetoric Review* 5 (1986): 71–81.

Ehrenreich, Barbara. "Teach Diversity—With a Smile." *Time* 8 Apr. 1991: 84.

Ehrmann, Stephen C., and Diane Balestri. "Learning to Design, Designing to Learn: A More Creative Role for Technology." *Machine-Mediated Learning* 2.1–2 (1987): 9–33.

Eisenstein, Elizabeth. *The Printing Press as an Agent of Change.* New York: Cambridge UP, 1979.

Elder, John, et al. *Word Processing in a Community of Writers.* New York: Garland, 1989.

Eldred, Janet M. "Computers, Composition Pedagogy, and the Social View." Hawisher and Selfe, *Critical Perspectives* 201–18.

Ellis, Havelock. "The Coming of Literate Communication in Western Culture." *Journal of Communication* 30.1 (1980): 90–98.

———. *Preface to Plato.* Cambridge: Belknap, 1963.

Ellsworth, Elizabeth. "Why Doesn't This Feel Empowering? Working through the Repressive Myths of Critical Pedagogy." *Harvard Educational Review* 59 (1989): 297–324.

Elwart-Keys, Mary, and Marjorie Horton. "Collaboration in the Capture Lab: Computer Support for Group Writing." *Bulletin of the Association of Business Communication* 53.2 (1990): 38–44.

Emerson, Richard M. "Power-Dependence Relations." *American Sociological Review* 27 (1962): 31–41.

Emig, Janet. "Non-magical Thinking: Presenting Writing Developmentally in Schools." *The Web of Meaning: Essays on Writing, Teaching, Learning, and Thinking.* Upper Montclair: Boynton/Cook, 1983. 132–44.

Englebart, Doug, and Kristina Hooper. "The Augmentation System Framework." *Interactive Multimedia: Visions of Multimedia for Developers, Educators, and Information Providers.* Ed. Sueann Ambron and Kristina Hooper. Redmond: Microsoft, 1988. 15–31.

English–Language Arts Curriculum Framework and Criteria Committee. *English–Language Arts Framework for California Public Schools, Kindergarten through Grade Twelve*. Sacramento: Dept. of Education, 1987.

Erickson, Ann. "An ACOT Experiment in Learning." *Computing Teacher* Apr. 1987: 31–32.

Erickson, Thomas D. "Interfaces for Cooperative Work: An Eclectic Look at CSCW '88." *SIGCHI Bulletin* 21.1 (1989): 56–64.

Erwin, Jim. "The Austra-Alaskan Project." *Computing Teacher* Apr. 1987: 34.

Everett, David. "Warlike Wizardry Could Be in Garage." *Detroit Free Press* 19 Jan. 1991: 6A.

Eylon, Bat-Sheva, and F. Reif. "Effects of Knowledge Organization on Task Performance." *Cognition and Instruction* 1.1 (1984): 5–44.

Fahnestock, Jeanne. "Connection and Understanding." Secor and Charney 235–56.

Fahnestock, Jeanne, and Marie Secor. "Teaching Argument: A Theory of Types." *College Composition and Communication* 34 (1983): 20–30.

Faigley, Lester. "Competing Theories of Process: A Critique and a Proposal." *College English* 48 (1986): 527–42.

———. "Nonacademic Writing: The Social Perspective." Odell and Goswami 231–80.

Faigley, Lester, and Thomas Miller. "What We Learn from Writing on the Job." *College English* 44 (1982): 557–69.

Farrell, Pamela. "Word Processing and High School Writing." *Computers and Composition* 2 (1984): 5–7.

Felker, Daniel, Frances Pickering, Veda Charrow, V. Melissa Holland, and Janice Redish. *Guidelines for Document Designers*. Washington: American Institutes for Research, 1981.

Felman, Shoshana. "Psychoanalysis and Education: Teaching Terminable and Interminable." *Yale French Studies* 63 (1982): 21–44.

Finn, Chester. "Why Can't Colleges Convey Our Diverse Culture's Unifying Themes?" Point of view. *Chronicle of Higher Education* 13 June 1990: A40.

Fish, Stanley. *Is There a Text in This Class? The Authority of Interpretive Communities*. Cambridge: Harvard UP, 1980.

Fishman, Andrea A. "Being Literate: A Lesson from the Amish." Lunsford, Moglen, and Slevin 29–38.

Fitschen, Kenneth. "Effective Advice to Beginning Writers: Revise the Hard Copy." *Teaching English in the Two-Year College* 13.2 (1986): 104–08.

Flammer, August, and Walter Kintsch. *Discourse Processing*. Amsterdam: North-Holland, 1982.

Flannery, Kathryn Thoms. "In Praise of the Local and Transitory." Lunsford, Moglen, and Slevin 208–14.

Flinn, Jane Zeni, and Chris Madigan. "Gateway Writing Project: Staff Development and Computers in St. Louis." Selfe, Rodrigues, and Oates 55–68.

Flores, Mary J. "Computer Conferencing: Composing a Feminist Community of Writers." Handa, *Computers and Community* 106–17.

Flower, Joe. "Of Tension, Harmony, and Dilemma-Busting." *Healthcare Forum Journal* (1990): 74–78.

Flower, Linda. "The Construction of Purpose in Writing and Reading." *College English* 50 (1988): 528–50.

———. "Writer-Based Prose: A Cognitive Basis for Problems in Writing." *College English* 41 (1979): 19–37.

Flower, Linda, and John R. Hayes. "The Cognition of Discovery: Defining a Rhetorical Problem." *College Composition and Communication* 21 (1980): 21–32.

Flynn, Elizabeth A. "Composing as a Woman." *College Composition and Communication* 39 (1988): 423–35.

Forester, Thomas, ed. *Computers in the Human Context: Information Technology, Productivity, and People.* Cambridge: MIT P, 1989.

Forman, Janis. "The Discourse Communities and Group Writing Practices of MBAs." *Worlds of Writing: Teaching and Learning in Discourse Communities at Work.* Ed. Carolyn Matalene. New York: Random, 1989. 247–54.

———. "Leadership Dynamics of Computer-Supported Writing Groups." *Computers and Composition* 7.2 (1990): 35–46.

———, ed. *New Visions of Collaborative Writing.* Portsmouth: Heinemann, 1992.

———. "Novices Work on Group Reports: Problems in Group Writing and in Computer-Supported Group Writing." *Journal of Business and Technical Communication* 5.1 (1991): 48–75.

Fortune, Ron. "Visual and Verbal Thinking: Drawing and Word Processing Software in Writing Instruction." Hawisher and Selfe, *Critical Perspectives* 145–61.

Foss, Carolyn. *Detecting Lost Users: Empirical Studies on Browsing Hypertext.* INRIA Tech. Rept. 972, Programme 8. Valbonne, France: L'Institut National de Récherche en Informatique et en Automatique, 1989.

Foucault, Michel. *The Archaeology of Knowledge and the Discourse on Language.* Trans. A. M. Sheridan Smith. New York: Pantheon, 1972.

———. *Discipline and Punish: The Birth of Prisons.* Trans. Alan Sheridan. New York: Vintage, 1979.

Frase, Lawrence. "The Influence of Sentence Order and Amount of Higher Level Text Processing upon Reproductive and Productive Memory." *American Educational Research Journal* 7 (1970): 307–19.

Freeman, Susan Tax. "An Anthropologist in Europe: Resources and Problems of Study." *Humanists at Work* 1–27.

Freire, Paulo. *Pedagogy of the Oppressed.* Trans. Myra Bergman Ramos. New York: Seabury, 1970; Penguin, 1980; Continuum, 1986.

———. *The Politics of Education.* Trans. Donaldo Macedo. South Hadley: Bergin, 1985.

Friedlander, Larry. "The Shakespeare Project: Experiments in Multimedia." *Academic Computing* May–June 1988: 1–6.

Frisse, Mark E. "Searching for Information in a Hypertext Medical Handbook." J. B. Smith et al. 57–67.

Frisse, Mark E., and Steve B. Cousins. "Information Retrieval from Hypertext: Update on the Dynamic Medical Handbook Project." Meyrowitz 199–212.

Fund for Improvement of Postsecondary Education Technology Study Group. *Ivory Towers, Silicon Basements: Learner-Centered Computing in Postsecondary Education.* McKinney: Academic Computing–EDUCOM, 1988.

Furlong, Mary S. "An Electronic Community for Older Adults: The Seniornet Network." *Journal of Communication* 39.3 (1989): 145–53.

Galegher, Jolene, and Robert E. Kraut. "Technology for Intellectual Teamwork: Perspectives on Research and Design." Galegher, Kraut, and Egido 1–20.

Galegher, Jolene, Robert E. Kraut, and Carmen Egido, eds. *Intellectual Teamwork: Social and Technological Foundations of Cooperative Work.* Hillsdale: Erlbaum, 1990.

Gandy, Oscar H., Jr. "The Surveillance Society: Information Technology and Bureaucratic Social Control." *Journal of Communication* 39.3 (1989): 61–76.

Gardner, Howard. *Frames of Mind: The Theory of Multiple Intelligences.* New York: Basic, 1985.

Gavrilovich, Peter. "Jobs for the '90s." *Detroit Free Press* 6 Nov. 1989: 1A+.

Geertz, Clifford. *The Interpretations of Cultures: Selected Essays.* New York: Basic, 1973.

———. *Local Knowledge: Further Essays in Interpretive Anthropology.* New York: Basic, 1983.

George, Diana. "The Politics of Social Construction and the Teaching of Writing." *Journal of Teaching Writing* 8 (1989): 1–10.

George, E. Laurie. "Taking Women Professors Seriously: Female Authority in the Computerized Classroom." Kremers and Peyton 45–52.

Gere, Anne Ruggles. "Composition and Literature: The Continuing Conversation." *College English* 52 (1989): 617–22.

———. *Writing Groups: History, Theory, and Implications.* Carbondale: Southern Illinois UP, 1987.

Gere, Anne Ruggles, and Laura Roop. "For Profit or Pleasure: Collaboration in Nineteenth Century Women's Clubs." Forman, *New Visions* 1–18.

"Get Smart." Editorial. *Detroit Free Press* 9 May 1989: 8A.

Getting a Job in the Computer Age. Princeton: Peterson's, 1986.

Gillespie, Andrew, and Kevin Robins. "Geographical Inequalities: The Spatial Bias of the New Communications Technologies." *Journal of Communication* 39.3 (1989): 7–18.

Gilligan, Carol. *In a Different Voice: Psychological Theory and Women's Development.* Cambridge: Harvard UP, 1982.

Giroux, Henry. "Liberal Arts Education and the Struggle for Public Life: Dreaming about Democracy." Gless and Smith 113–38.

———. *Theory and Resistance in Education: A Pedagogy for the Opposition.* South Hadley: Bergin, 1983.

Giroux, Henry, and Peter McLaren, eds. *Critical Pedagogy, the State, and Cultural Struggle.* Albany: State U of New York P, 1989.

Glaser, Barney, and Anselm Strauss. *The Discovery of Grounded Theory*. New York: de Gruyter, 1967.

Gless, Darryl, and Barbara Herrnstein Smith, eds. *The Politics of Liberal Education*. Spec. issue of *South Atlantic Quarterly* 89.1 (1990): 1–236.

Glossbrenner, Alfred. *The Complete Handbook of Personal Computer Communications*. New York: St. Martin's, 1985.

Glushko, Robert J. "Design Issues for Multi-document Hypertexts." Meyrowitz 213–24.

Glynn, Shawn M., Bruce K. Britton, K. Denise Muth, and Nukhet Dogan. "Writing and Revising Persuasive Documents: Cognitive Demands." *Journal of Educational Psychology* 74 (1982): 557–67.

Glynn, Shawn, and Francis J. Di Vesta. "Outline and Hierarchical Organization as Aids for Study and Retrieval." *Journal of Educational Psychology* 69 (1977): 89–95.

Goethals, Gregor. *The TV Ritual: Worship at the Video Altar*. Boston: Beacon, 1981.

Gomez, Mary Louise. "The Equitable Teaching of Composition with Computers: A Case for Change." Hawisher and Selfe, *Evolving Perspectives* 318–35.

Goody, Jack, and Ian Watt. "The Consequences of Literacy." *Comparative Studies in Society and History* 5 (1962–63): 304–26, 332–45. Rpt. in *Language and Social Context*. Ed. Pier Giglioli. Harmondsworth, Eng.: Penguin, 1972. 311–57.

Gordon, Sallie, and Vicki Lewis. "Enhancing Hypertext Documents to Support Learning from Text." *Technical Communication* 39 (1992): 305–08.

———. "Knowledge Engineering for Hypertext Instructional Systems." *Proceedings of the Human Factors Society, 34th Annual Meeting*. Anaheim, 1990.

Gordon, Sallie, Jill Gustavel, Jana Moore, and Jon Hankey. "The Effects of Hypertext on Reader Knowledge Representation." *Proceedings of the Human Factors Society, 32nd Annual Meeting*. Anaheim, 24–28 Oct. 1988. Santa Monica: Human Factors Soc., 1989.

Gould, John, and Nancy Grischkowsky. "Doing the Same Work with Hard Copy and with CRT Terminals." *Human Factors* 26 (1984): 323–37.

Graff, Gerald. "Colleges Are Depriving Students of a Connected View of Scholarship." Point of view. *Chronicle of Higher Education* 13 Feb. 1991: A48.

———. *Professing Literature: An Institutional History*. Chicago: U of Chicago P, 1987.

Graff, Harvey, ed. *Literacy and Social Development in the West: A Reader*. Cambridge: Cambridge UP, 1981.

Grafton, A. T. "The Importance of Being Printed." *Journal of Interdisciplinary History* 11 (1980): 265–86.

Graves, Donald. *Writing: Teachers and Children at Work*. Portsmouth: Heinemann, 1983.

Gray, Paul. "Whose America?" *Time* 8 July 1991: 12–17.

Greenbaum, Joan. "The Head and the Heart: Using Gender Analysis to Study the Social Construction of Computer Systems." *Computers and Society* 20.2 (1990): 9–17.

Greenberg, Saul, ed. *Computer-Supported Cooperative Work and Groupware.* London: Harcourt, 1991.

Greenberger, Martin, ed. *On Multimedia: Technologies for the Twenty-first Century.* Santa Monica: Voyager, 1990.

Grice, Roger. "On-line Information: What Do People Want? What Do People Need?" Barrett, *Society of Text* 22–44.

Griffith, Gary, and Lucy Maddox. "Letting Them Teach Each Other: An Experiment in Classroom Networking." Unpublished ms.

Grimes, Joseph. *The Thread of Discourse.* Hague: Mouton, 1975.

Guyer, Carolyn, and Martha Petry. "Notes for *Izme Pass* Exposé." *Writing on the Edge* 2.2 (1991): 82–89.

Haas, Christina. "Composing in Technological Contexts: A Study of Note-Making." *Written Communication* 7 (1990): 512–47.

———. "Does the Medium Make a Difference?: Two Studies of Writing with Pen and Paper and with Computers." *Human-Computer Interaction* 4 (1989): 149–69.

———. " 'Seeing It on the Screen Isn't Really Seeing It': Computer Writers' Reading Problems." Hawisher and Selfe, *Critical Perspectives* 16–29.

Haas, Christina, and John R. Hayes. " 'What Did I Just Say?': Reading Problems in Writing with the Machine." *Research in the Teaching of English* 20.1 (1986): 22–35.

Hairston, Maxine. "The Winds of Change: Thomas Kuhn and the Revolution in the Teaching of Writing." *College Composition and Communication* 33 (1982): 76–88.

Halasz, Frank. "Reflections on Notecards: Seven Issues for the Next Generation of Hypermedia Systems." J. B. Smith et al. 345–65.

Halio, Marcia Peoples. "Student Writing: Can the Machine Maim the Message?" *Academic Computing* 4.4 (1990): 16 + .

Halliday, Michael, and R. Hasan. *Cohesion in English.* London: Longman, 1976.

Handa, Carolyn, ed. *Computers and Community: Teaching Composition in the Twenty-first Century.* Portsmouth: Boynton/Cook, 1990.

———. "Politics, Ideology, and the Strange, Slow Death of the Isolated Composer; Or, Why We Need Community in the Writing Classroom." *Computers and Community* 160–84.

Haraway, Donna. "A Manifesto for Cyborgs: Science, Technology, and Socialist Feminism in the 1980s." *Socialist Review* 80 (1985): 65–105.

Harding, Sandra, and Merrill B. Hintikka, eds. *Discovering Reality: Feminist Perspectives on Epistemology, Metaphysics, Methodology, and Philosophy of Science.* London: Reidel, 1983.

Harpold, Terence. "Hypertext and Hypermedia: A Selected Bibliography." Berk and Devlin 555–71.

———. "Threnody: Psychoanalytic Digressions on the Subject of Hypertexts." Delany and Landow, *Hypermedia* 171–81.

Harris, Jacqueline. *Henry Ford.* New York: Watts, 1984.

Harris, Joseph. "The Idea of Community in the Study of Writing." *College Composition and Communication* 40 (1990): 11–22.

Hartman, Karen, et al. "Patterns of Social Interaction in Learning to Write: Some Effects of Network Technologies." *Written Communication* 8 (1991): 79–113.

Harvard, Robert. *Eli Whitney*. Chicago: Follett, 1966.

Hassan, Ihab. *The Postmodern Turn: Essays in Postmodern Theory and Culture*. Columbus: Ohio State UP, 1987.

Hawisher, Gail E. "Connecting the Visual and the Verbal." *Lessons for the Computer Age*. Ed. William Wresch. Urbana: NCTE, 1991. 129–32.

———. "The Effects of Word Processing on the Revision Strategies of College Freshmen." *Research in the Teaching of English* 21.1 (1987): 145–59.

———. "Reading and Writing Connections: Composition Pedagogy and Word Processing." Holdstein and Selfe 71–83.

———. "Research and Recommendations for Computers and Composition." Hawisher and Selfe, *Critical Perspectives* 44–69.

———. "Studies in Word Processing." *Computers and Composition* 4 (1986): 6–35.

Hawisher, Gail E., and Paul LeBlanc, eds. *Re-imagining Computers and Composition: Teaching and Research in the Virtual Age*. Portsmouth: Boynton/Cook, 1992.

Hawisher, Gail E., and Cynthia L. Selfe, eds. *Critical Perspectives on Computers and Composition Instruction*. New York: Teachers Coll. P, 1989.

———. *Evolving Perspectives on Computers and Composition Studies: Questions for the 1990s*. Urbana: NCTE, 1991.

———. Letter from the Editors. *Selected Papers from the Fifth Computers and Composition Conference, May 1989*. Spec. issue of *Computers and Composition* 7 (1990): 5–14.

———. "The Rhetoric of Technology and the Electronic Writing Class." *College Composition and Communication* 42 (1991): 55–65.

———. "Tradition and Change in Computer-Supported Writing Environments." *Theoretical and Critical Perspectives on Teacher Change*. Ed. Phyllis Kahaney, Joseph Janangelo, and Linda A. M. Perry. Norwood: Ablex, forthcoming.

Hayes, John R. *Cognitive Psychology: Thinking and Creating*. Homewood: Dorsey, 1978.

———. Personal communication. 5 Feb. 1993.

Hays, Wilma. *Eli Whitney, Founder of Modern Industry*. New York: Watts, 1965.

Heath, Shirley Brice. "The Fourth Vision: Literate Language at Work." Lunsford, Moglen, and Slevin 289–306.

———. *Ways with Words: Language, Life, and Work in Communities and Classrooms*. Cambridge: Cambridge UP, 1983.

Heath, Shirley Brice, and Leslie Mangiola. *Children of Promise: Literate Activity in Linguistically and Culturally Diverse Classrooms*. Washington: NEA, Center for the Study of Writing and Literacy, American Educational Research Assn., 1991.

Heath, Stephen, ed. and trans. *Image-Music-Text*. New York: Hill, 1977.

———. "On Suture." *Questions of Cinema*. Bloomington: Indiana UP, 1981. 76–112. Rpt. of "Notes on Suture." *Screen* 18.4 (1977–78): 48–76.

Heidegger, Martin. *The Question concerning Technology and Other Essays*. New York: Harper, 1977.

Heller, Scott. "Changing Trends in Literary Scholarship Modify the Appearance of English Institute as It Celebrates Fiftieth Meeting at Harvard U." *Chronicle of Higher Education* 11 Sept. 1991: A9–11.

———. "Colleges Becoming Havens of 'Political Correctness,' Some Scholars Say." *Chronicle of Higher Education* 21 Nov. 1990: A1+.

———. "Scholars Form Group to Combat 'Malicious Distortions' by Conservatives." *Chronicle of Higher Education* 18 Sept. 1991: A19+.

Henry, William. "Upside Down in the Groves of Academe." *Time* 1 Apr. 1991: 66–69.

Hentoff, Nat. "Whitewashing PC on College Campuses." *Detroit News* 29 Sept. 1991: 12C.

Herrmann, Andrea. "Computers and Writing Research: Shifting Our 'Governing Gaze.' " Holdstein and Selfe 124–34.

———. "Computers in Public Schools: Are We Being Realistic?" Hawisher and Selfe, *Critical Perspectives* 109–25.

Herron, Jerry. *Universities and the Myth of Cultural Decline*. Detroit: Wayne State UP, 1988.

Herrstrom, David S., and David G. Massey. "Hypertext in Context." Barrett, *Society of Text* 45–58.

Hillocks, George, Jr. *Research on Written Composition: New Directions for Teaching*. Urbana: NCTE, 1986.

Hinds, Julie. "Ivory Terror." *Detroit News* 16 Mar. 1991: 1C+.

Hirsch, E. D. *Cultural Literacy: What Every American Needs to Know*. New York: Random, 1987.

Hobbs, Jerry. *Literature and Cognition*. Menlo Park: CSLI, 1990.

Holdstein, Deborah H., and Cynthia L. Selfe, eds. *Computers and Writing: Theory, Research, Practice*. New York: MLA, 1990.

Hollander, Paul. "Communism's Collapse Won't Faze the Marxists in Academe." Point of view. *Chronicle of Higher Education* 23 May 1990: A44.

Holt, Thomas. " 'Knowledge Is Power': The Black Struggle for Literacy." Lunsford, Moglen, and Slevin 91–102.

Holzman, Michael. "Nominal and Active Literacy." *Writing as Social Action*. Ed. Marilyn Cooper and Michael Holzman. Portsmouth: Boynton/Cook, 1989. 157–65.

Horn, Robert E. *Mapping Hypertext: The Analysis, Organization, and Display of Knowledge for the Next Generation of On-line Text and Graphics*. Waltham: Lexington Institute, 1990.

Horowitz, Irving Louis. *Communicating Ideas: The Crisis of Publishing in a Post-industrial Society*. New York: Oxford UP, 1986.

Horowitz, P. "Telecommunications: An Electronic Interstate School Newspaper." *Electronic Learning* May–June 1984: 48.

Horton, William K. *Designing and Writing Online Documentation: From Help Files to Hypertext*. New York: Wiley, 1990.

Hubbard, Ruth. Foreword. Rothschild vii–viii.

Hufford, Jon R. "Elements of the Bibliographic Record Used by Reference Staff Members at Three ARL Libraries." *College Research Libraries* 52 (1991): 54–64.

Hull, Glynda, and Mike Rose. "Toward a Social-Cognitive Understanding of Problematic Reading and Writing." Lunsford, Moglen, and Slevin 235–45.

Hult, Christine, and Jeannette Harris. *A Writer's Introduction to Word Processing*. Belmont: Wadsworth, 1987.

Humanists at Work: Papers Presented at a Symposium Held at the University of Illinois at Chicago on April 27–28, 1989. Chicago: University Library, U of Illinois, 1989.

Humphrey, David. "Computers and Collaboration: Writing as a Social Skill." *Assembly on Computers in English Newsletter* July–Sept. 1987: 3.

Irish, Peggy, and Randall Trigg. "Supporting Collaboration in Hypermedia: Issues and Experiences." Barrett, *Society of Text* 90–106.

Iser, Wolfgang. *The Act of Reading: A Theory of Aesthetic Response*. Baltimore: Johns Hopkins UP, 1978.

Jackson, Luther. "Manufacturing Study Finds Poorly Educated Work Force." *Detroit Free Press* 26 Mar. 1990: 4E.

Jansen, Sue Curry. "Gender and the Information Society: A Socially Structured Silence." *Journal of Communication* 39.3 (1989): 196–215. Rpt. in Siefert, Gerbner, and Fisher 196–215.

Jaynes, Joseph. "Limited Freedom: Linear Reflections on Nonlinear Texts." Barrett, *Society of Text* 148–61.

Jessup, Emily. "Feminism and Computers in Composition Instruction." Hawisher and Selfe, *Evolving Perspectives* 336–55.

Johansen, Robert. *Groupware: Computer Support for Business Teams*. New York: Free, 1988.

Johnson, Bonnie, Geraldine Weaver, Margrethe H. Olson, and Robert Dunham. "Using a Computer-Based Tool to Support Collaboration: A Field Experiment." *Proceedings of the Conference on Computer Supported Cooperative Work*. Austin, 1986. 343–52.

Johnson-Eilola, Johndan. " 'Click Here . . . No Here . . . Maybe Here': Anarchy and Hypertext." Conference on College Composition and Communication. Boston, 21–23 Mar. 1991. ERIC ED 331 060.

———. "Structure and Text: *Writing Space* and *Storyspace*." *Computers and Composition* 9.2 (1992): 95–129.

———. " 'Trying to See the Garden': Interdisciplinary Perspectives on Hypertext Use in Composition Instruction." *Writing on the Edge* 2.2 (1991): 92–111.

Joyce, Michael. "Mind and History: Hypertext Narrative." Hypertext '89 Conference. Pittsburgh, 6 Nov. 1989.

———. "Siren Shapes: Exploratory and Constructive Hypertexts." *Academic Computing* Nov. 1988: 10 + .

Julyan, Candace. "National Geographic Kids Network: Real Science in the Elementary Classroom." *Classroom Computer Learning* 10.2 (1989): 30–37.

Just, Marcel, and Patricia Carpenter. *The Psychology of Reading and Language Comprehension.* Boston: Allyn, 1987.

Kaestle, Carl F. "The History of Literacy and the History of Readers." *Review of Research in Education* 12 (1985): 11–53.

Kalmbach, James. "Hypermedia and the Book: A Mediation." Conference on College Composition and Communication. Boston, 21–23 Mar. 1991.

Kapisovsky, Peggy. "Real Science Is Happening in Secondary Schools, Too." *Classroom Computer Learning* Oct. 1989: 37.

Kaplan, Nancy. "Ideology, Technology, and the Future of Writing Instruction." Hawisher and Selfe, *Evolving Perspectives* 11–42.

Kaplan, Nancy, and Stuart Moulthrop."Other Ways of Seeing." *Computers and Composition* 7 (1990): 89–102.

———."Something to Imagine: Literature, Composition, and Interactive Fiction." *Computers and Composition* 8 (1991): 7–23.

Karis, Bill. "Conflict in Collaboration: A Burkean Perspective." *Rhetoric Review* 8 (1989): 113–26.

Katz, Daniel. "Are Newspapers Yesterday's News?" *Esquire* Jan. 1990: 39–40.

———. "Don't Be Mean to Your Machine: Have Computers Become Too Complex to Keep Their Users Friendly?" *Esquire* May 1990: 181–82.

Keller, Evelyn Fox. *Reflections on Gender and Science.* New Haven: Yale UP, 1985.

Kelly, Michelle. Interview. Springfield, MA, 1989.

Kemp, Fred. "Freeing the Student Voice: Establishing Discourse Communities through Networked Computers." Penn State Conference on Rhetoric and Composition. State College, July 1987.

Kernan, Alvin. *The Death of Literature.* New Haven: Yale UP, 1990.

———. *Samuel Johnson and the Impact of Print.* Princeton: Princeton UP, 1987.

Kerr, Stephen. "Transition from Page to Screen." *CD-ROM: The New Papyrus.* Ed. Steve Lambert and Suzanne Ropiequet. Vol. 1. New York: Harper, 1986. 321–43.

Kidder, Tracy. *The Soul of a New Machine.* New York: Avon, 1981.

Kieras, David. "Initial Mention as a Signal to Thematic Content in Technical Passages." *Memory and Cognition* 8.4 (1980): 345–53.

———. "A Model of Reader Strategies for Abstracting Main Ideas from Simple Technical Prose." *Text* 2.1 (1982): 47–81.

———. *The Role of Prior Knowledge in Operating Equipment from Written Instructions.* Tech. Rept. 19. Ann Arbor: U of Michigan, 1985.

Kieras, David, and Christiane Dechert. *Rules for Comprehensible Technical Prose: A Survey of the Psycholinguistic Literature.* Tech. Rept. 21. Ann Arbor: U of Michigan, 1985.

Kiesler, Sara, Jane Siegel, and Timothy W. McGuire. "Social Psychological Aspects of Computer-Mediated Communication." *American Psychologist* 39 (1984): 1123–34.

Kimball, Roger. *Tenured Radicals: How Politics Has Corrupted Our Higher Education.* New York: Harper, 1990.

Kintgen, Eugene, Barry Kroll, and Mike Rose, eds. *Perspectives on Literacy.* Carbondale: Southern Illinois UP, 1988.

Kintsch, Walter. "The Representation of Knowledge and the Use of Knowledge in Discourse Comprehension." *Language Processing in Social Context.* Ed. R. Dietrich and C. F. Graumann. New York: Elsevier, 1989. 185–209.

———. "The Role of Knowledge in Discourse Comprehension: A Construction-Integration Model." *Psychological Review* 95 (1988): 163–82.

———. "Text Processing: A Psychological Model." *Handbook of Discourse Analysis.* Vol. 2. Ed. T. A. van Dijk. London: Academic, 1985. 231–43.

Kintsch, Walter, and Teun A. van Dijk. "Toward a Model of Text Comprehension and Production." *Psychological Review* 85 (1978): 363–94.

Kling, Rob. "Value Conflicts in Computing Developments: Developed and Developing Countries." *Telecommunication Policy* Mar. 1983: 12–34.

Kling, Rob, and Walt Scacchi. "The Web of Computing: Computer Technology and Social Organization." *Advances in Computers* 21 (1982): 2–60.

Knoblauch, C. H. "Literacy and the Politics of Education." Lunsford, Moglen, and Slevin 74–80.

Knox-Quinn, Carolyn. "Collaboration in the Writing Classroom: An Interview with Ken Kesey." *College Composition and Communication* 41 (1990): 309–17.

Kohlberg, Lawrence, and R. Mayer. "Development as an Aim of Education." *Harvard Educational Review* 42 (1972): 449–96.

Kovanis, Georgea. "The Day of Living Correctly." *Detroit Free Press* 8 Nov. 1991: 3F+.

———. "PC or Not PC, Who Decides?" *Detroit Free Press* 8 Nov. 1991: 3F.

Kramarae, Cheris. *Technology and Women's Voices: Keeping in Touch.* London: Routledge, 1988.

Kramer, Pamela E., and Sheila Lehman. "Measuring Women: A Critique of Research on Computer Ability and Avoidance." *Signs* 16 (1990): 158–77.

Kremers, Marshall. "Adams Sherman Hill Meets ENFI: An Inquiry and a Retrospective." *Computers and Composition* 5 (1988): 69–77.

———. "Sharing Authority on a Synchronous Network: The Case for Riding the Beast." Kremers and Peyton 33–44.

Kremers, Marshall, and Joy Kreeft Peyton, eds. *Papers from the Fifth Computers and Writing Conference.* Spec. issue of *Computers and Composition* 7 (1990).

Krendl, Kathy A., Mary C. Broihier, and Cynthia Fleetwood. "Children and Computers: Do Sex-Related Differences Persist?" *Journal of Communication* 39.3 (1989): 85–93. Rpt. in Siefert, Gerbner, and Fisher 85–93.

Krikelas, James. "Catalog Use Studies and Their Implications." *Advances in Librarianship.* Vol. 3. Ed. Melvin J. Voigt. New York: Seminar, 1972. 195–220.

Kroll, Barry. "Cognitive Egocentrism and the Problem of Audience Awareness in Written Discourse." *Research in the Teaching of English* 12 (1978): 269–81.

Kuhn, Thomas S. *The Structure of Scientific Revolutions*. 2nd ed. Chicago: U of Chicago P, 1970.

Kurshan, Barbara. "Educational Telecommunications Connections for the Classroom—Part 2." *Computing Teacher* Apr. 1990: 51–52.

Kurth, R. "Using Word Processing to Enhance Revision Strategies during Student Writing Activities." *Educational Technology* 27 (1987): 13–19.

Lake, Dan. "Two Projects That Worked: Using Telecommunications as a Resource in the Classroom—Part 2." *Computing Teacher* Dec.–Jan. 1989–90: 17–19.

Lakoff, George. *Women, Fire, and Dangerous Things: What Categories Reveal about the Mind*. Chicago: U of Chicago P, 1987.

Lampton, Christopher. *Thomas Alva Edison*. New York: Watts, 1988.

Lancaster, Frederick W. "Has Technology Failed Us?" *Information Technology and Library Management, Thirteenth International Essen Symposium*. 22–25 Oct. 1990. Ed. Ahmed H. Helal and Joachim W. Weiss. Essen: Universitätsbibliothek Essen, 1991. 2–13.

Landow, George P. *Hypertext: The Convergence of Contemporary Critical Theory and Technology*. Baltimore: Johns Hopkins UP, 1992.

———. "The Rhetoric of Hypermedia: Some Rules for Authors." Delany and Landow, *Hypermedia* 105–18.

Landow, George P., and Paul Delany. "Hypertext, Hypermedia, and Literary Studies: The State of the Art." Delany and Landow, *Hypermedia* 1–50.

Langer, Judith. "Understanding Literature." *Language Arts* 67 (1990): 812–16.

Langer, Susanne K. *Feeling and Form: A Theory of Art*. New York: Scribner's, 1953.

———. *Mind: An Essay on Human Feeling*. Baltimore: Johns Hopkins UP, 1967.

Lanham, Richard A. "The Electronic Word: Literary Study and the Digital Revolution." *New Literary History* 20 (1989): 265–89.

———. "The Extraordinary Convergence: Democracy, Technology, Theory, and the University Curriculum." Gless and Smith 27–50.

———. Foreword. Handa, *Computers and Community* xii–xv.

Lapham, Lewis. "Acceptable Opinions." *Harper's* Dec. 1990: 10–14.

Lay, Mary M. "The Androgynous Collaborator: The Impact of Feminist Theory on Collaboration." Forman, *New Visions* 82–104.

———. "Feminist Theory and the Redefinition of Technical Communication." *Journal of Business and Technical Communication* 5.4 (1991): 348–70.

———. "Interpersonal Conflict in Collaborative Writing: What We Can Learn from Gender Studies." *Journal of Business and Technical Communication* 3.2 (1989): 5–28.

LeFevre, Karen Burke. *Invention as a Social Act*. Carbondale: Southern Illinois UP, 1987.

Lentz, Tony M. *Orality and Literacy in Hellenic Greece*. Carbondale: Southern Illinois UP, 1989.

Lesk, Michael. "What to Do When There's Too Much Information." Meyrowitz 305–18.

Levin, Henry, and Gail Meister. "Is CAI Cost Effective?" *Phi Delta Kappan* 67.10 (1986): 748+.

Levin, James, et al. "Microcomputer Communication Networks for Education."

Quarterly Newsletter of the Laboratory of Comparative Cognition 4.2 (1982): 32–34.

———. "Observations of Electronic Networks: Appropriate Activities for Learning." *Computing Teacher* May 1989: 17–21.

Levin, James, Haesum Kim, and Margaret Riel. "Instructional Interactions on Electronic Message Networks." Annual Meeting of the American Educational Research Assn. New Orleans, Apr. 1988.

Levin, James, M. Riel, M. Boruta, and R. Rowe. "Muktuk Meets Jacuzzi: Computer Networks and Elementary Schools." *The Acquisition of Written Language.* Ed. Sarah Freedman. New York: Ablex, 1984. 160–71.

Levy, Steven. "Does the Mac Make You Stupid?" *Macworld* Nov. 1990: 69–78.

Lieberman, Seymour. "The Effects of Changes in Roles on the Attitudes of Role Occupants." *Human Relations* 9 (1956): 385–402.

Lindemann, Shirlee, and Jeannette Willert. "Word Processing in High School Writing Classes." Collins and Sommers 47–54.

Lloyd-Jones, Richard, and Andrea A. Lunsford, eds. *The English Coalition Conference: Democracy through Language.* Urbana: NCTE; New York: MLA, 1989.

Lodewijks, Hans. "Self-Regulated versus Teacher-Provided Sequencing of Information in Learning from Text." Flammer and Kintsch 509–20.

Lofty, John S. "Time to Write: Resistance to Literacy in a Maine Fishing Community." Lunsford, Moglen, and Slevin 39–49.

Lunsford, Andrea A., Helene Moglen, and James Slevin, eds. *The Right to Literacy.* New York: MLA, 1990.

Lynn, Stephanie. "Hi-Tech Kid Talk." *Instructor* 95.2 (1985): 66–68.

Lynn, Steven. "A Passage into Critical Theory." *College English* 52 (1990): 258–71.

Mabrito, Mark. "Annotated Bibliography of Resources in Computer Networking." *Computers and Composition* 7.3 (1990): 23–39.

MacKensie, Donald, and Judy Wajcman, eds. *The Social Shaping of Technology.* Philadelphia: Open University, 1985.

Mackenzie, G. Calvin. "Fallacies of PC." Opinion. *Chronicle of Higher Education* 4 Sept. 1991: B1–2.

Mageau, Therese. "Teaching and Learning Online." *Electronic Learning* Nov.–Dec. 1990: 26–30.

Magner, Denise. "Ideological Foes in 'PC' Debates Open Dialogue." *Chronicle of Higher Education* 2 Oct. 1991: A17+.

Mahoney, J. L. *The Enlightenment and English Poetry.* Lexington: Heath, 1980.

Maki, Ruth. "Memory for Script Actions: Effects of Relevance and Detail Expectancy." *Memory and Cognition* 18 (1990): 5–14.

Malinowitz, Harriet. "The Rhetoric of Empowerment in Writing Programs." Lunsford, Moglen, and Slevin 152–62.

Malone, Thomas W., et al. "Semistructured Messages Are Surprisingly Useful for Computer-Supported Coordination." *Computer-Supported Cooperative Work.* Ed. Irene Greif. San Mateo: Morgan Kaufmann, 1988. 311–31.

Mandl, Heinz, Nancy L. Stein, and Thomas Trabasso, eds. *Learning and Comprehension of Texts.* Hillsdale: Erlbaum, 1984.

Mandler, Jean Matter. *Stories, Scripts, and Scenes: Aspects of Schema Theory.* Hillsdale: Erlbaum, 1984.

Mannes, Suzanne M., and Walter Kintsch. "Knowledge Organization and Text Organization." *Cognition and Instruction* 4.2 (1987): 91–115.

Marchionini, Gary, and Ben Shneiderman. "Finding Facts vs. Browsing Knowledge in Hypertext Systems." *IEEE Computer* 21.1 (1988): 70–80.

Marcus, Stephen. "What Are *Hypercard*?" Part 1. *Writing Notebook* Sept.–Oct. 1989: 16–18. Part 3. Jan.–Feb. 1990: 24–25.

Marcuse, Herbert. *One-Dimensional Man: Studies in the Ideology of Advanced Industrial Society.* Boston: Beacon, 1964.

Markus, M. Lynne, and Janis Forman. "Individual Interests and Collective Choice: The Adoption and Use of Group Support Tools." Working paper. U of California, Los Angeles, 1990.

Marling, William. "Grading Essays on a Microcomputer." *College English* 46 (1984): 797–810.

Martin, Biddy. "Feminism, Criticism, and Foucault." *Feminism and Foucault: Reflections on Resistance.* Ed. Irene Diamond and Lee Quinby. Boston: Northeastern UP, 1983. 3–19.

Mayer, Richard E. "Some Conditions of Meaningful Learning for Computer Programming: Advance Organizers and Subject Control of Frame Order." *Journal of Educational Psychology* 68 (1976): 143–50.

Mayer, Richard E., Linda K. Cook, and Jennifer L. Dyck. "Techniques That Help Readers Build Mental Models from Scientific Text: Definitions Pretraining and Signaling." *Journal of Educational Psychology* 76.6 (1984): 1089–105.

McAleese, Ray. "Navigation and Browsing in Hypertext." *Hypertext: Theory into Practice.* Ed. McAleese. Norwood: Ablex, 1989. 6–44.

McCarthy, Robert. "Behind the Scenes at Bank Street College." *Electronic Learning* Oct. 1989: 30–34.

McCormick, Kathleen, Gary Waller, and Linda Flower. *Reading Texts: Reading, Responding, Writing.* Lexington: Heath, 1987.

McDaid, John. "Toward an Ecology of Hypermedia." Hawisher and Selfe, *Evolving Perspectives* 203–23.

McDaniel, Ellen. "Assessing the Professional Role of the English Department 'Computer Person.' " Holdstein and Selfe 84–94.

———. "A Comparative Study of First-Generation Invention Software." *Computers and Composition* 3.3 (1986): 7–21.

McGrath, Joseph E. *Groups: Interaction and Performance.* Englewood Cliffs: Prentice, 1984.

Meese, Elizabeth. "Women and Writing: A Re/turn." *College English* 52 (1990): 375–84.

Meyer, Bonnie J. F. "Text Dimensions and Cognitive Processing." Mandl, Stein, and Trabasso 3–51.

Meyer, Bonnie J. F., and Roy O. Freedle. "Effects of Discourse Type on Recall." *American Educational Research Journal* 21.1 (1984): 121–43.

Meyrowitz, Norman, ed. *Hypertext '89 Proceedings.* Pittsburgh, 5–8 Nov. 1989. New York: Assn. for Computing Machinery, 1989.

Millar, Jeff, and Bill Hinds. "Tank McNamara." Cartoon. *Detroit Free Press* 21 Feb. 1991: 12E.

Miller, James. *The Amazing Story of Henry Ford, the Ideal American and the World's Most Famous Private Citizen: A Complete and Authentic Account of His Life and Surpassing Achievements.* Chicago: Donahue, 1922.

Miller, John. "Political Correctness Threatens Free Discourse on Campus." *Detroit News* 31 Mar. 1991: 3B.

Mitterer, John, Gary Oland, and J. S. Schankula. *Hypermedia Bibliography.* Computer Science Tech. Rept. CS-88-02. Saint Catherines, Ont.: Brock U, 1988.

Moberg, Goran. *Writing on Computers in English Composition.* New York: Writing Consultant, 1986.

Moffett, James. *Active Voice.* Portsmouth: Boynton/Cook, 1981.

———. "Censorship and Spiritual Education." Lunsford, Moglen, and Slevin 113–19.

Montgomery, Elizabeth. *Henry Ford: Automotive Pioneer.* Champaign: Garrard, 1969.

Mooney, Carolyn. "Academic Group Fighting the 'Politically Correct Left' Gains Momentum." *Chronicle of Higher Education* 12 Dec. 1990: A1+ .

———. "Activist Dean at Yale Brings Controversy to His Post with Strong Views on Study of Western Civilization." *Chronicle of Higher Education* 19 June 1991: A1–12.

———. "Scholars Decry Campus Hostility to Western Culture at a Time When More Nations Embrace Its Values." *Chronicle of Higher Education* 30 Jan. 1991: A15–16.

Moore, M. A. "The Effect of Word Processing Technology in a Developmental Writing Program on Writing Quality, Attitude towards Composing, and Revision Strategies of Fourth and Fifth Grade Students." Diss. U of South Florida, 1987.

Moran, Charles. "The Computer-Writing Room: Authority and Control." *Computers and Composition* 7 (1990): 61–69.

———. "The Word-Processor and the Writer." *Computers and Composition* 2 (1984): 1–5.

Morton, Herbert C., and Anne J. Price. *The ACLS Survey of Scholars: Final Report of Views on Publications, Computers, and Libraries.* Washington: Office of Scholarly Communication and Technology, American Council of Learned Soc., 1989.

Moulthrop, Stuart. "Forking Paths." Unpublished hypertext, 1987.

———. "Hypertext and 'the Hyperreal.' " Meyrowitz 259–67.

———. "In the Zones: Hypertext and the Politics of Interpretation." *Writing on the Edge* 1.1 (1989): 18–27.

———. "Reading from the Map: Metonymy and Metaphor in the Fiction of Forking Paths." Delany and Landow, *Hypermedia* 119–32.

———. "Toward a Paradigm for Reading Hypertexts: Making Nothing Happen in Hypermedia Fiction." Berk and Devlin 65–78.

———. "Writing on the Hypertextual Edge." *Writing on the Edge* 2.2 (1991): 79–81.

Moulthrop, Stuart, and Nancy Kaplan. "Something to Imagine: Literature, Composition, and Interactive Fiction." *Computers and Composition* 9 (1991): 7–23.

Murray, Denise. "The Composing Process for Computer Conversation." *Written Communication* 8.1 (1991): 35–55.

Murray, Donald. *A Writer Teaches Writing*. 2nd ed. Boston: Houghton, 1985.

Myers, Greg. "Reality, Consensus, and Reform in the Rhetoric of Composition Teaching." *College English* 48 (1986): 154–74.

Naisbett, John. *Megatrends: Ten New Directions Transforming Our Lives*. New York: Warner, 1982.

Nelson, Theodor H. *Computer Lib/Dream Machines*. 1974. Redmond: Tempus, 1987.

———. *Literary Machines*. South Bend: Distributors, 1987.

———. "A New Home for the Mind." *Datamation* 28.2 (1982): 168–80.

Neuwirth, Christine M., and David S. Kaufer. "Computers and Composition Studies: Articulating a Pattern of Discovery." Hawisher and LeBlanc 173–90.

———. "The Role of External Representations in the Writing Process: Implications for the Design of Hypertext-Based Writing Tools." Meyrowitz 319–41.

Neuwirth, Christine M., David S. Kaufer, Ravinder Chandhok, and James H. Morris. "Issues in the Design of Computer Support for Coauthoring and Commenting." *Third Conference on Computer Supported Cooperative Work (CSCW '90)*. Baltimore: Assn. for Computing Machinery, 1990. 193–95.

Neuwirth, Christine M., David S. Kaufer, Rick Chimera, and Terilyn Gillespie. "The Notes Program: A Hypertext Application for Writing from Source Texts." J. B. Smith et al. 121–41.

Neuwirth, Christine M., David Kaufer, Gary Keim, and Terilyn Gillespie. *The Comments Program: Computer Support for Response to Writing*. Tech. Rept. CMU-CECE-TR-2. Pittsburgh: Carnegie Mellon U, 1988.

Neuwirth, Christine M., Michael Palmquist, Cynthia Cochran, Terilyn Gillespie, Karen Hartman, and Thomas Hajduk. "Why Write—Together—Concurrently on a Computer Network?" *Situated Evaluation of ENFI*. Ed. Bertram Bruce, Joy Peyton, and Trent Batson. Cambridge: Cambridge UP, in press.

Neuwirth, Christine M., Michael Palmquist, and Terilyn Gillespie. *An Instructor's Guide to Collaborative Writing with CECE Talk: A Computer Network Tool*. Tech. Rept. CMU-CECE-TR-8. Pittsburgh: Carnegie Mellon U, Dept. of English, Center for Educational Computing in English, 1988.

Nickell, Samila. "Composition Students Experience Word Processing." *Computers and Composition* 2 (1984): 11–14.

Nielsen, Jakob. *Hypertext and Hypermedia*. Boston: Academic, 1990.

Nydahl, Joel. "Teaching Word Processors to Be CAI Programs." *College English* 52 (1990): 904–15.

Nystrand, Martin. "Sharing Words: The Effects of Readers on Developing Writers." *Written Communication* 7.1 (1990): 3–24.

Oakley, Francis. "Despite Its Critics, Undergraduate Education Is a Success." Point of view. *Chronicle of Higher Education* 14 Mar. 1990: A52.

Odell, Lee, and Dixie Goswami, eds. *Writing in Nonacademic Settings*. New York: Guilford, 1985.

Odell, Lee, Dixie Goswami, and Doris Quick. "Writing outside the English Composition Class: Implications for Teaching and for Learning." Bailey and Fosheim 175–96.

Ohmann, Richard. "Literacy, Technology, and Monopoly Capital." *College English* 47 (1985): 675–89.

Olson, C. Paul. "Who Computes?" *Critical Pedagogy and Cultural Power*. Ed. David W. Livingstone. South Hadley: Bergin, 1987. 179–204.

Ong, Walter. *Interfaces of the Word: Studies in the Evolution of Consciousness and Culture*. Ithaca: Cornell UP, 1977.

———. *Orality and Literacy: The Technologizing of the Word*. London: Methuen, 1982.

———. *Rhetoric, Romance, and Technology: Studies in the Interaction of Expression and Culture*. Ithaca: Cornell UP, 1971.

Paine, Charles. "Relativism, Radical Pedagogy, and the Ideology of Paralysis." *College English* 51 (1989): 557–70.

Papert, Seymour. "Background to the Proposal." Cannings, Polin, et al. i–iv.

———. *Mindstorms: Children, Computers, and Powerful Ideas*. New York: Basic, 1980.

Paradis, James, David Dobrin, and Richard Miller. "Writing at Exxon ITD." Odell and Goswami 281–307.

Parsaye, Kamran, Mark Chignell, Setrag Khoshafian, and Harry Wong. *Intelligent Databases: Object-Oriented, Deductive Hypermedia Technologies*. New York: Wiley, 1989.

Pea, Roy D., and D. Midian Kurland. "Cognitive Technologies for Writing." *Review of Research in Education*. Vol. 14. Ed. Ernst Rothkopf. Washington: American Educational Research Assn., 1987. 277–326.

Perrow, Charles. "On Not Using Libraries." *Humanists at Work* 29–42.

Perry, Ruth, and Lisa Greber. "Women and Computers: An Introduction." *From Hard Drive to Software: Gender, Computers, and Difference*. Spec. issue of *Signs* 16 (1990): 74–101.

Personal Computers in the Home—A Marketing Report. Dataquest, 1988.

Phelps, Louise Wetherbee. *Composition as a Human Science: Contributions to the Self-understanding of a Discipline*. New York: Oxford UP, 1988.

Piaget, Jean. *Six Psychological Studies*. Trans. Anita Tenzer. New York: Vintage, 1968.

Polin, Linda. "Coming Attractions." *Writing Notebook* 8.1 (1990): 33–34.

Poster, Mark. *The Mode of Information: Poststructuralism and Social Context*. Chicago: U of Chicago P, 1990.

Postman, Neil. *Amusing Ourselves to Death: Public Discourse in the Age of Show Business*. New York: Penguin, 1985.

———. *Technopoly: The Surrender of Culture to Technology*. New York: Knopf, 1992.

Pratt, Mary Louise. "Humanities for the Future: Reflections on the Western Culture Debate at Stanford." Gless and Smith 7–25.

Pufahl, John. "Response to Richard Collier." *College Composition and Communication* 35 (1984): 191–93.

Pugh, Emerson. *Memories That Shaped an Industry: Decisions Leading to IBM System/360.* Cambridge: MIT P, 1984.

Purdy, Matthew, Karl Stark, and Tim Weiner. "High-Tech Payoff." *Detroit Free Press* 19 Jan. 1991: 6A.

Purves, Alan C., and William C. Purves. "Viewpoints: Cultures, Text Models, and the Activity of Writing." *Research in the Teaching of English* 20 (1986): 174–97.

Raskin, Jef. "The Hype in Hypertext: A Critique." J. B. Smith et al. 325–30.

Raubitschek, A. E. Letter to L. M. Dryden. 20 Dec. 1990.

Rauch, Esther Nettles. "Student/Teacher Computer Conferences: Their Effect on Privacy and Power." Unpublished ms.

Ravitch, Diane. "Multiculturalism Yes, Particularism, No." Point of view. *Chronicle of Higher Education* 24 Oct. 1990: A44.

Ray, Ruth, and Ellen Barton. "Technology and Authority." Hawisher and Selfe, *Evolving Perspectives* 279–99.

Raymond, Darrell R., and Frank W. Tompa. "Hypertext and the *New Oxford English Dictionary*." J. B. Smith et al. 143–54.

Reinking, David, and Robert Schreiner. "The Effects of Computer-Mediated Text on Measures of Reading Comprehension and Reading Behavior." *Reading Research Quarterly* 20 (1985): 536–52.

Reither, James A., and Douglas Vipond. "Writing as Collaboration." *College English* 51 (1989): 855–67.

Remde, Joel R., Louis M. Gomez, and Thomas K. Landauer. "Superbook: An Automatic Tool for Information Exploration—Hypertext?" J. B. Smith et al. 175–88.

Riel, Margaret. "Building a New Foundation for Global Communities." *Writing Notebook* Jan.–Feb. 1990: 35–37.

———. "The *Computer Chronicles* Newswire: A Functional Learning Environment for Acquiring Literacy Skills." *Journal of Educational Computing Research* 1 (1985): 317–37.

———. "The Intercultural Learning Network." *Computing Teacher* Apr. 1987: 27–30.

Ritchie, Joy S. "Resistance to Reading: Another View of the Minefield." *Journal of Advanced Composition* 12 (1992): 117–36.

Robertson, G. Kamilla, Don McCracken, and Alan Newell. *The ZOG Approach to Man-Machine Communication.* Computer Science Tech. Rept. CMU-CS-79-148. Pittsburgh: Carnegie Mellon U, 1979.

Robinson, Jay, ed. *Conversations on the Written Word: Essays on Language and Literacy.* Portsmouth: Boynton/Cook, 1990.

Rodrigues, Dawn. "Developing and Implementing Computer-Training Programs for English Teachers: A Game Plan." Selfe, Rodrigues, and Oates 179–95.

Rodrigues, Dawn, and Raymond Rodrigues. *Teaching Writing with a Word Processor.* Urbana: NCTE, 1986.

Rogers, Sharon, and Charlene S. Hurt. "How Scholarly Communication

Should Work in the Twenty-first Century." *Chronicle of Higher Education* 18 Oct. 1990: A56.

Rorty, Richard. *Philosophy and the Mirror of Nature.* Princeton: Princeton UP, 1979.

———. "Two Cheers for the Cultural Left." Gless and Smith 227–34.

Rose, Mike. *Lives on the Boundary: The Struggles and Achievements of America's Underprepared.* New York: Free, 1989.

———. "Narrowing the Mind and Page: Remedial Writers and Cognitive Reductionism." *College Composition and Communication* 39.3 (1988): 267–302.

Rosenblatt, Louise M. *Literature as Exploration.* 4th ed. New York: MLA, 1983.

Ross, Myron. "Professor Predicts an Economy in the Pink." Interview. With Luther Jackson. *Detroit Free Press* 20 Nov. 1989: 3C.

Roth, Lorie. "Introducing the Word Processor." *Computers and Composition* 2 (1984): 10–11.

Rothschild, Joan. *Machina ex Dea: Feminist Perspectives on Technology.* New York: Pergamon, 1983.

Rouet, Jean-François. "Initial Domain Knowledge and Comprehension Strategies in the Use of an Interactive Reading Software." Third European Conference on Learning and Instruction. Madrid, 4–7 Sept. 1989.

———. "Interactive Text Processing by Inexperienced (Hyper-) Readers." Streitz, Rizk, and André 250–60.

Royster, Jacqueline Jones. "Perspectives on the Intellectual Tradition of Black Women Writers." Lunsford, Moglen, and Slevin 103–12.

Rubin, Andee, and Bertram Bruce. *Alternate Realizations of Purpose in Computer-Supported Writing.* Tech. Rept. 492. Champaign: Center for the Study of Writing, 1990.

Rubin, Donald. "Introduction: Four Dimensions of Social Construction in Written Communication." *The Social Construction of Written Communication.* Ed. Donald Rubin and Bennett Rafoth. Norwood: Ablex, 1988. 1–33.

Ruskiewicz, John. "Word and Image: The Next Revolution." *Computers and Composition* 5 (1988): 9–16.

Sabin, Louis. *Thomas Alva Edison, Young Inventor.* Natwah: Troll, 1983.

Salvio, Paula M. "The World, the Text, and the Reader." Lunsford, Moglen, and Slevin 269–75.

Sanford, Anthony, and Simon Garrod. *Understanding Written Language: Exploration in Comprehension beyond the Sentence.* Chichester, Eng.: Wiley, 1981.

Scardamalia, Marlene, and Carl Bereiter. "Assimilative Processes in Composition Planning." *Educational Psychologist* 17.3 (1982): 165–71.

Scardamalia, Marlene, et al. "Computer-Supported Intentional Learning Environments." *Journal of Educational Computing Research* 5 (1989): 51–68.

Schank, Roger. *Reading and Understanding: Teaching from the Perspective of Artificial Intelligence.* Hillsdale: Erlbaum, 1982.

Schilb, John. "The Sociological Imagination and the Ethics of Collaboration." Forman, *New Visions* 105–19.

Schilling, Nancy, and Jack Gittinger, Jr. "The Eastern Navajo Agency Network:

Computer Networking for Native American Schools." *Winds of Change* 2.2 (1989): 47+.

Schmitt, Marilyn. "Scholars Must Take the Lead in Computerization in the Humanities." *Chronicle of Higher Education* 21 Nov. 1990: A44.

Schnotz, Wolfgang. "Comparative Instructional Text Organization." Mandl, Stein, and Trabasso 53–81.

———. "How Do Different Readers Learn with Different Text Organizations?" *Discourse Processing*. Flammer and Kintsch 87–97.

Scholes, Robert. *Protocols of Reading*. New Haven: Yale UP, 1989.

———. *Textual Power: Literary Theory and the Teaching of English*. New Haven: Yale UP, 1985.

Schrum, Lynne. "Telecommunications: A Window to the World." *Instructor* Oct. 1988: 31–32.

Schuster, Charles. "The Ideology of Literacy: A Bakhtinian Perspective." Lunsford, Moglen, and Slevin 225–32.

Schwartz, Helen. *Interactive Writing: Composing with a Word Processor*. New York: Holt, 1985.

———. "Monsters and Mentors: Computer Applications for Humanistic Education." *College English* 44 (1982): 141–52.

Schwartz, Jeffrey. "Using an Electronic Network to Play the Scales of Discourse." *English Journal* 70 (1990): 16–24.

Schwarz, Maria N., and August Flammer. "Text Structure and Title—Effects on Comprehension and Recall." *Journal of Verbal Learning and Verbal Behavior* 20 (1981): 61–66.

Schweickart, Patrocinio P. "Reading Ourselves: Toward a Feminist Theory of Reading." *Gender and Reading*. Ed. Elizabeth Flynn and Patrocinio P. Schweickart. Baltimore: Johns Hopkins UP, 1986. 31–62.

Scribner, Sylvia. "Literacy in Three Metaphors." *American Journal of Education* 93 (1984): 6–21.

Scribner, Sylvia, and Michael Cole. *The Psychology of Literacy*. Cambridge: Harvard UP, 1981.

Searle, John. "The Storm over the University." *New York Review* 6 Dec. 1990: 34–42.

Secor, Marie, and Davida Charney, eds. *Constructing Rhetorical Education*. Carbondale: Southern Illinois UP, 1992.

Seguin, Armand. "Networking Educators across the Expanses of Alaska." *T.H.E. Journal* Apr. 1988: 81–84.

Selfe, Cynthia L. "Computer-Based Conversations and the Changing Nature of Collaboration." Forman, *New Visions* 147–69.

———. "Creating a Computer Lab That Composition Teachers Can Live With." *Collegiate Microcomputer* 5 (1987): 149–58.

———. "English Teachers and the Humanization of Computers: Networking Communities of Writers." *On Literacy and Its Teaching: Issues in English Education*. Ed. Gail E. Hawisher and Anna O. Soter. Albany: State U of New York P, 1990. 190–205.

———. "Preparing English Teachers for the Virtual Age: The Case for Technology Critics." Hawisher and LeBlanc 24–42.

———. "Redefining Literacy: The Multi-layered Grammars of Computers." Hawisher and Selfe, *Critical Perspectives* 3–15.

———. "Technology in the English Classroom: Computers through the Lens of Feminist Theory." Handa, *Computers and Community* 118–39.

Selfe, Cynthia L., Dawn Rodrigues, and William R. Oates, eds. *Computers in English and the Language Arts: The Challenge of Teacher Education.* Urbana: NCTE, 1989.

Selfe, Cynthia, and Billie J. Wahlstrom. "Computer-Supported Writing Classes: Lessons for Teachers." Selfe, Rodrigues, and Oates 257–68.

Shirk, Henrietta Nickels. "Hypertext and Composition Studies." Hawisher and Selfe, *Evolving Perspectives* 177–202.

Shneiderman, Ben. "Reflections on Authoring, Editing, and Managing Hypertext." Barrett, *Society of Text* 115–31.

———. "User Interface Design for the Hyperties Electronic Encyclopedia." J. B. Smith et al. 189–94.

Shonk, William. *Working in Teams: A Practical Manual for Improving Work Groups.* New York: Amacom, 1982.

Shor, Ira. *Critical Teaching and Everyday Life.* Chicago: U of Chicago P, 1987.

Shumway, David R. "Introduction." *Poetics Today* 9 (1988): 687–98.

Siefert, Marsha, George Gerbner, and Janice Fisher, eds. *The Information Gap: How Computers and Other New Communication Technologies Affect the Social Distribution of Power.* New York: Oxford UP, 1989.

Sirc, Geoffrey, and Tom Reynolds. "The Face of Collaboration in the Networked Writing Classroom." Kremers and Peyton 53–70.

Sizer, Theodore R. "Public Literacy: Puzzlements of a High School Watcher." Lunsford, Moglen, and Slevin 9–12.

Slack, Jennifer Daryl. *Communication Technologies and Society: Conceptions of Causality and the Politics of Technological Intervention.* Norwood: Ablex, 1984.

Slatin, John M. "Hypertext and the Teaching of Writing." Barrett, *Text, Context, and Hypertext* 111–29.

———. "Reading Hypertext: Order and Coherence in a New Medium." *College English* 52 (1990): 870–83.

Sledd, Andrew. "Readin' not Riotin': The Politics of Literacy." *College English* 50 (1988): 495–508.

Smagorinsky, Peter. *Expressions: Multiple Intelligences in the English Class.* Urbana: NCTE, 1991.

Smit, David W. "Some Difficulties with Collaborative Learning." *Journal of Advanced Composition* 9 (1989): 45–58.

Smith, Barbara Herrnstein. *Contingencies of Value: Alternative Perspectives for Critical Theory.* Cambridge: Harvard UP, 1988.

———. "Cult-Lit: Hirsch, Literacy, and the 'National Culture.'" Gless and Smith 69–88.

Smith, Catherine F. "Reconceiving Hypertext." Hawisher and Selfe, *Evolving Perspectives* 224–52.

Smith, Catherine F., et al. *Multiple Perspectives: Courseware Development Using Hypercard*. Research Rept. 1. Syracuse: Writing Program, Syracuse U, 1990.

Smith, Eldred. *The Librarian, the Scholar, and the Future of the Research Library*. New York: Greenwood, 1990.

Smith, Frank. *Insult to Intelligence: The Bureaucratic Invasion of Our Classrooms*. Portsmouth: Heinemann, 1988.

———. *Understanding Reading: A Psychoanalytic Analysis of Reading and Learning to Read*. New York: Holt, 1971.

Smith, John B., and Catherine Smith. "Writing, Thinking, Computing." *Poetics* 19 (1990): 121–42.

Smith, John B., et al., eds. *Hypertext '87 Papers*. U of North Carolina, Chapel Hill, 13–15 Nov. 1987. New York: Assn. for Computing Machinery, 1989.

Smith, John B., Stephen F. Weiss, and Gordon J. Ferguson. "A Hypertext Writing Environment and Its Cognitive Basis." J. B. Smith et al. 195–214.

Smith, Lou. "An Evolving Logic of Participant Observation, Educational Ethnography, and Other Case Studies." *Review of Research in Education*. Vol. 6. Ed. Lee Shulman. Chicago: Peacock, 1979. 316–77.

Smith, Page. *Killing the Spirit: Higher Education in America*. New York: Viking, 1990.

Smitherman, Geneva. *Talkin and Testifyin: The Language of Black America*. Detroit: Wayne State UP, 1977.

Spitzer, Michael. "Computer Conferencing: An Emerging Technology." Hawisher and Selfe, *Critical Perspectives* 187–200.

———. "Writing Style in Computer Conferences." Spec. issue of *IEEE Transactions on Professional Communication*. Ed. V. Arms. 29.1 (1986): 19–22.

Sprecher, Jerry W. "The Future of Software Development in Higher Education." *Facilitating Academic Software Development*. Ed. Sprecher. McKinney: Academic Computing, 1988.

Stefik, Mark, et al. "Beyond the Chalkboard: Computer Support for Collaboration and Problem Solving in Meetings." *Communications of the ACM* 30 (1987): 32–47.

Stewart, Donald C. "Collaborative Learning and Composition: Boon or Bane?" *Rhetoric Review* 7 (1988): 58–83.

Stieg, Margaret. "The Information Needs of Historians." *College and Research Libraries* 42 (1981): 547–60.

Stillman, Peter. "A Writer (and Teacher of Writing) Confronts Word Processing." Collins and Sommers 19–28.

Stimpson, Catharine. "New 'Politically Correct' Metaphors Insult History and Our Campuses." Point of view. *Chronicle of Higher Education* 29 May 1991: A40.

Stoan, Stephen K. "Research and Information Retrieval among Academic Researchers: Implications for Library Instruction." *Library Trends* 39 (1991): 238–57.

———. "Research and Library Skills: An Analysis and Interpretation." *College and Research Libraries* 45 (1984): 99–109.

Stone, Sue. "Humanities Scholars: Information Needs and Uses." *Journal of Documentation* 38 (1982): 291–313.

Street, Brian. *Literacy in Theory and Practice.* Cambridge: Cambridge UP, 1984.

Streitz, N., A. Rizk, and J. André, eds. *Hypertext: Concepts, Systems, Applications. Proceedings of the European Conference on Hypertext. INRIA.* Versailles, France, Nov. 1990. Cambridge: Cambridge UP, 1990.

Strickland, James. "Prewriting and Composing." Collins and Sommers 67–74.

Stumbo, Carol. "The World Class Environmental Conference." *Bread Loaf News* Spring 1990: 7–8.

Sullivan, Patricia. "Taking Control of the Page: Electronic Writing and Word Publishing." Hawisher and Selfe, *Evolving Perspectives* 43–64.

Swearingen, C. Jan. "Bloomsday: Doomsday Book for Literacy?" Lunsford, Moglen, and Slevin 215–24.

Sykes, Charles. *Profscam: Professors and the Demise of Higher Education.* Washington: Regnery, 1988.

Talbert, Bob. "Are the Media Surrendering to Word Police?" *Detroit Free Press* 30 Jan. 1991: 6E.

Taylor, John. "Are You Politically Correct?" *New York* 21 Jan. 1991: 33–40.

Taylor, Robert. *The Computer in the School: Tutor, Tool, and Tutee.* New York: Teachers Coll. P, 1980.

Thomas, Lloyd S., Mel Grubb, and Phillip C. Gonzales. *A Description of the California Literature Project Multimedia Institute Training: A Report by the MMI Directors.* Downey: Los Angeles County Office of Education, 1991.

Thompson, Diane. "Conversational Networking: Why the Teacher Gets Most of the Lines." *Collegiate Microcomputer* 6.3 (1988): 193–201.

———. "Electronic Bulletin Boards: A Timeless Place for Collaborative Writing Projects." *Computers and Composition* 7 (1990): 43–53.

———. "Interactive Networking: Creating Bridges between Speech, Writing, and Composition." *Computers and Composition* 5 (1988): 17–28.

Thompson, James D. *Organizations in Action.* New York: McGraw, 1969.

Thornburg, David D. *Edutrends 2010: Restructuring, Technology, and the Future of Education.* San Carlos: Starsong, 1992.

Tifft, Susan. "A Crisis Looms in Science." *Time* 9 Sept. 1989: 68–70.

Toffler, Alvin. *The Third Wave.* New York: Morrow, 1980.

Tompkins, Jane. "A Short Course in Post-structuralism." *College English* 50 (1988): 733–47.

Trigg, Randall, and Peggy Irish. "Hypertext Habitats: Experiences of Writers in Notecards." J. B. Smith et al. 89–108.

Trigg, Randall H., Lucy A. Suchman, and Frank G. Halasz. "Supporting Collaboration in Notecards." *Proceedings of the Conference on Computer Supported Cooperative Work.* Austin, 3–5 Dec. 1986.

Trimbur, John. "Consensus and Difference in Collaborative Learning." *College English* 51 (1988): 602–16.

Trimbur, John, and Lundy A. Braun. "Laboratory Life and the Determination of Authorship." Forman, *New Visions* 19–36.

Tulonen, Joanne. "Pollution Control: Planning for Productive Telecomputing." *Bread Loaf and the Schools* Fall–Winter 1988: 17–19.

Tuman, Myron C. Rev. of *Writing Space*, by Jay David Bolter. *College Composition and Communication* 43 (1992): 261–63.

———. "Words, Tools, and Technology." Rev. of *Orality and Literacy*, by Walter Ong. *College English* 45 (1983): 769–79.

Turkle, Sherry, and Seymour Papert. "Epistemological Pluralism: Styles and Voices within the Computer Culture." *Signs* 16 (1990): 128–57.

Ulmer, Gregory. "Grammatology Hypermedia." *Postmodern Culture* 1.2 (1991): n.p.

———. "Textshop for Psychoanalysis: On De-programming Freshmen Platonists." *College English* 49 (1987): 757–69.

Utting, Kenneth, and Nicole Yankelovich. "Context and Orientation in Hypermedia Networks." *ACM Transactions on Information Systems* 7.1 (1989): 58–84.

van Dijk, Teun A. "Relevance Assignment in Discourse Comprehension." *Discourse Processes* 2 (1979): 113–26.

van Dijk, Teun A., and Walter Kintsch. *Strategies of Discourse Comprehension*. New York: Academic, 1983.

Volti, Rudi. *Society and Technological Change*. New York: St. Martin's, 1988.

Vygotsky, Lev S. *Mind in Society: The Development of Higher Psychological Processes*. Cambridge: Harvard UP, 1978.

———. *Thought and Language*. Ed. Eugenia Hanfmann. Trans. Gertrude Vakar. Cambridge: MIT P, 1962.

Waddell, Craig. "PC-Write: Quality Word Processing at a Price That's Hard to Beat." *Computers and Composition* 2 (1985): 77–82.

Wahlstrom, Billie. "Desktop Publishing: Perspectives, Potentials, and Politics." Hawisher and Selfe, *Critical Perspectives* 162–86.

Walker, Janet H. "Authoring Tools for Complex Documents." Barrett, *Society of Text* 132–47.

———. "Document Examiner: Delivery Interface for Hypertext Documents." J. B. Smith et al. 307–24.

Walters, Keith. "Language, Logic, and Literacy." Lunsford, Moglen, and Slevin 173–88.

White, James Boyd. "The Invisible Discourse of the Law: Reflection on Legal Literacy and General Education." Bailey and Fosheim 137–50.

Whiteside, John, Sandra Jones, Paula Levy, and Dennis Wixon. "User Performance with Command, Menu, and Iconic Interfaces." *Human Factors in Computing Systems*. Proceedings of the CHI '85 conference. San Francisco, 14–18 Apr. 1985. Ed. Lorraine Borman and Bill Curtis. New York: Assn. for Computing Machinery, 1985. 185–91.

"Who Needs the Great Works?" *Harper's* Sept. 1989: 43–52.

Wiberley, Stephen E., Jr., and William G. Jones. "Patterns of Information Seeking in the Humanities." *College and Research Libraries* 50 (1989): 638–45.

Wilhite, Stephen. "Headings as Memory Facilitators." *Practical Aspects of Memory: Current Research and Issues*. Vol. 2. Ed. Michael Gruneberg, Peter Morris, and Robert Sykes. Chichester, Eng.: Wiley, 1988. 531–36.

Will, George. "Academia Suffers the Diversity Enforcers." *Detroit News* 22 Apr. 1991: 3B.

———. "Political Correctness—The Sequel." *Detroit News* 20 Oct. 1991: 3B.

Williams, Raymond. *Television: Technology and Cultural Form*. New York: Schocken, 1975.

Wilshire, Bruce. *The Moral Collapse of the University: Professionalism, Purity, and Alienation*. Albany: State U of New York P, 1990.

Winograd, Terry, and Fernando Flores. *Understanding Computers and Cognition: A New Foundation for Design*. Reading: Addison, 1987.

Wright, Patricia, and Ann Lickorish. "The Influence of Discourse Structure on Display and Navigation in Hypertexts." *Computers and Writing*. Ed. N. Williams and P. Holt. Norwood: Ablex, 1989. 90–124.

Wright, William. "On-line with an Expert: A World Class Interview." *Bread Loaf News* Spring 1990: 10–12.

———. "Telecommunications and Social Action: The Birth of World Class." *Bread Loaf News* Spring 1990: 4–6.

Wurman, Richard. *Information Anxiety*. New York: Doubleday, 1988.

Yankelovich, Nicole, Norman Meyrowitz, and Andries van Dam. "Reading and Writing the Electronic Book." *IEEE Computer* 18.10 (1985): 15–30.

Young, Iris Marion. "The Ideal of Community and the Politics of Difference." *Social Theory and Practice* 12 (1986): 1–26.

Young, Richard E., Alton L. Becker, and Kenneth L. Pike. *Rhetoric: Discovery and Change*. New York: Harcourt, 1970.

Younggren, Geri. "Using an Object-Oriented Programming Language to Create Audience-Driven Hypermedia Environments." Barrett, *Text, Context, and Hypertext* 77–92.

Zebroski, James Thomas. "The English Department and Social Class: Resisting Education." Lunsford, Moglen, and Slevin 81–90.

Zellweger, Polle T. "Scripted Documents: A Hypermedia Path Mechanism." Meyrowitz 1–14.

Zeni, Jane. *Writinglands: Composing with Old and New Writing Tools*. Urbana: NCTE, 1990.

Ziegler, Bart. "Think That Computer Message You Just Sent Is Secret? Think Again." *Detroit News and Free Press* 26 Aug. 1990: 1D.

Zimmerman, Jan, ed. *The Technological Woman: Interfacing with Tomorrow*. New York: Praeger, 1983.

Zuboff, Shoshana. *In the Age of the Smart Machine: The Future of Work and Power*. New York: Basic, 1988.

Zukav, Gary. *The Dancing Wu-Li Masters: An Overview of the New Physics*. Toronto: Bantam, 1979.

Computer Software

Access. For information, write Lillian S. Bridwell-Bowles and Donald Ross, Program in Composition and Communication, 209 Lind Hall, Univ. of Minnesota, Minneapolis 55455. IBM and compatibles.

Bolter, Jay David, Michael Joyce, and John B. Smith. *Storyspace*. Eastgate Systems, 1990.

Collymore, J. C., et al. *Writer's Workbench*. AT&T, 1982. IBM.

Commentary. For information, write Thomas Barker, Dept. of English, Texas Tech Univ., Lubbock 79409.

Daedalus Integrated Writing Environment (DIWE). For information, write Daedalus Group, 1106 Clayton Ln., Suite 248W, Austin, TX 78723. IBM and Macintosh.

Dodge, B. J. *Irrawaddy: A Tool for Creating Branching Stories and Simulations with Hypercard.* Educational Technology Department, San Diego State Univ., 1992.

Free. For information, write James Strickland, Dept. of English, Slippery Rock Univ., Slippery Rock, PA 16057.

Grammatik. Reference Software, 1983. IBM and compatibles.

HBJ Writer (originally *Wandah*). Harcourt, 1986. IBM.

Hypercard. Claris, 1988. Macintosh.

Interactive Nova: Race to Save the Planet. Scholastic, 1992. Videodisc and hypermedia.

Interchange. For information, write Daedalus Group, 1106 Clayton Ln., Suite 248W, Austin, TX 78723. IBM and Macintosh.

Intermedia. Eastgate, 1992. Macintosh.

Joyce, Michael. "Afternoon: A Story." Eastgate, 1990. Macintosh.

McDaid, John. "Uncle Buddy's Phantom Funhouse." Eastgate, 1993. Macintosh.

Papert, Seymour. "School of the Future." *MIT Media Laboratory.* Ed. Guy Guillet. Pioneer, n.d. Videodisc.

Point of View. Scholastic, 1990. Videodisc and hypermedia.

Polin, Linda. *The Literature Navigator.* Interactive Multimedia, 1992. Videodisc and hypermedia.

Prewrite. For information, write Mimi Schwartz, Stockton State Coll., Pomona, NJ 07042.

PROSE. McGraw-Hill, 1986. Macintosh.

Quest. For information, write James Strickland, Dept. of English, Slippery Rock Univ., Slippery Rock, PA 16057.

Schwartz, Helen. *Seen.* Conduit, 1986. Macintosh.

Topoi. For information, write Hugh Burns, Dept. of English, Univ. of Texas, Austin 78701.

Ulysses. Version 1.1. IBM, 1992. CD-ROM.

Winter, Robert. *Ludwig van Beethoven: Symphony No. 9 CD Companion.* Voyager, 1991. CD-ROM.

Wordbench. For information, write D. Midian Kurland, Education Development Center, 55 Chapel St., Newton, MA 02158.

Writewell Series. For information, write Deborah H. Holdstein, Governors State Univ., University Park, IL 60466.

"

Index